# MAGI
## The labyrinth of magic

5

Story & Art by
**SHINOBU OHTAKA**

# MAGI
### The labyrinth of magic

## ⑤

# CONTENTS

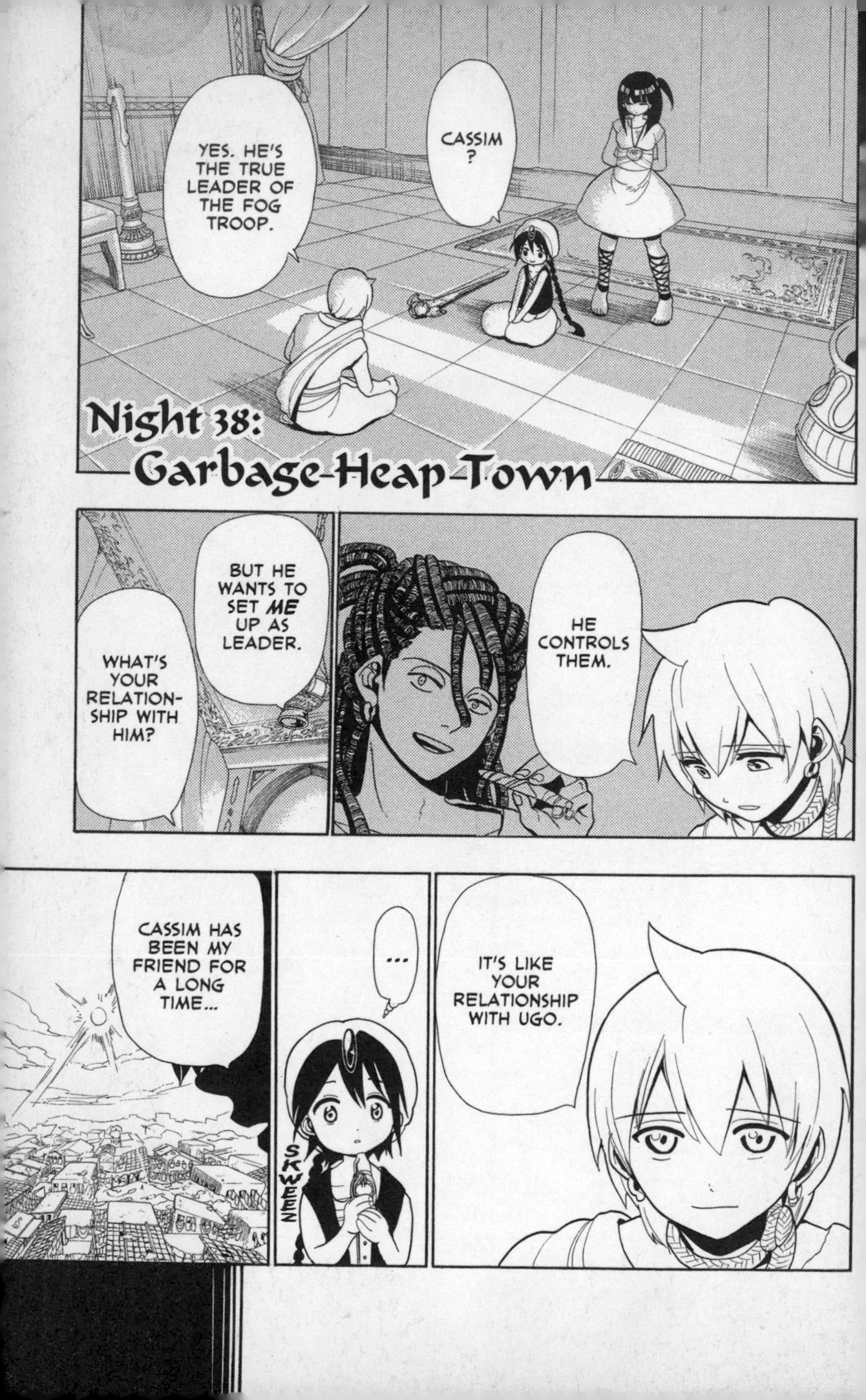
CASSIM ?
YES. HE'S THE TRUE LEADER OF THE FOG TROOP.
Night 38: Garbage-Heap-Town
HE CONTROLS THEM.
BUT HE WANTS TO SET *ME* UP AS LEADER.
WHAT'S YOUR RELATIONSHIP WITH HIM?
IT'S LIKE YOUR RELATIONSHIP WITH UGO.
...
SKWEEZ
CASSIM HAS BEEN MY FRIEND FOR A LONG TIME...

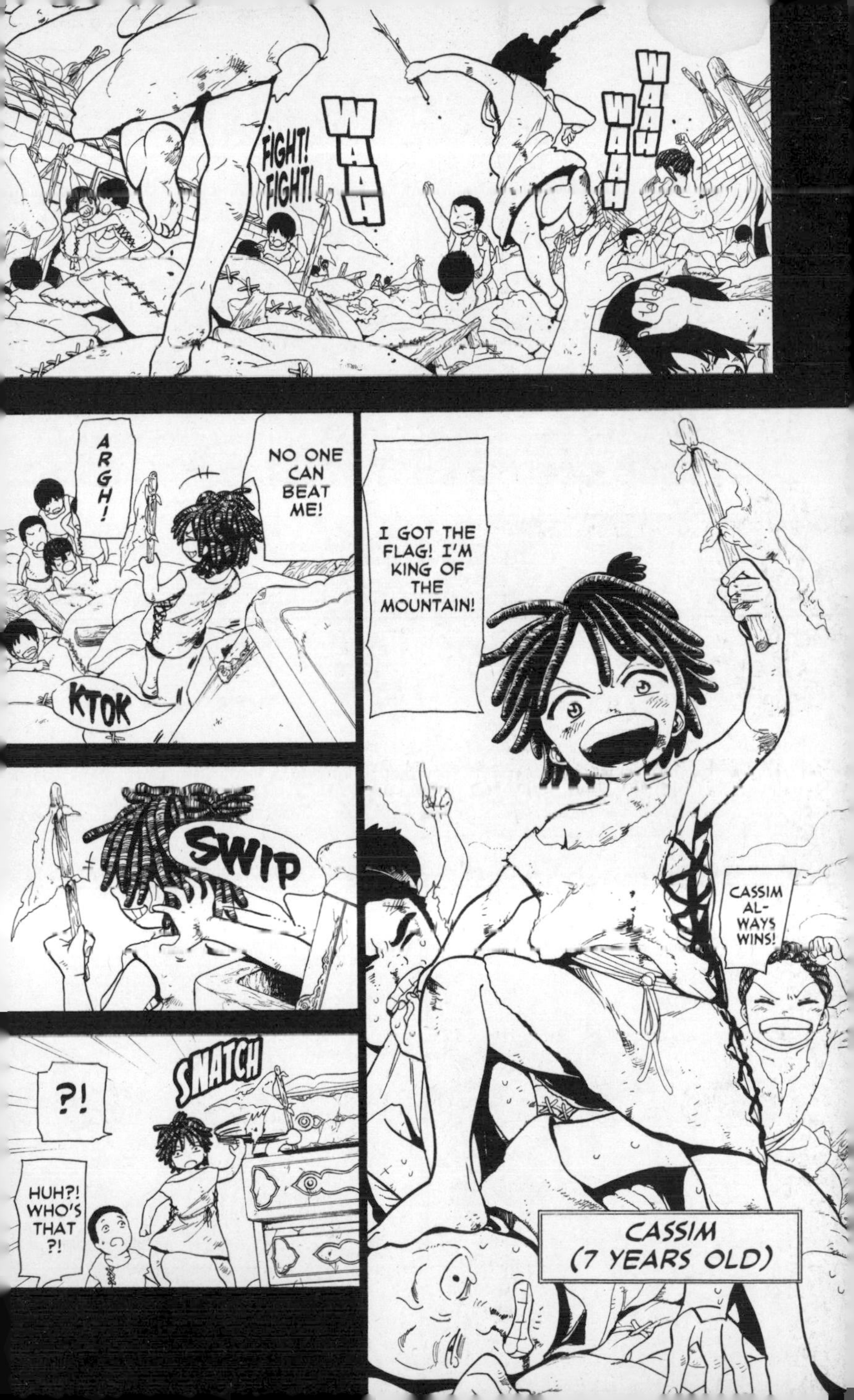
WAAH
WAAH
WAAH
FIGHT! FIGHT!
I GOT THE FLAG! I'M KING OF THE MOUNTAIN!
CASSIM AL-WAYS WINS!
CASSIM (7 YEARS OLD)
NO ONE CAN BEAT ME!
ARGH!
KTOK
SWIP
SNATCH
?!
HUH?! WHO'S THAT?!

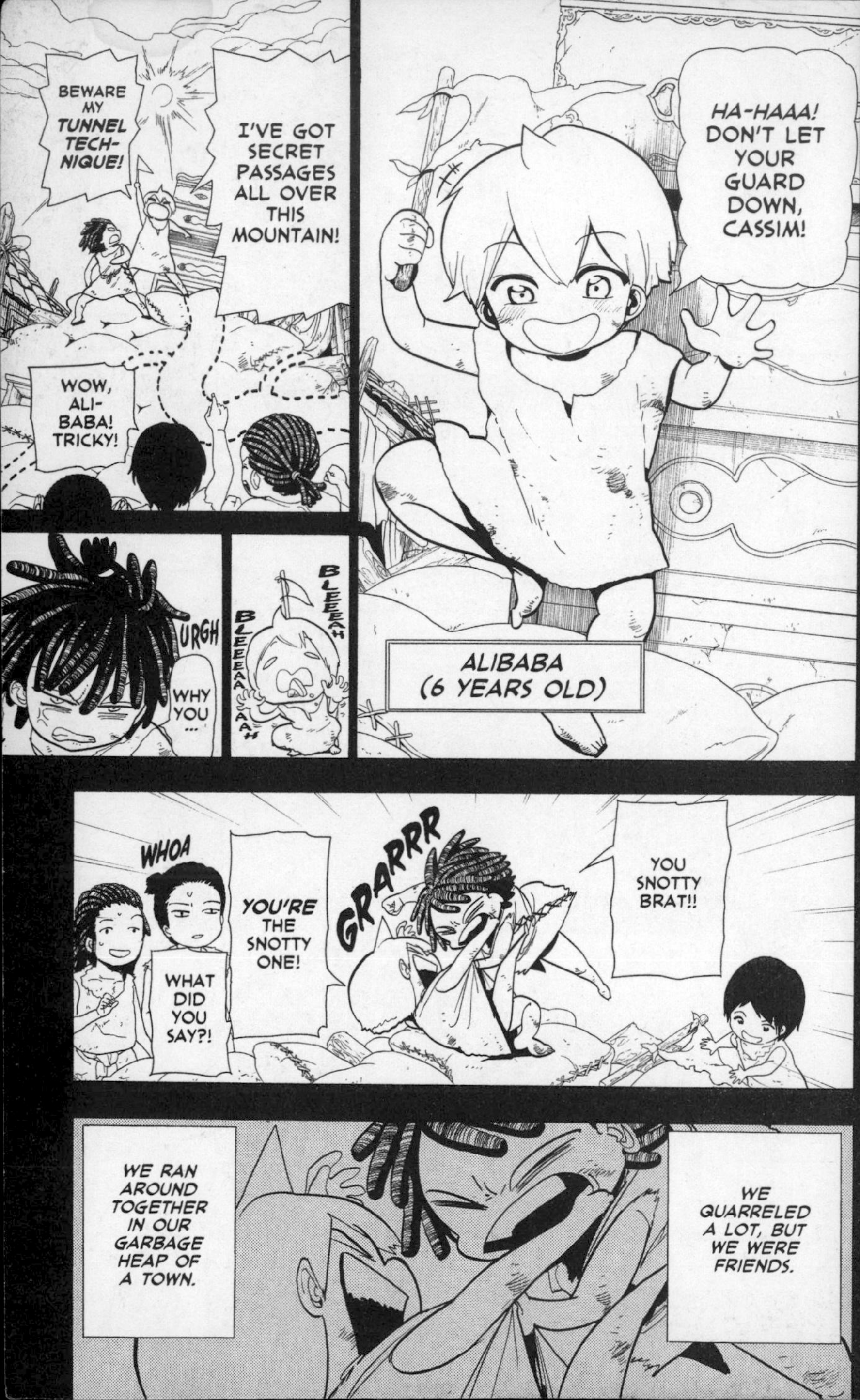
HA-HAAA! DON'T LET YOUR GUARD DOWN, CASSIM!
ALIBABA (6 YEARS OLD)
I'VE GOT SECRET PASSAGES ALL OVER THIS MOUNTAIN!
BEWARE MY TUNNEL TECH-NIQUE!
WOW, ALI-BABA! TRICKY!
BLEEEAH
BLEEEEAAAAH
URGH
WHY YOU ...
YOU SNOTTY BRAT!!
GRARRR
YOU'RE THE SNOTTY ONE!
WHOA
WHAT DID YOU SAY?!
WE QUARRELED A LOT, BUT WE WERE FRIENDS.
WE RAN AROUND TOGETHER IN OUR GARBAGE HEAP OF A TOWN.

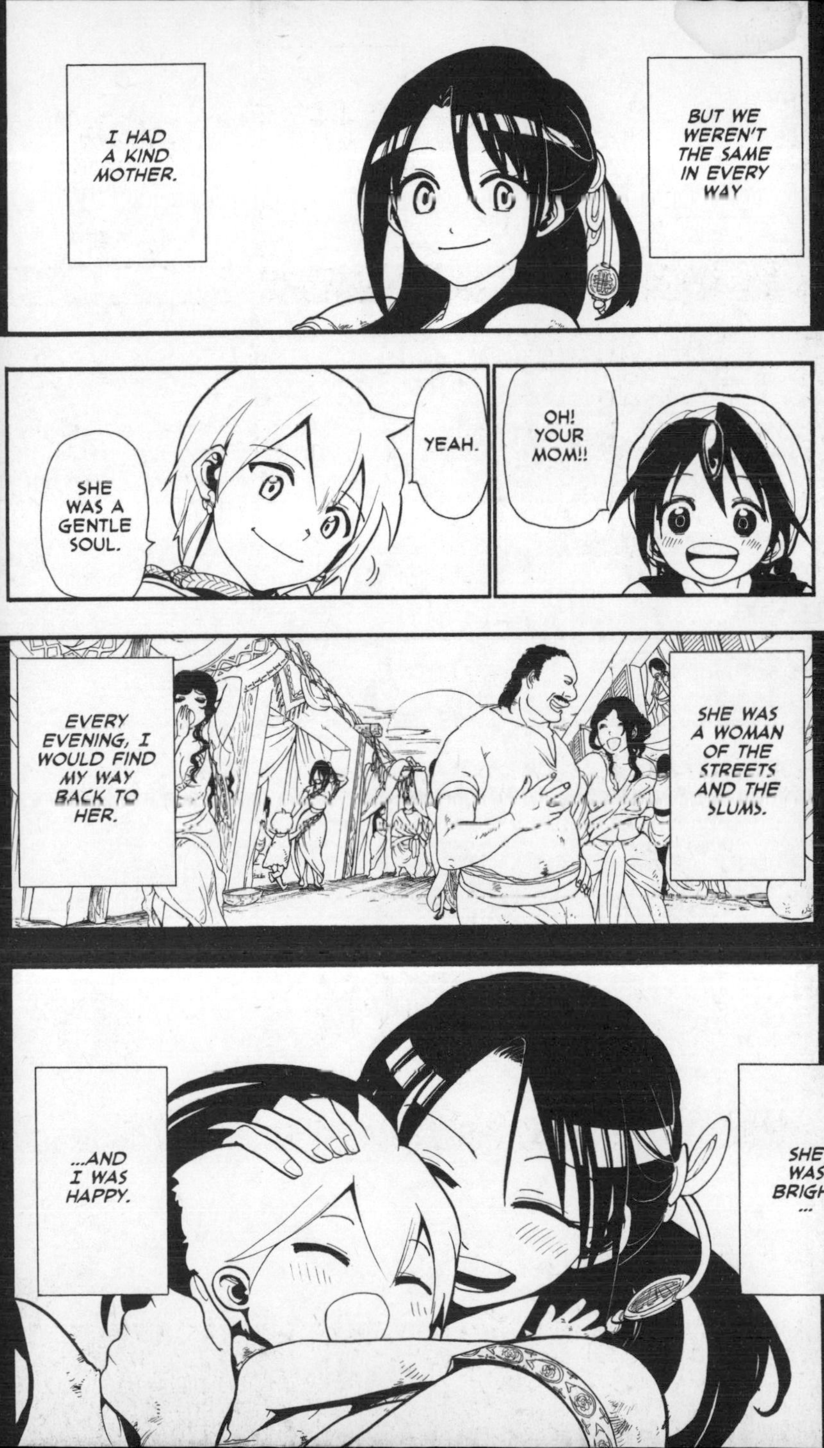
BUT WE WEREN'T THE SAME IN EVERY WAY
I HAD A KIND MOTHER.
OH! YOUR MOM!!
YEAH.
SHE WAS A GENTLE SOUL.
SHE WAS A WOMAN OF THE STREETS AND THE SLUMS.
EVERY EVENING, I WOULD FIND MY WAY BACK TO HER.
SHE WAS BRIGHT...
...AND I WAS HAPPY.

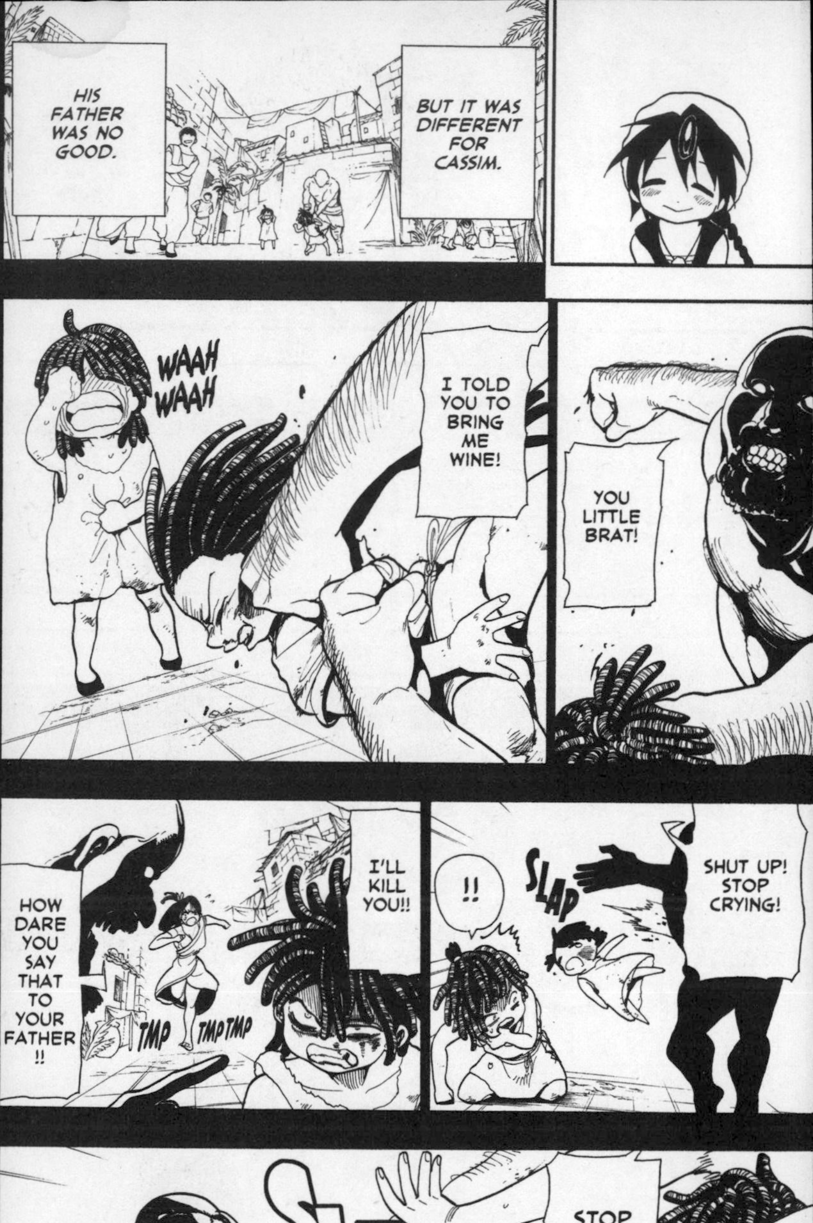
BUT IT WAS DIFFERENT FOR CASSIM.
HIS FATHER WAS NO GOOD.
YOU LITTLE BRAT!
I TOLD YOU TO BRING ME WINE!
WAAH WAAH
SHUT UP! STOP CRYING!
SLAP
!!
I'LL KILL YOU!!
HOW DARE YOU SAY THAT TO YOUR FATHER!!
TMP
TMPTMP
STOP IT!!
SLAM

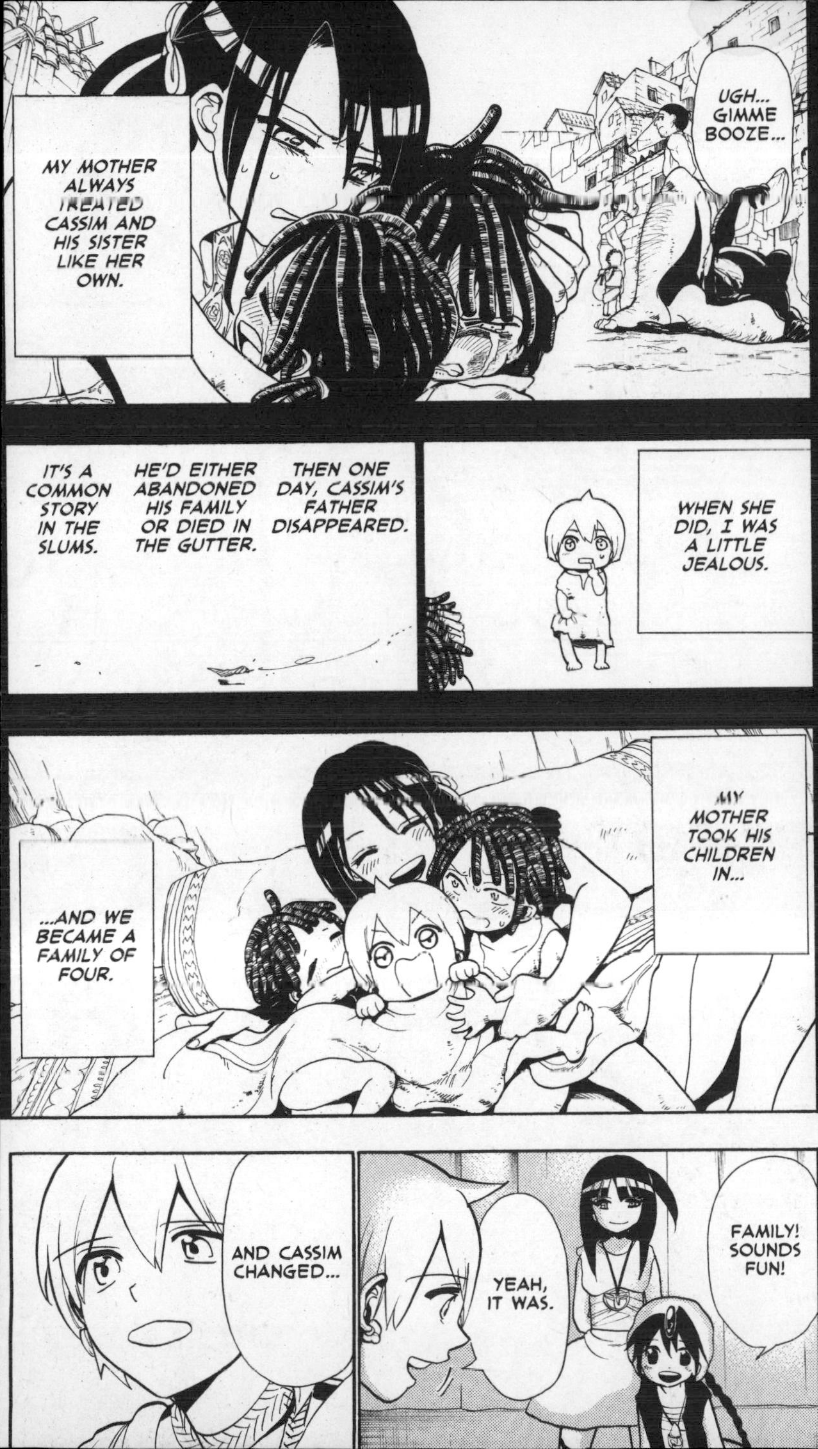
UGH... GIMME BOOZE...
MY MOTHER ALWAYS TREATED CASSIM AND HIS SISTER LIKE HER OWN.
WHEN SHE DID, I WAS A LITTLE JEALOUS.
THEN ONE DAY, CASSIM'S FATHER DISAPPEARED.
HE'D EITHER ABANDONED HIS FAMILY OR DIED IN THE GUTTER.
IT'S A COMMON STORY IN THE SLUMS.
MY MOTHER TOOK HIS CHILDREN IN...
...AND WE BECAME A FAMILY OF FOUR.
FAMILY! SOUNDS FUN!
YEAH, IT WAS.
AND CASSIM CHANGED...

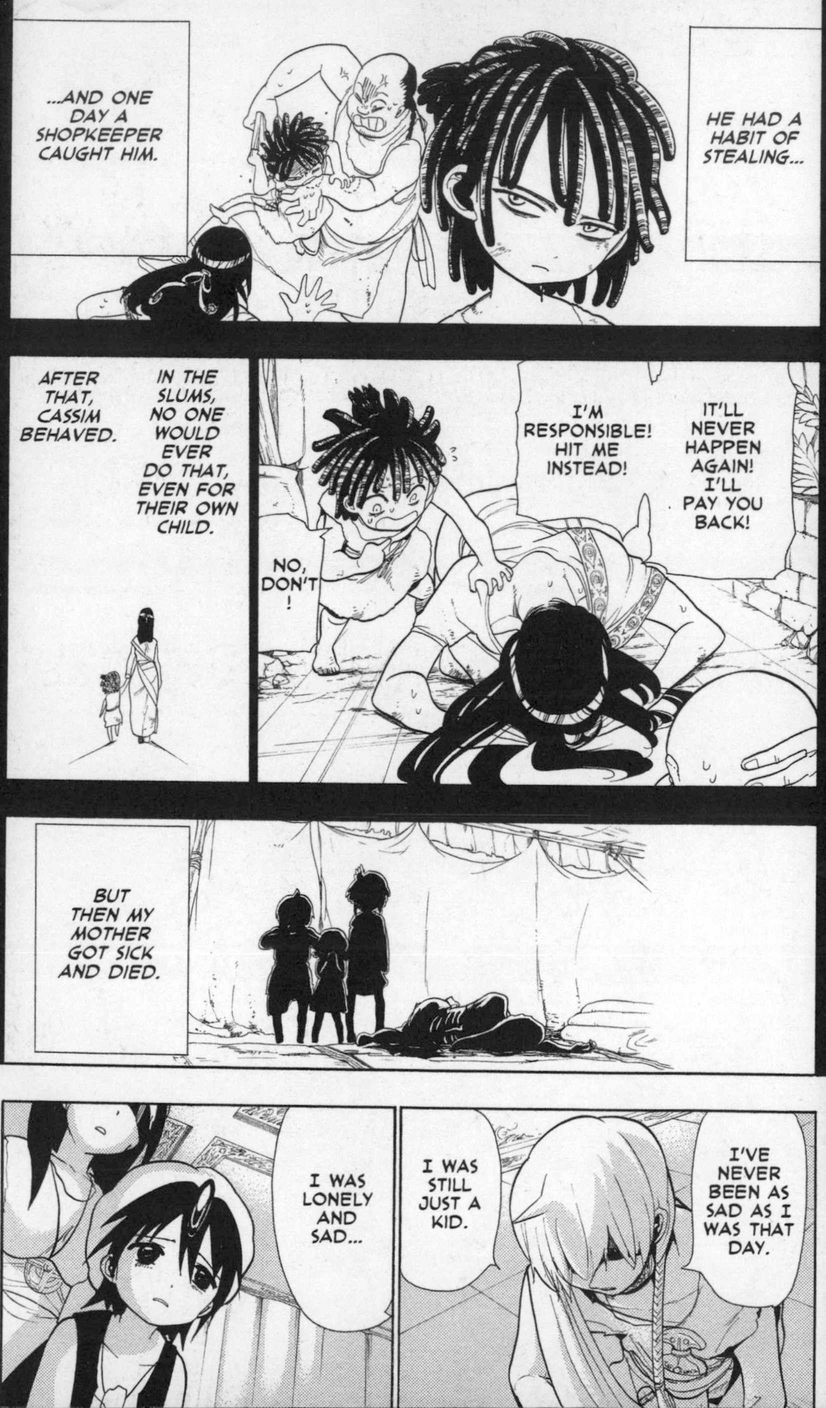
HE HAD A HABIT OF STEALING...
...AND ONE DAY A SHOPKEEPER CAUGHT HIM.
IT'LL NEVER HAPPEN AGAIN! I'LL PAY YOU BACK!
I'M RESPONSIBLE! HIT ME INSTEAD!
NO, DON'T!
IN THE SLUMS, NO ONE WOULD EVER DO THAT, EVEN FOR THEIR OWN CHILD.
AFTER THAT, CASSIM BEHAVED.
BUT THEN MY MOTHER GOT SICK AND DIED.
I'VE NEVER BEEN AS SAD AS I WAS THAT DAY.
I WAS STILL JUST A KID.
I WAS LONELY AND SAD...

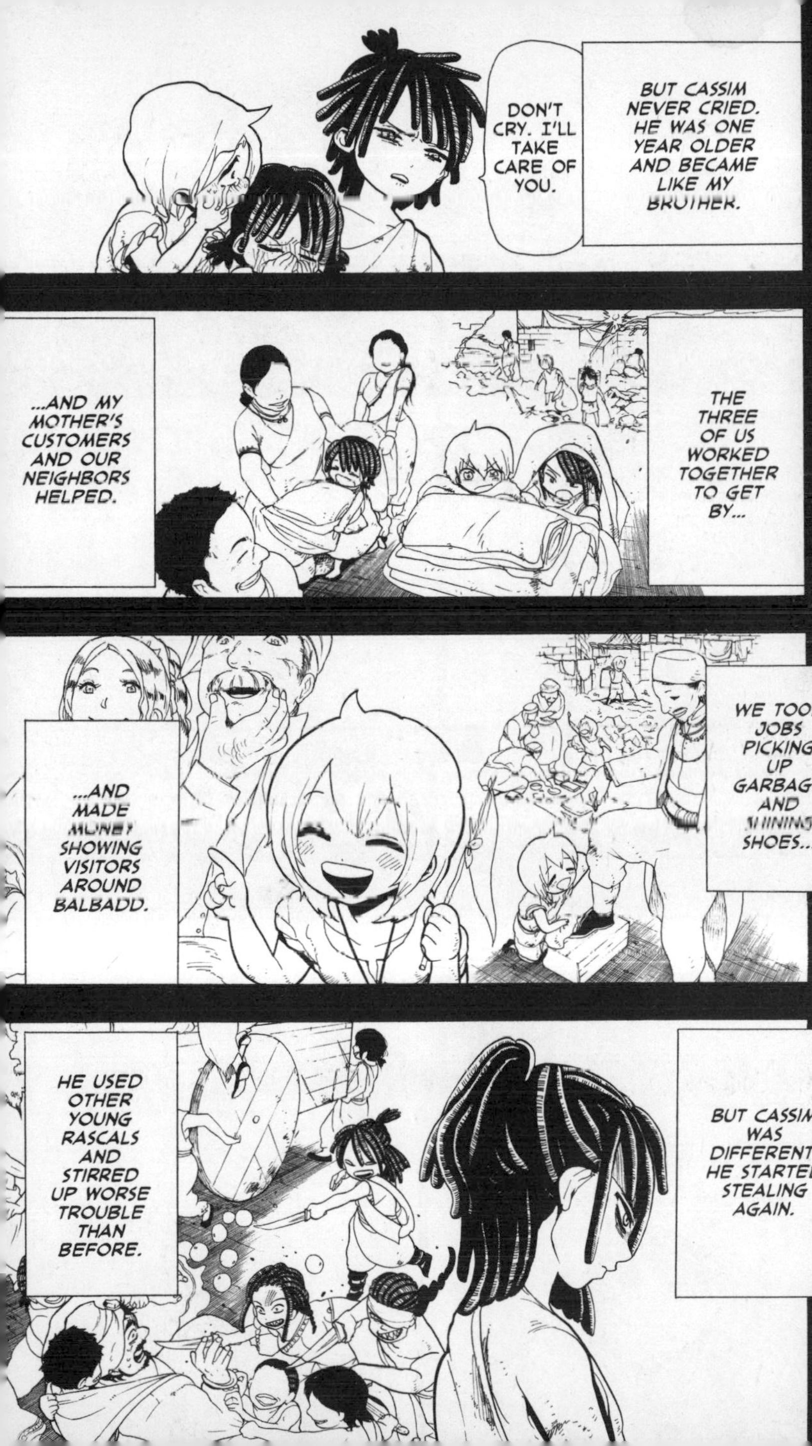

BUT CASSIM NEVER CRIED. HE WAS ONE YEAR OLDER AND BECAME LIKE MY BROTHER.
DON'T CRY. I'LL TAKE CARE OF YOU.
THE THREE OF US WORKED TOGETHER TO GET BY...
...AND MY MOTHER'S CUSTOMERS AND OUR NEIGHBORS HELPED.
WE TOOK JOBS PICKING UP GARBAGE AND SHINING SHOES...
...AND MADE MONEY SHOWING VISITORS AROUND BALBADD.
BUT CASSIM WAS DIFFERENT. HE STARTED STEALING AGAIN.
HE USED OTHER YOUNG RASCALS AND STIRRED UP WORSE TROUBLE THAN BEFORE.

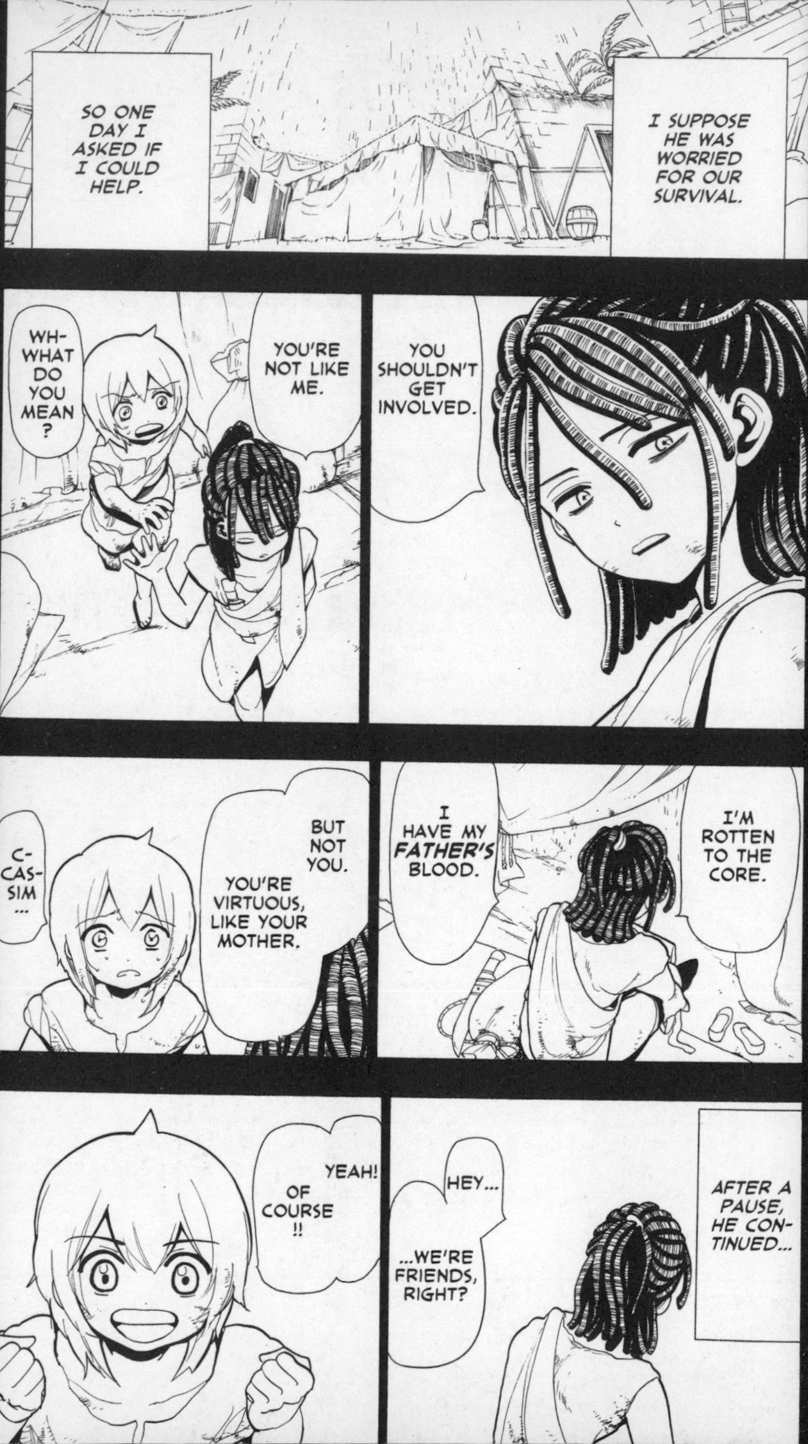
I SUPPOSE HE WAS WORRIED FOR OUR SURVIVAL.
SO ONE DAY I ASKED IF I COULD HELP.
YOU SHOULDN'T GET INVOLVED.
YOU'RE NOT LIKE ME.
WH-WHAT DO YOU MEAN?
I'M ROTTEN TO THE CORE.
I HAVE MY *FATHER'S* BLOOD.
BUT NOT YOU.
YOU'RE VIRTUOUS, LIKE YOUR MOTHER.
C-CASSIM...
AFTER A PAUSE, HE CONTINUED...
HEY...
...WE'RE FRIENDS, RIGHT?
YEAH!
OF COURSE!!

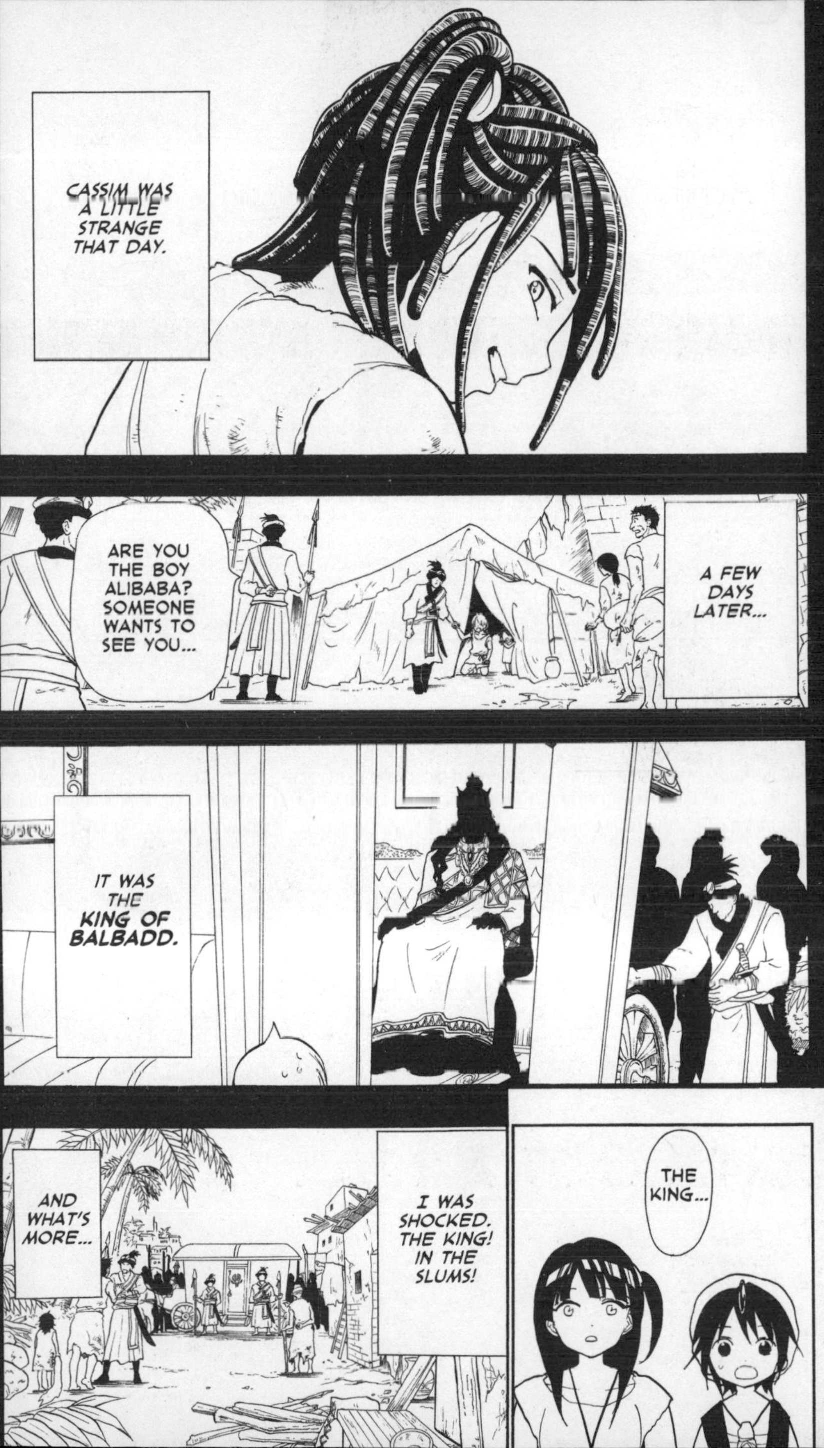
CASSIM WAS A LITTLE STRANGE THAT DAY.
A FEW DAYS LATER...
ARE YOU THE BOY ALIBABA? SOMEONE WANTS TO SEE YOU...
IT WAS THE KING OF BALBADD.
THE KING...
I WAS SHOCKED. THE KING! IN THE SLUMS!
AND WHAT'S MORE...

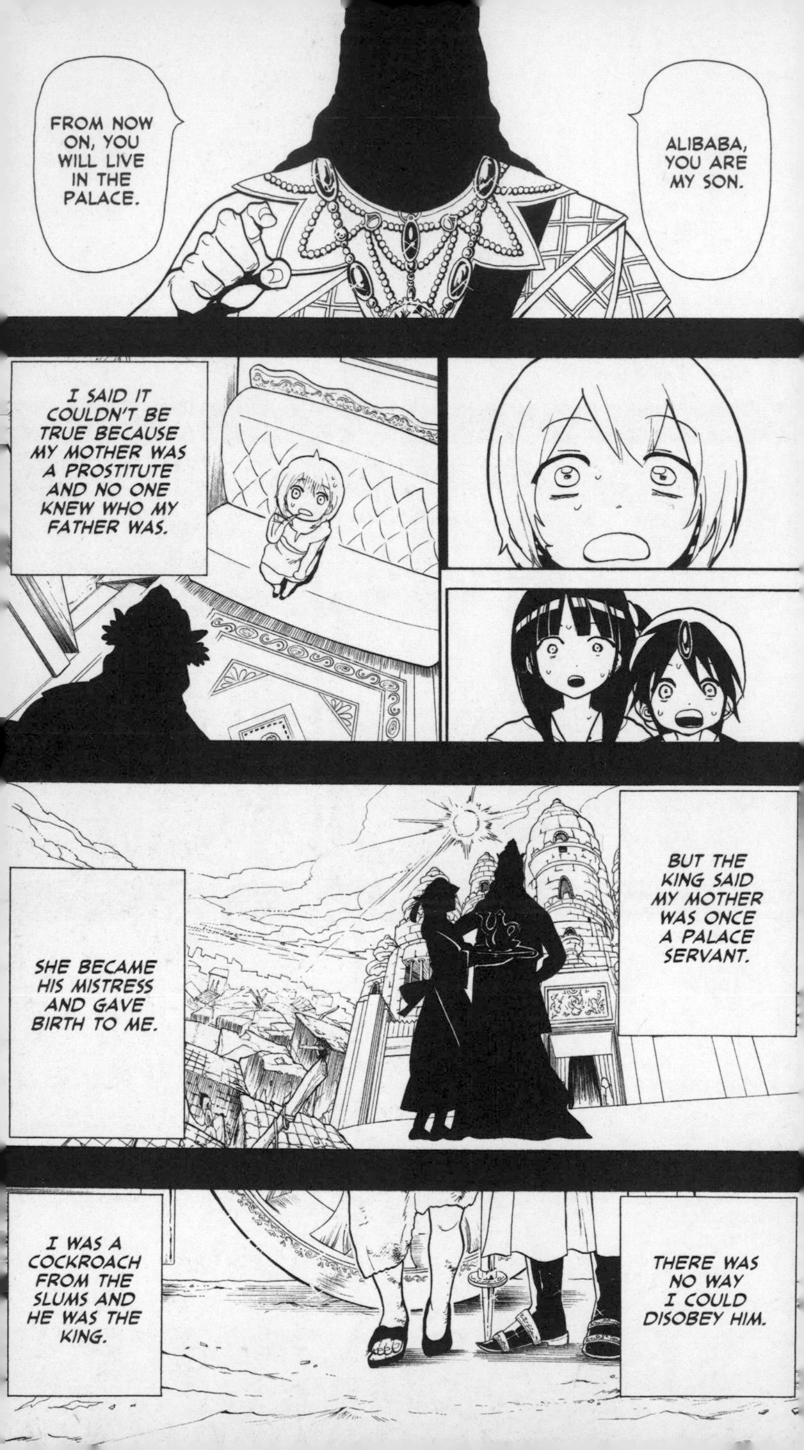
ALIBABA, YOU ARE MY SON.
FROM NOW ON, YOU WILL LIVE IN THE PALACE.
I SAID IT COULDN'T BE TRUE BECAUSE MY MOTHER WAS A PROSTITUTE AND NO ONE KNEW WHO MY FATHER WAS.
BUT THE KING SAID MY MOTHER WAS ONCE A PALACE SERVANT.
SHE BECAME HIS MISTRESS AND GAVE BIRTH TO ME.
THERE WAS NO WAY I COULD DISOBEY HIM.
I WAS A COCKROACH FROM THE SLUMS AND HE WAS THE KING.

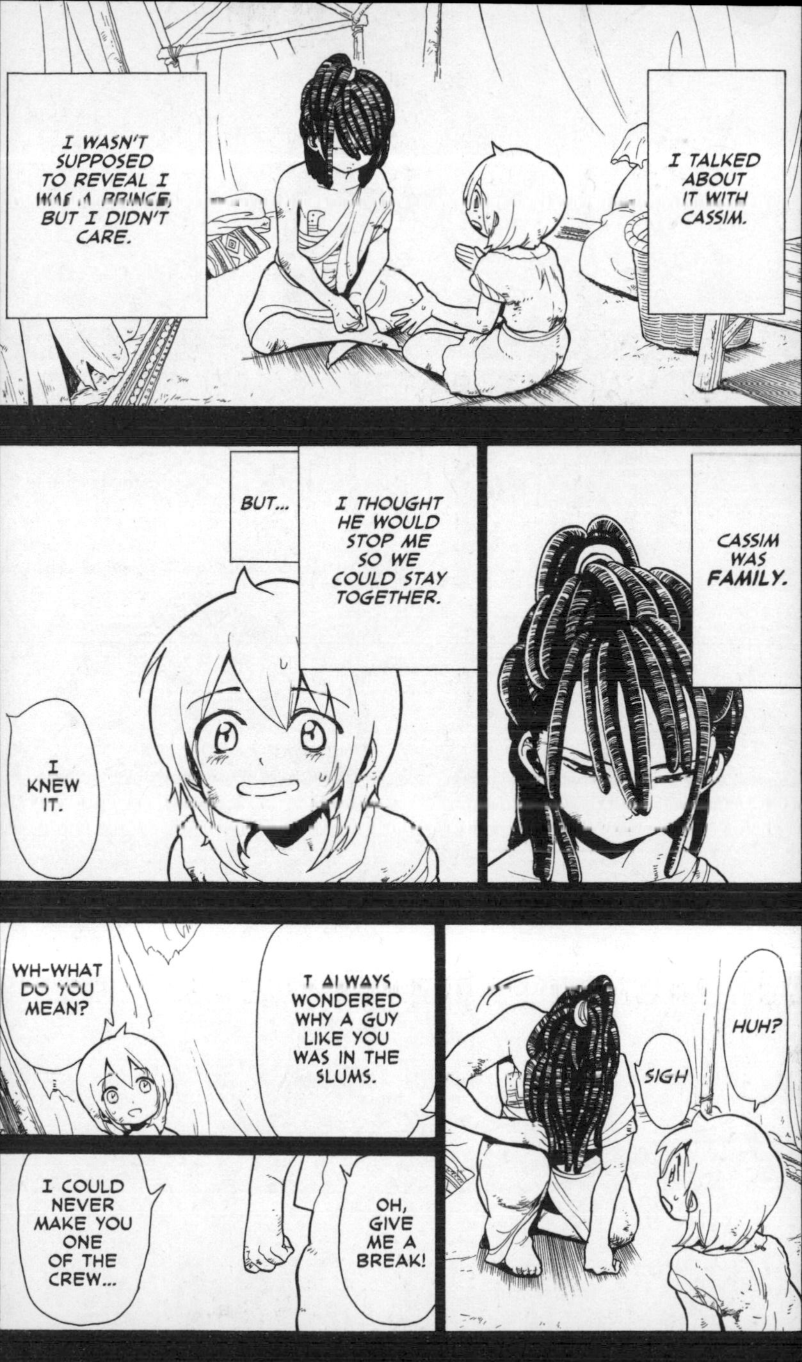
I TALKED ABOUT IT WITH CASSIM.
I WASN'T SUPPOSED TO REVEAL I WAS A PRINCE, BUT I DIDN'T CARE.
CASSIM WAS FAMILY.
I THOUGHT HE WOULD STOP ME SO WE COULD STAY TOGETHER.
BUT...
I KNEW IT.
HUH?
SIGH
I ALWAYS WONDERED WHY A GUY LIKE YOU WAS IN THE SLUMS.
WH-WHAT DO YOU MEAN?
OH, GIVE ME A BREAK!
I COULD NEVER MAKE YOU ONE OF THE CREW...

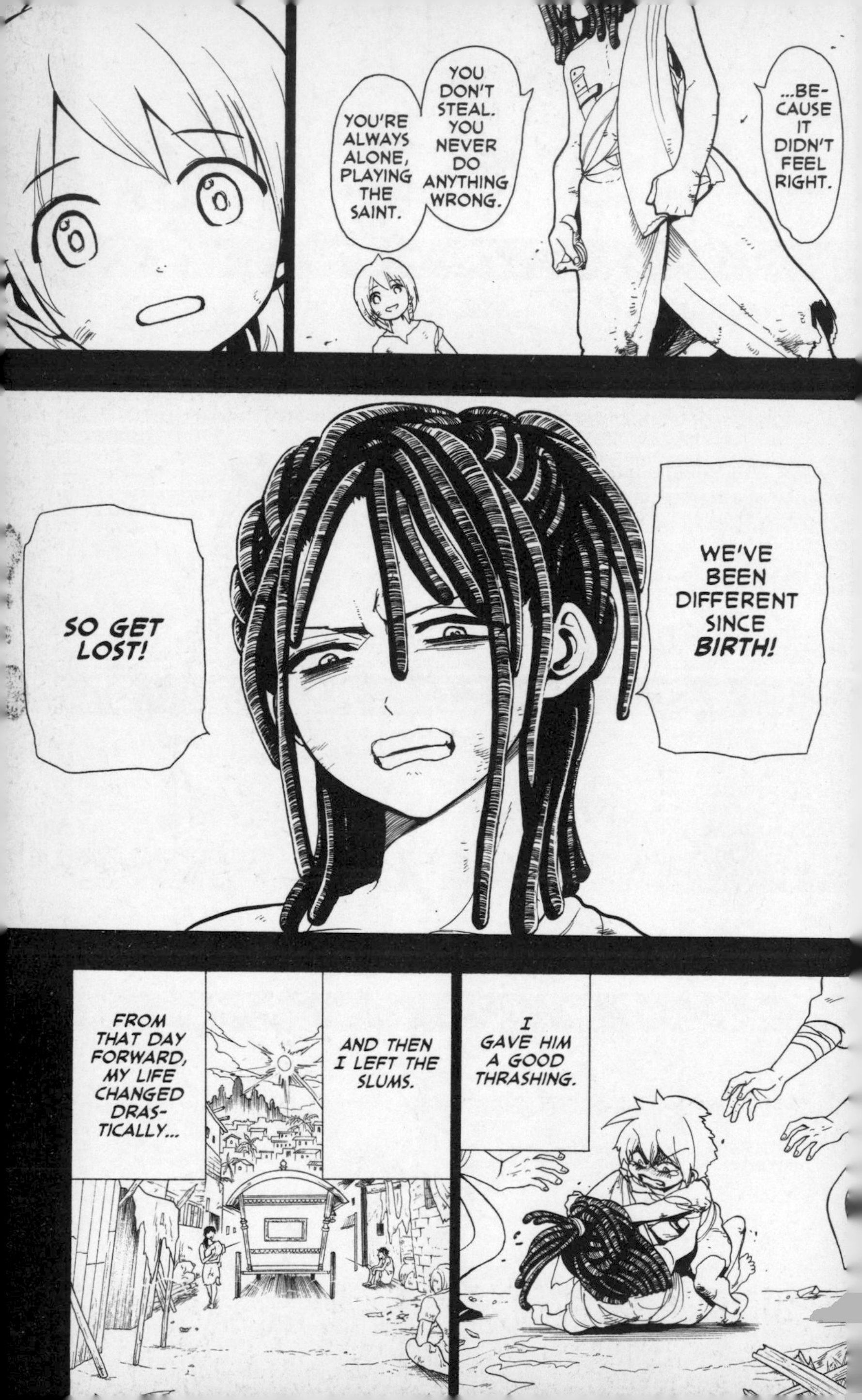
...BECAUSE IT DIDN'T FEEL RIGHT.
YOU DON'T STEAL. YOU NEVER DO ANYTHING WRONG.
YOU'RE ALWAYS ALONE, PLAYING THE SAINT.
WE'VE BEEN DIFFERENT SINCE *BIRTH!*
SO GET LOST!
I GAVE HIM A GOOD THRASHING.
AND THEN I LEFT THE SLUMS.
FROM THAT DAY FORWARD, MY LIFE CHANGED DRASTICALLY...

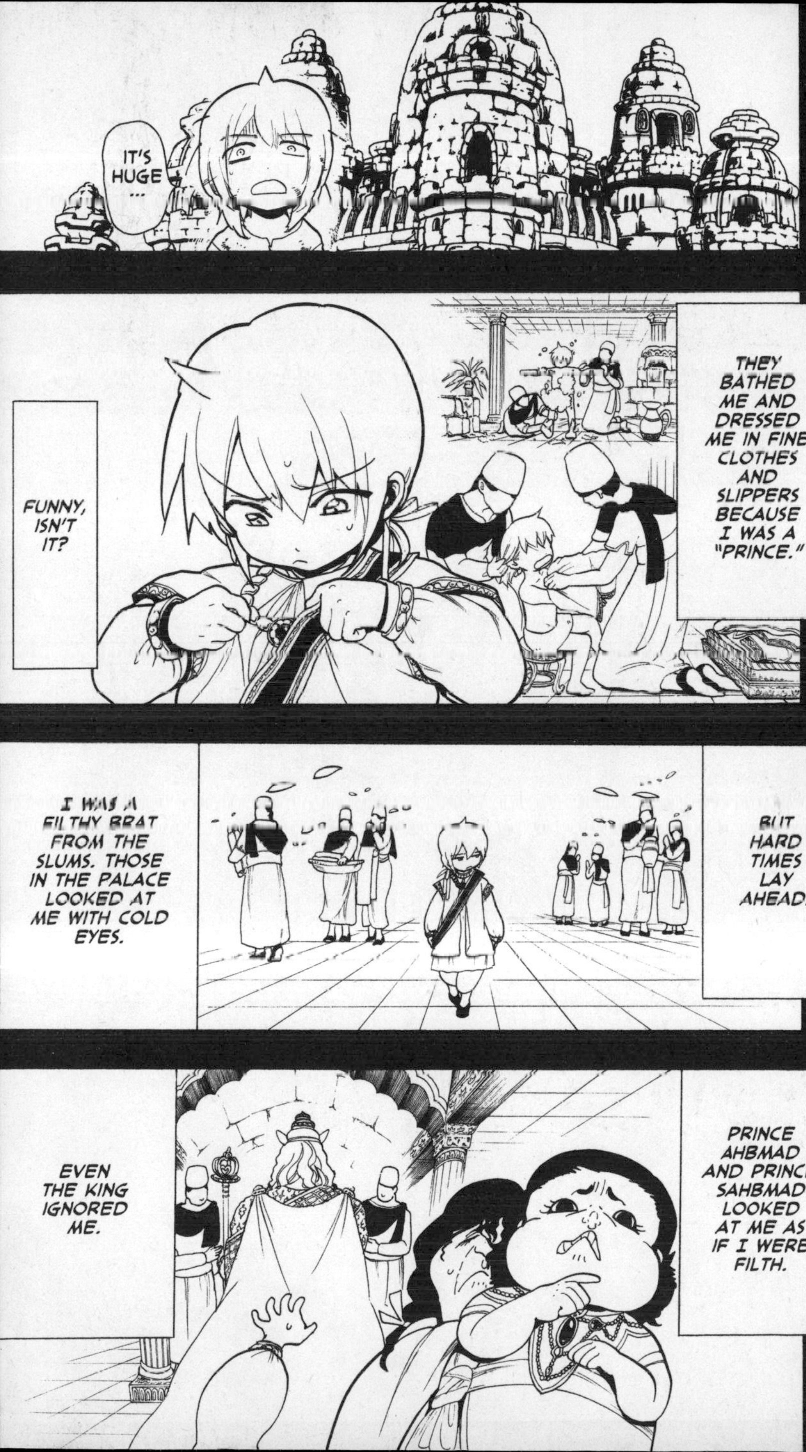
IT'S HUGE ...
THEY BATHED ME AND DRESSED ME IN FINE CLOTHES AND SLIPPERS BECAUSE I WAS A "PRINCE."
FUNNY, ISN'T IT?
BUT HARD TIMES LAY AHEAD.
I WAS A FILTHY BRAT FROM THE SLUMS. THOSE IN THE PALACE LOOKED AT ME WITH COLD EYES.
PRINCE AHBMAD AND PRINCE SAHBMAD LOOKED AT ME AS IF I WERE FILTH.
EVEN THE KING IGNORED ME.

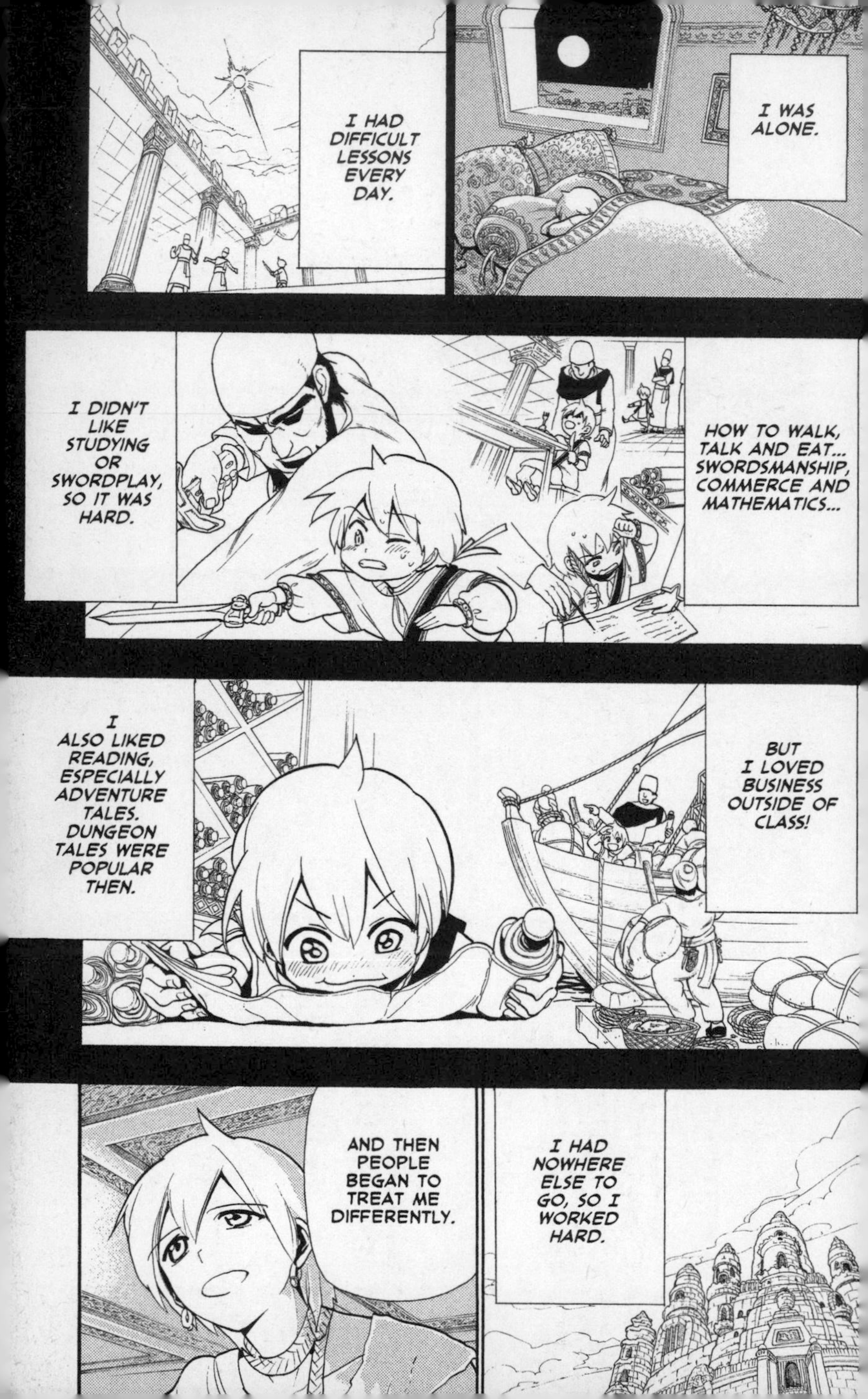
I WAS ALONE.
I HAD DIFFICULT LESSONS EVERY DAY.
HOW TO WALK, TALK AND EAT... SWORDSMANSHIP, COMMERCE AND MATHEMATICS...
I DIDN'T LIKE STUDYING OR SWORDPLAY, SO IT WAS HARD.
BUT I LOVED BUSINESS OUTSIDE OF CLASS!
I ALSO LIKED READING, ESPECIALLY ADVENTURE TALES. DUNGEON TALES WERE POPULAR THEN.
I HAD NOWHERE ELSE TO GO, SO I WORKED HARD.
AND THEN PEOPLE BEGAN TO TREAT ME DIFFERENTLY.

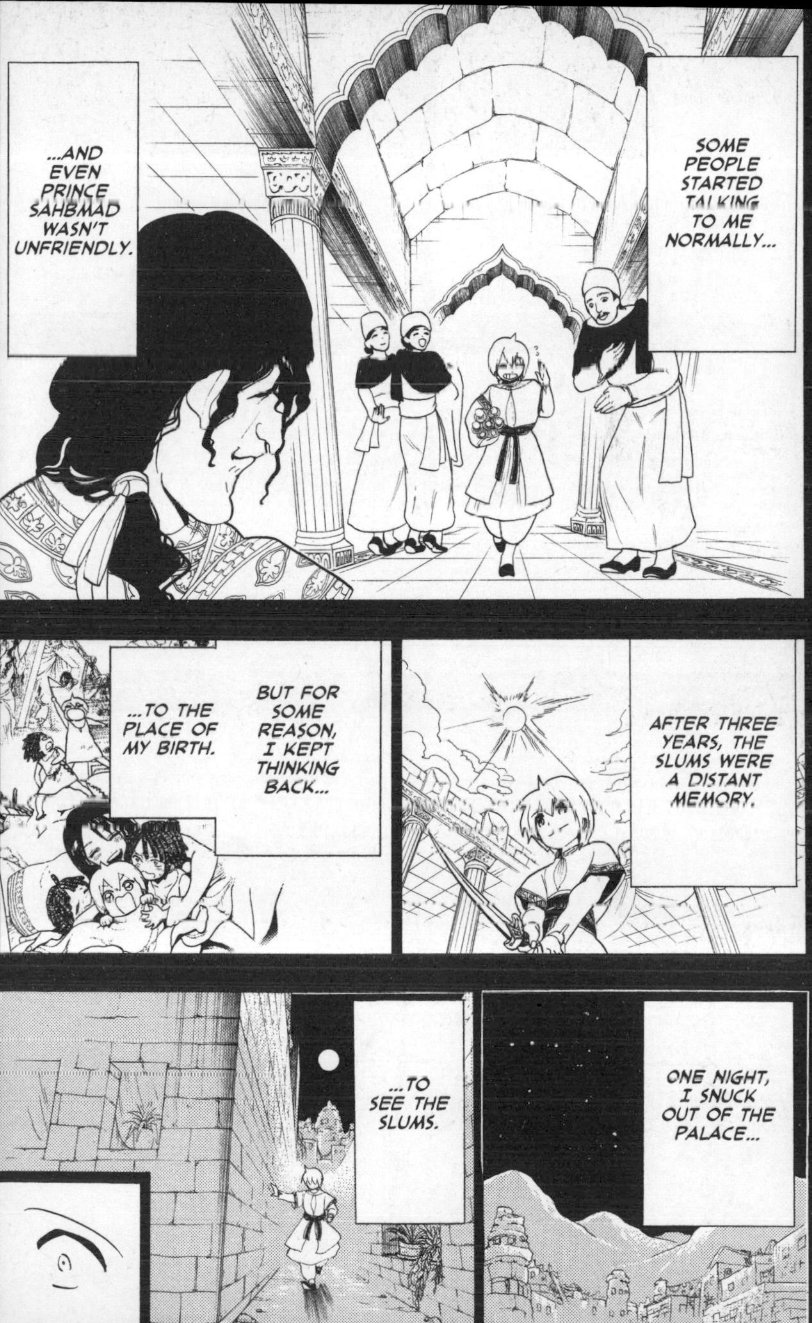
SOME PEOPLE STARTED TALKING TO ME NORMALLY...
...AND EVEN PRINCE SAHBMAD WASN'T UNFRIENDLY.
AFTER THREE YEARS, THE SLUMS WERE A DISTANT MEMORY.
BUT FOR SOME REASON, I KEPT THINKING BACK...
...TO THE PLACE OF MY BIRTH.
ONE NIGHT, I SNUCK OUT OF THE PALACE...
...TO SEE THE SLUMS.

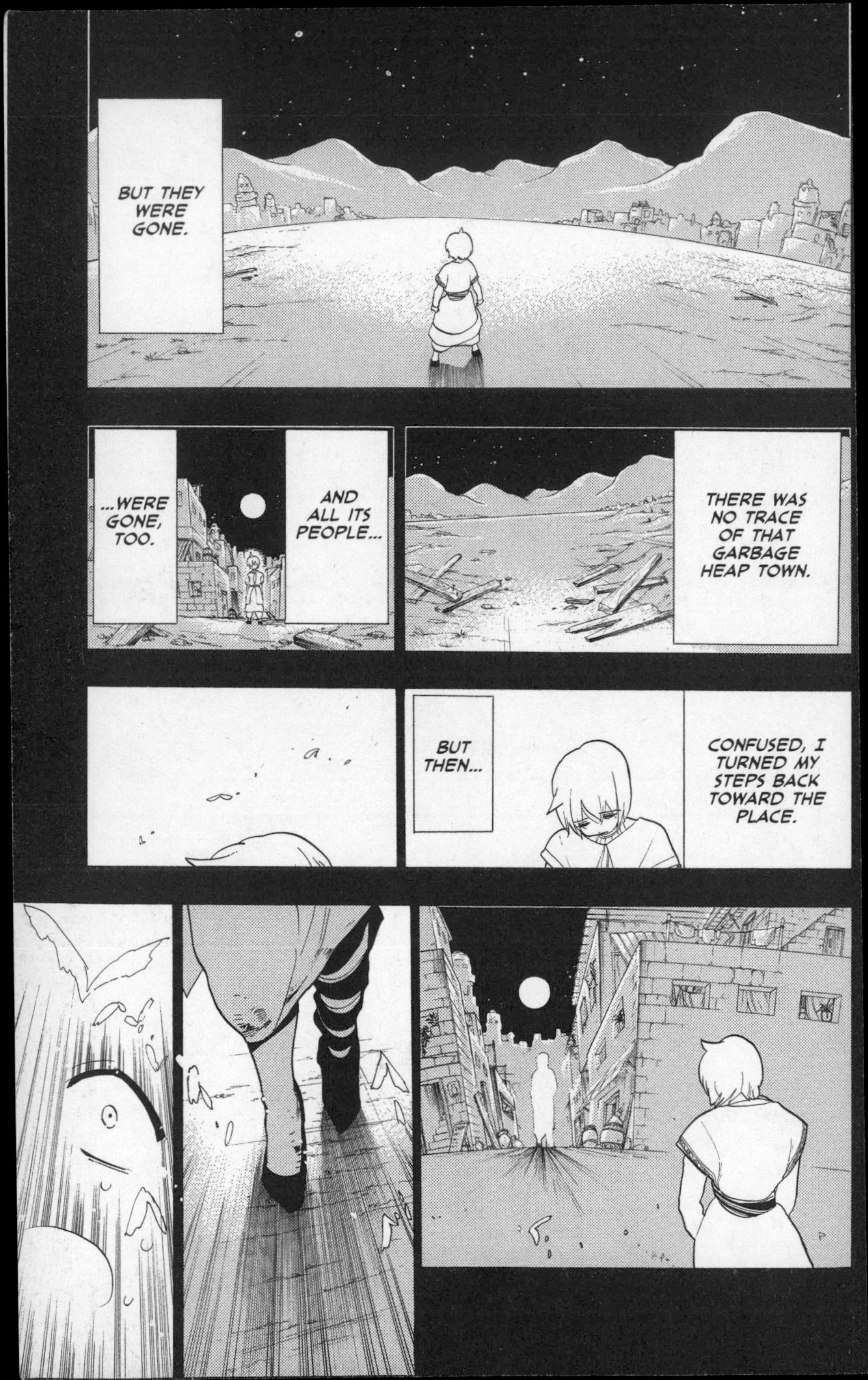
BUT THEY WERE GONE.
THERE WAS NO TRACE OF THAT GARBAGE HEAP TOWN.
AND ALL ITS PEOPLE...
...WERE GONE, TOO.
CONFUSED, I TURNED MY STEPS BACK TOWARD THE PLACE.
BUT THEN...

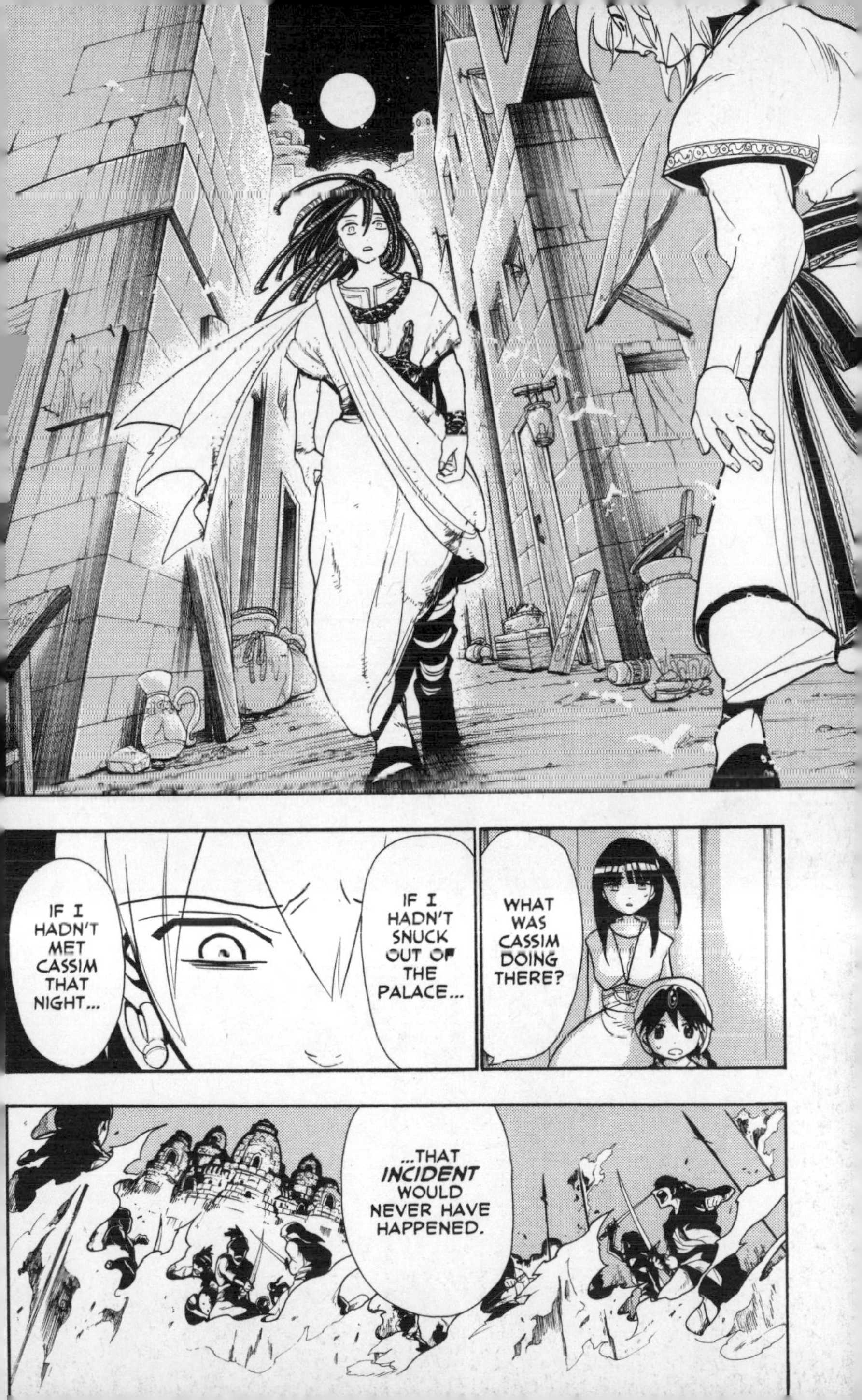
WHAT WAS CASSIM DOING THERE?
IF I HADN'T SNUCK OUT OF THE PALACE...
IF I HADN'T MET CASSIM THAT NIGHT...
...THAT *INCIDENT* WOULD NEVER HAVE HAPPENED.

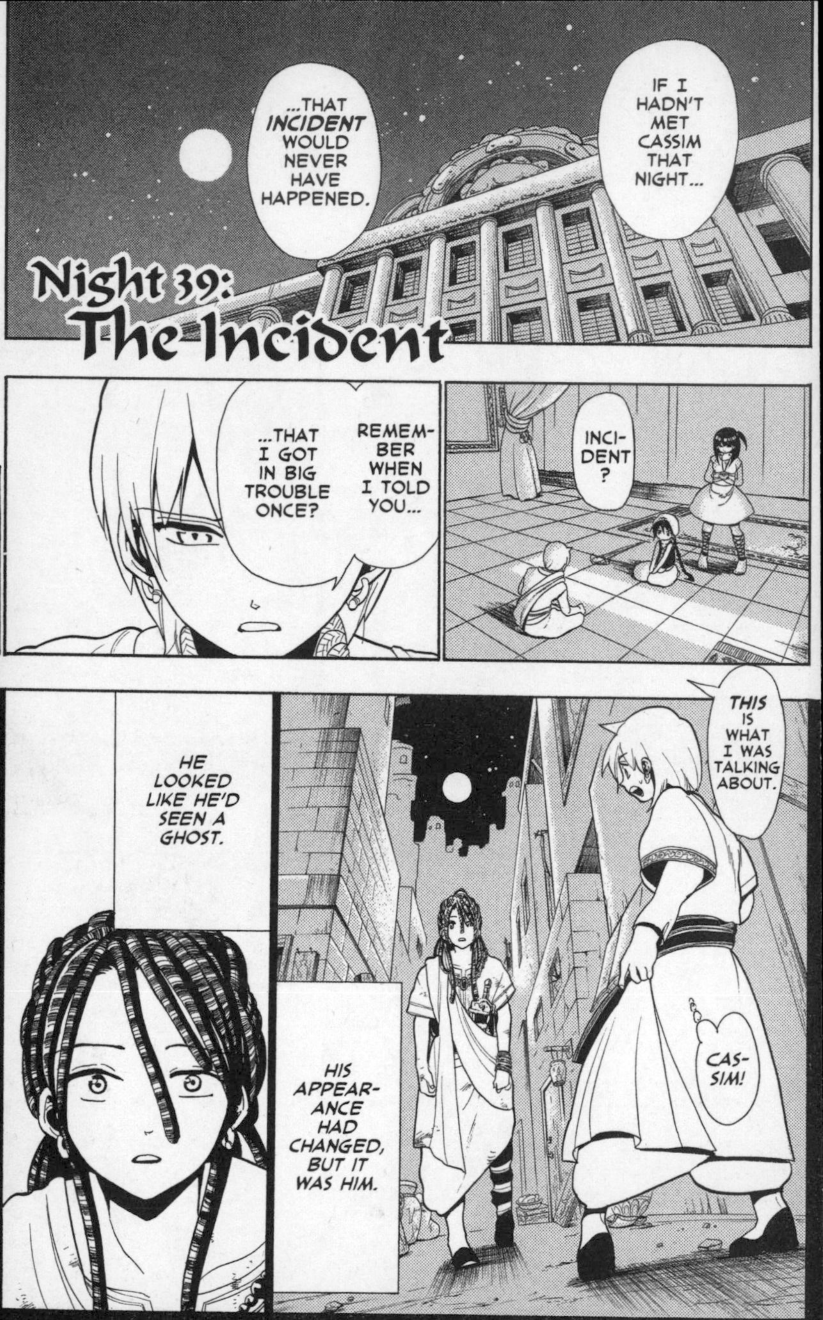
IF I HADN'T MET CASSIM THAT NIGHT...
...THAT INCIDENT WOULD NEVER HAVE HAPPENED.
Night 39: The Incident
INCIDENT?
REMEMBER WHEN I TOLD YOU...
...THAT I GOT IN BIG TROUBLE ONCE?
THIS IS WHAT I WAS TALKING ABOUT.
CASSIM!
HIS APPEARANCE HAD CHANGED, BUT IT WAS HIM.
HE LOOKED LIKE HE'D SEEN A GHOST.

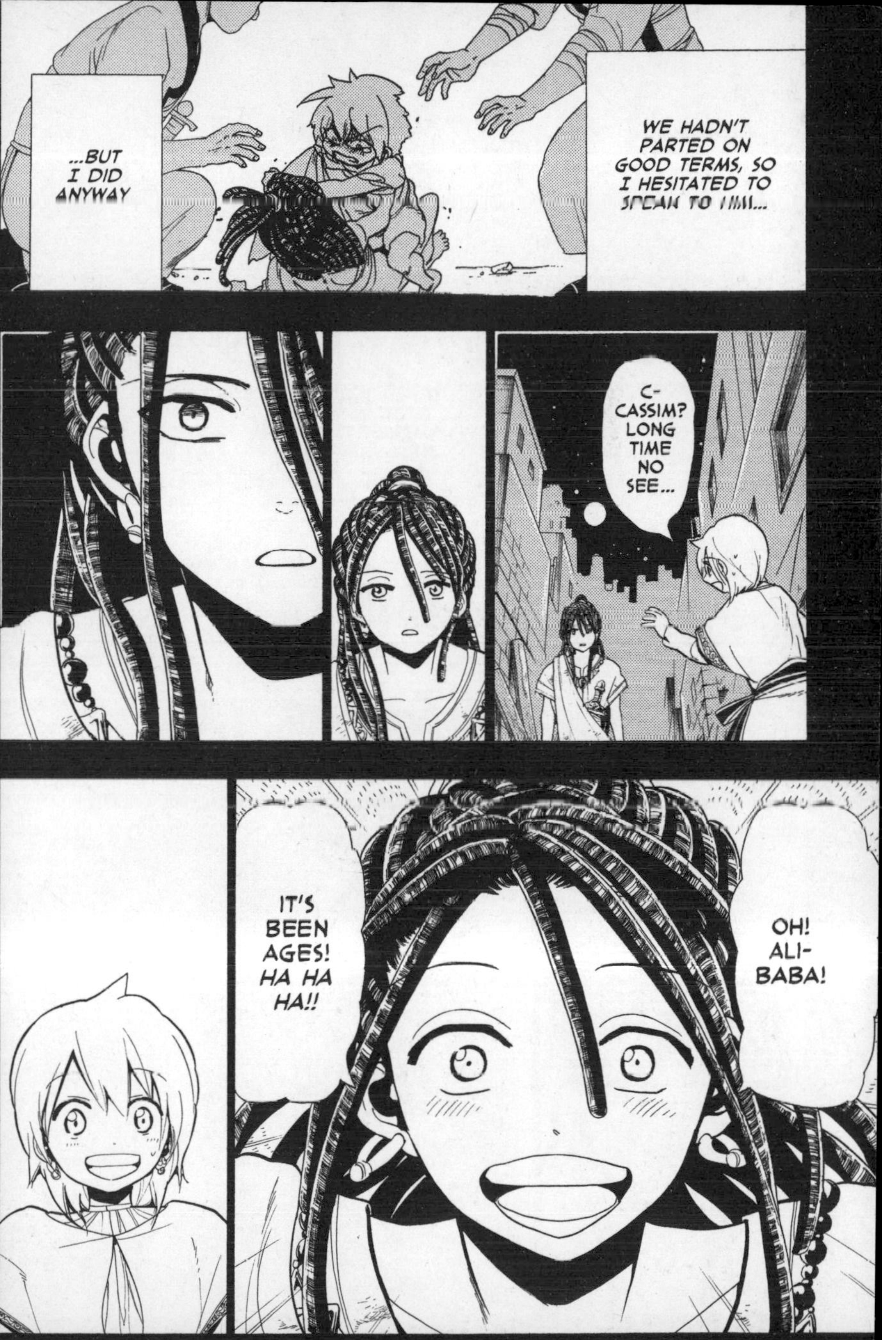
WE HADN'T PARTED ON GOOD TERMS, SO I HESITATED TO SPEAK TO HIM...
...BUT I DID ANYWAY
C-CASSIM? LONG TIME NO SEE...
OH! ALI-BABA!
IT'S BEEN AGES! HA HA HA!!

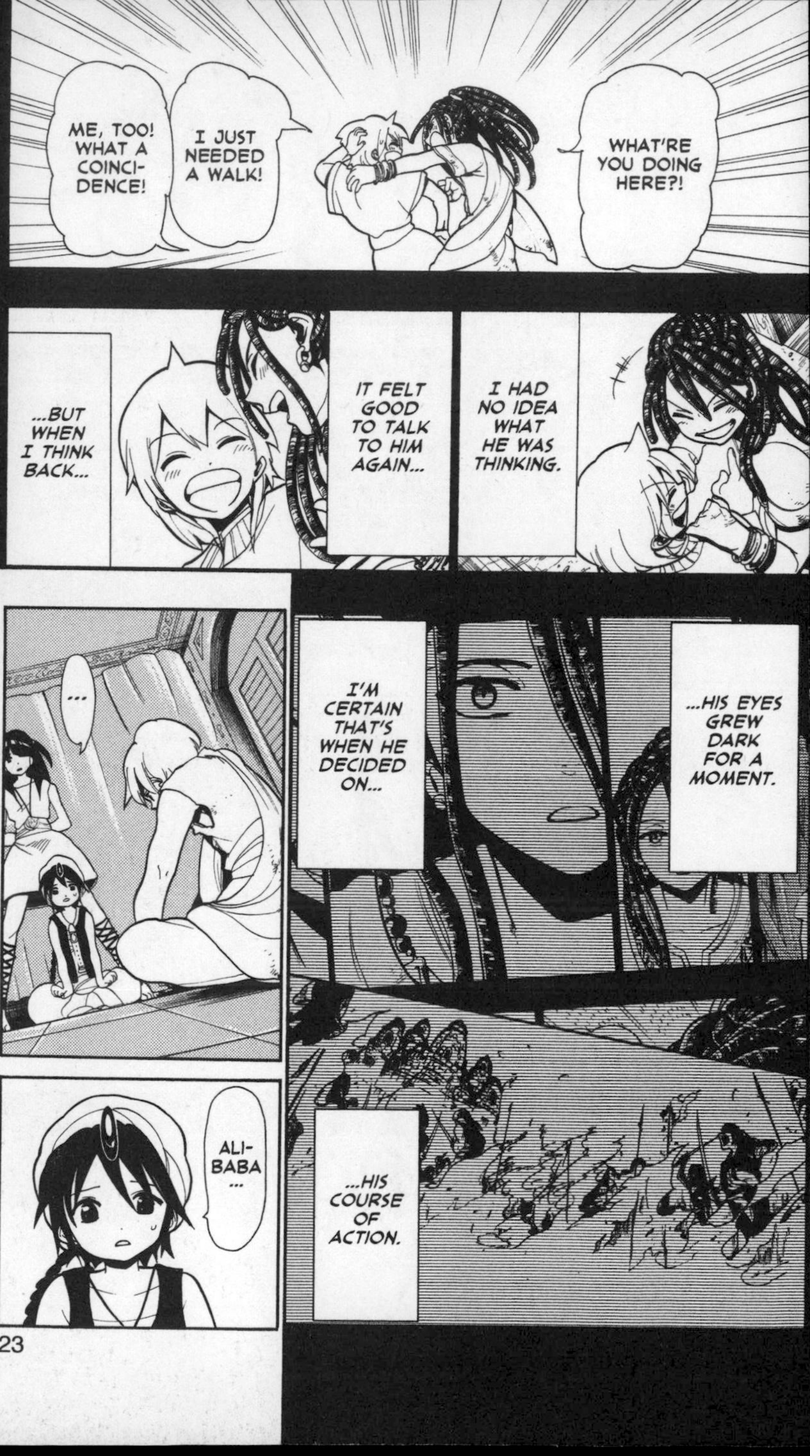
WHAT'RE YOU DOING HERE?!
I JUST NEEDED A WALK!
ME, TOO! WHAT A COINCI-DENCE!
I HAD NO IDEA WHAT HE WAS THINKING.
IT FELT GOOD TO TALK TO HIM AGAIN...
...BUT WHEN I THINK BACK...
...HIS EYES GREW DARK FOR A MOMENT.
I'M CERTAIN THAT'S WHEN HE DECIDED ON...
...HIS COURSE OF ACTION.
...
ALI-BABA...

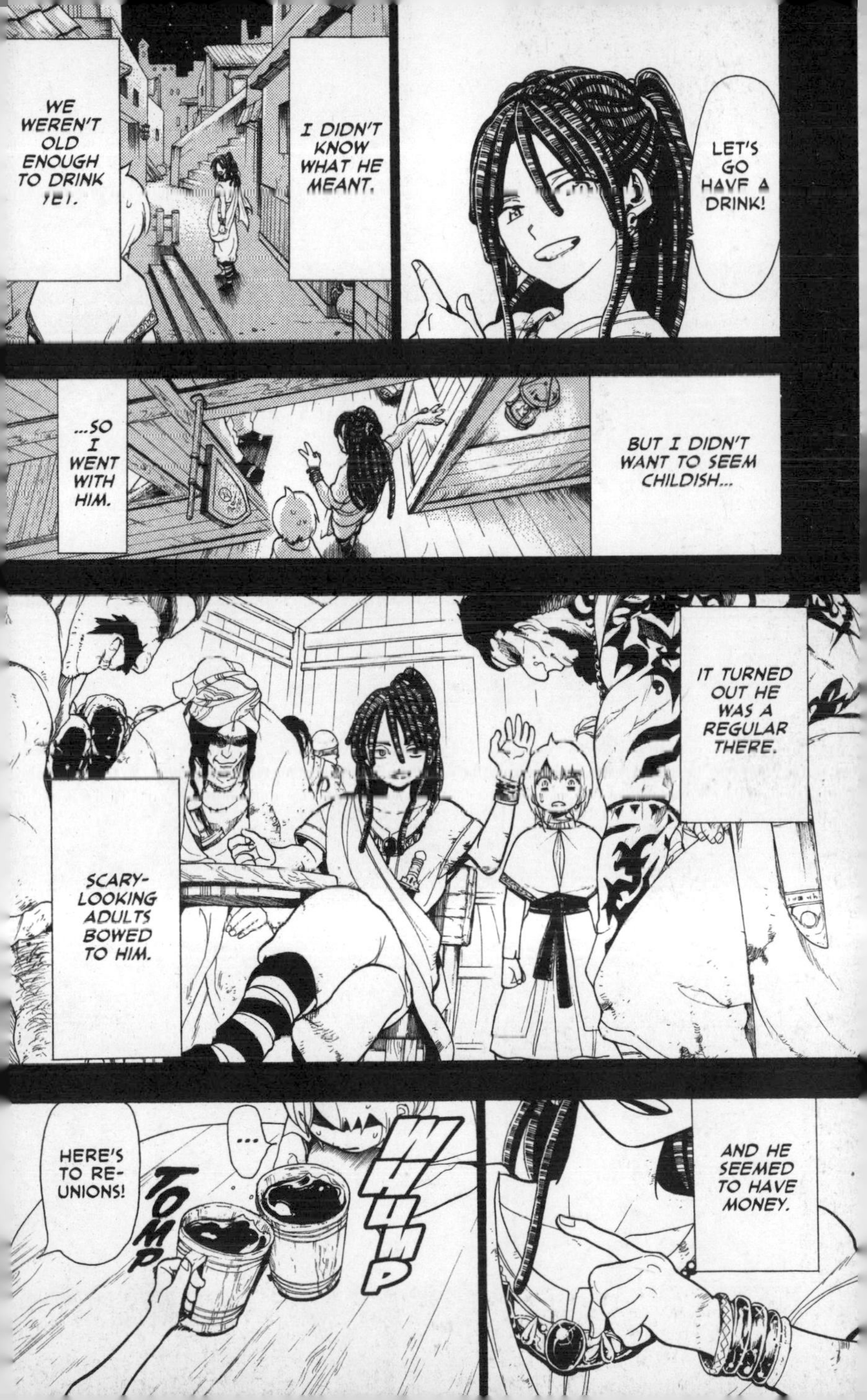
LET'S GO HAVE A DRINK!
I DIDN'T KNOW WHAT HE MEANT.
WE WEREN'T OLD ENOUGH TO DRINK YET.
BUT I DIDN'T WANT TO SEEM CHILDISH...
...SO I WENT WITH HIM.
IT TURNED OUT HE WAS A REGULAR THERE.
SCARY-LOOKING ADULTS BOWED TO HIM.
AND HE SEEMED TO HAVE MONEY.
WHUMP
...
HERE'S TO RE-UNIONS!
TOMP

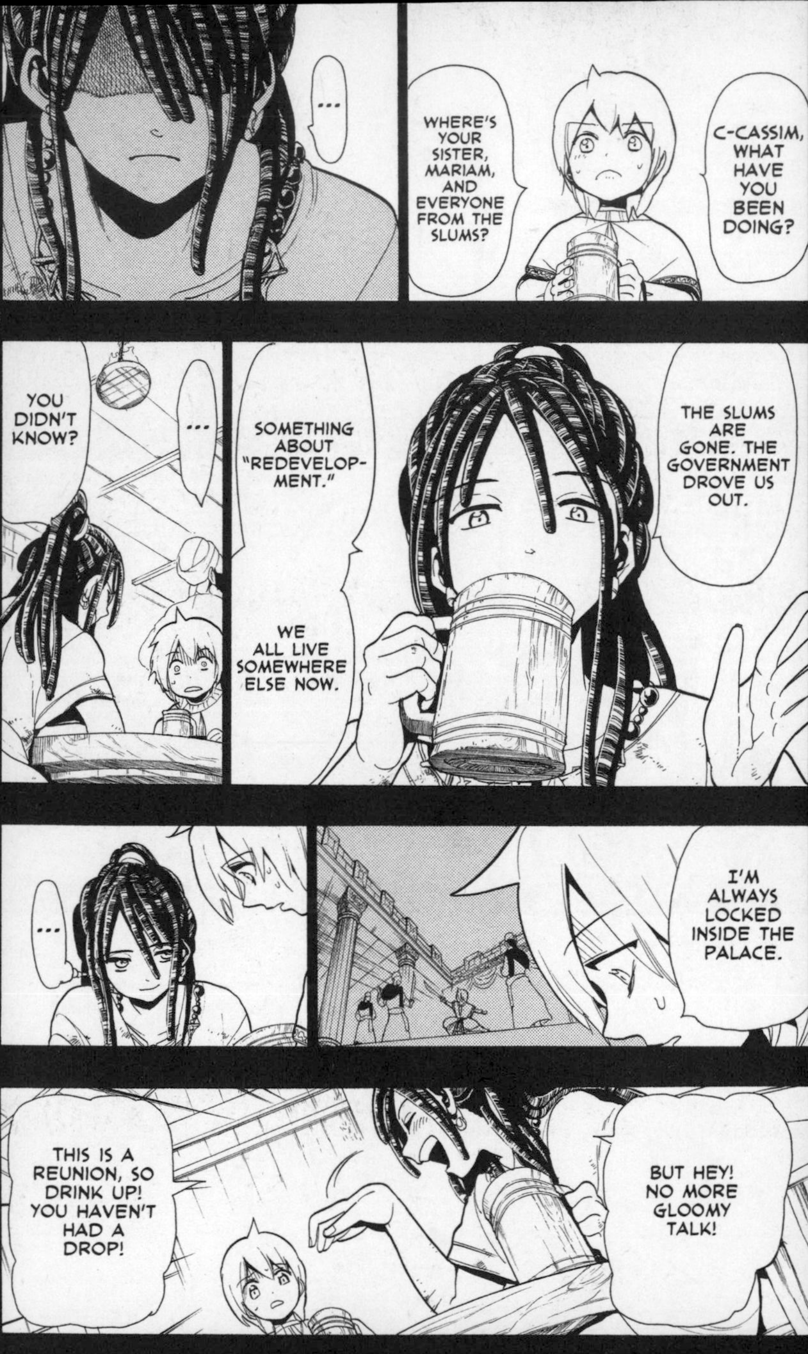
C-CASSIM, WHAT HAVE YOU BEEN DOING?
WHERE'S YOUR SISTER, MARIAM, AND EVERYONE FROM THE SLUMS?
...
THE SLUMS ARE GONE. THE GOVERNMENT DROVE US OUT.
SOMETHING ABOUT "REDEVELOPMENT."
WE ALL LIVE SOMEWHERE ELSE NOW.
...
YOU DIDN'T KNOW?
I'M ALWAYS LOCKED INSIDE THE PALACE.
...
BUT HEY! NO MORE GLOOMY TALK!
THIS IS A REUNION, SO DRINK UP! YOU HAVEN'T HAD A DROP!

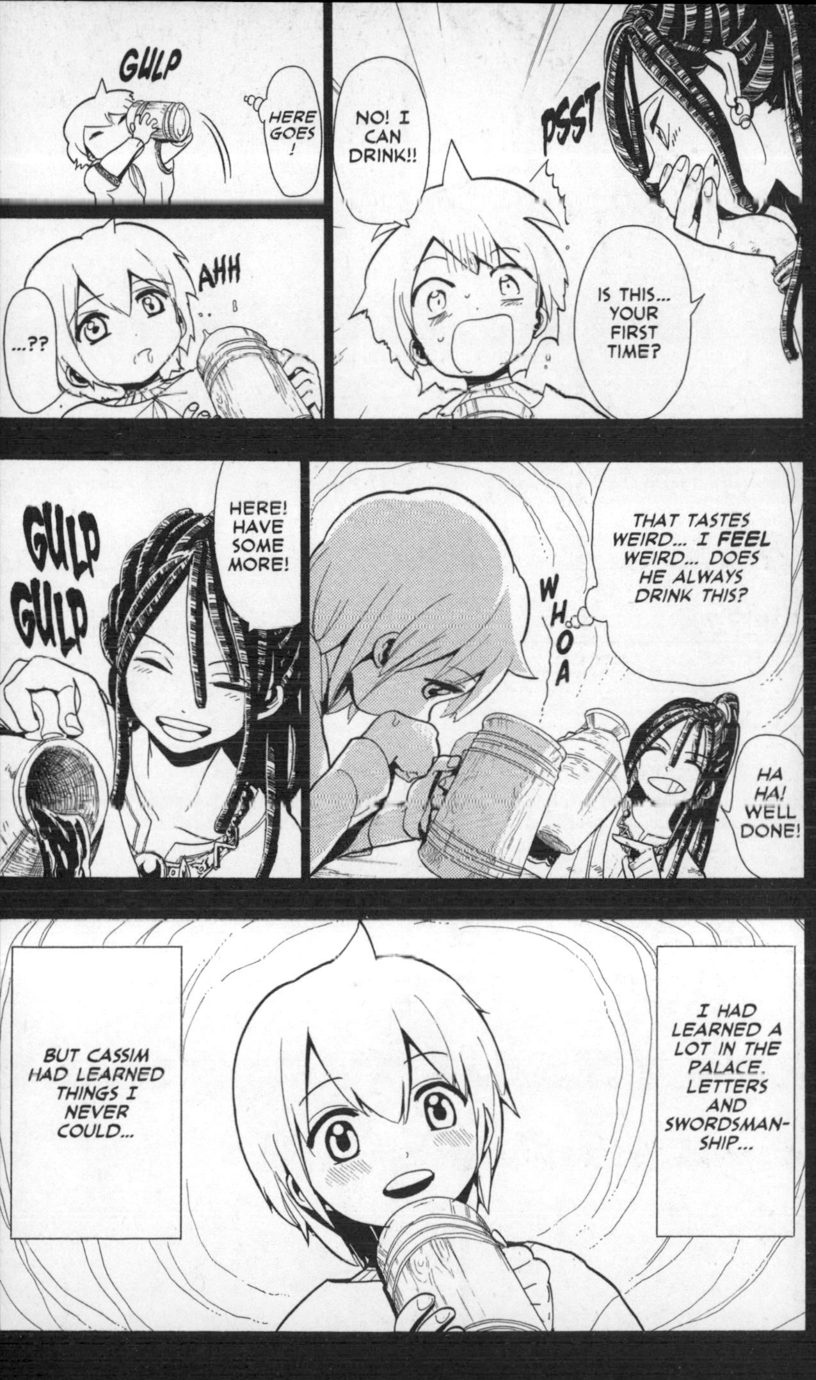
PSST
IS THIS... YOUR FIRST TIME?
NO! I CAN DRINK!!
HERE GOES!
GULP
AHH
...??
THAT TASTES WEIRD... I FEEL WEIRD... DOES HE ALWAYS DRINK THIS?
WHOA
HA HA! WELL DONE!
HERE! HAVE SOME MORE!
GULP GULP
I HAD LEARNED A LOT IN THE PALACE. LETTERS AND SWORDSMAN-SHIP...
BUT CASSIM HAD LEARNED THINGS I NEVER COULD...

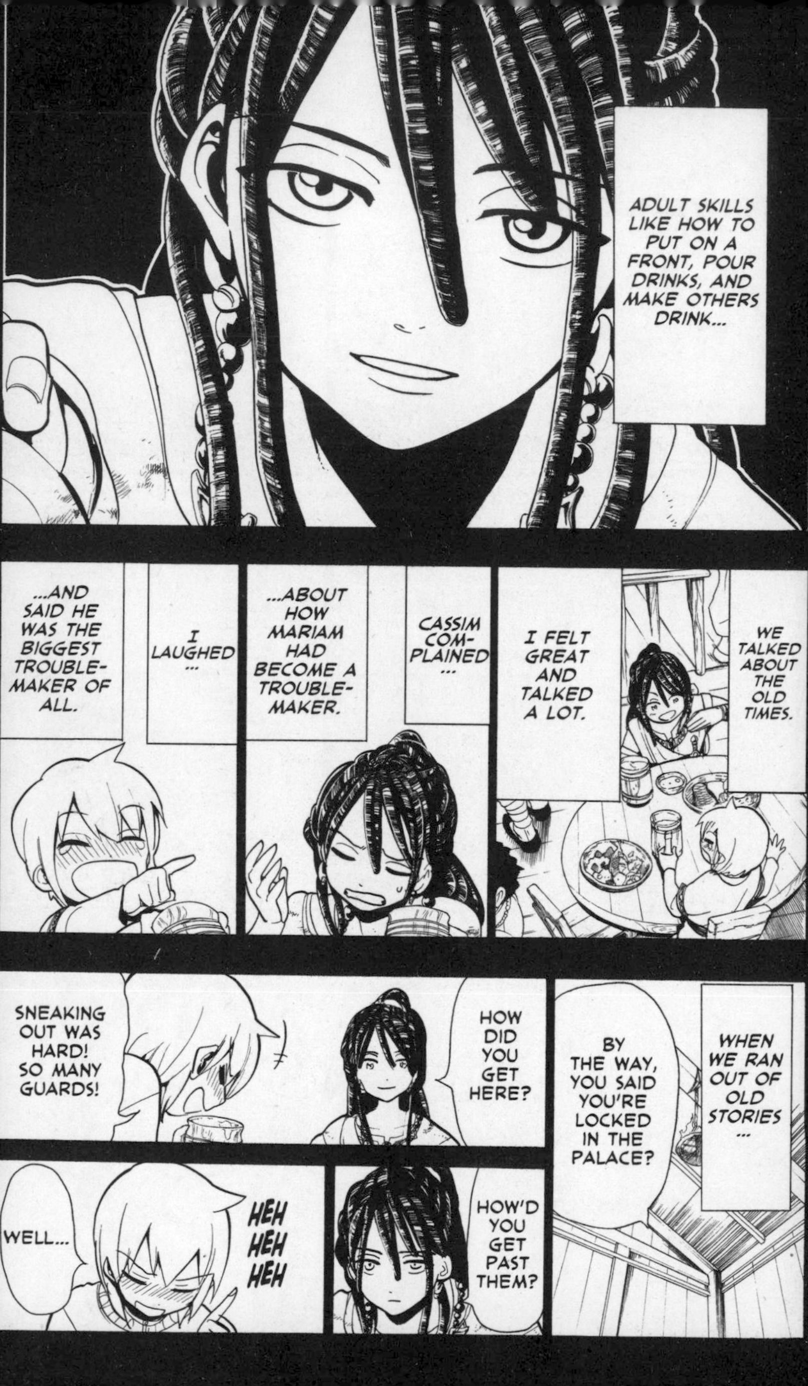

ADULT SKILLS LIKE HOW TO PUT ON A FRONT, POUR DRINKS, AND MAKE OTHERS DRINK...
WE TALKED ABOUT THE OLD TIMES.
I FELT GREAT AND TALKED A LOT.
CASSIM COM-PLAINED...
...ABOUT HOW MARIAM HAD BECOME A TROUBLE-MAKER.
I LAUGHED...
...AND SAID HE WAS THE BIGGEST TROUBLE-MAKER OF ALL.
WHEN WE RAN OUT OF OLD STORIES...
BY THE WAY, YOU SAID YOU'RE LOCKED IN THE PALACE?
HOW DID YOU GET HERE?
SNEAKING OUT WAS HARD! SO MANY GUARDS!
HOW'D YOU GET PAST THEM?
HEH HEH HEH
WELL...

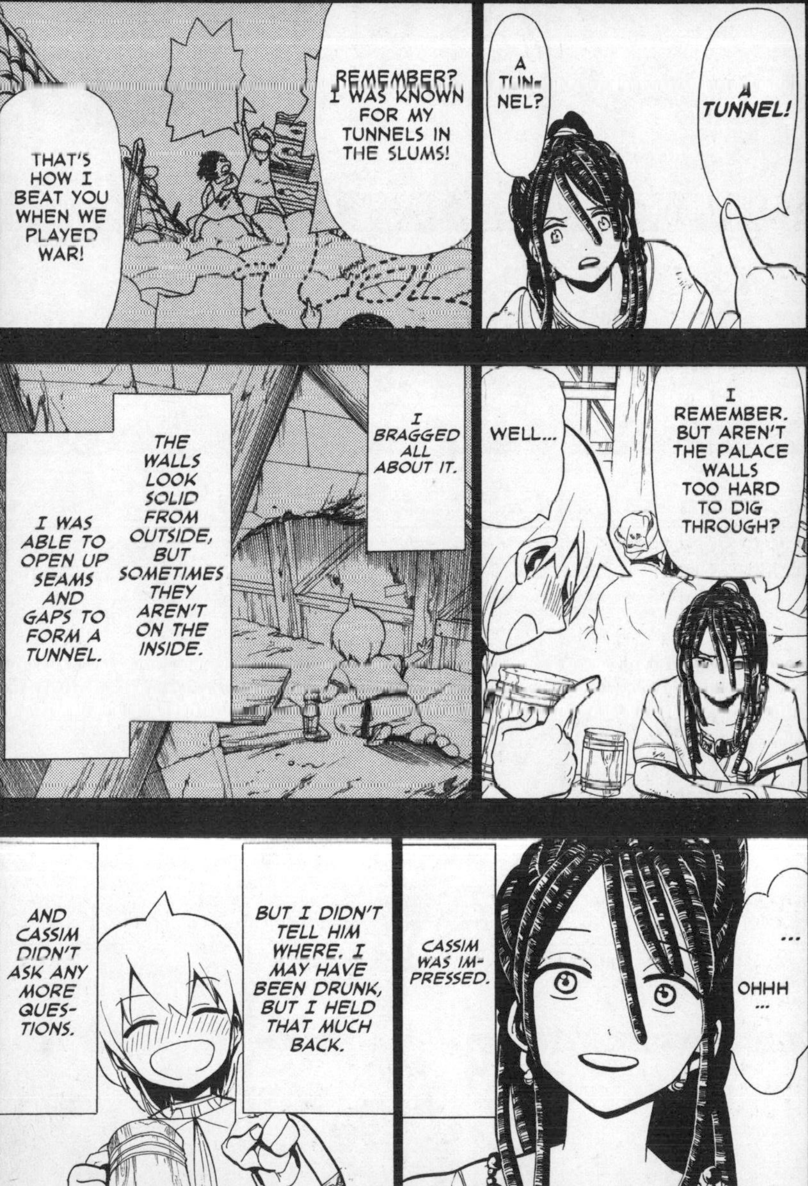
A TUNNEL!
A TUN-NEL?
REMEMBER? I WAS KNOWN FOR MY TUNNELS IN THE SLUMS!
THAT'S HOW I BEAT YOU WHEN WE PLAYED WAR!
I REMEMBER. BUT AREN'T THE PALACE WALLS TOO HARD TO DIG THROUGH?
WELL...
I BRAGGED ALL ABOUT IT.
THE WALLS LOOK SOLID FROM OUTSIDE, BUT SOMETIMES THEY AREN'T ON THE INSIDE.
I WAS ABLE TO OPEN UP SEAMS AND GAPS TO FORM A TUNNEL.
...
OHHH ...
CASSIM WAS IM-PRESSED.
BUT I DIDN'T TELL HIM WHERE. I MAY HAVE BEEN DRUNK, BUT I HELD THAT MUCH BACK.
AND CASSIM DIDN'T ASK ANY MORE QUES-TIONS.

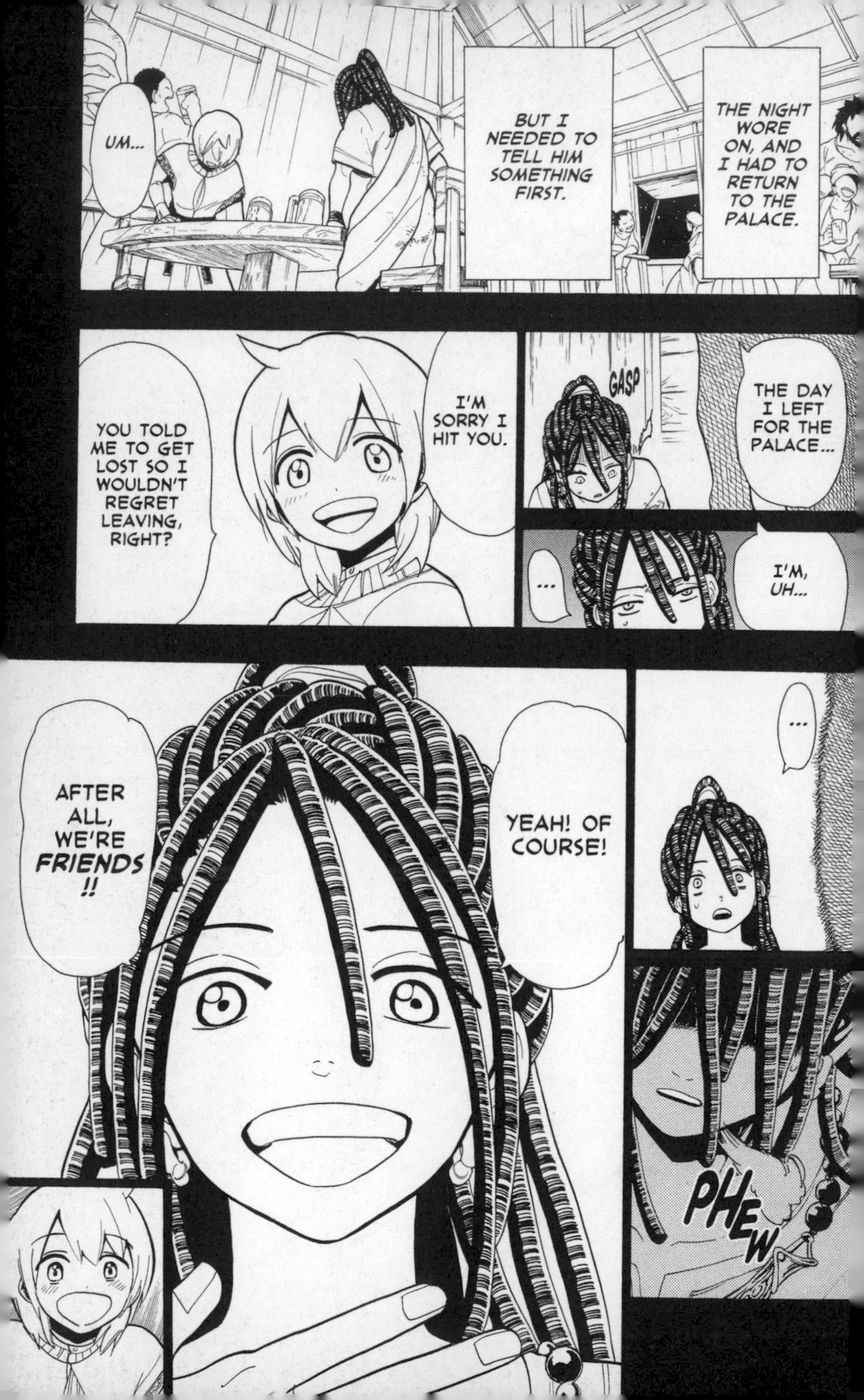
THE NIGHT WORE ON, AND I HAD TO RETURN TO THE PALACE.
BUT I NEEDED TO TELL HIM SOMETHING FIRST.
UM...
THE DAY I LEFT FOR THE PALACE...
GASP
I'M, UH...
...
I'M SORRY I HIT YOU.
YOU TOLD ME TO GET LOST SO I WOULDN'T REGRET LEAVING, RIGHT?
...
PHEW
YEAH! OF COURSE!
AFTER ALL, WE'RE FRIENDS!!

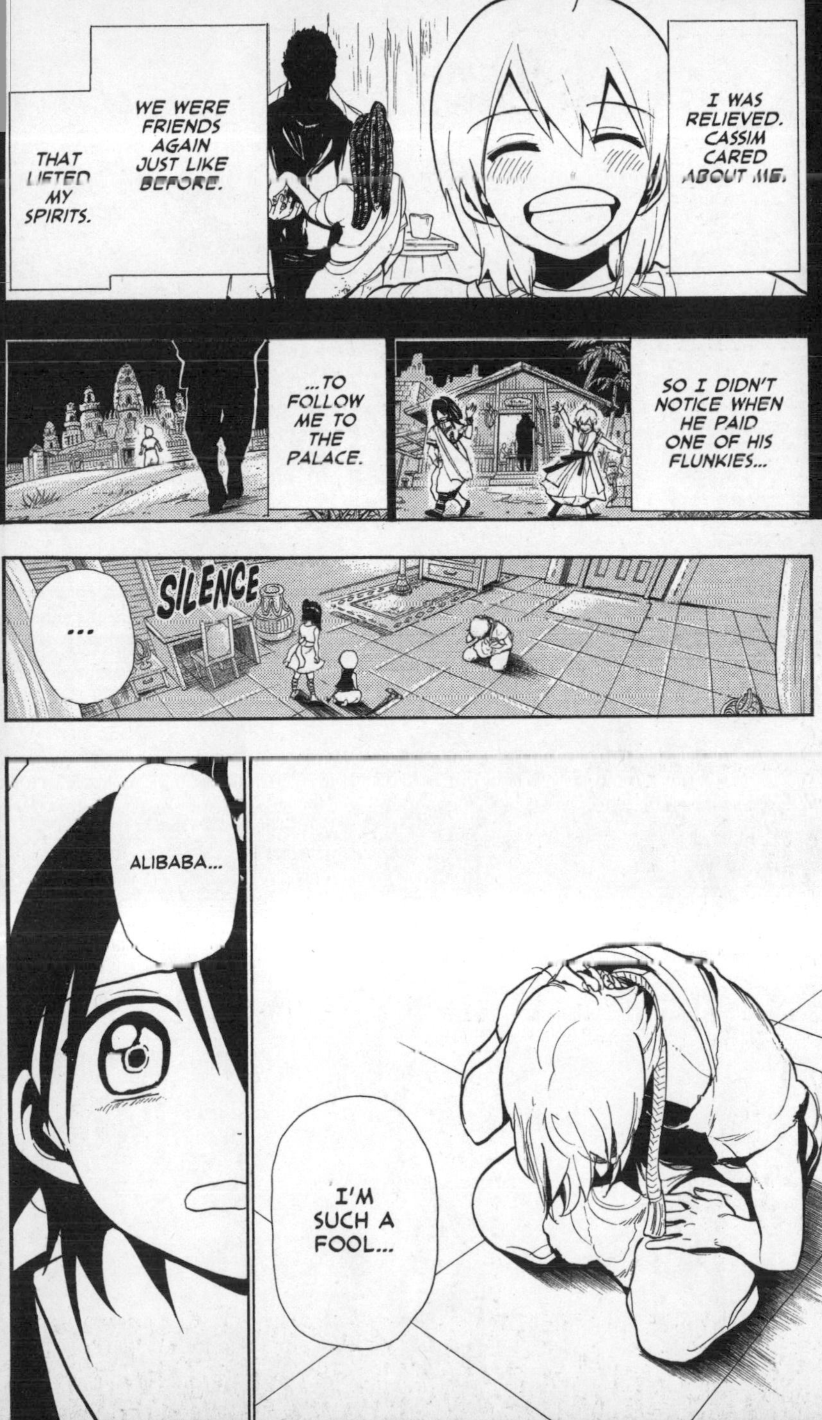
I WAS RELIEVED. CASSIM CARED ABOUT ME.
WE WERE FRIENDS AGAIN JUST LIKE BEFORE.
THAT LIFTED MY SPIRITS.
SO I DIDN'T NOTICE WHEN HE PAID ONE OF HIS FLUNKIES...
...TO FOLLOW ME TO THE PALACE.
SILENCE
...
I'M SUCH A FOOL...
ALIBABA...

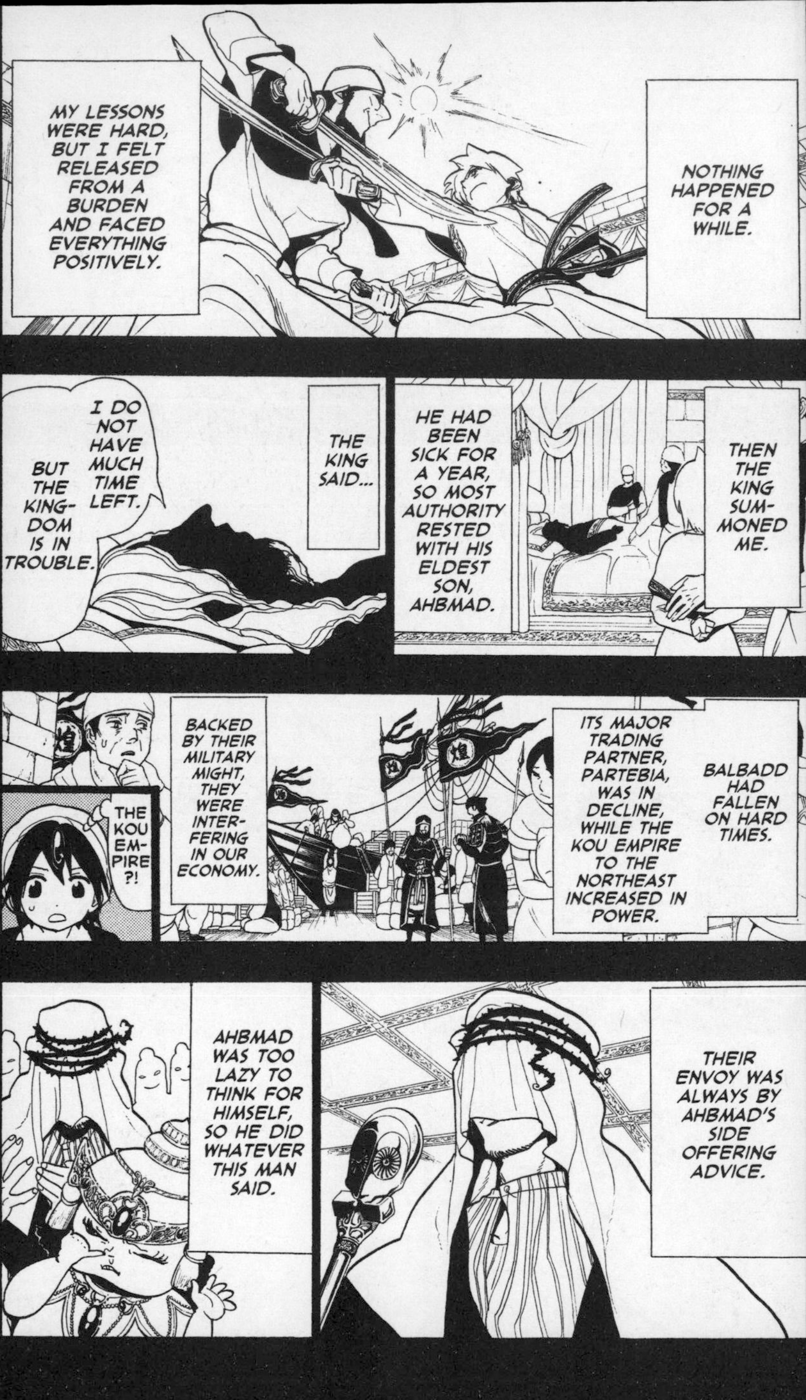

NOTHING HAPPENED FOR A WHILE.
MY LESSONS WERE HARD, BUT I FELT RELEASED FROM A BURDEN AND FACED EVERYTHING POSITIVELY.
THEN THE KING SUMMONED ME.
HE HAD BEEN SICK FOR A YEAR, SO MOST AUTHORITY RESTED WITH HIS ELDEST SON, AHBMAD.
THE KING SAID...
I DO NOT HAVE MUCH TIME LEFT.
BUT THE KINGDOM IS IN TROUBLE.
BALBADD HAD FALLEN ON HARD TIMES.
ITS MAJOR TRADING PARTNER, PARTEBIA, WAS IN DECLINE, WHILE THE KOU EMPIRE TO THE NORTHEAST INCREASED IN POWER.
BACKED BY THEIR MILITARY MIGHT, THEY WERE INTERFERING IN OUR ECONOMY.
THE KOU EMPIRE?!
THEIR ENVOY WAS ALWAYS BY AHBMAD'S SIDE OFFERING ADVICE.
AHBMAD WAS TOO LAZY TO THINK FOR HIMSELF, SO HE DID WHATEVER THIS MAN SAID.

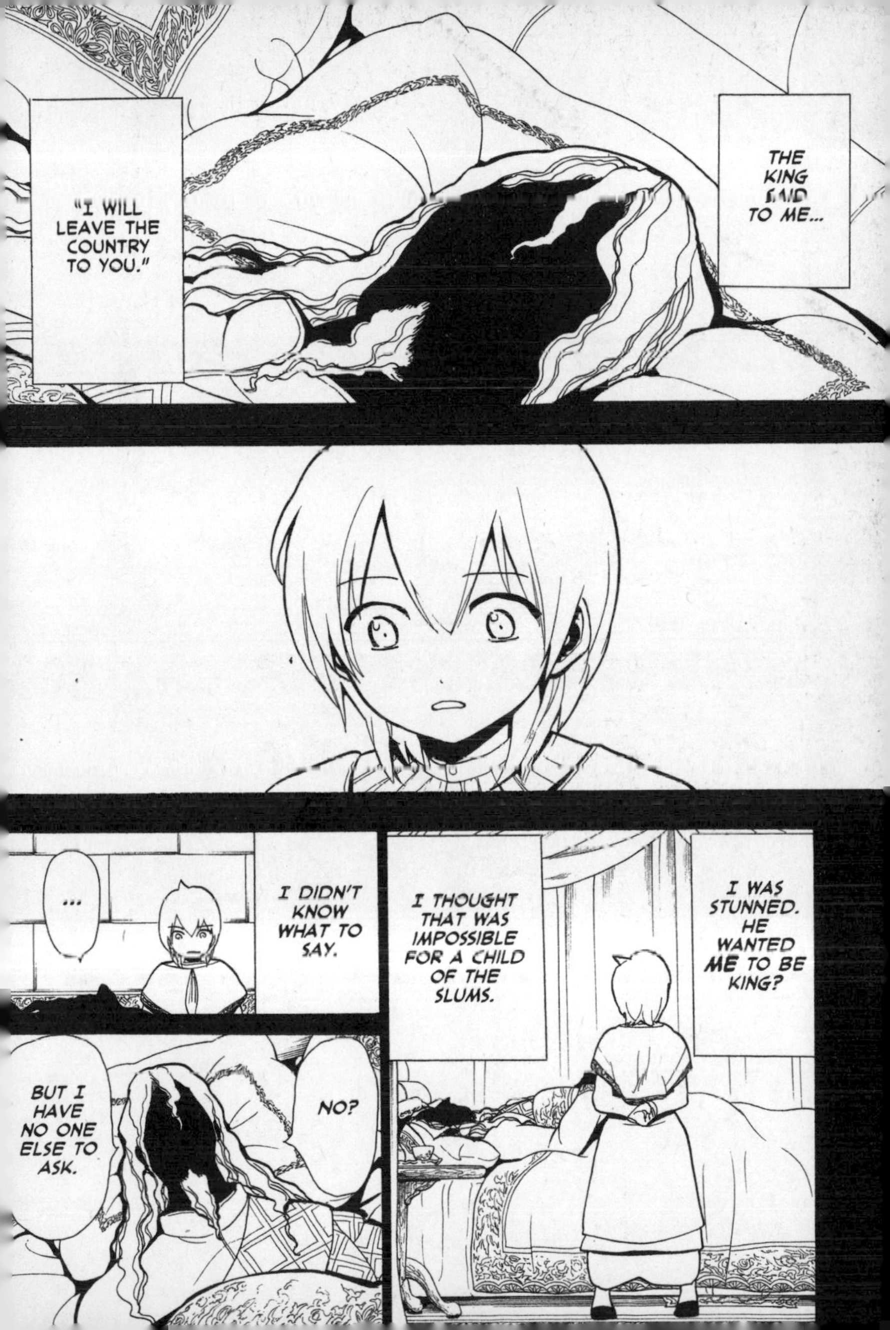
THE KING SAID TO ME...
"I WILL LEAVE THE COUNTRY TO YOU."
I WAS STUNNED. HE WANTED ME TO BE KING?
I THOUGHT THAT WAS IMPOSSIBLE FOR A CHILD OF THE SLUMS.
I DIDN'T KNOW WHAT TO SAY.
...
NO?
BUT I HAVE NO ONE ELSE TO ASK.

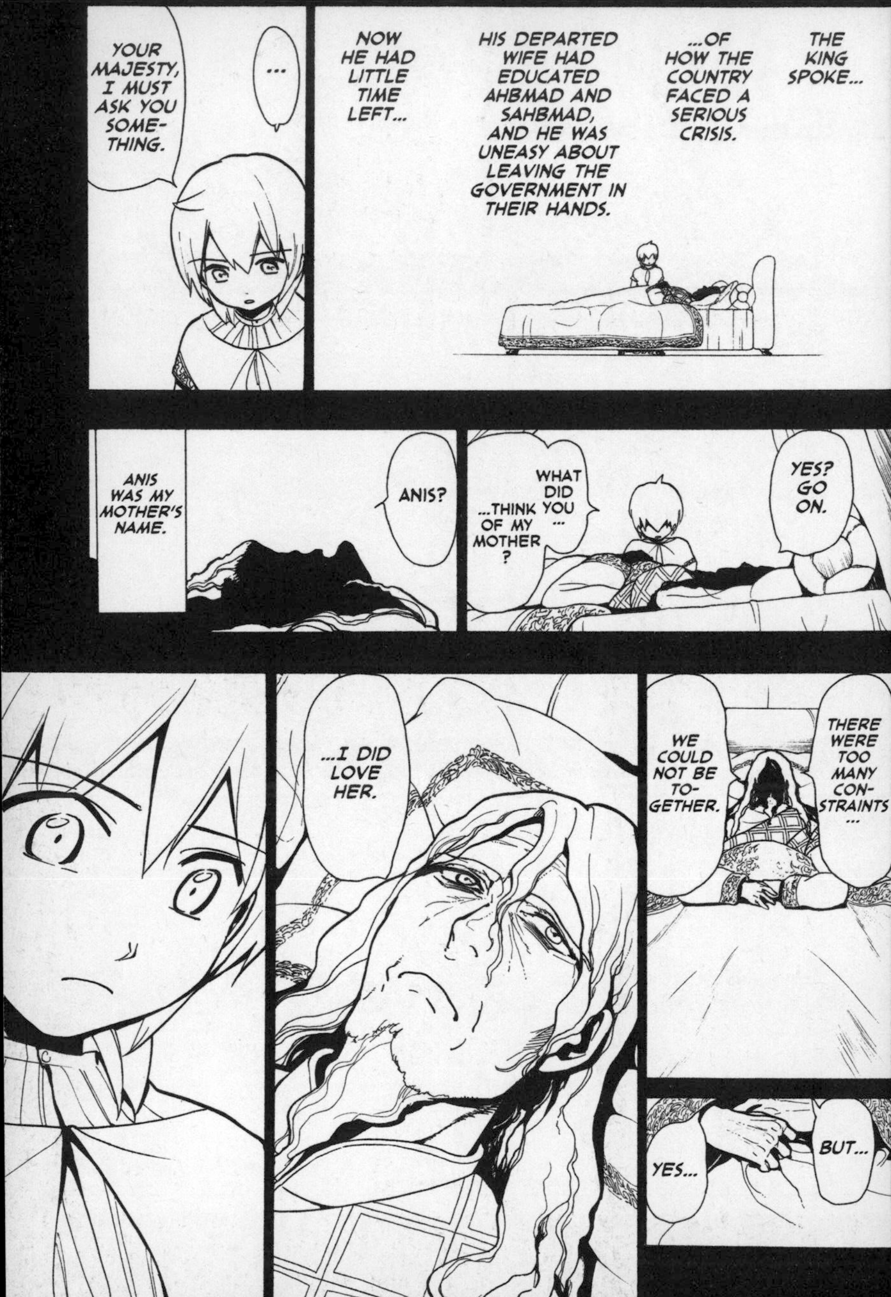
THE KING SPOKE...
...OF HOW THE COUNTRY FACED A SERIOUS CRISIS.
HIS DEPARTED WIFE HAD EDUCATED AHBMAD AND SAHBMAD, AND HE WAS UNEASY ABOUT LEAVING THE GOVERNMENT IN THEIR HANDS.
NOW HE HAD LITTLE TIME LEFT...
...
YOUR MAJESTY, I MUST ASK YOU SOME-THING.
YES? GO ON.
WHAT DID YOU ...
...THINK OF MY MOTHER ?
ANIS?
ANIS WAS MY MOTHER'S NAME.
THERE WERE TOO MANY CON-STRAINTS ...
WE COULD NOT BE TO-GETHER.
BUT...
YES...
...I DID LOVE HER.

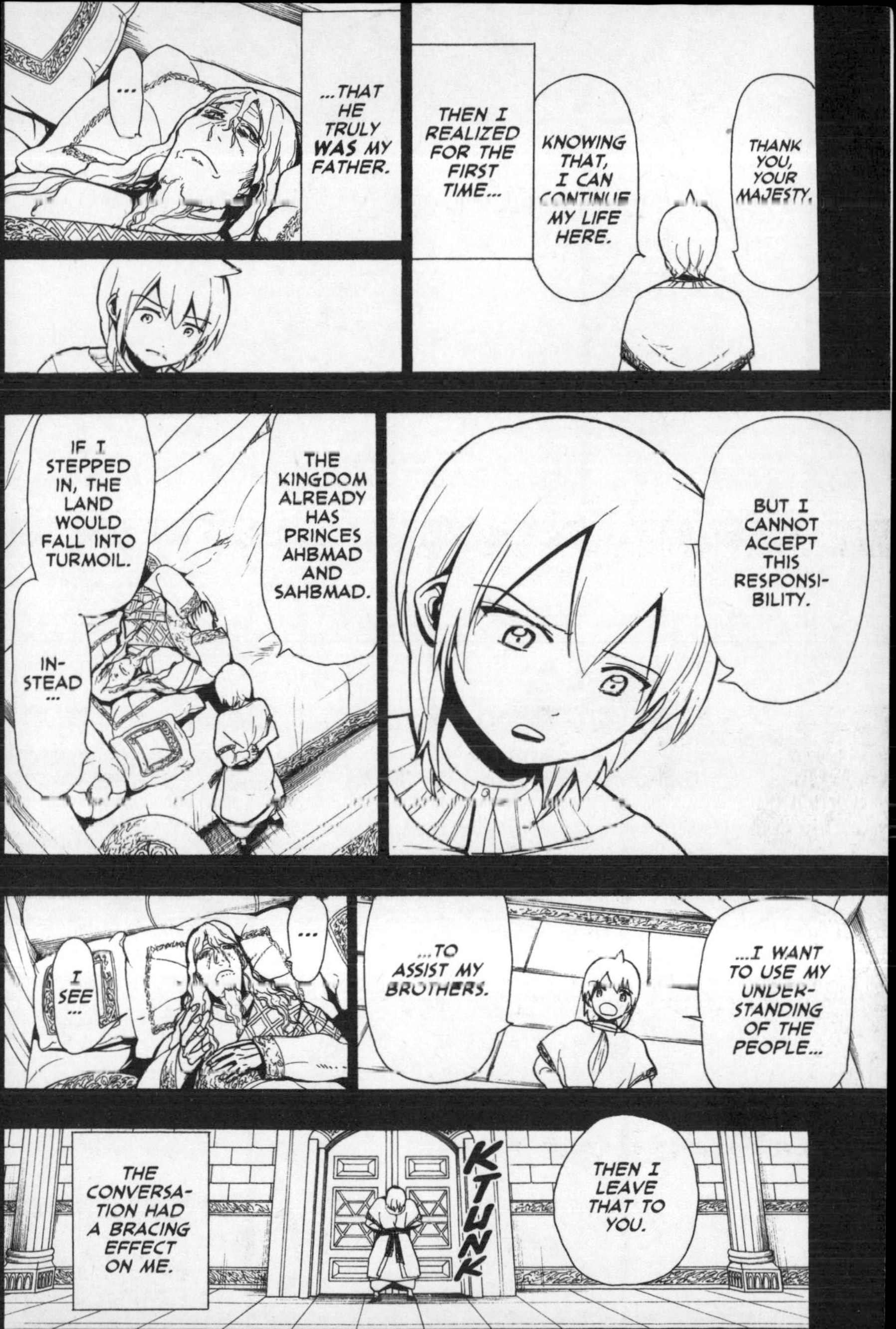
THANK YOU, YOUR MAJESTY.
KNOWING THAT, I CAN CONTINUE MY LIFE HERE.
THEN I REALIZED FOR THE FIRST TIME...
...THAT HE TRULY WAS MY FATHER.
...
BUT I CANNOT ACCEPT THIS RESPONSIBILITY.
THE KINGDOM ALREADY HAS PRINCES AHBMAD AND SAHBMAD.
IF I STEPPED IN, THE LAND WOULD FALL INTO TURMOIL.
INSTEAD...
...I WANT TO USE MY UNDERSTANDING OF THE PEOPLE...
...TO ASSIST MY BROTHERS.
...
I SEE...
THEN I LEAVE THAT TO YOU.
KTUNK
THE CONVERSATION HAD A BRACING EFFECT ON ME.

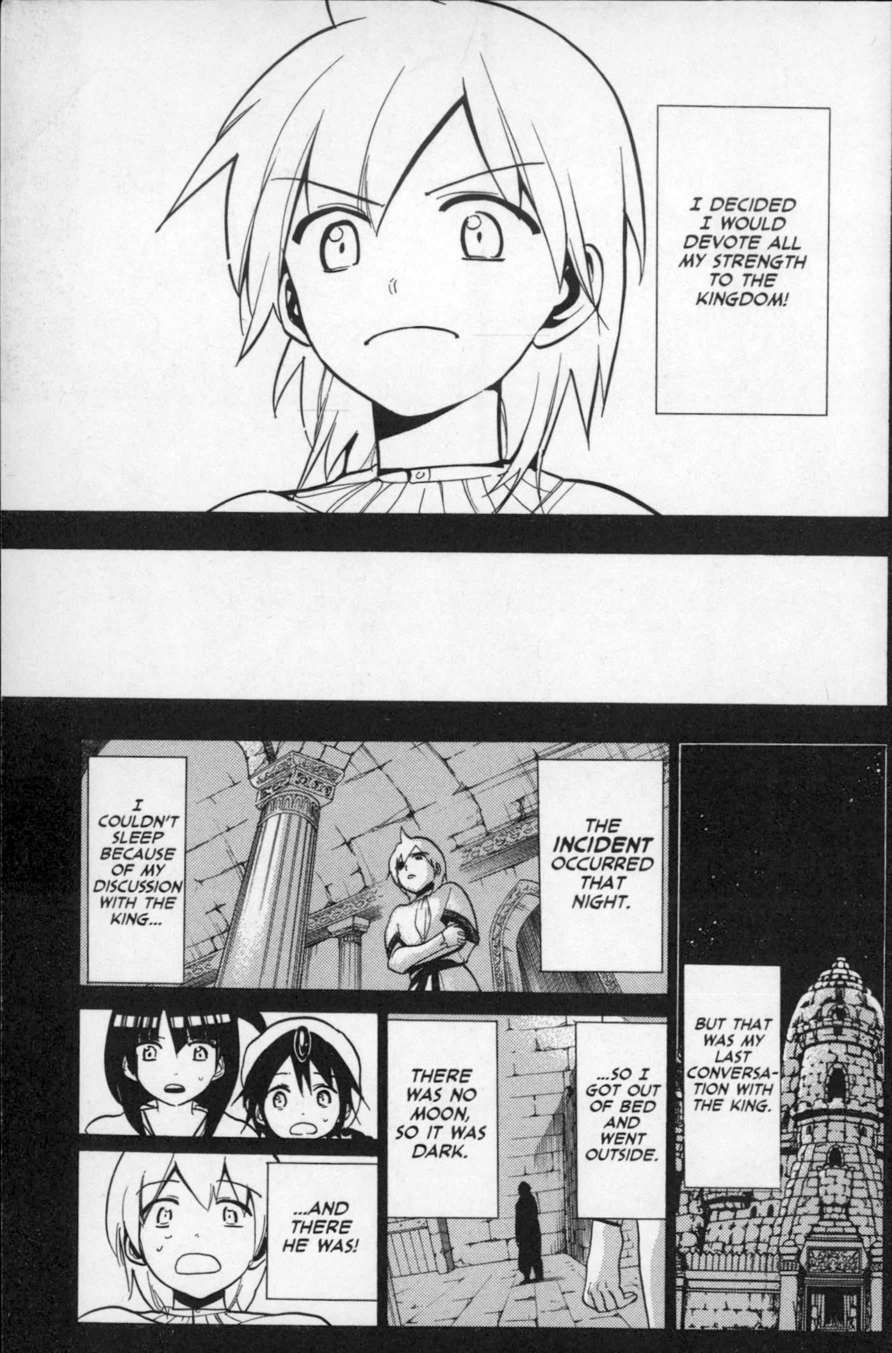
I DECIDED I WOULD DEVOTE ALL MY STRENGTH TO THE KINGDOM!
BUT THAT WAS MY LAST CONVERSA-TION WITH THE KING.
THE INCIDENT OCCURRED THAT NIGHT.
I COULDN'T SLEEP BECAUSE OF MY DISCUSSION WITH THE KING...
...SO I GOT OUT OF BED AND WENT OUTSIDE.
THERE WAS NO MOON, SO IT WAS DARK.
...AND THERE HE WAS!

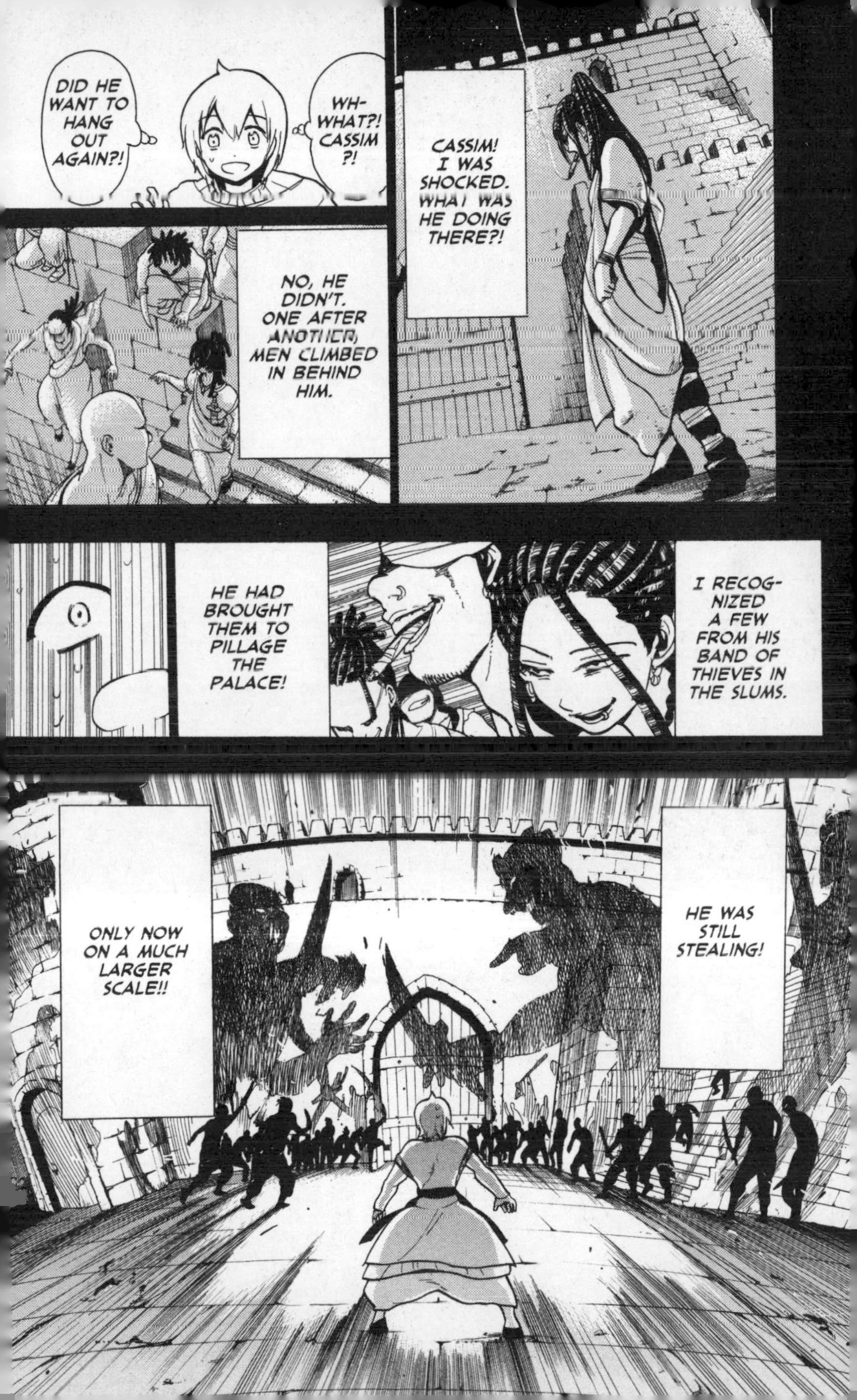
CASSIM! I WAS SHOCKED. WHAT WAS HE DOING THERE?!
WH- WHAT?! CASSIM?!
DID HE WANT TO HANG OUT AGAIN?!
NO, HE DIDN'T. ONE AFTER ANOTHER, MEN CLIMBED IN BEHIND HIM.
I RECOG-NIZED A FEW FROM HIS BAND OF THIEVES IN THE SLUMS.
HE HAD BROUGHT THEM TO PILLAGE THE PALACE!
HE WAS STILL STEALING!
ONLY NOW ON A MUCH LARGER SCALE!!

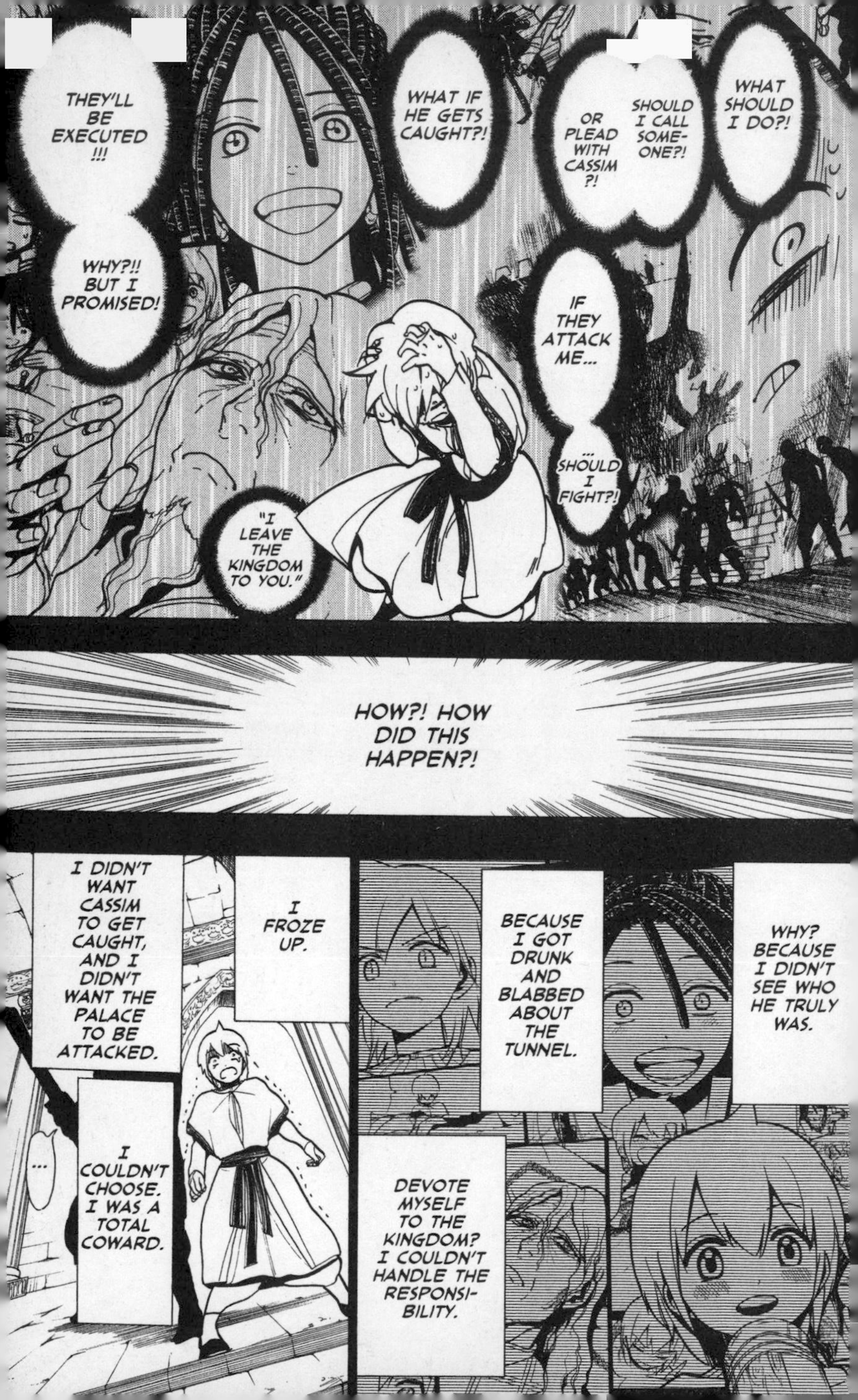
WHAT SHOULD I DO?!
SHOULD I CALL SOMEONE?!
OR PLEAD WITH CASSIM?!
WHAT IF HE GETS CAUGHT?!
THEY'LL BE EXECUTED!!!
IF THEY ATTACK ME...
...SHOULD I FIGHT?!
WHY?!! BUT I PROMISED!
"I LEAVE THE KINGDOM TO YOU."
HOW?! HOW DID THIS HAPPEN?!
WHY? BECAUSE I DIDN'T SEE WHO HE TRULY WAS.
BECAUSE I GOT DRUNK AND BLABBED ABOUT THE TUNNEL.
DEVOTE MYSELF TO THE KINGDOM? I COULDN'T HANDLE THE RESPONSIBILITY.
I FROZE UP.
I DIDN'T WANT CASSIM TO GET CAUGHT, AND I DIDN'T WANT THE PALACE TO BE ATTACKED.
I COULDN'T CHOOSE. I WAS A TOTAL COWARD.
...

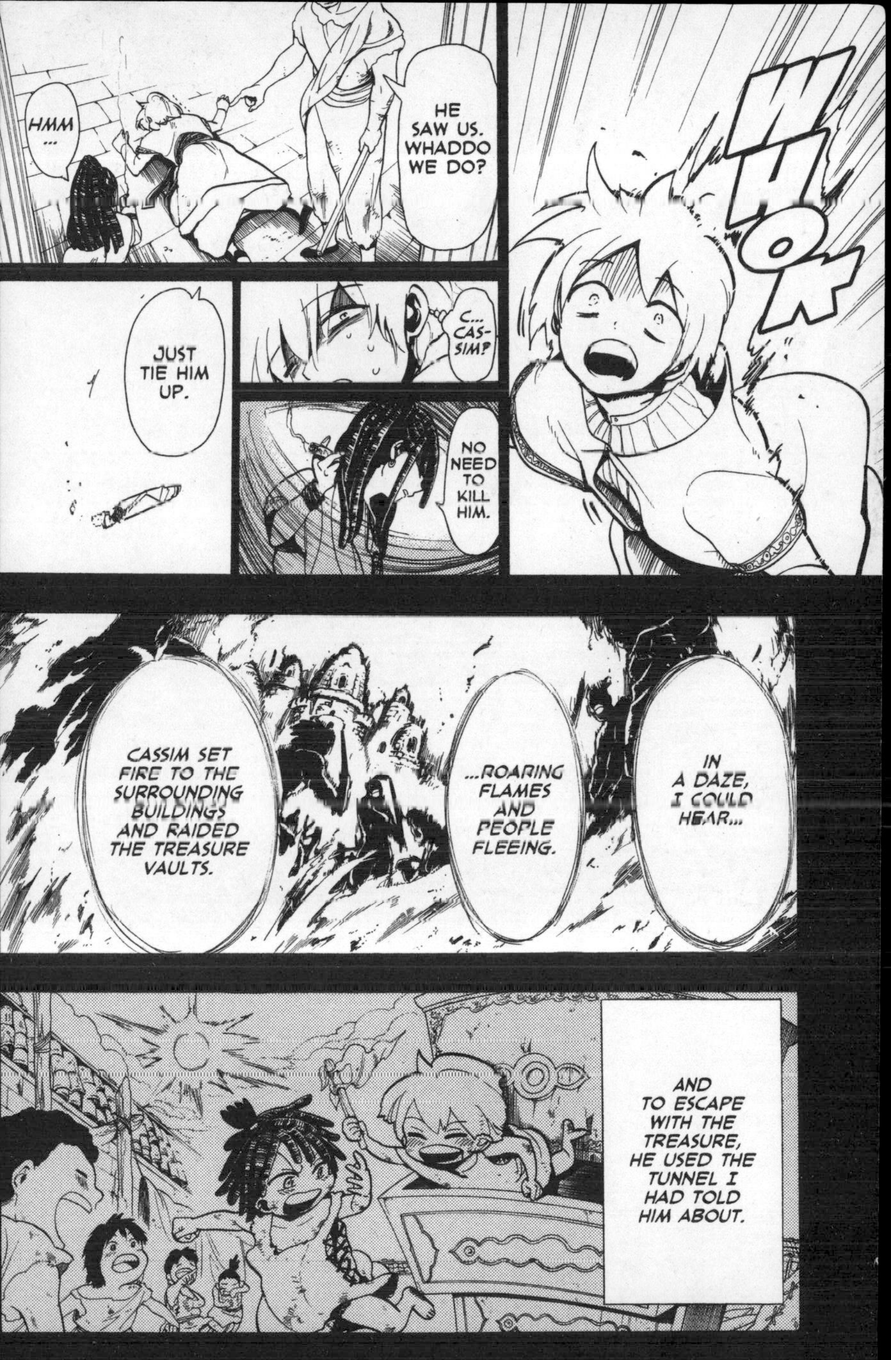
WHOK
HE SAW US. WHADDO WE DO?
HMM...
C... CASSIM?
NO NEED TO KILL HIM.
JUST TIE HIM UP.
IN A DAZE, I COULD HEAR...
...ROARING FLAMES AND PEOPLE FLEEING.
CASSIM SET FIRE TO THE SURROUNDING BUILDINGS AND RAIDED THE TREASURE VAULTS.
AND TO ESCAPE WITH THE TREASURE, HE USED THE TUNNEL I HAD TOLD HIM ABOUT.

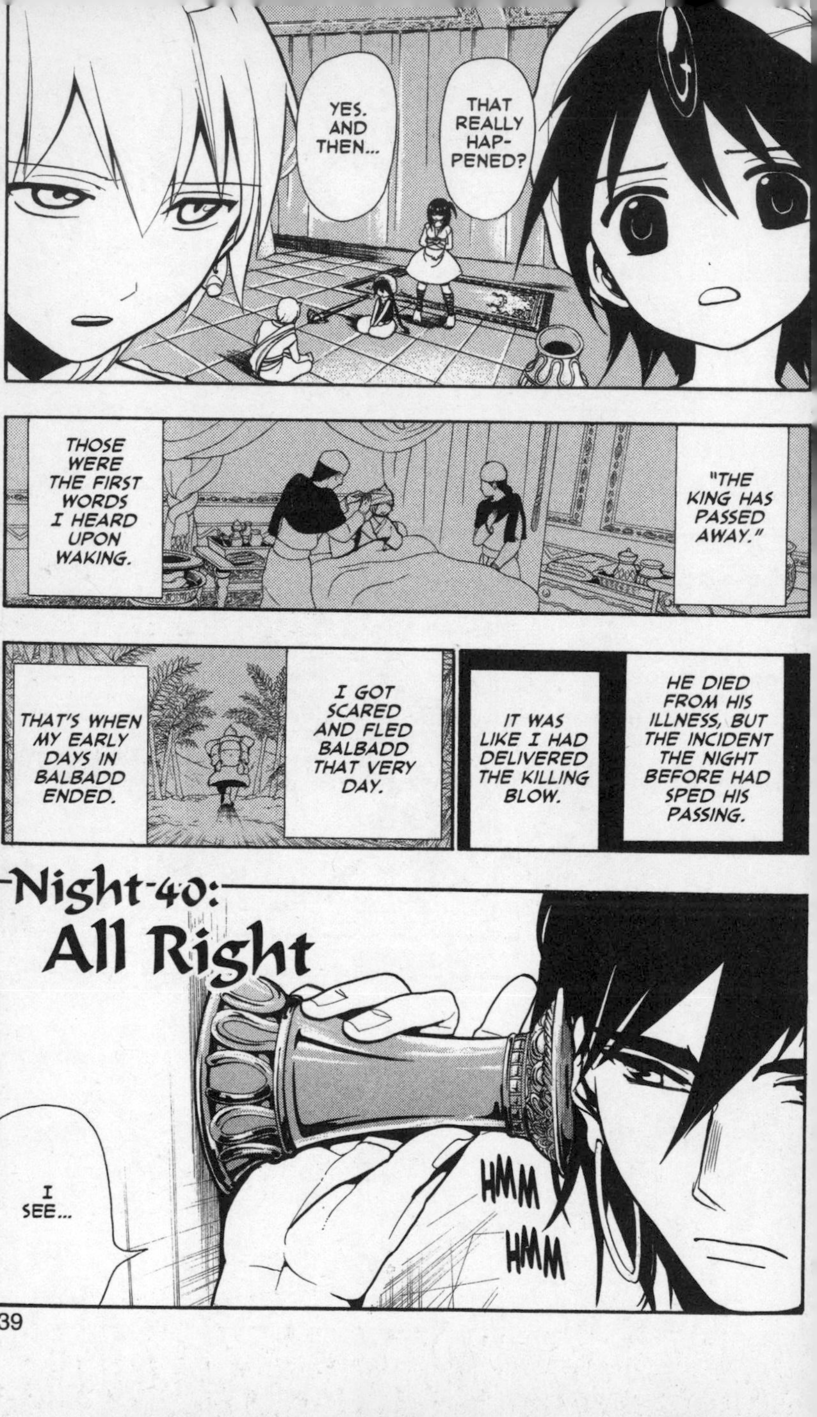
THAT REALLY HAP-PENED?
YES. AND THEN...
"THE KING HAS PASSED AWAY."
THOSE WERE THE FIRST WORDS I HEARD UPON WAKING.
HE DIED FROM HIS ILLNESS, BUT THE INCIDENT THE NIGHT BEFORE HAD SPED HIS PASSING.
IT WAS LIKE I HAD DELIVERED THE KILLING BLOW.
I GOT SCARED AND FLED BALBADD THAT VERY DAY.
THAT'S WHEN MY EARLY DAYS IN BALBADD ENDED.
Night 40: All Right
HMM
HMM
I SEE...

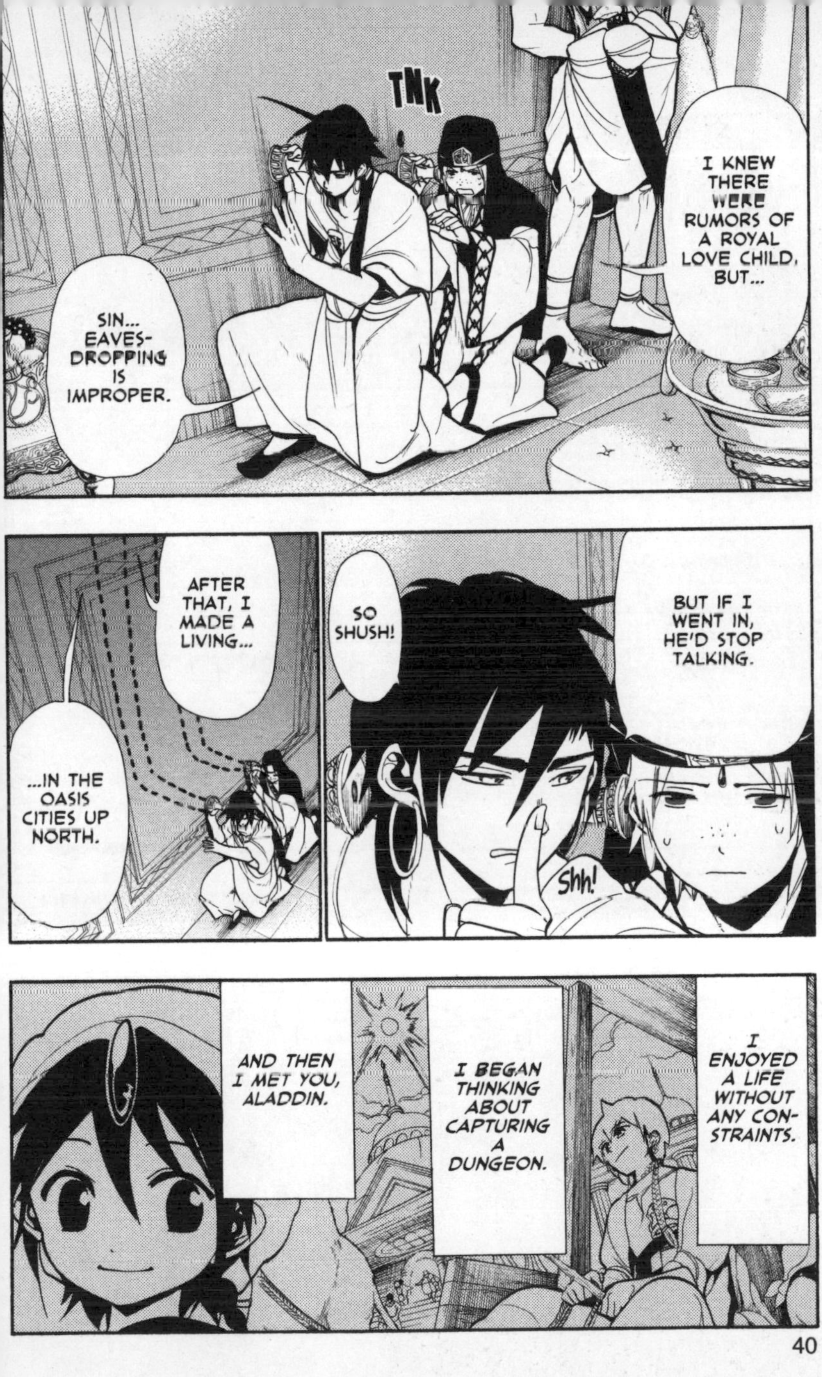
I KNEW THERE WERE RUMORS OF A ROYAL LOVE CHILD, BUT...
TNK
SIN... EAVES-DROPPING IS IMPROPER.
BUT IF I WENT IN, HE'D STOP TALKING.
SO SHUSH!
Shh!
AFTER THAT, I MADE A LIVING...
...IN THE OASIS CITIES UP NORTH.
I ENJOYED A LIFE WITHOUT ANY CON-STRAINTS.
I BEGAN THINKING ABOUT CAPTURING A DUNGEON.
AND THEN I MET YOU, ALADDIN.

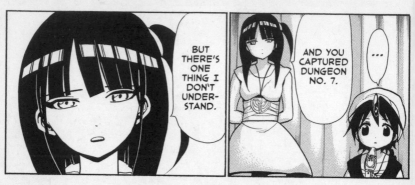

...
AND YOU CAPTURED DUNGEON NO. 7.
BUT THERE'S ONE THING I DON'T UNDER-STAND.
CASSIM BETRAYED YOU, SO WHY DID YOU JOIN THE FOG TROOP?
I RETURNED TO BALBADD TO SET MATTERS RIGHT.
I HAD CAPTURED A DUN-GEON...
...AND MADE A PROMISE TO ALADDIN.
BEFORE MAKING A FRESH START, I DECIDED TO RETURN TO THE PALACE...
...AND REVEAL THE TRUTH ABOUT THE RAID.

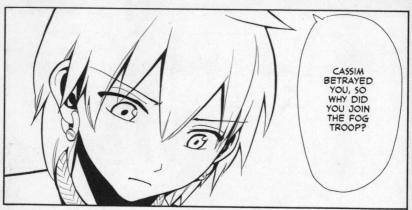

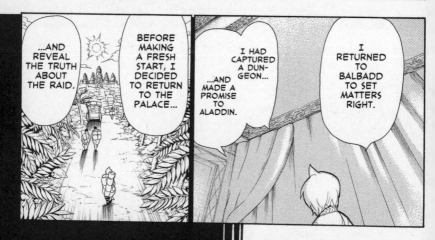

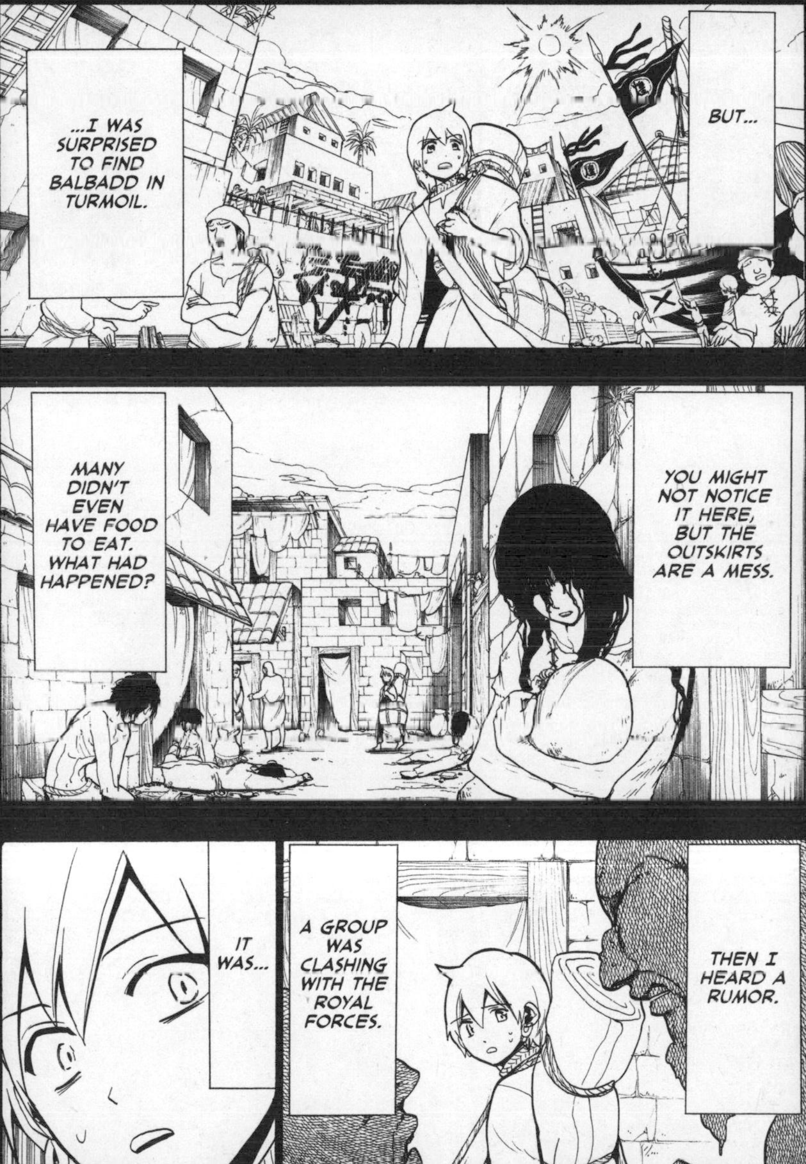
BUT...
...I WAS SURPRISED TO FIND BALBADD IN TURMOIL.
YOU MIGHT NOT NOTICE IT HERE, BUT THE OUTSKIRTS ARE A MESS.
MANY DIDN'T EVEN HAVE FOOD TO EAT. WHAT HAD HAPPENED?
THEN I HEARD A RUMOR.
A GROUP WAS CLASHING WITH THE ROYAL FORCES.
IT WAS...

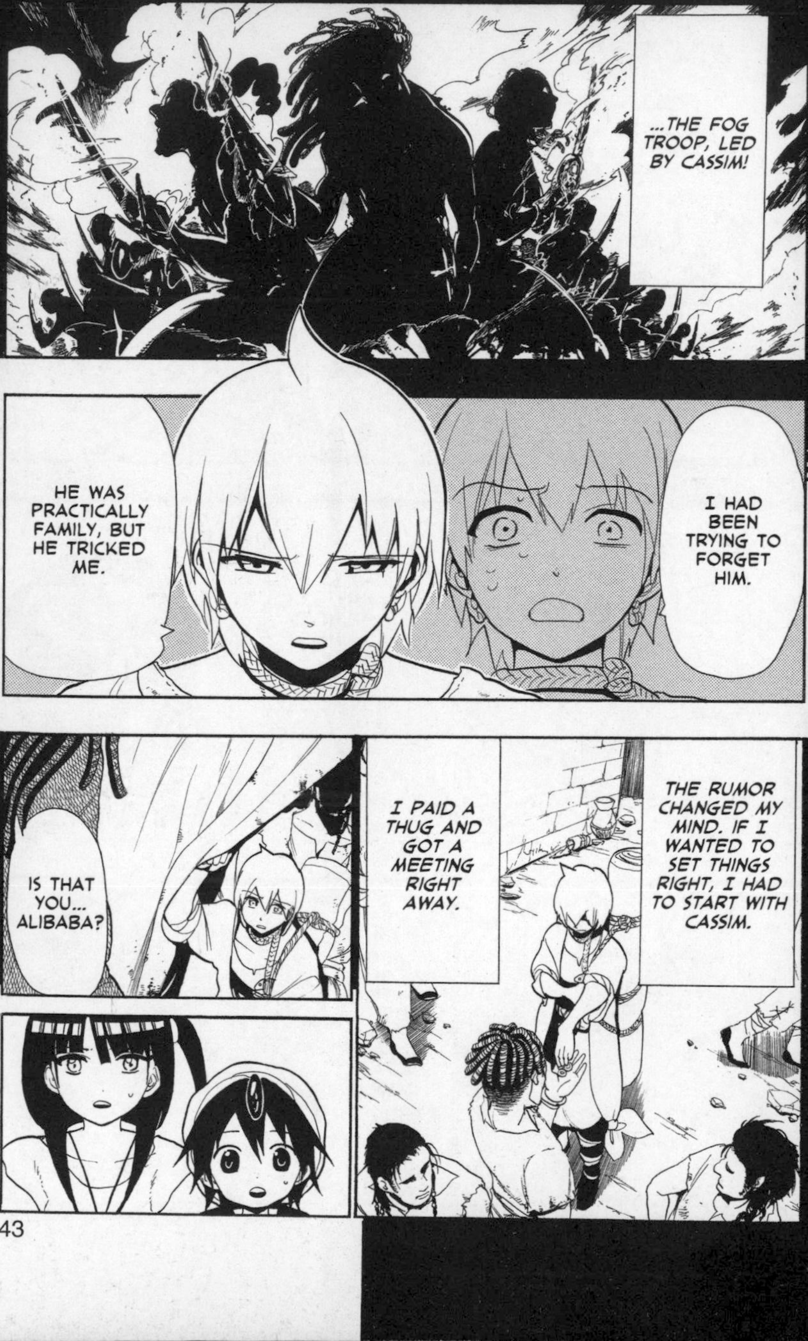
...THE FOG TROOP, LED BY CASSIM!
I HAD BEEN TRYING TO FORGET HIM.
HE WAS PRACTICALLY FAMILY, BUT HE TRICKED ME.
THE RUMOR CHANGED MY MIND. IF I WANTED TO SET THINGS RIGHT, I HAD TO START WITH CASSIM.
I PAID A THUG AND GOT A MEETING RIGHT AWAY.
IS THAT YOU... ALIBABA?

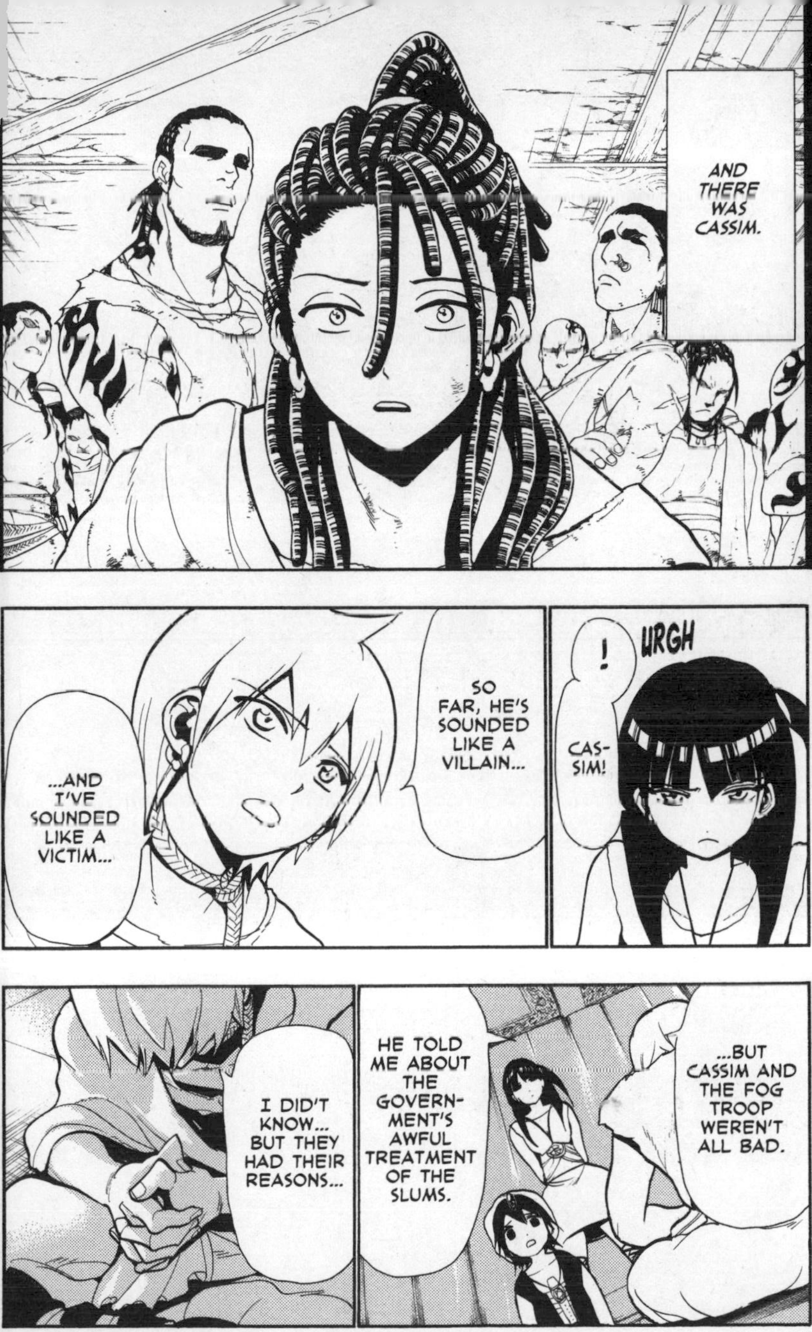
AND THERE WAS CASSIM.
!
URGH
CAS-SIM!
SO FAR, HE'S SOUNDED LIKE A VILLAIN...
...AND I'VE SOUNDED LIKE A VICTIM...
...BUT CASSIM AND THE FOG TROOP WEREN'T ALL BAD.
HE TOLD ME ABOUT THE GOVERN-MENT'S AWFUL TREATMENT OF THE SLUMS.
I DIDN'T KNOW... BUT THEY HAD THEIR REASONS...

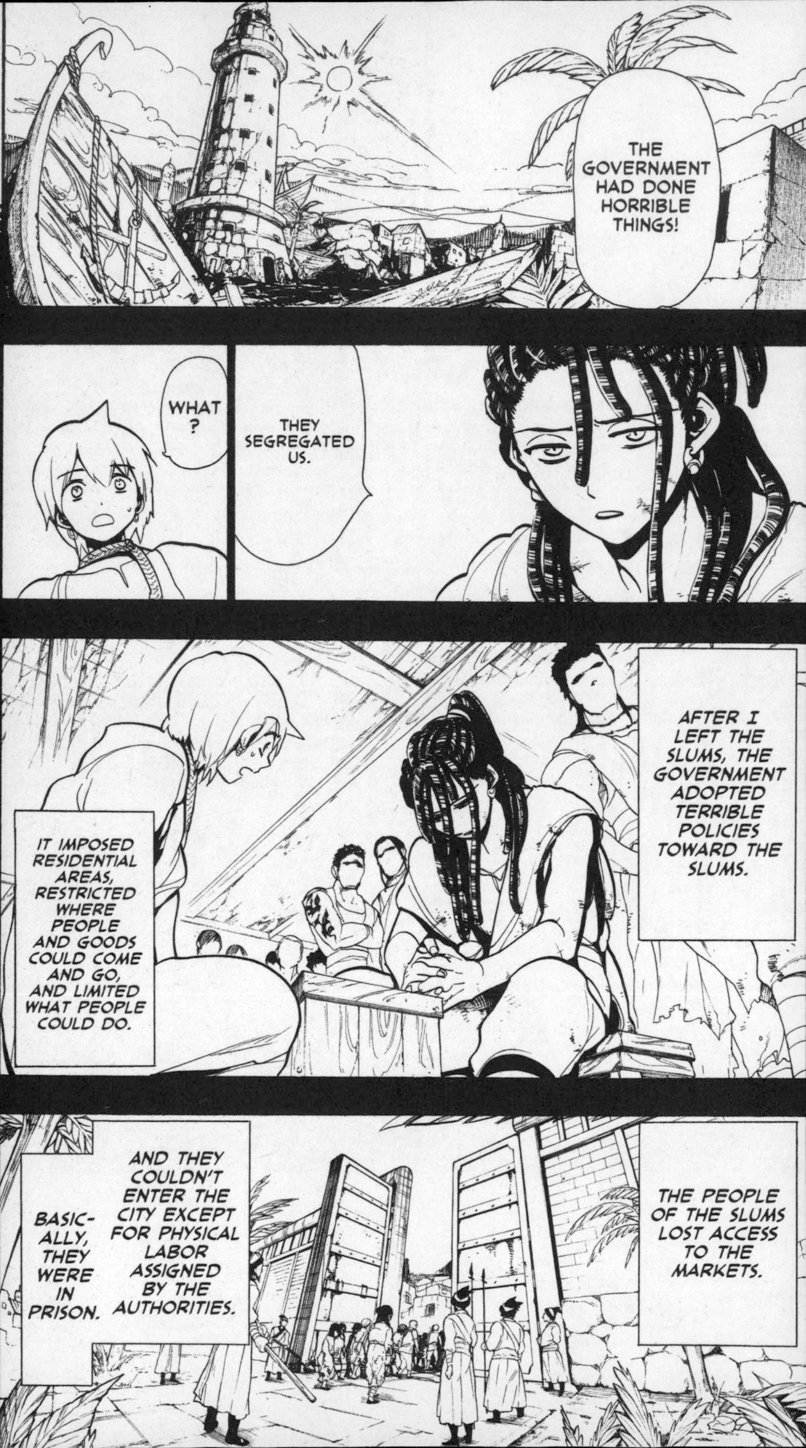
THE GOVERNMENT HAD DONE HORRIBLE THINGS!
THEY SEGREGATED US.
WHAT?
AFTER I LEFT THE SLUMS, THE GOVERNMENT ADOPTED TERRIBLE POLICIES TOWARD THE SLUMS.
IT IMPOSED RESIDENTIAL AREAS, RESTRICTED WHERE PEOPLE AND GOODS COULD COME AND GO, AND LIMITED WHAT PEOPLE COULD DO.
THE PEOPLE OF THE SLUMS LOST ACCESS TO THE MARKETS.
AND THEY COULDN'T ENTER THE CITY EXCEPT FOR PHYSICAL LABOR ASSIGNED BY THE AUTHORITIES.
BASIC-ALLY, THEY WERE IN PRISON.

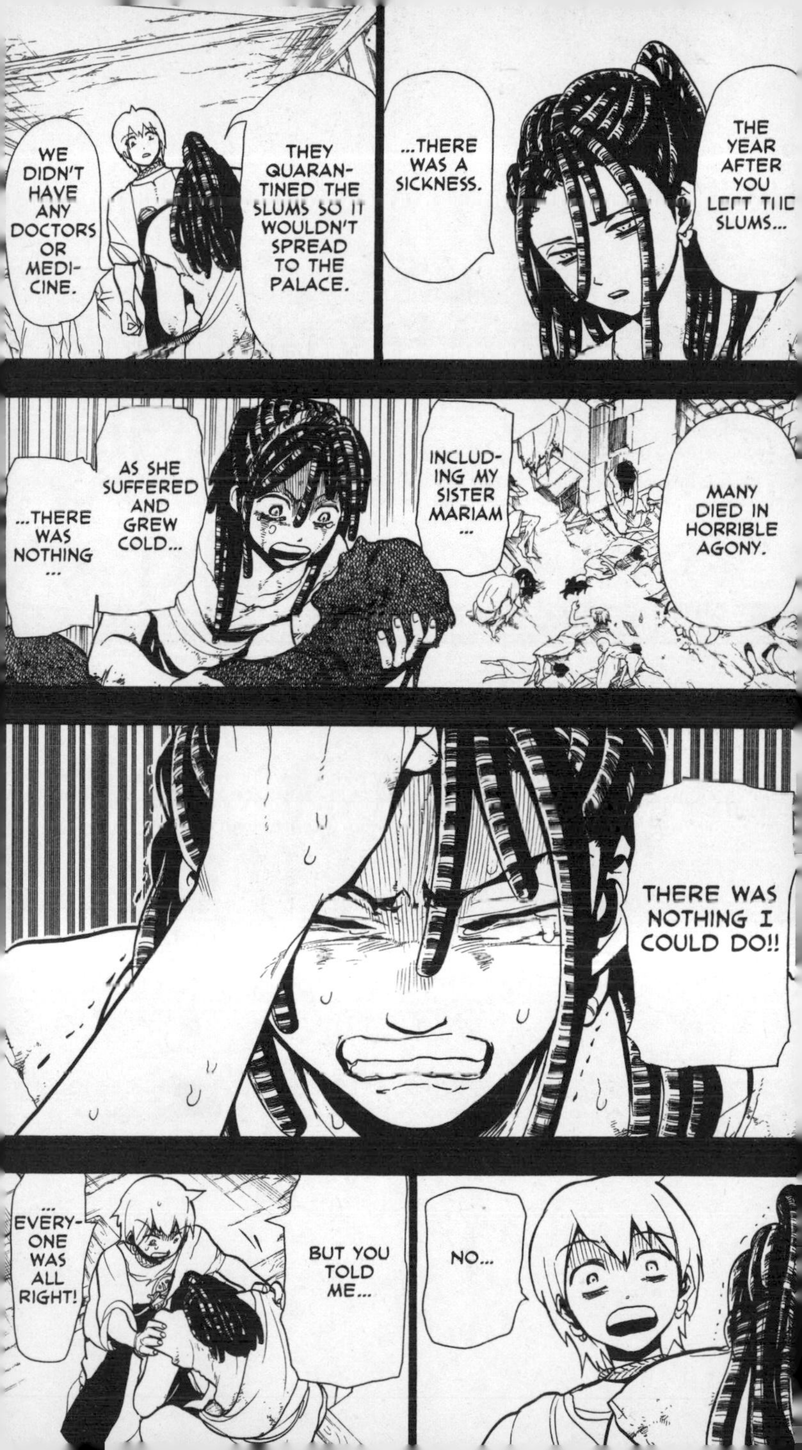
THE YEAR AFTER YOU LEFT THE SLUMS...
...THERE WAS A SICKNESS.
THEY QUARANTINED THE SLUMS SO IT WOULDN'T SPREAD TO THE PALACE.
WE DIDN'T HAVE ANY DOCTORS OR MEDICINE.
MANY DIED IN HORRIBLE AGONY.
INCLUDING MY SISTER MARIAM...
AS SHE SUFFERED AND GREW COLD...
...THERE WAS NOTHING...
THERE WAS NOTHING I COULD DO!!
NO...
BUT YOU TOLD ME...
...EVERYONE WAS ALL RIGHT!

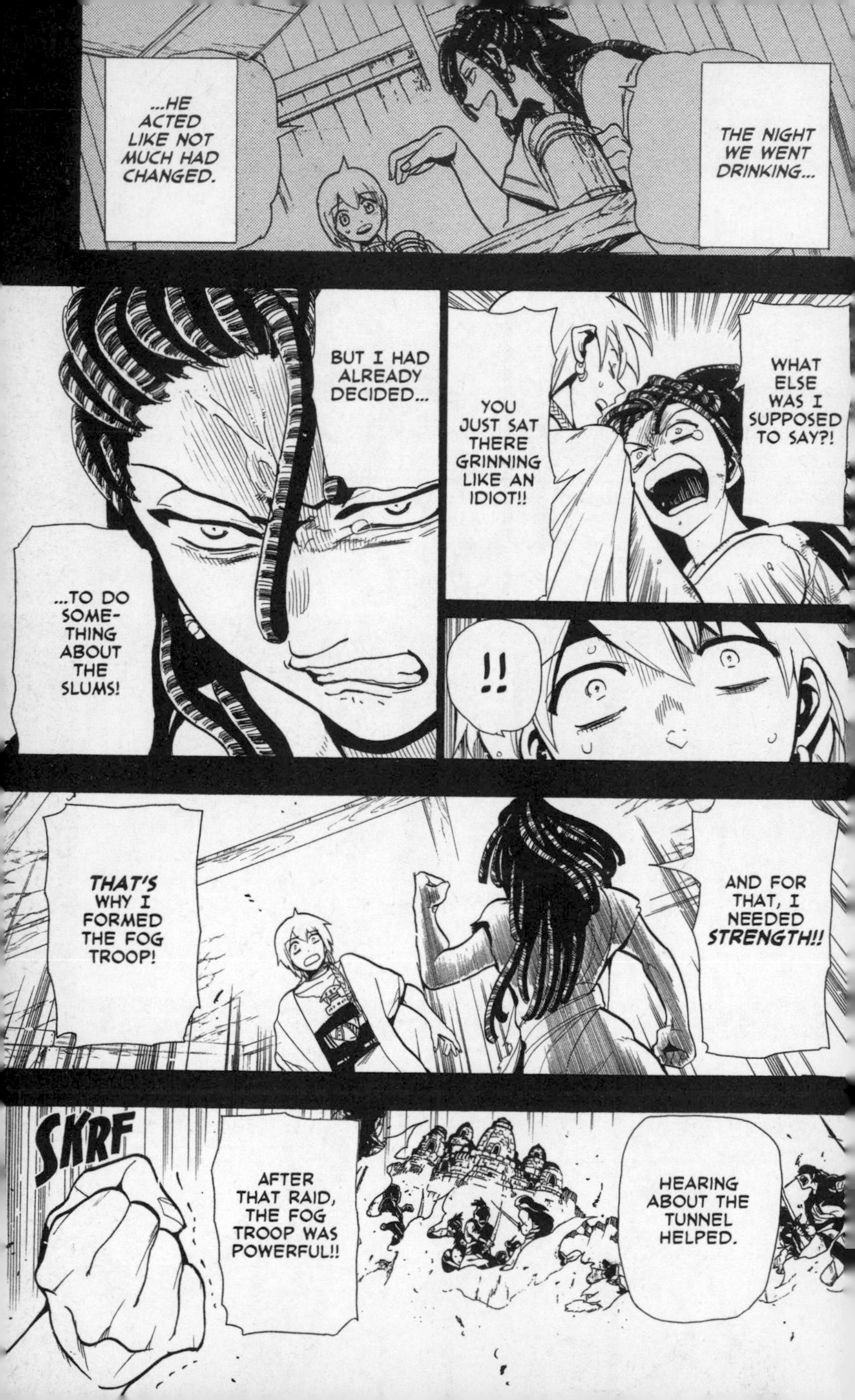
THE NIGHT WE WENT DRINKING...
...HE ACTED LIKE NOT MUCH HAD CHANGED.
WHAT ELSE WAS I SUPPOSED TO SAY?!
YOU JUST SAT THERE GRINNING LIKE AN IDIOT!!
!!
BUT I HAD ALREADY DECIDED...
...TO DO SOME-THING ABOUT THE SLUMS!
AND FOR THAT, I NEEDED *STRENGTH!!*
*THAT'S* WHY I FORMED THE FOG TROOP!
HEARING ABOUT THE TUNNEL HELPED.
AFTER THAT RAID, THE FOG TROOP WAS POWERFUL!!
SKRF

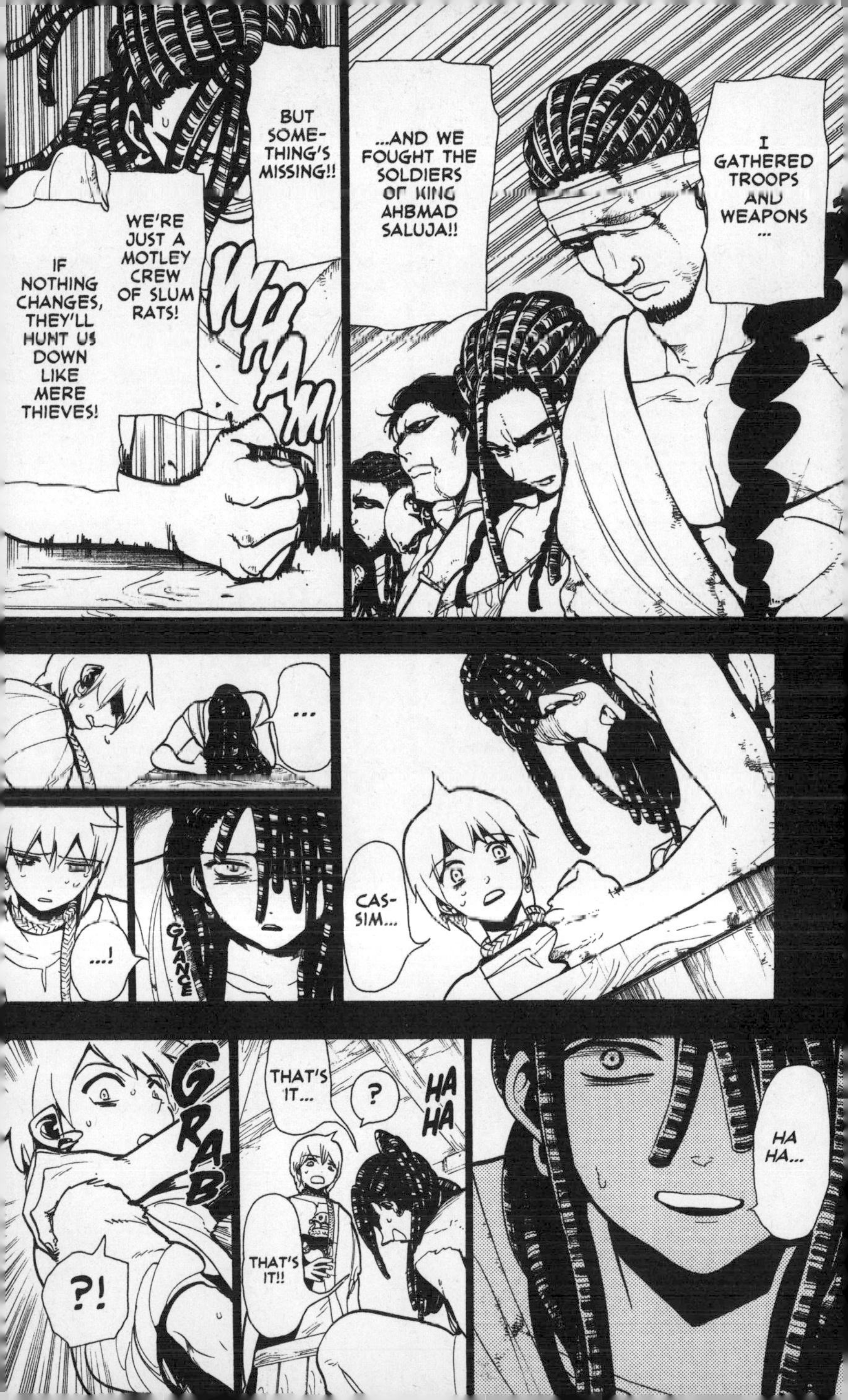
I GATHERED TROOPS AND WEAPONS...
...AND WE FOUGHT THE SOLDIERS OF KING AHBMAD SALUJA!!
BUT SOMETHING'S MISSING!!
WE'RE JUST A MOTLEY CREW OF SLUM RATS!
IF NOTHING CHANGES, THEY'LL HUNT US DOWN LIKE MERE THIEVES!
WHAM
CASSIM...
...
GLANCE
...!
HA HA...
HA HA
?
THAT'S IT...
THAT'S IT!!
GRAB
?!

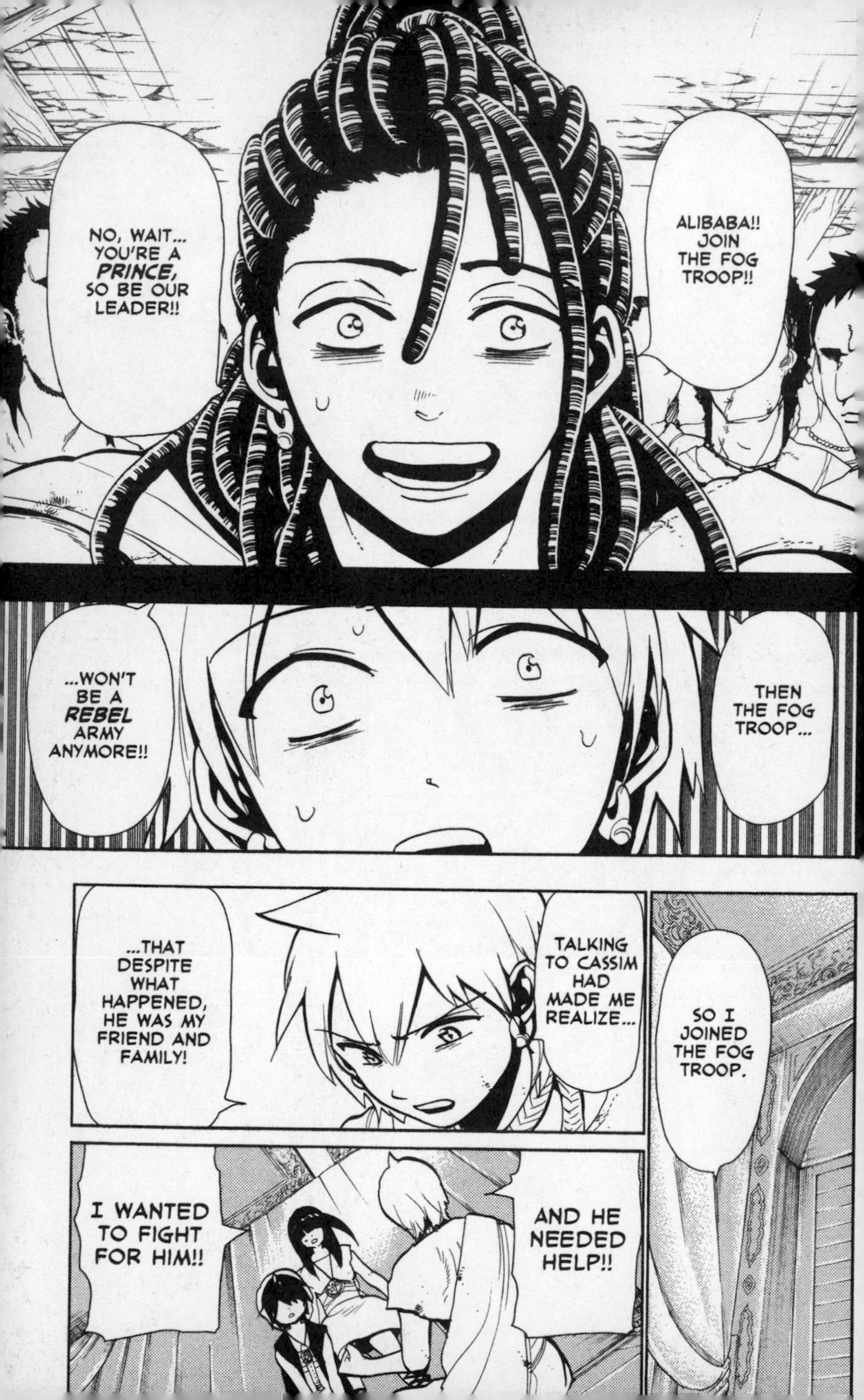
ALIBABA!! JOIN THE FOG TROOP!!
NO, WAIT... YOU'RE A *PRINCE*, SO BE OUR LEADER!!
THEN THE FOG TROOP...
...WON'T BE A *REBEL* ARMY ANYMORE!!
SO I JOINED THE FOG TROOP.
TALKING TO CASSIM HAD MADE ME REALIZE...
...THAT DESPITE WHAT HAPPENED, HE WAS MY FRIEND AND FAMILY!
AND HE NEEDED HELP!!
I WANTED TO FIGHT FOR HIM!!

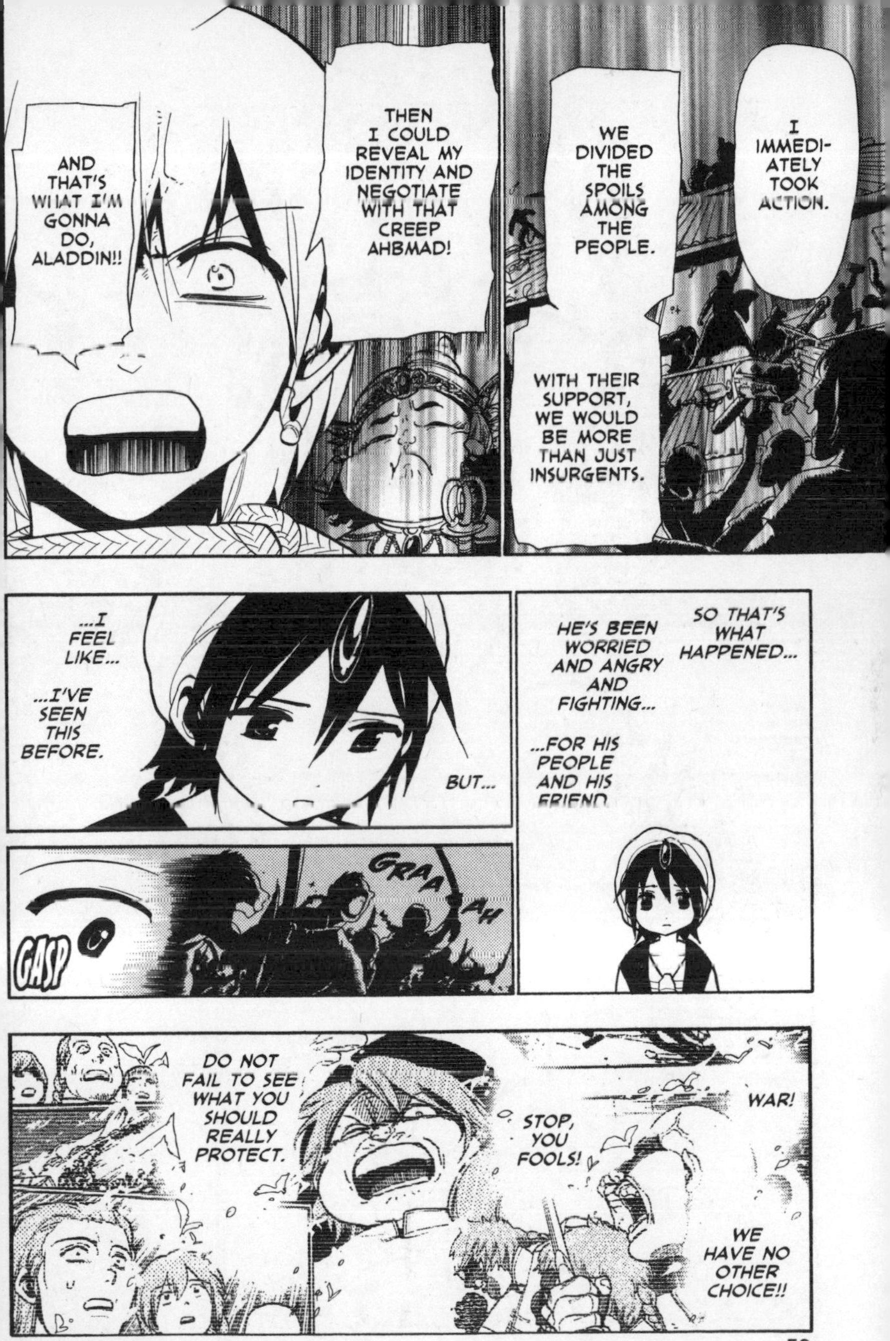
I IMMEDIATELY TOOK ACTION.
WE DIVIDED THE SPOILS AMONG THE PEOPLE.
WITH THEIR SUPPORT, WE WOULD BE MORE THAN JUST INSURGENTS.
THEN I COULD REVEAL MY IDENTITY AND NEGOTIATE WITH THAT CREEP AHBMAD!
AND THAT'S WHAT I'M GONNA DO, ALADDIN!!
SO THAT'S WHAT HAPPENED...
HE'S BEEN WORRIED AND ANGRY AND FIGHTING...
...FOR HIS PEOPLE AND HIS FRIEND
...I FEEL LIKE...
...I'VE SEEN THIS BEFORE.
BUT...
GRAAAAH
GASP
WAR!
WE HAVE NO OTHER CHOICE!!
STOP, YOU FOOLS!
DO NOT FAIL TO SEE WHAT YOU SHOULD REALLY PROTECT.

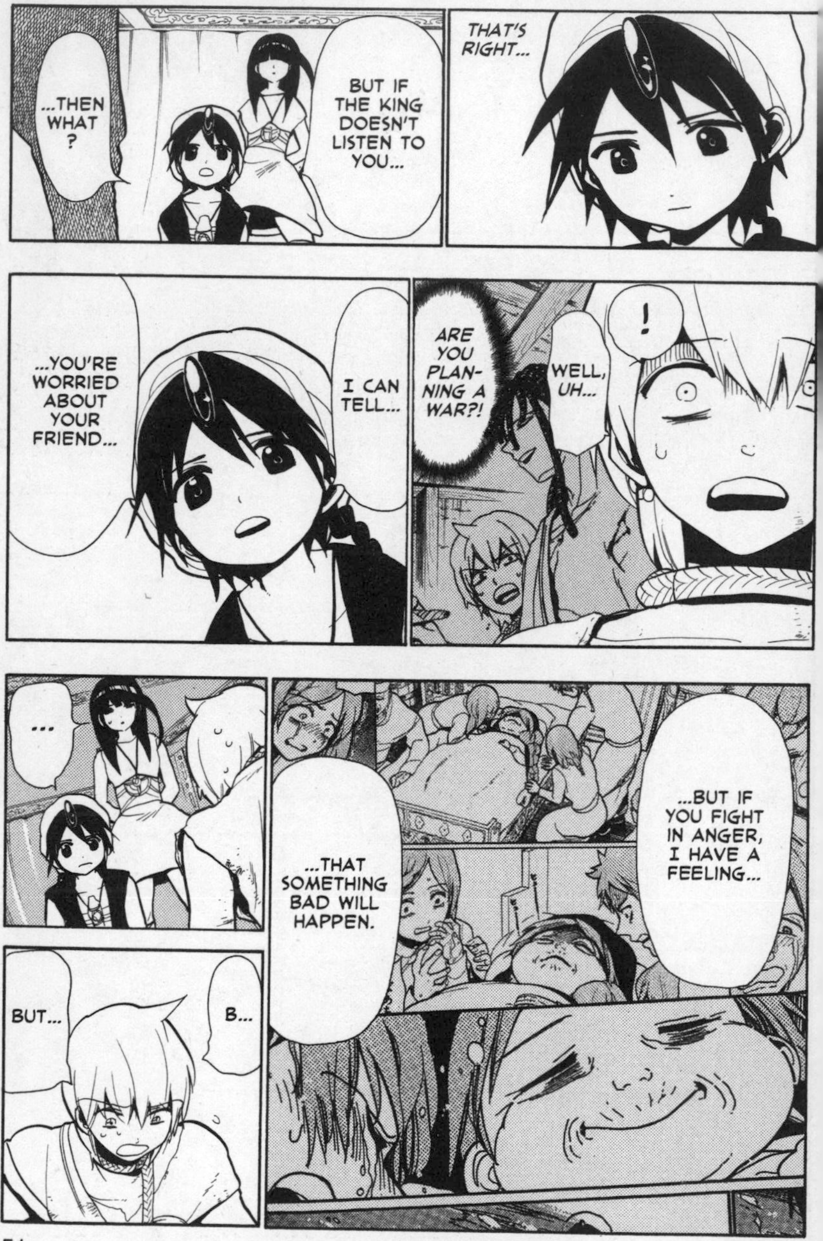
THAT'S RIGHT...
BUT IF THE KING DOESN'T LISTEN TO YOU...
...THEN WHAT?
!
WELL, UH...
ARE YOU PLAN-NING A WAR?!
I CAN TELL...
...YOU'RE WORRIED ABOUT YOUR FRIEND...
...BUT IF YOU FIGHT IN ANGER, I HAVE A FEELING...
...THAT SOMETHING BAD WILL HAPPEN.
...
B...
BUT...

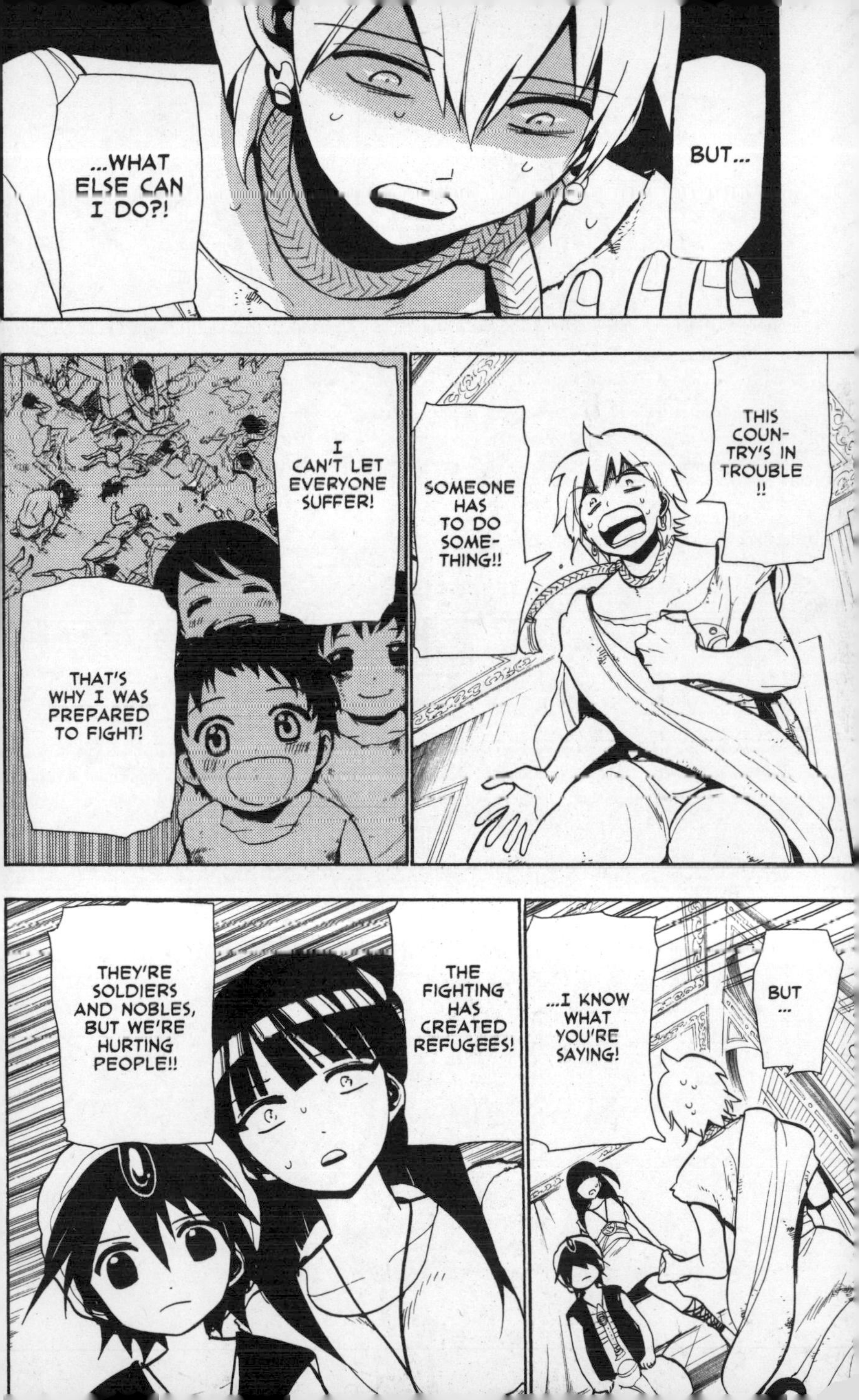
BUT...
...WHAT ELSE CAN I DO?!
THIS COUNTRY'S IN TROUBLE!!
SOMEONE HAS TO DO SOMETHING!!
I CAN'T LET EVERYONE SUFFER!
THAT'S WHY I WAS PREPARED TO FIGHT!
BUT...
...I KNOW WHAT YOU'RE SAYING!
THE FIGHTING HAS CREATED REFUGEES!
THEY'RE SOLDIERS AND NOBLES, BUT WE'RE HURTING PEOPLE!!

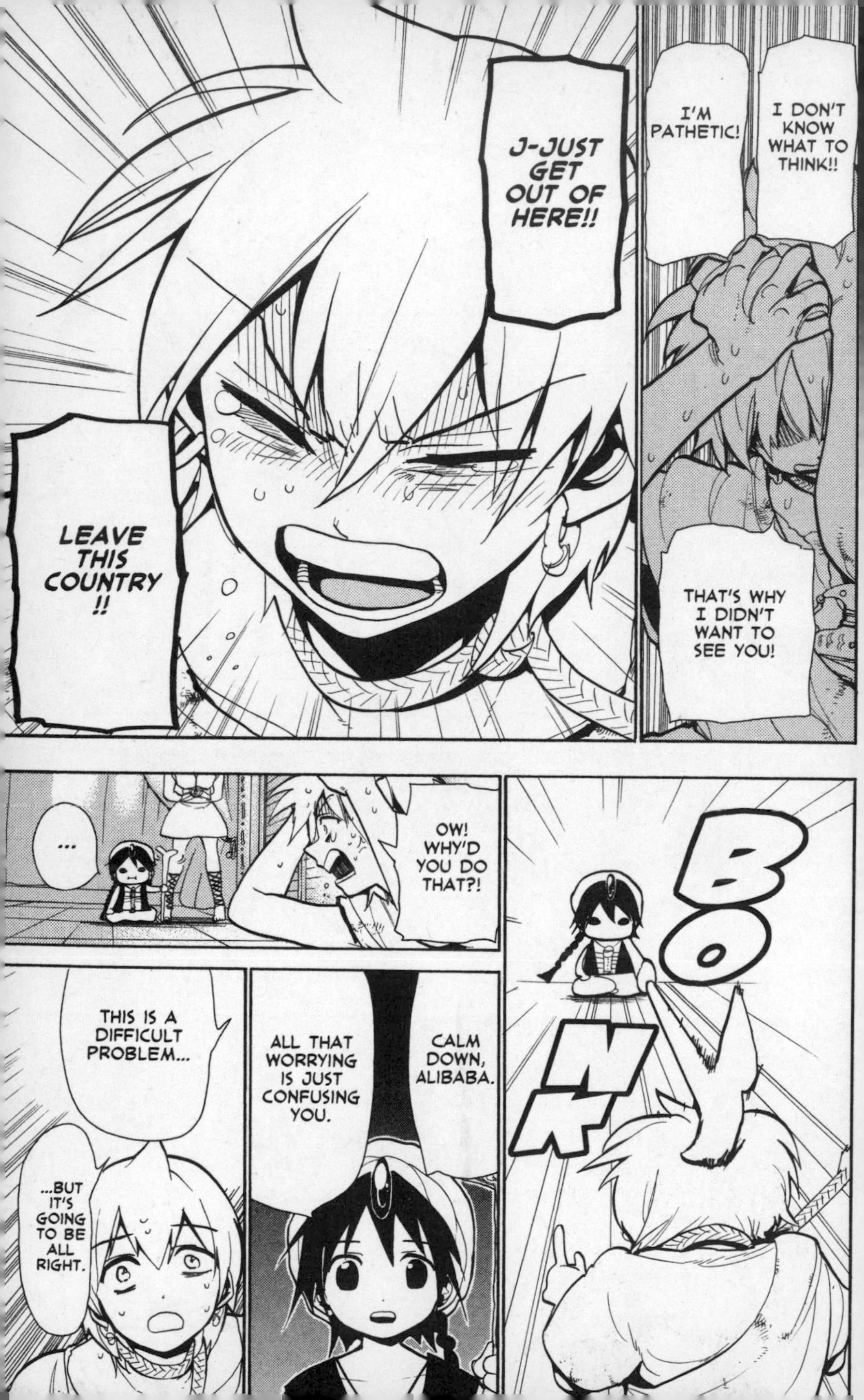
I DON'T KNOW WHAT TO THINK!!
I'M PATHETIC!
THAT'S WHY I DIDN'T WANT TO SEE YOU!
J-JUST GET OUT OF HERE!!
LEAVE THIS COUNTRY !!
BONK
OW! WHY'D YOU DO THAT?!
...
CALM DOWN, ALIBABA.
ALL THAT WORRYING IS JUST CONFUSING YOU.
THIS IS A DIFFICULT PROBLEM...
...BUT IT'S GOING TO BE ALL RIGHT.

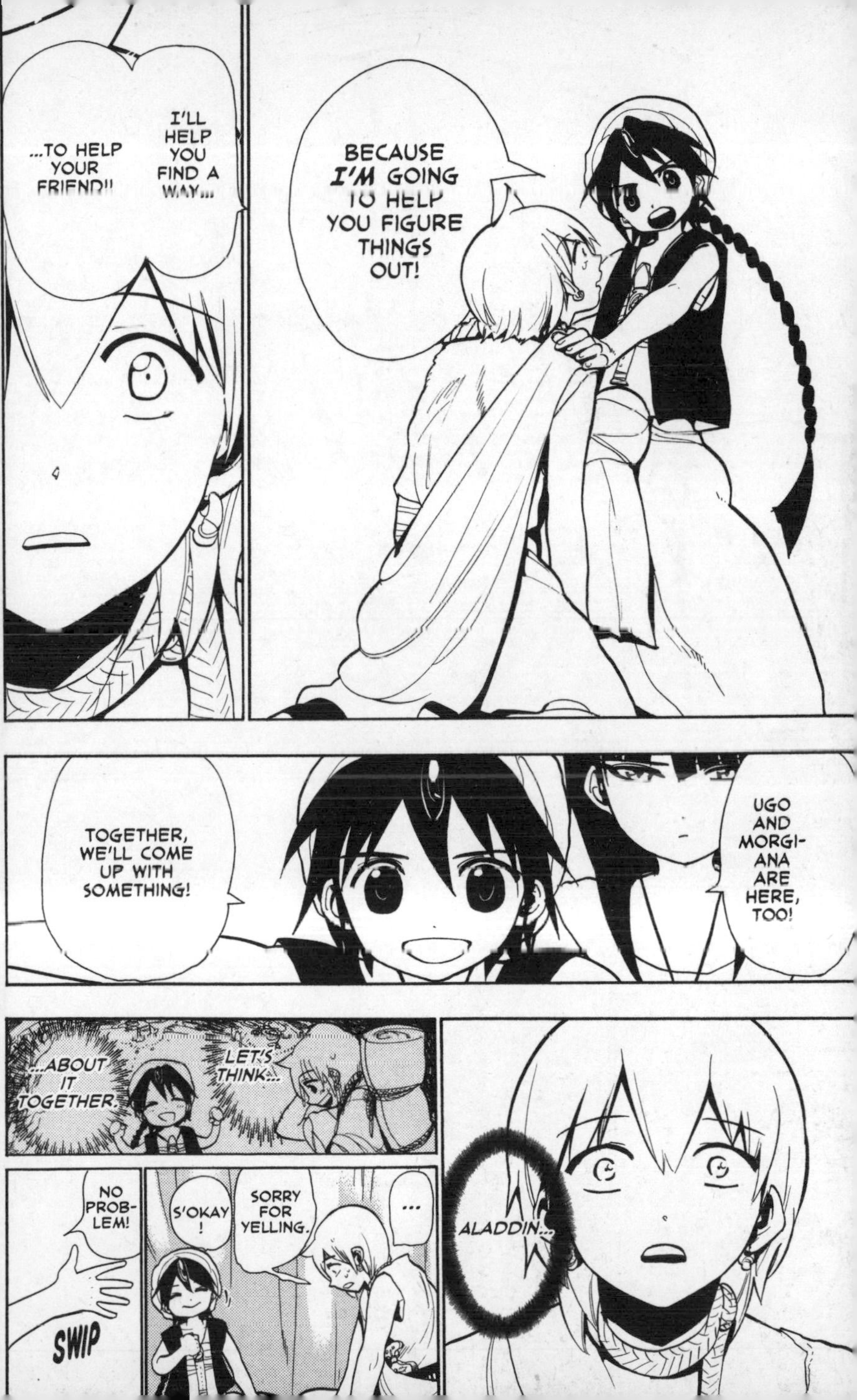
BECAUSE I'M GOING TO HELP YOU FIGURE THINGS OUT!
I'LL HELP YOU FIND A WAY...
...TO HELP YOUR FRIEND!!
UGO AND MORGIANA ARE HERE, TOO!
TOGETHER, WE'LL COME UP WITH SOMETHING!
ALADDIN...
LET'S THINK...
...ABOUT IT TOGETHER.
...
SORRY FOR YELLING.
S'OKAY!
NO PROBLEM!
SWIP

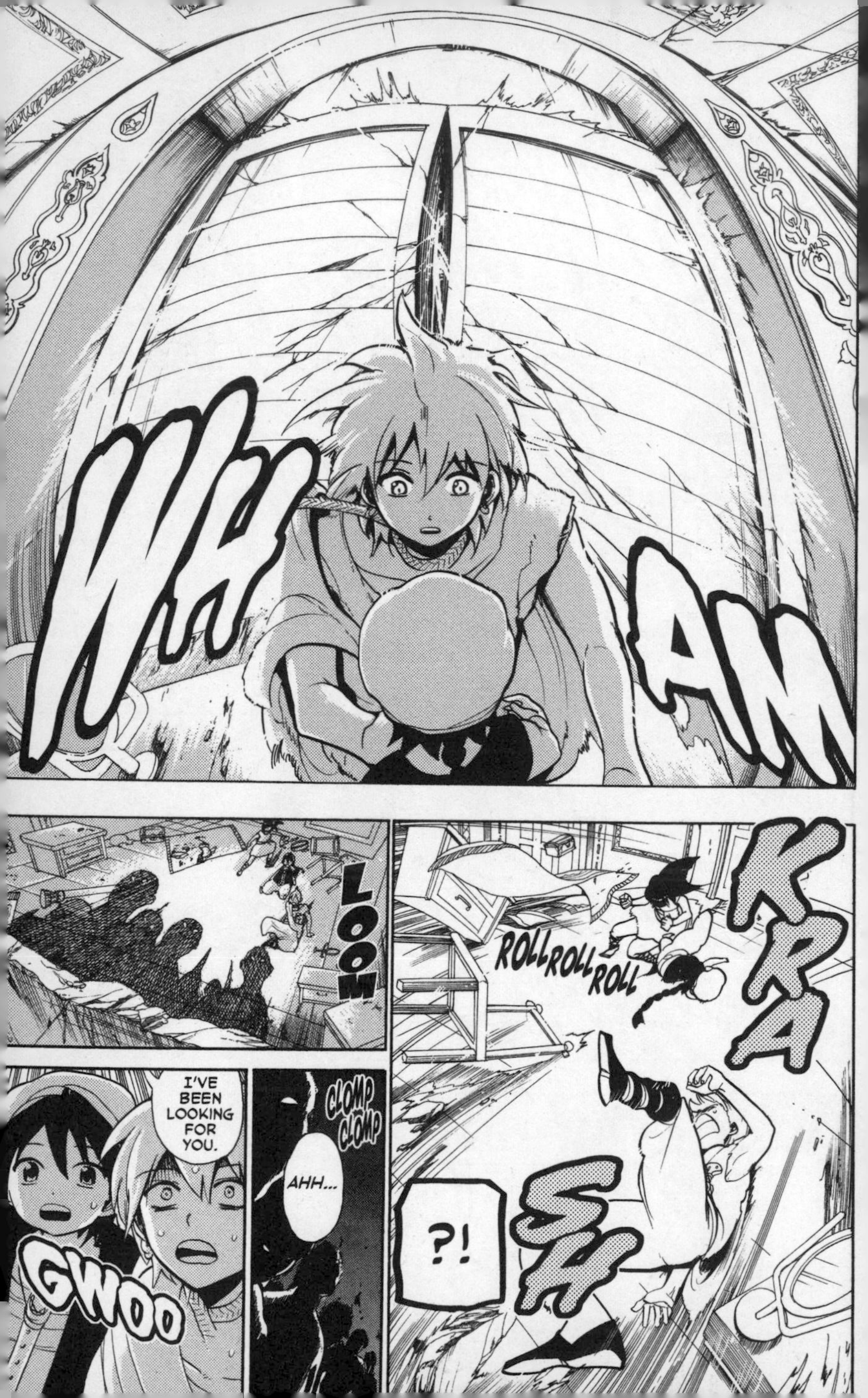
WHAM
KRA
ROLL ROLL ROLL
?!
SH
LOOOM
CLOMP CLOMP
AHH...
I'VE BEEN LOOKING FOR YOU.
GWOO

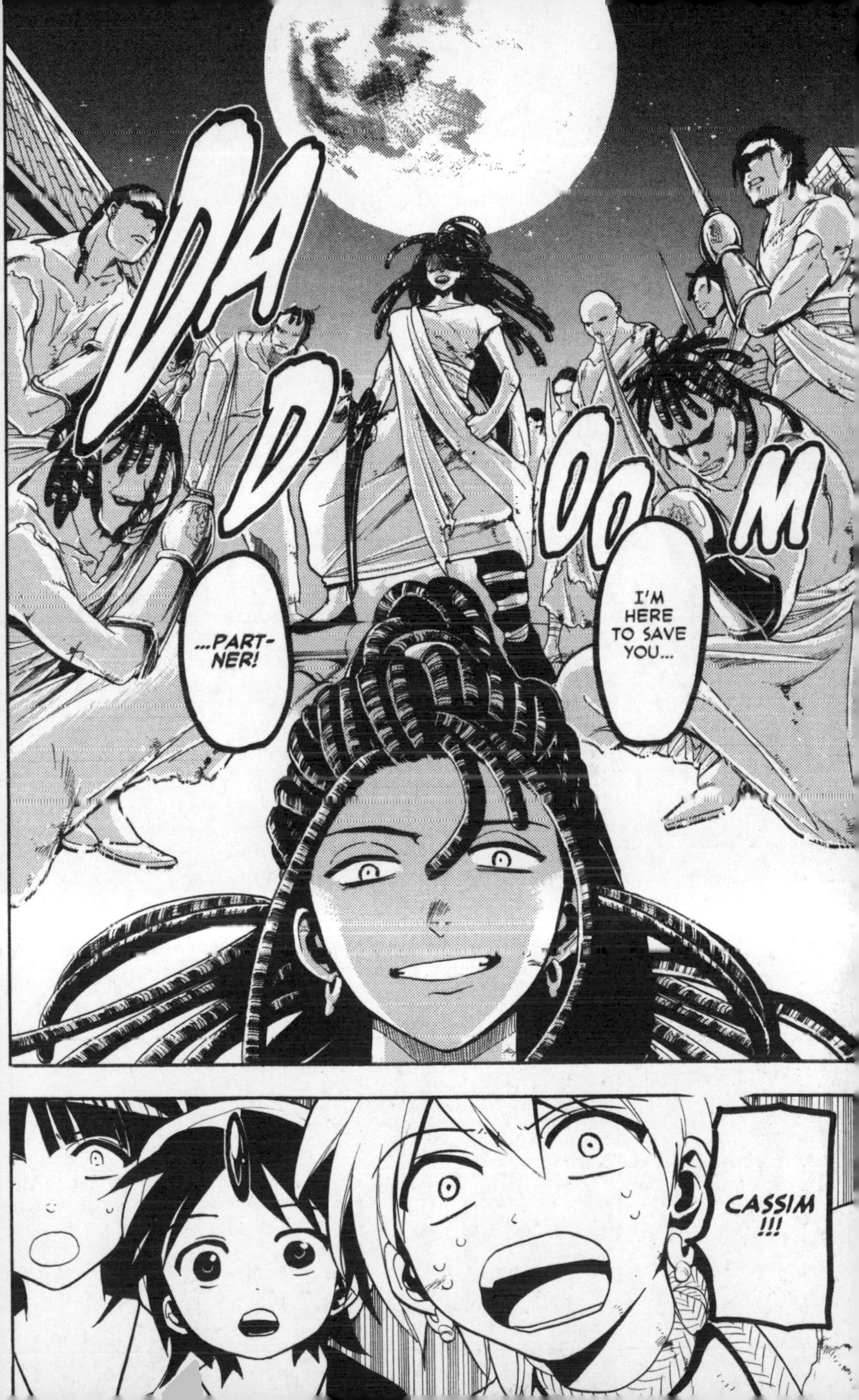
DADOOOM
I'M HERE TO SAVE YOU...
...PARTNER!
CASSIM!!!

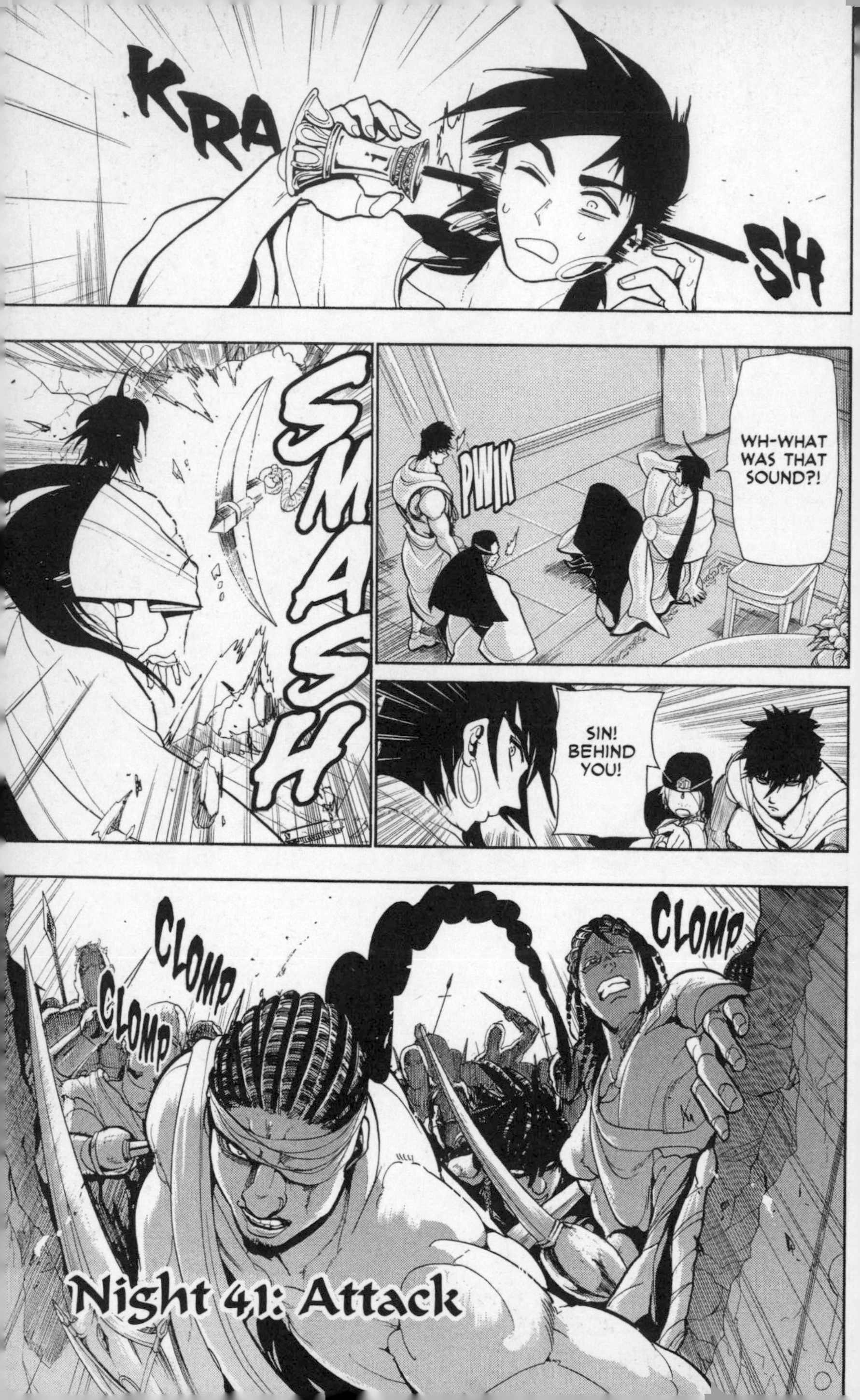
KRA-
SH
WH-WHAT WAS THAT SOUND?!
PWIK
SIN! BEHIND YOU!
SMASH
CLOMP
CLOMP
CLOMP
Night 41: Attack

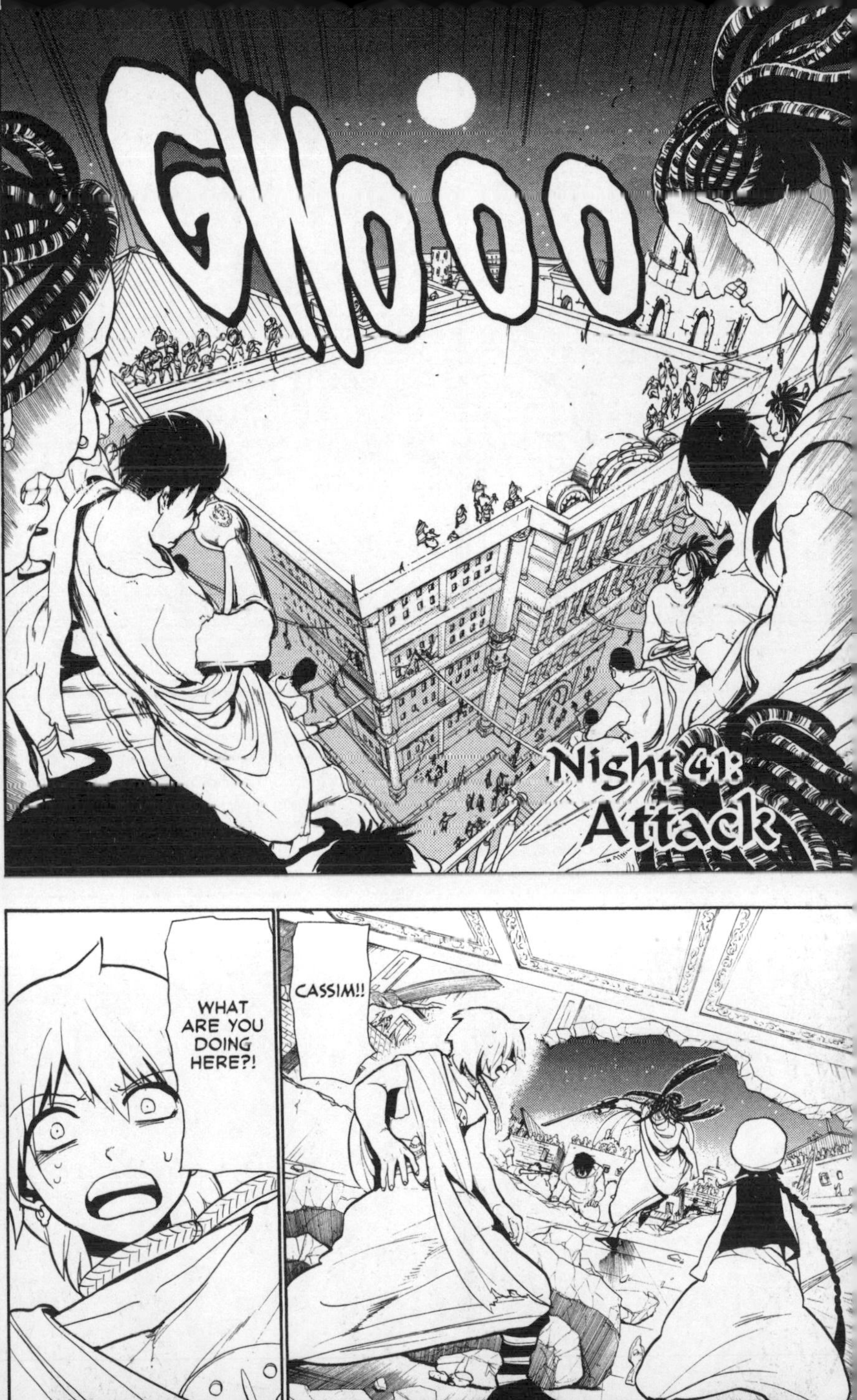
GWOOOO
Night 41:
Attack
CASSIM!!
WHAT ARE YOU DOING HERE?!

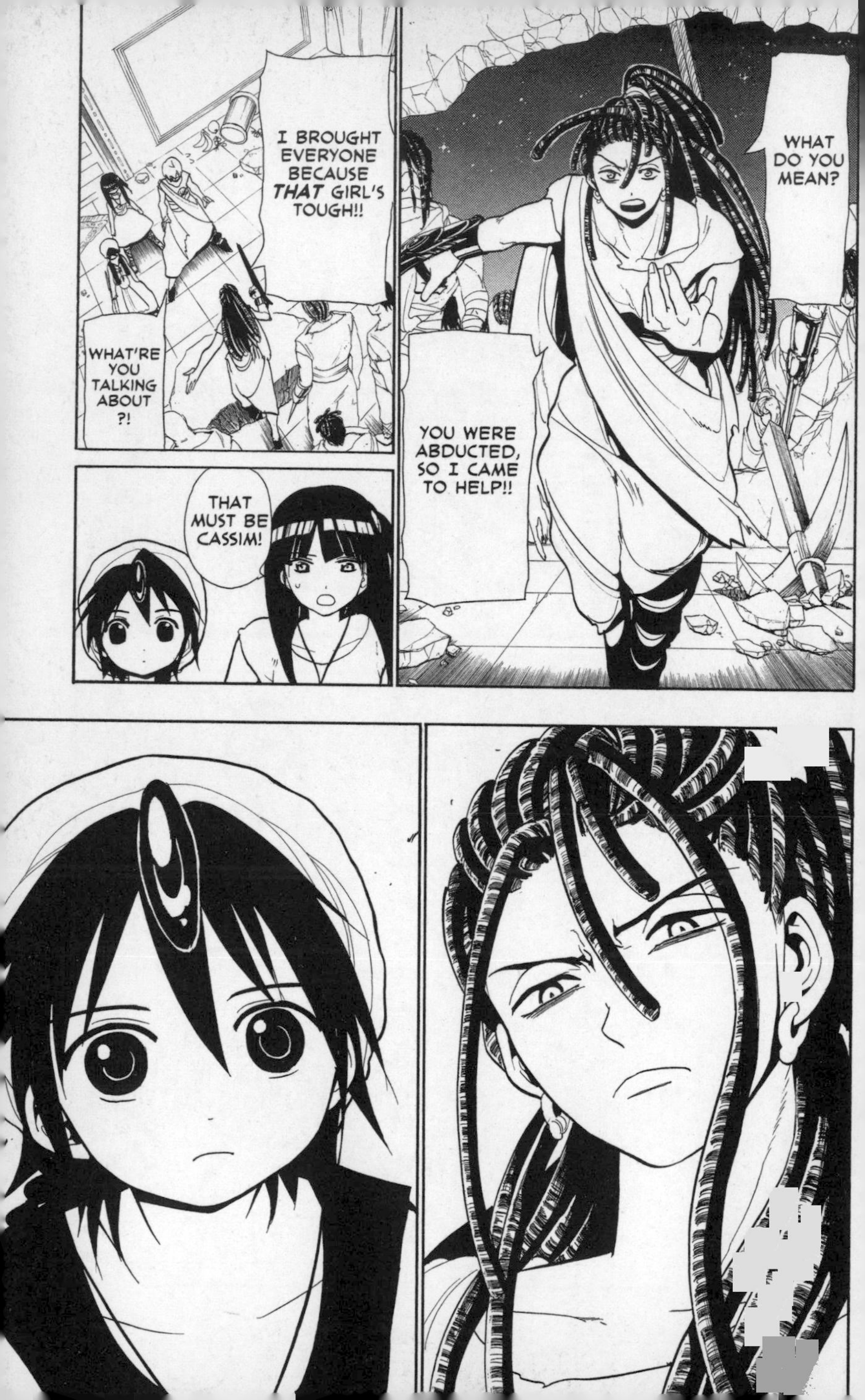
WHAT DO YOU MEAN?
YOU WERE ABDUCTED, SO I CAME TO HELP!!
I BROUGHT EVERYONE BECAUSE *THAT* GIRL'S TOUGH!!
WHAT'RE YOU TALKING ABOUT ?!
THAT MUST BE CASSIM!

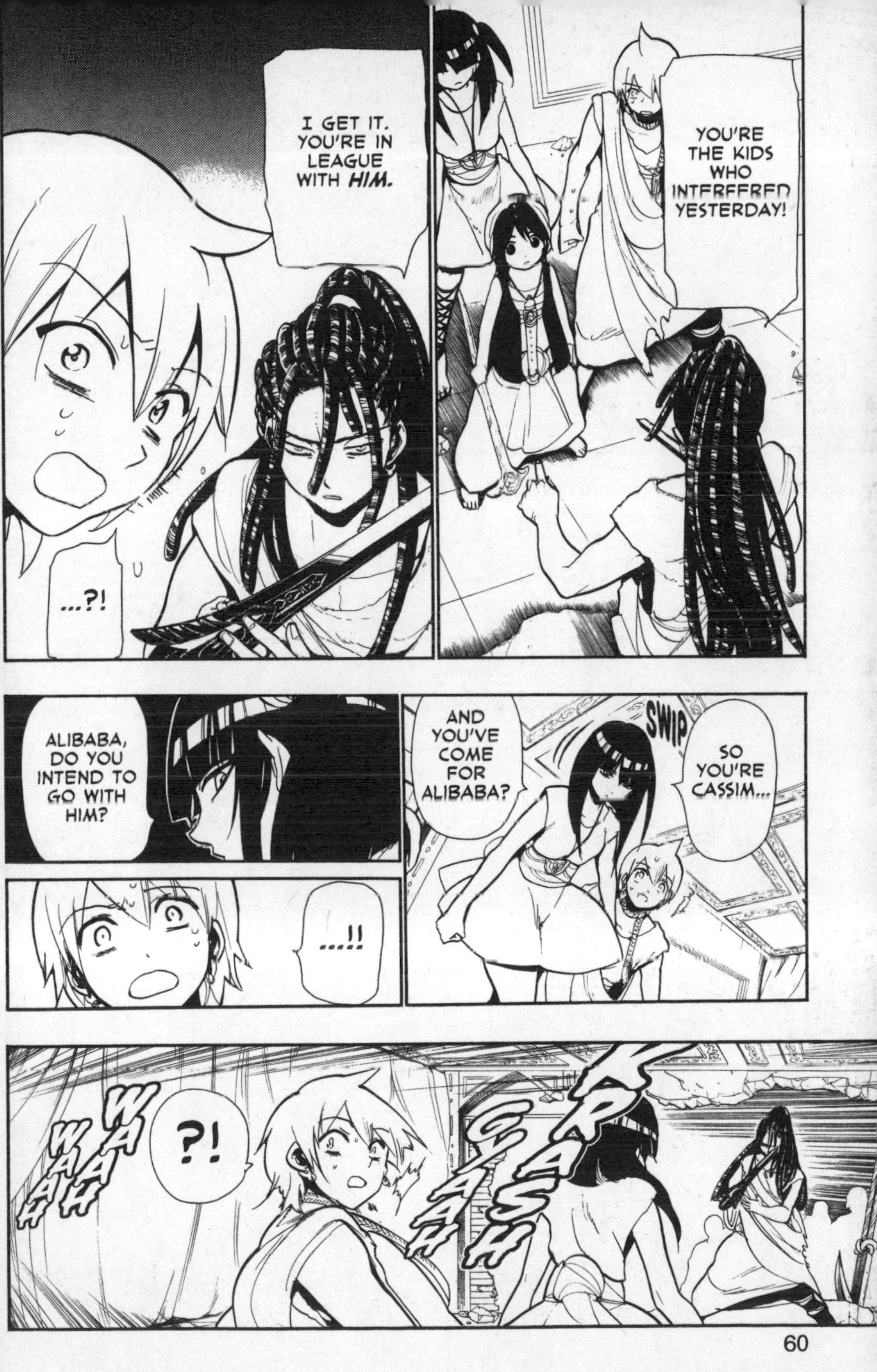
YOU'RE THE KIDS WHO INTERFERED YESTERDAY!
I GET IT. YOU'RE IN LEAGUE WITH HIM.
...?!
SO YOU'RE CASSIM...
SWIP
AND YOU'VE COME FOR ALIBABA?
ALIBABA, DO YOU INTEND TO GO WITH HIM?
...!!
KRASH
GYAAAH
?!
WAAAH
WAAAH

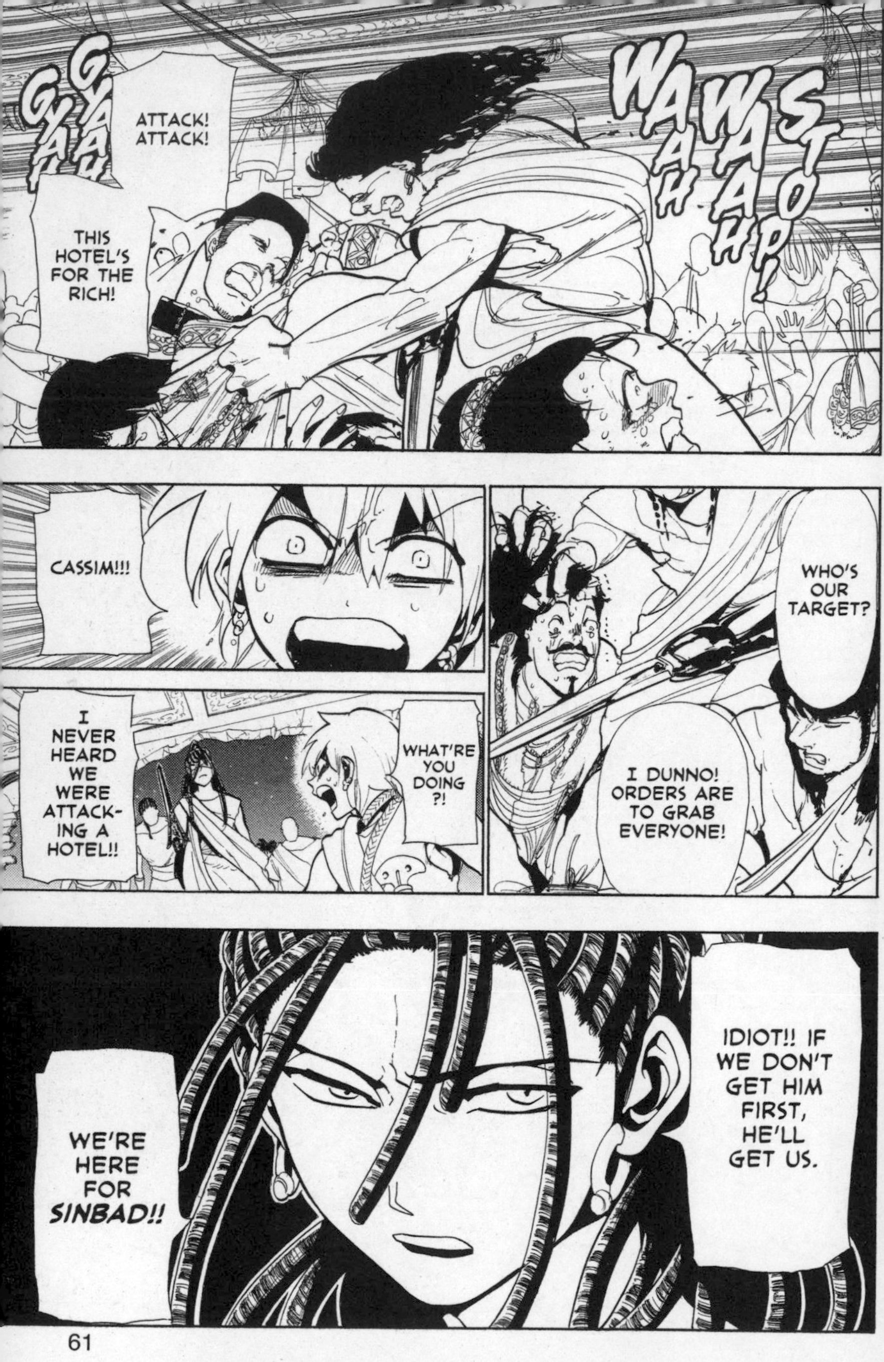
STOP!
WAAH
WAAH
ATTACK! ATTACK!
THIS HOTEL'S FOR THE RICH!
GYAA
GYAA
WHO'S OUR TARGET?
I DUNNO! ORDERS ARE TO GRAB EVERYONE!
CASSIM!!!
WHAT'RE YOU DOING?!
I NEVER HEARD WE WERE ATTACKING A HOTEL!!
IDIOT!! IF WE DON'T GET HIM FIRST, HE'LL GET US.
WE'RE HERE FOR *SINBAD!!*

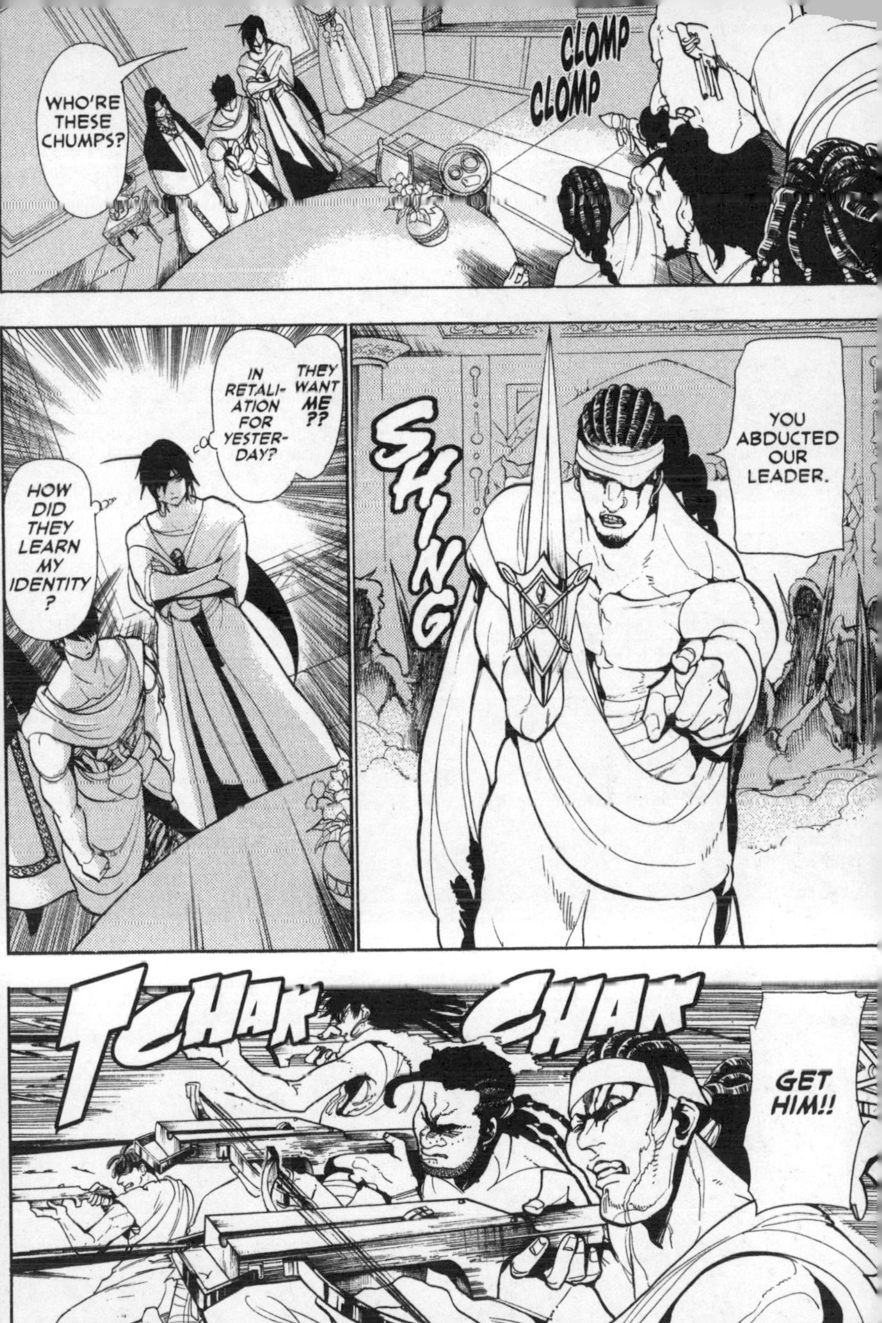
CLOMP CLOMP
WHO'RE THESE CHUMPS?
SHING
YOU ABDUCTED OUR LEADER.
THEY WANT ME??
IN RETALIATION FOR YESTERDAY?
HOW DID THEY LEARN MY IDENTITY?
GET HIM!!
TCHAK CHAK

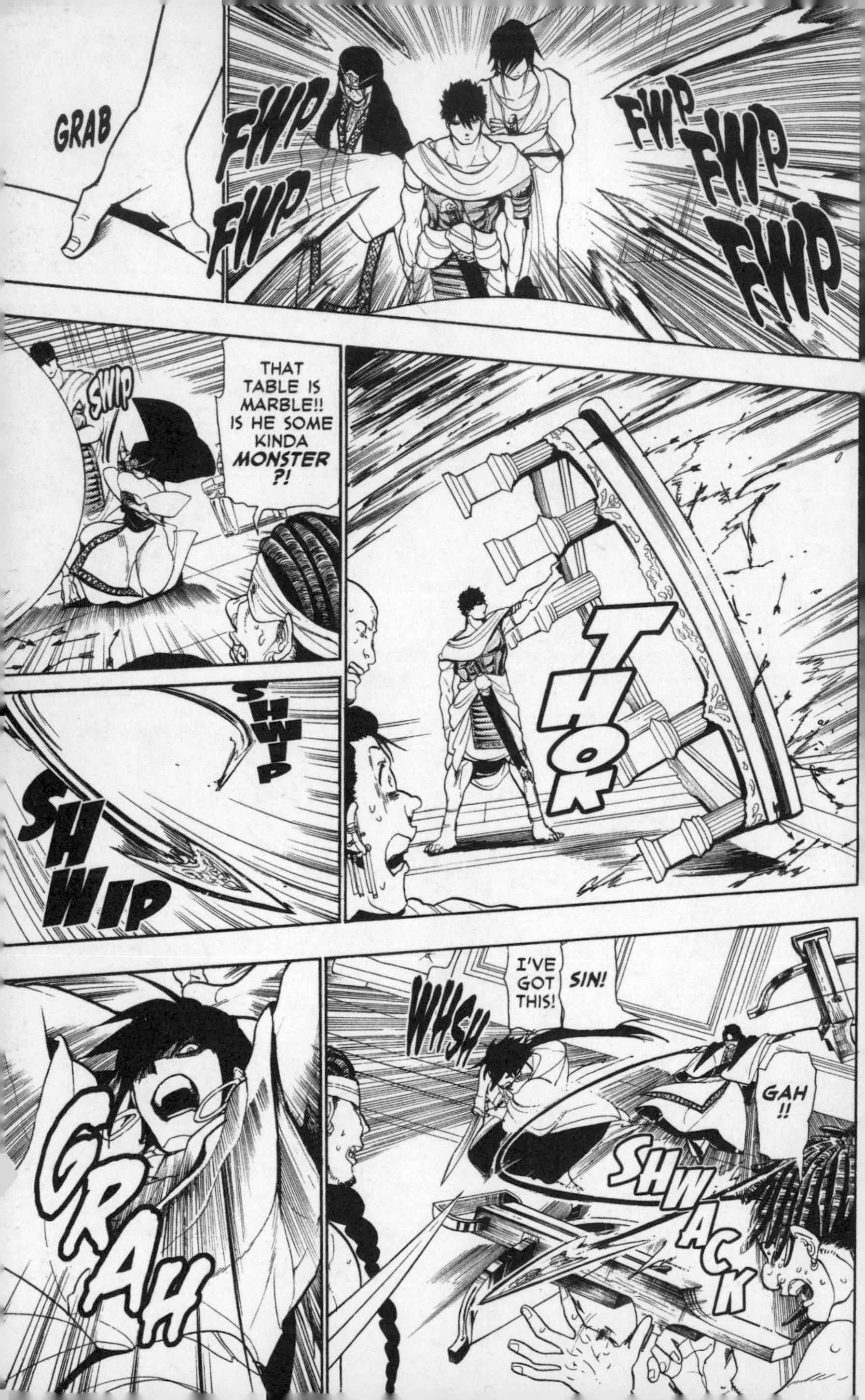

FWP
FWP
FWP
FWP
FWP
FWP
GRAB
THOK
THAT TABLE IS MARBLE!! IS HE SOME KINDA MONSTER?!
SWIP
SHWIP
SHWIP
SIN!
I'VE GOT THIS!
WHSH
GAH!!
SHWACK
GRAH

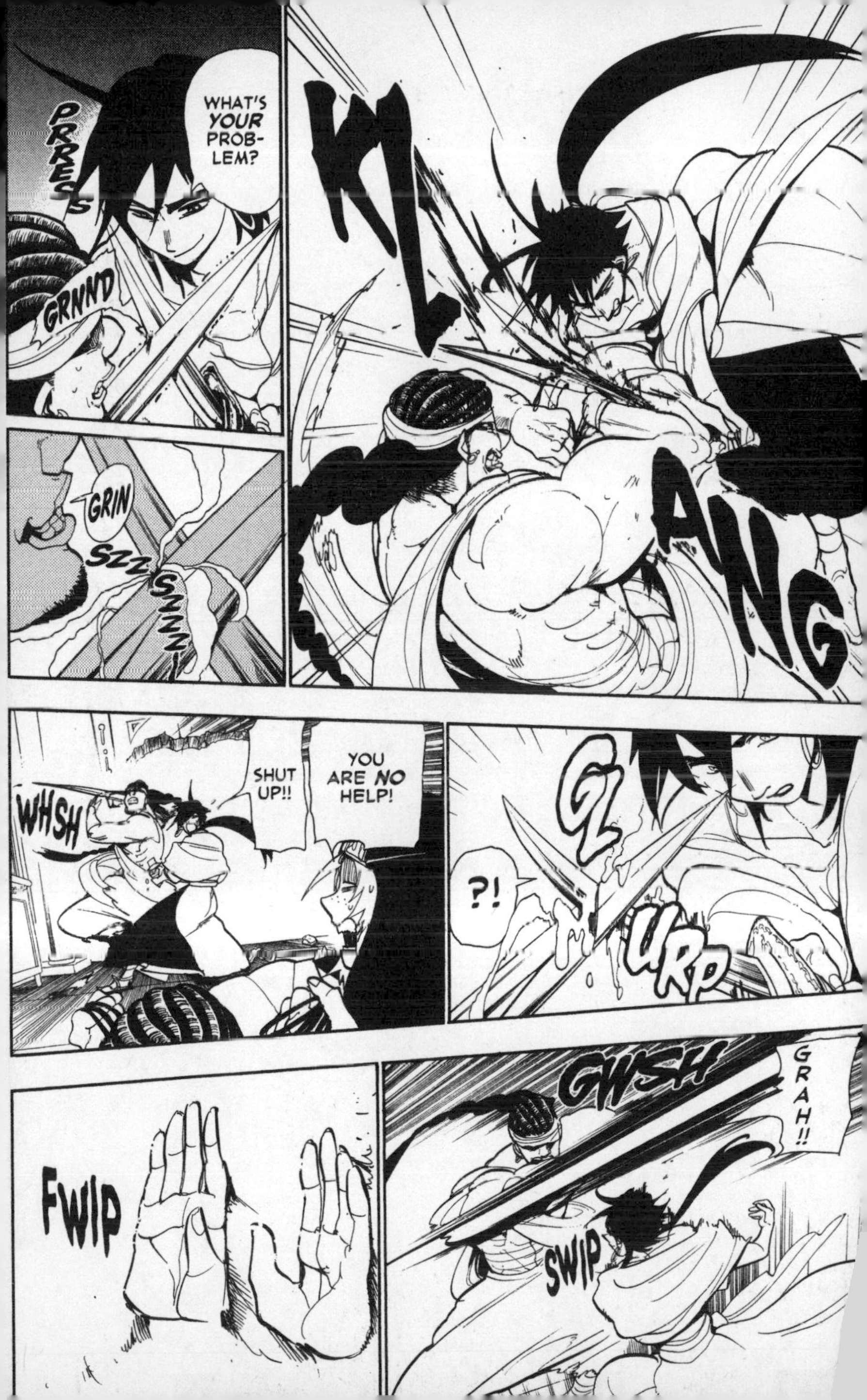
KL
ANG
PRRECS
WHAT'S *YOUR* PROB-LEM?
GRNND
GRIN
SZZ
SZZZ
GL
?!
URP
YOU ARE *NO* HELP!
SHUT UP!!
WHSH
GWSH
GRAH!!
SWIP
FWIP

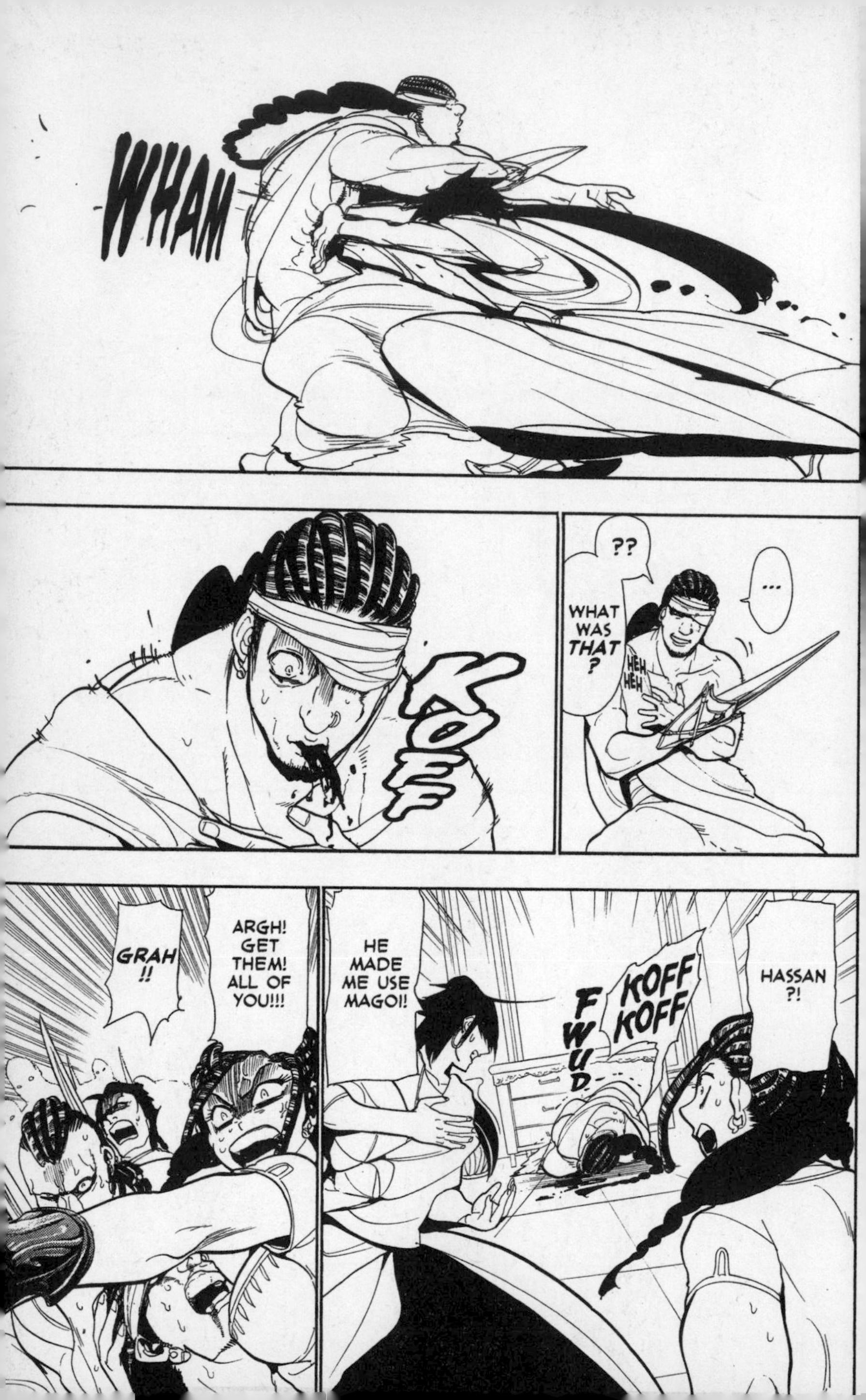
WHAM
...
??
WHAT WAS THAT?
HEH HEH
KOFF
HASSAN ?!
KOFF KOFF
FWUD
HE MADE ME USE MAGOI!
ARGH! GET THEM! ALL OF YOU!!!
GRAH !!

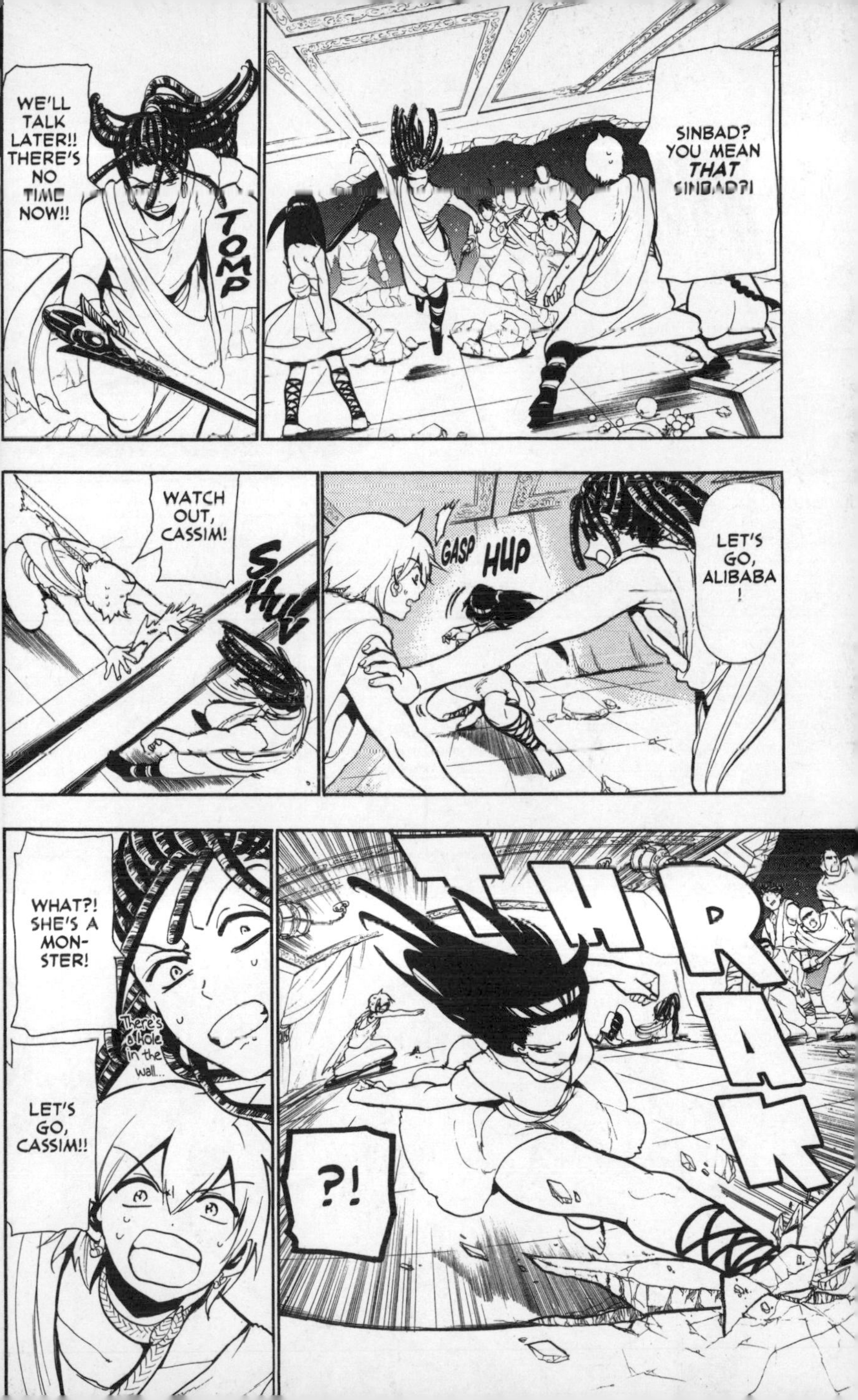
SINBAD? YOU MEAN THAT SINBAD?!
WE'LL TALK LATER!! THERE'S NO TIME NOW!!
TOMP
LET'S GO, ALIBABA!
HUP
GASP
WATCH OUT, CASSIM!
SHUV
THRAK
?!
WHAT?! SHE'S A MONSTER!
There's a hole in the wall...
LET'S GO, CASSIM!!

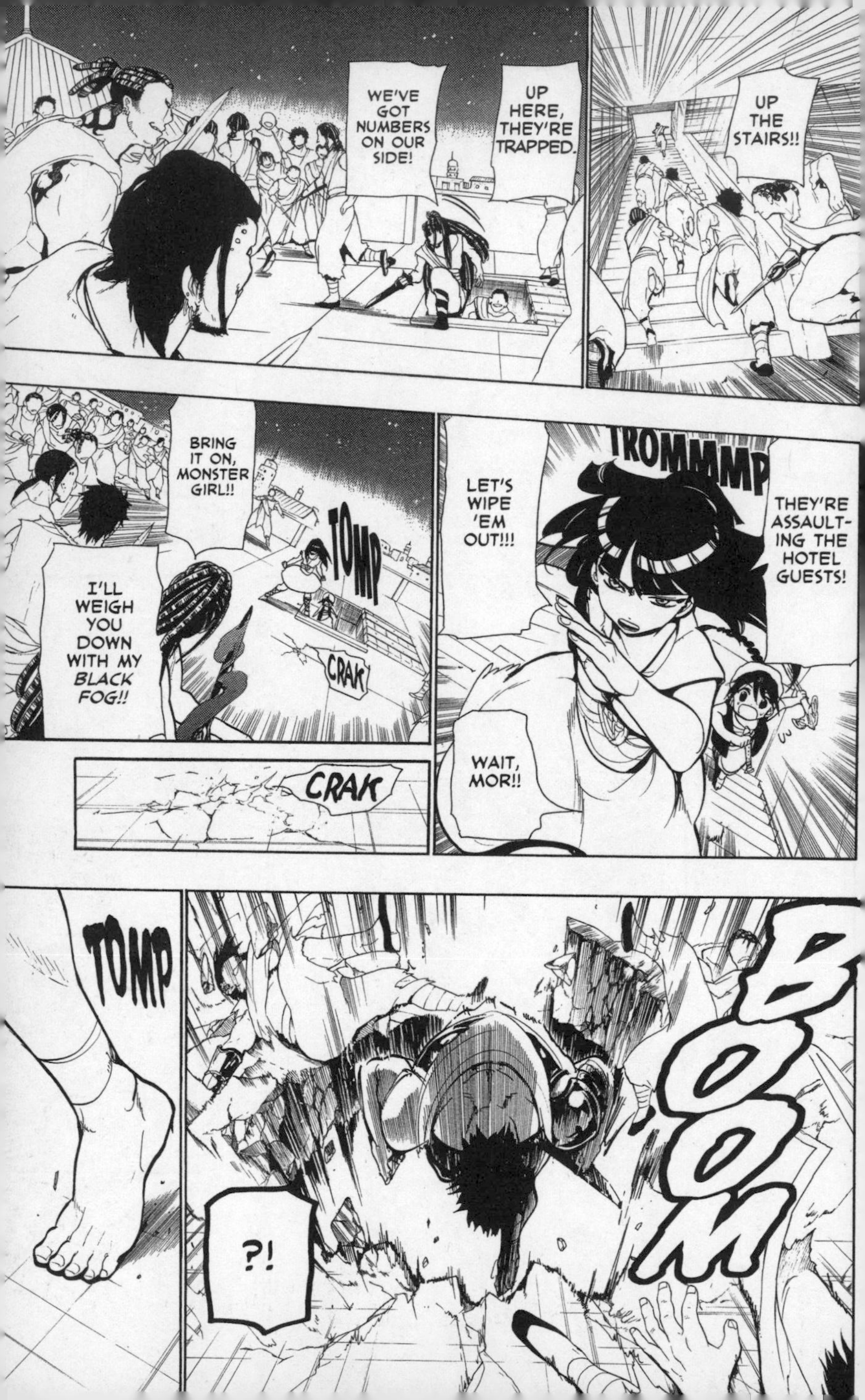
UP THE STAIRS!!
UP HERE, THEY'RE TRAPPED.
WE'VE GOT NUMBERS ON OUR SIDE!
TROMMMP
THEY'RE ASSAULT-ING THE HOTEL GUESTS!
LET'S WIPE 'EM OUT!!!
WAIT, MOR!!
BRING IT ON, MONSTER GIRL!!
TOMP
I'LL WEIGH YOU DOWN WITH MY *BLACK FOG!!*
CRAK
CRAK
BOOM
?!
TOMP

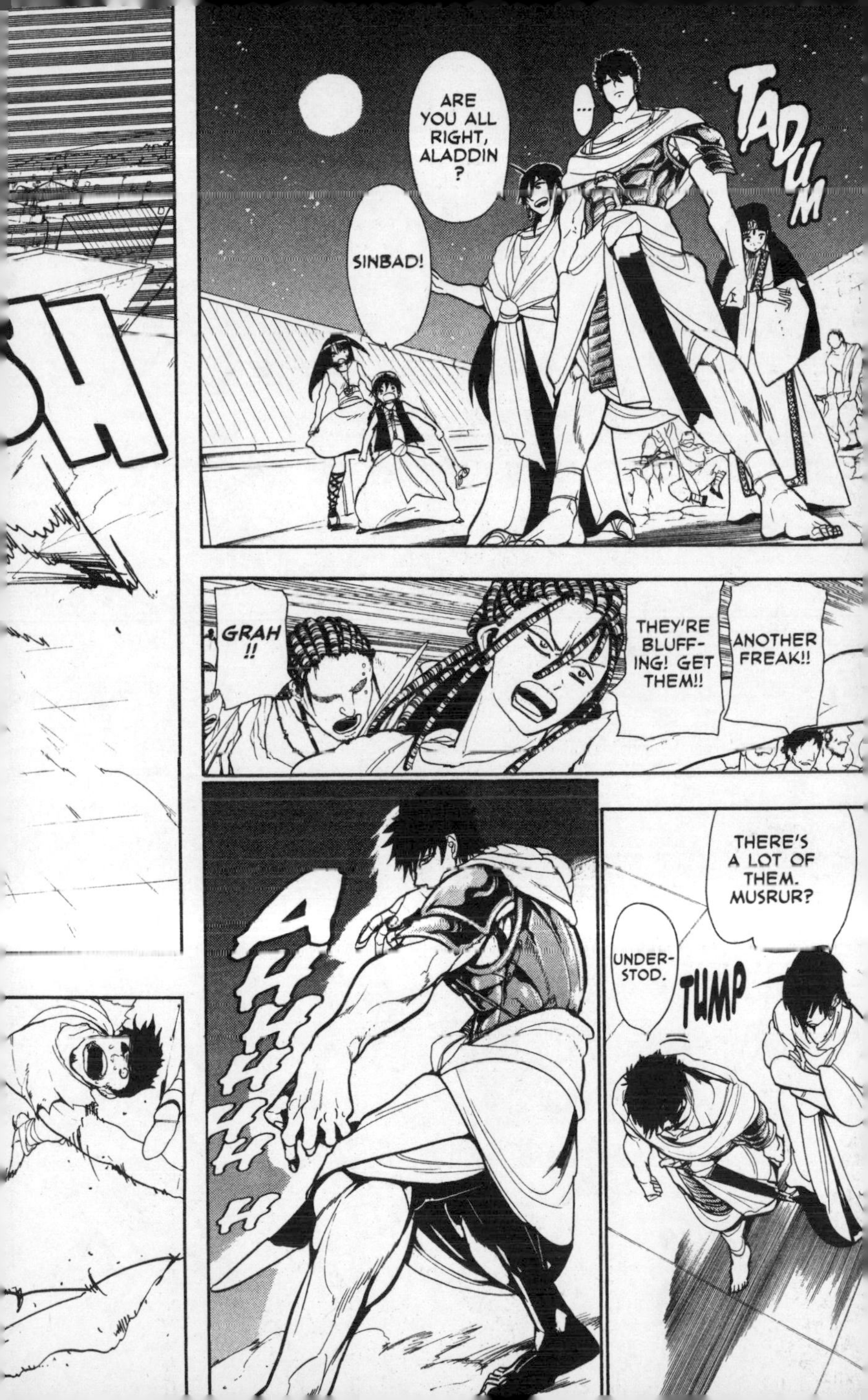
TADUM
...
ARE YOU ALL RIGHT, ALADDIN?
SINBAD!
ANOTHER FREAK!!
THEY'RE BLUFF-ING! GET THEM!!
GRAH!!
THERE'S A LOT OF THEM. MUSRUR?
UNDER-STOD.
TUMP
AHHHHHH
SH

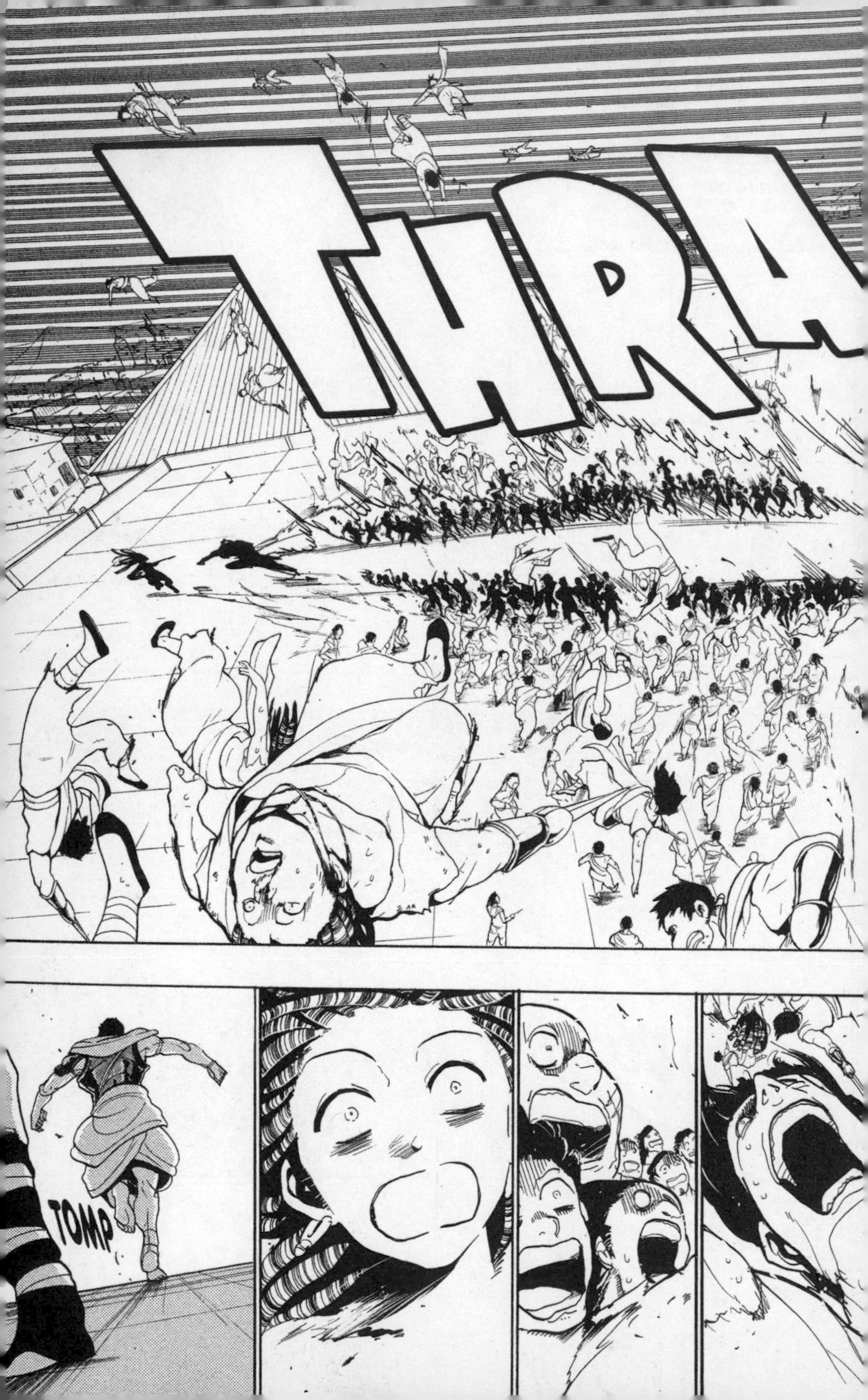
THRA
TOMP

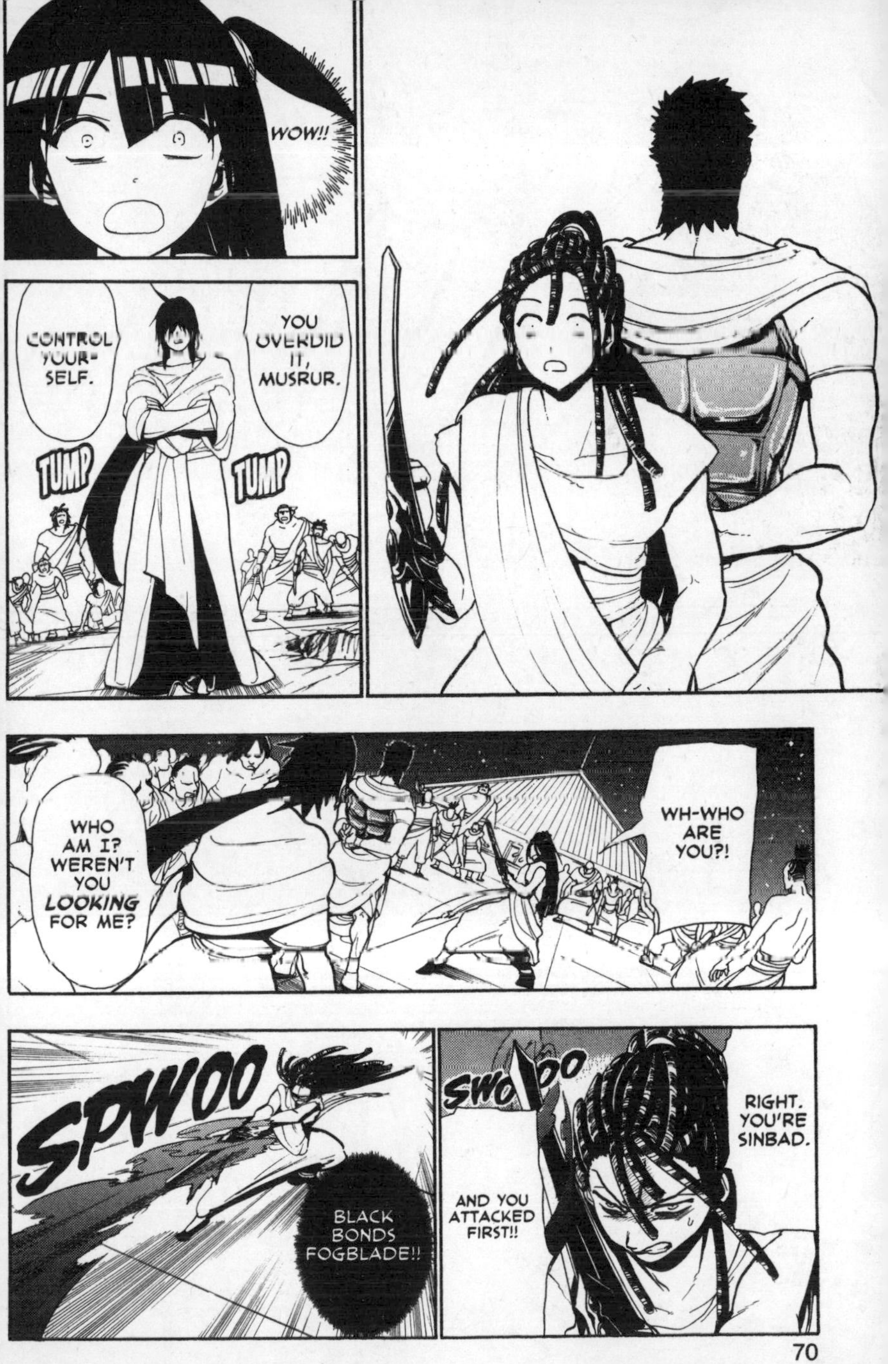
WOW!!
YOU OVERDID IT, MUSRUR.
CONTROL YOUR-SELF.
TUMP
TUMP
WH-WHO ARE YOU?!
WHO AM I? WEREN'T YOU LOOKING FOR ME?
RIGHT. YOU'RE SINBAD.
AND YOU ATTACKED FIRST!!
SPWOO
BLACK BONDS FOGBLADE!!

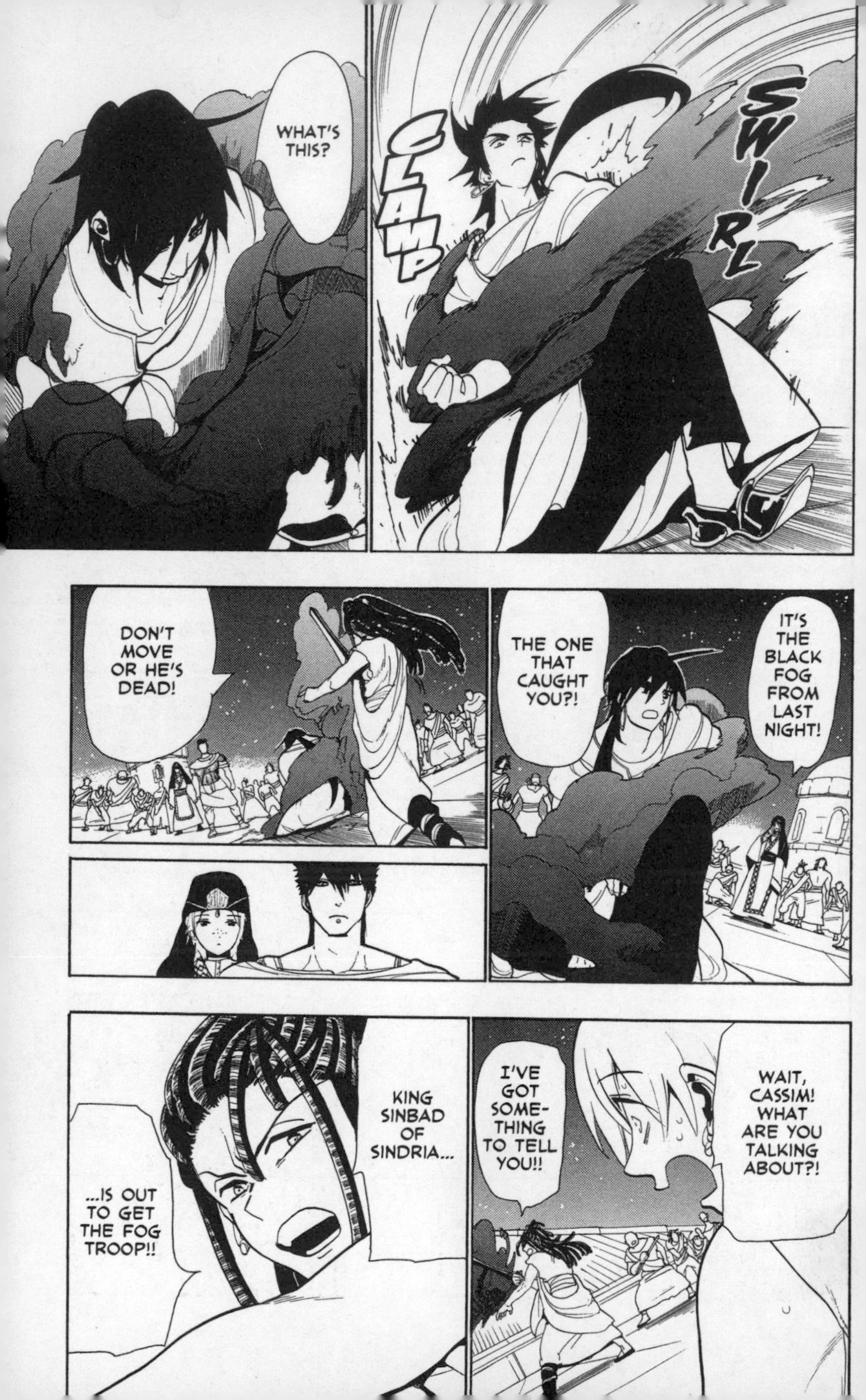
SWIRL
CLAMP
WHAT'S THIS?
IT'S THE BLACK FOG FROM LAST NIGHT!
THE ONE THAT CAUGHT YOU?!
DON'T MOVE OR HE'S DEAD!
WAIT, CASSIM! WHAT ARE YOU TALKING ABOUT?!
I'VE GOT SOME-THING TO TELL YOU!!
KING SINBAD OF SINDRIA...
...IS OUT TO GET THE FOG TROOP!!

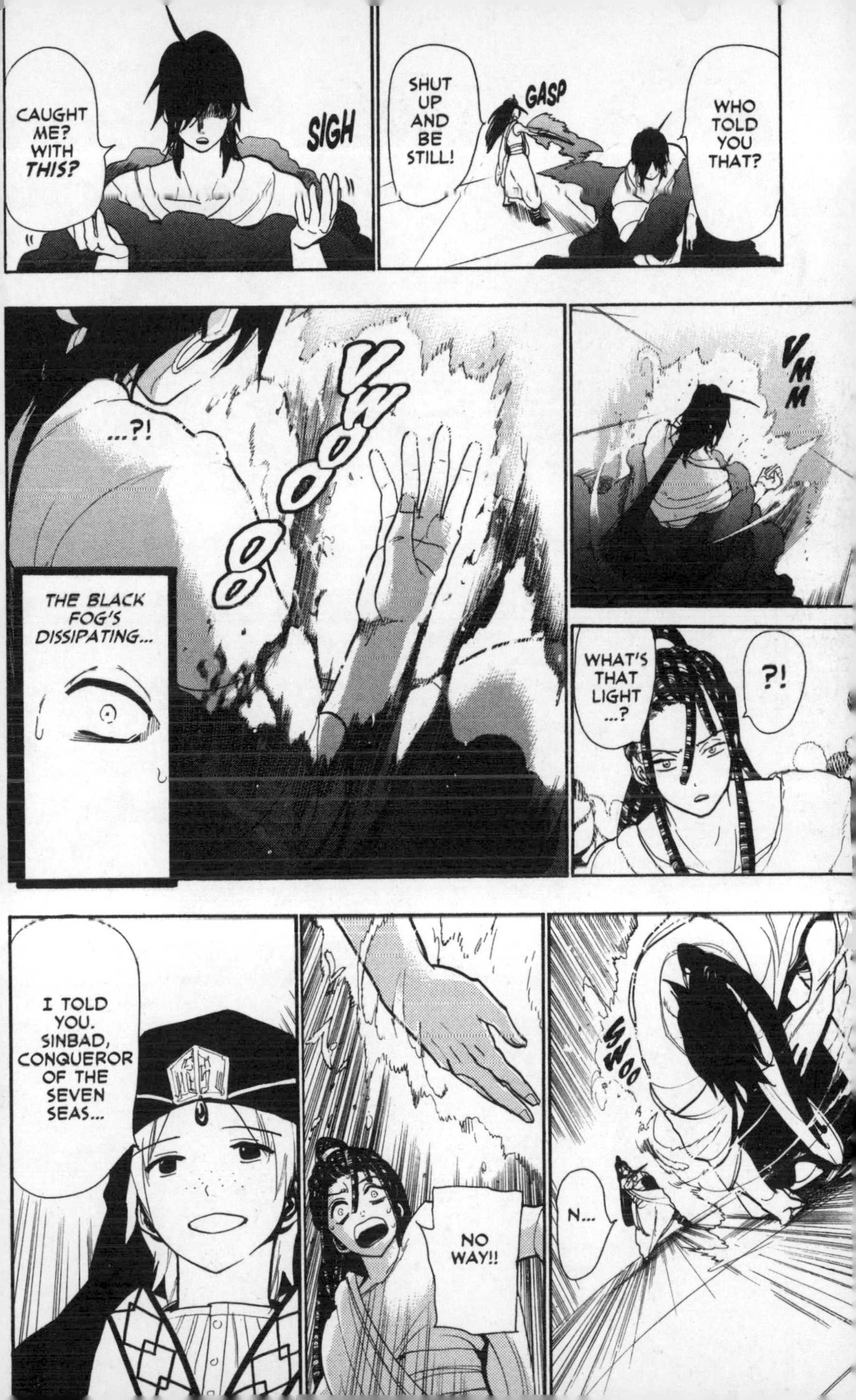
WHO TOLD YOU THAT?
SHUT UP AND BE STILL!
GASP
CAUGHT ME? WITH *THIS?*
SIGH
VMM
?!
WHAT'S THAT LIGHT ...?
VWOOOOO
...?!
THE BLACK FOG'S DISSIPATING...
SWOO
N...
NO WAY!!
I TOLD YOU. SINBAD, CONQUEROR OF THE SEVEN SEAS...

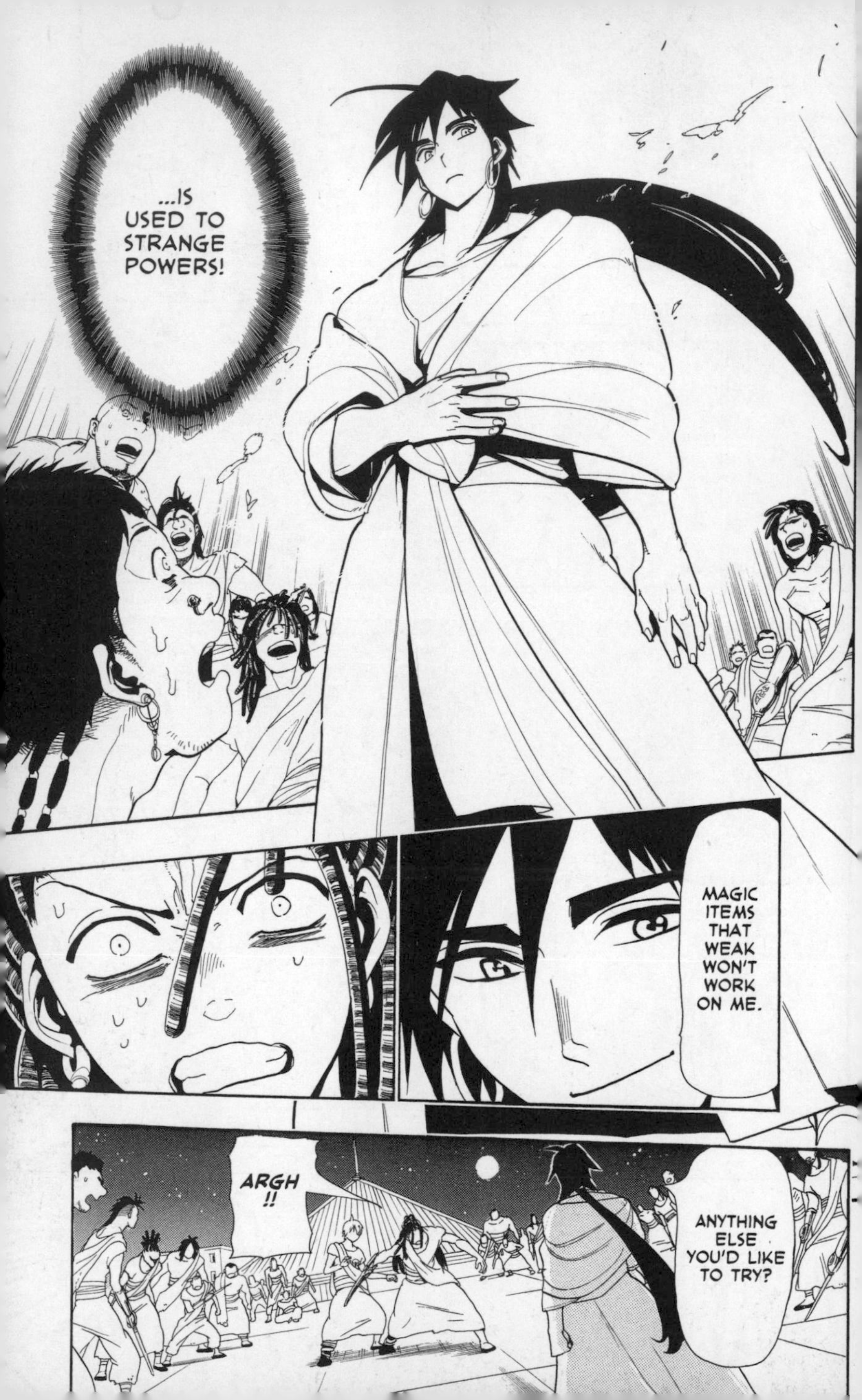
...IS USED TO STRANGE POWERS!
MAGIC ITEMS THAT WEAK WON'T WORK ON ME.
ANYTHING ELSE YOU'D LIKE TO TRY?
ARGH !!

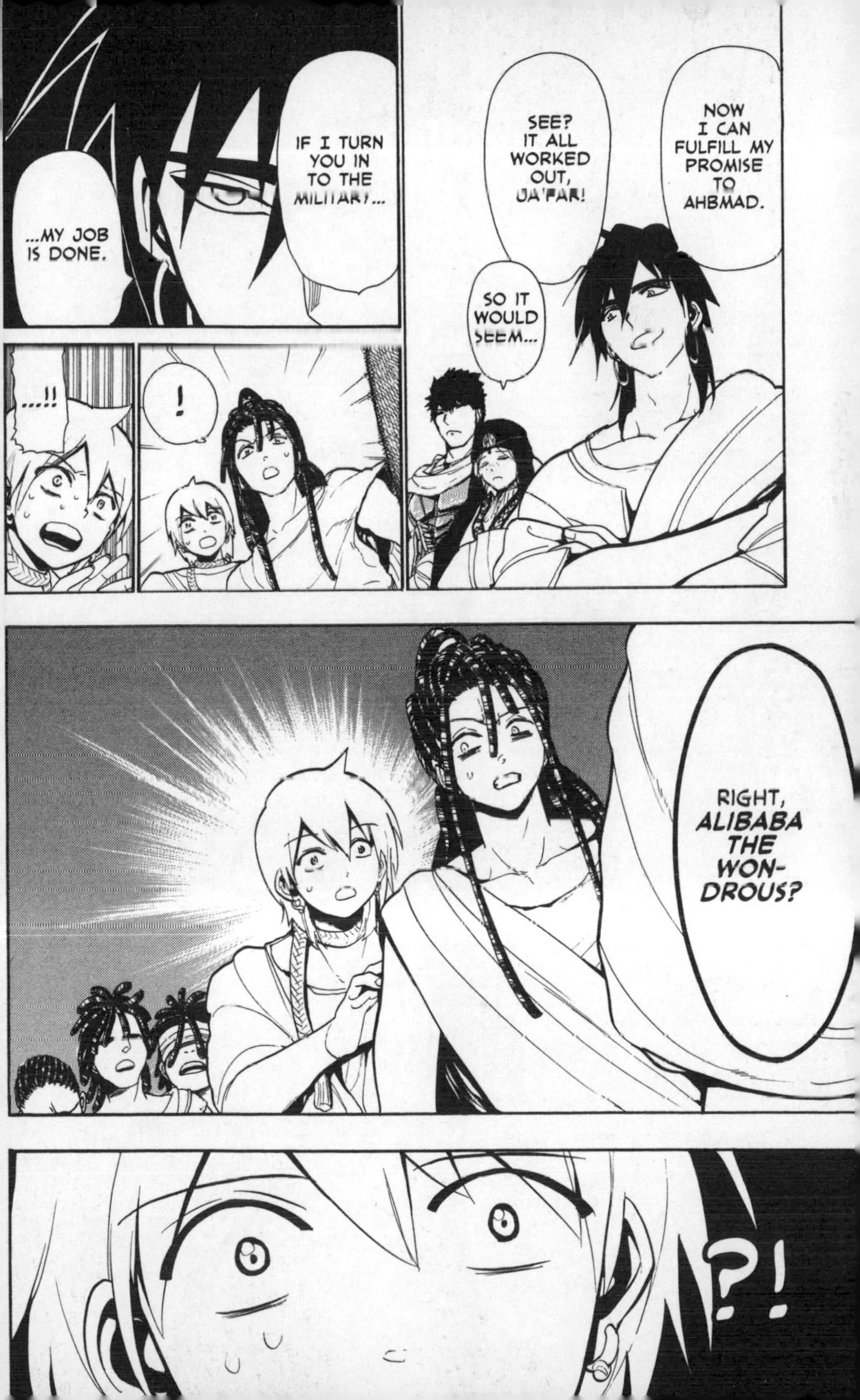
NOW I CAN FULFILL MY PROMISE TO AHBMAD.
SEE? IT ALL WORKED OUT, JA'FAR!
SO IT WOULD SEEM...
IF I TURN YOU IN TO THE MILITARY...
...MY JOB IS DONE.
!
...!!
RIGHT, ALIBABA THE WON-DROUS?
?!

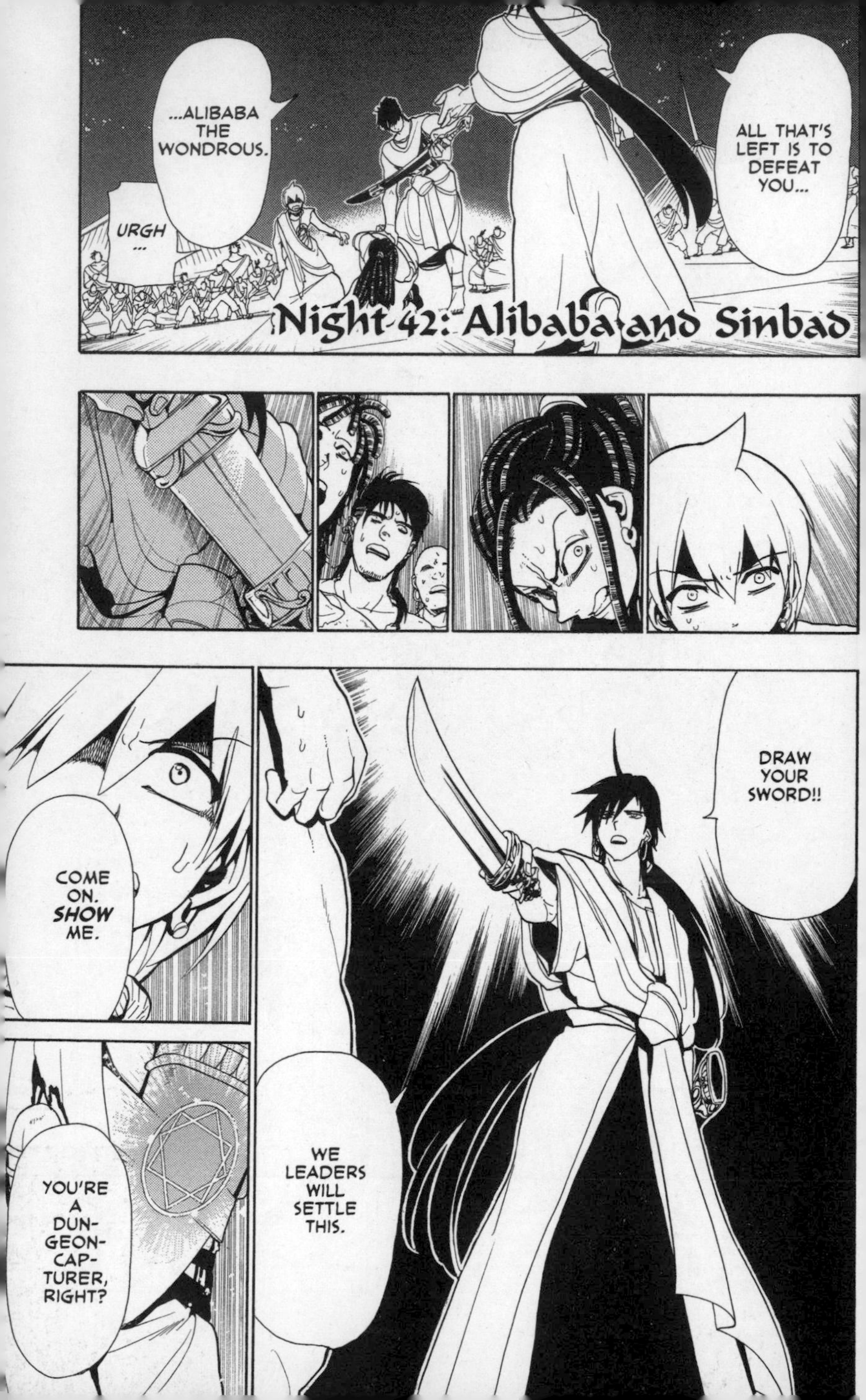
ALL THAT'S LEFT IS TO DEFEAT YOU...
...ALIBABA THE WONDROUS.
URGH...
Night 42: Alibaba and Sinbad
DRAW YOUR SWORD!!
WE LEADERS WILL SETTLE THIS.
COME ON. *SHOW* ME.
YOU'RE A DUNGEON-CAPTURER, RIGHT?

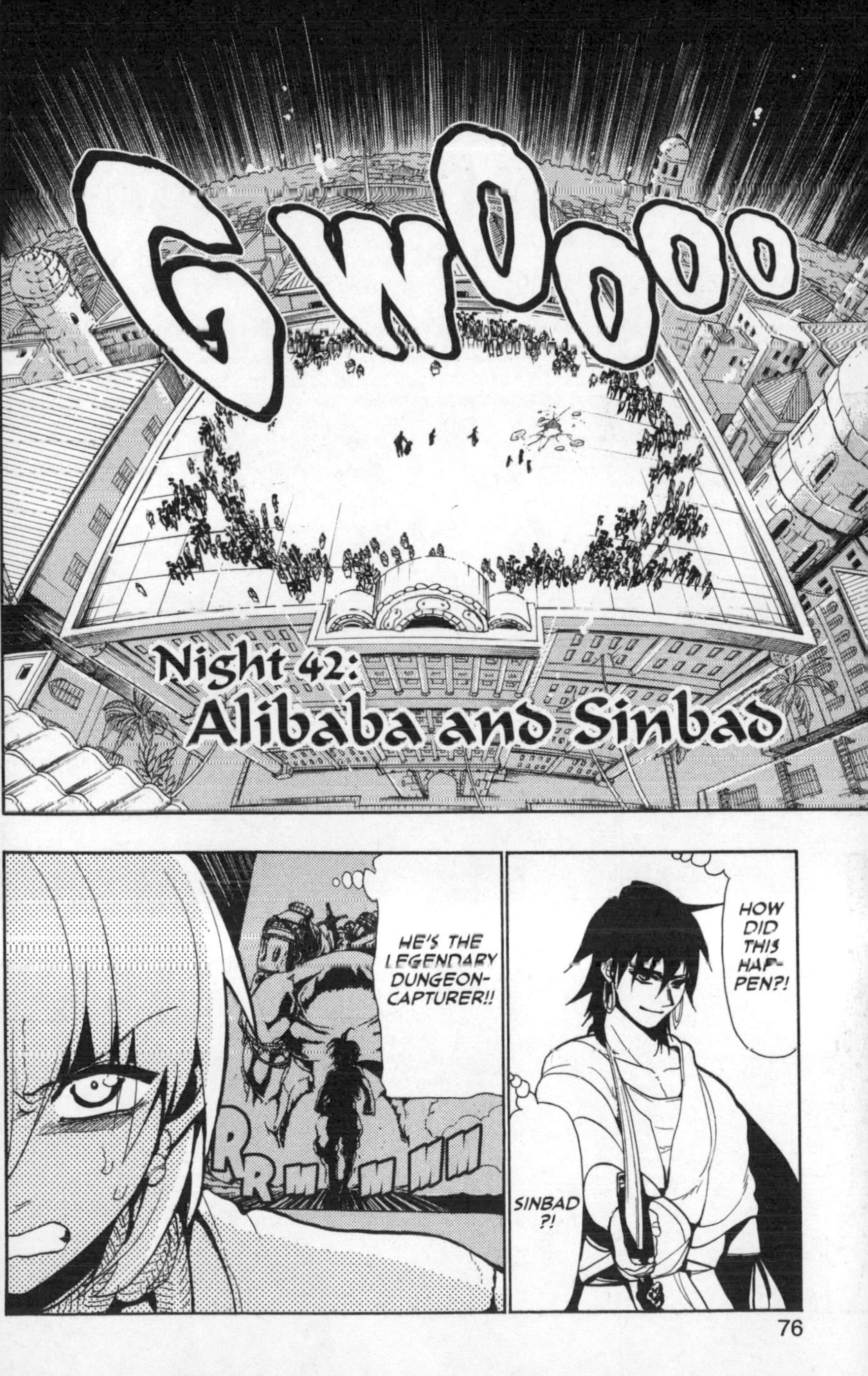
GWOOOO
Night 42: Alibaba and Sinbad
HOW DID THIS HAP-PEN?!
SINBAD?!
HE'S THE LEGENDARY DUNGEON-CAPTURER!!
RRMMMMM

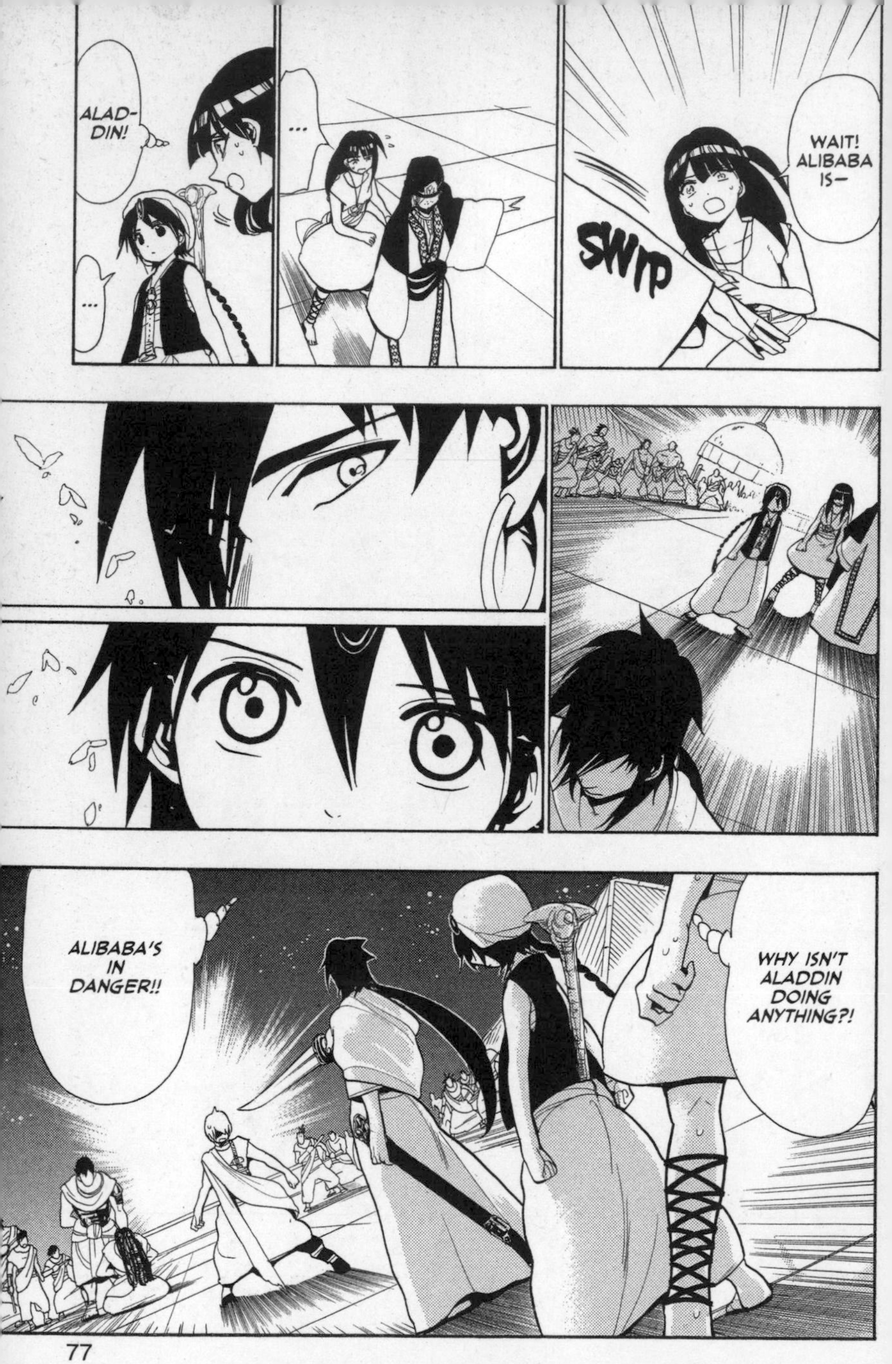
WAIT! ALIBABA IS—
SWIP
...
ALAD-DIN!
...
WHY ISN'T ALADDIN DOING ANYTHING?!
ALIBABA'S IN DANGER!!

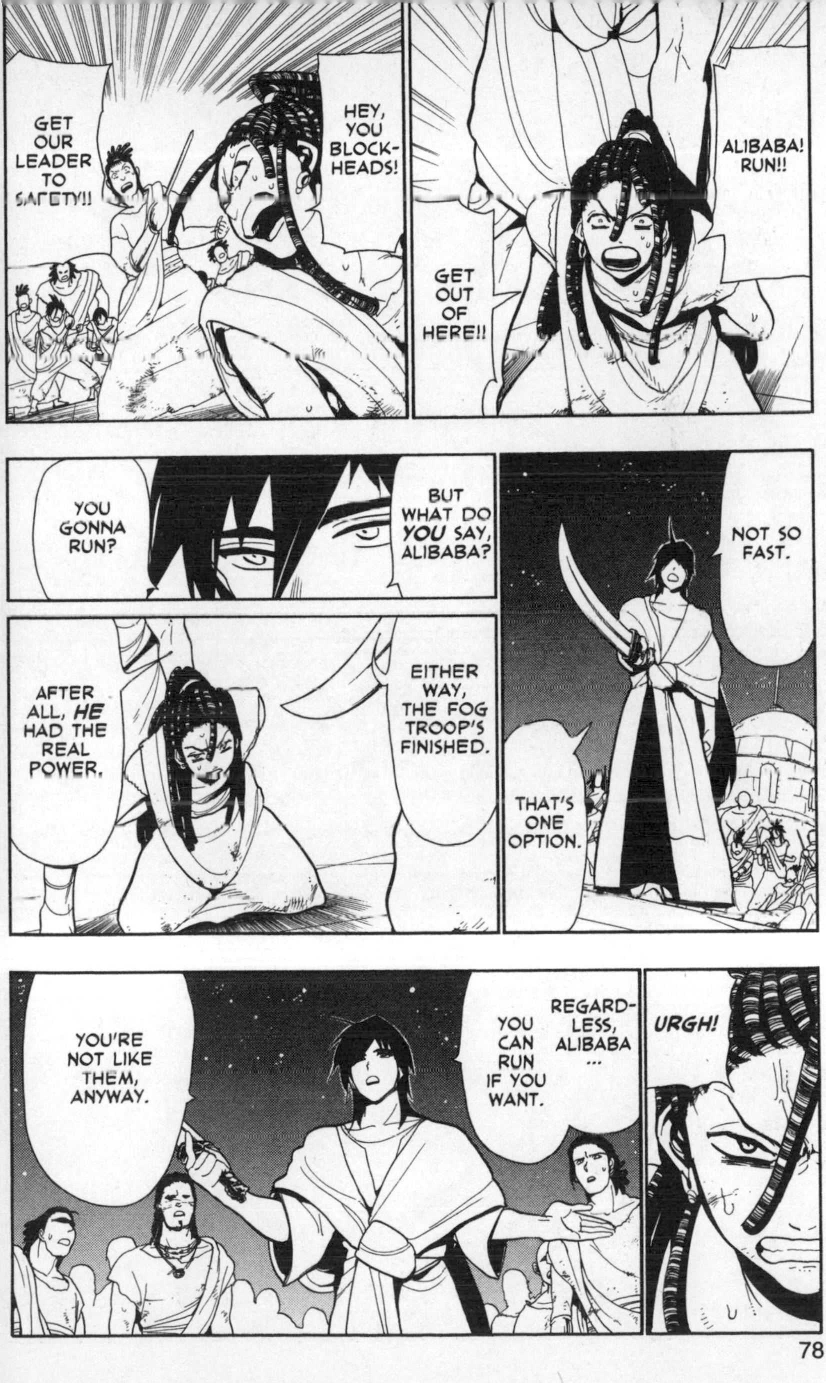
ALIBABA! RUN!!
GET OUT OF HERE!!
HEY, YOU BLOCKHEADS!
GET OUR LEADER TO SAFETY!!
NOT SO FAST.
THAT'S ONE OPTION.
BUT WHAT DO *YOU* SAY, ALIBABA?
YOU GONNA RUN?
EITHER WAY, THE FOG TROOP'S FINISHED.
AFTER ALL, *HE* HAD THE REAL POWER.
*URGH!*
REGARDLESS, ALIBABA...
YOU CAN RUN IF YOU WANT.
YOU'RE NOT LIKE THEM, ANYWAY.

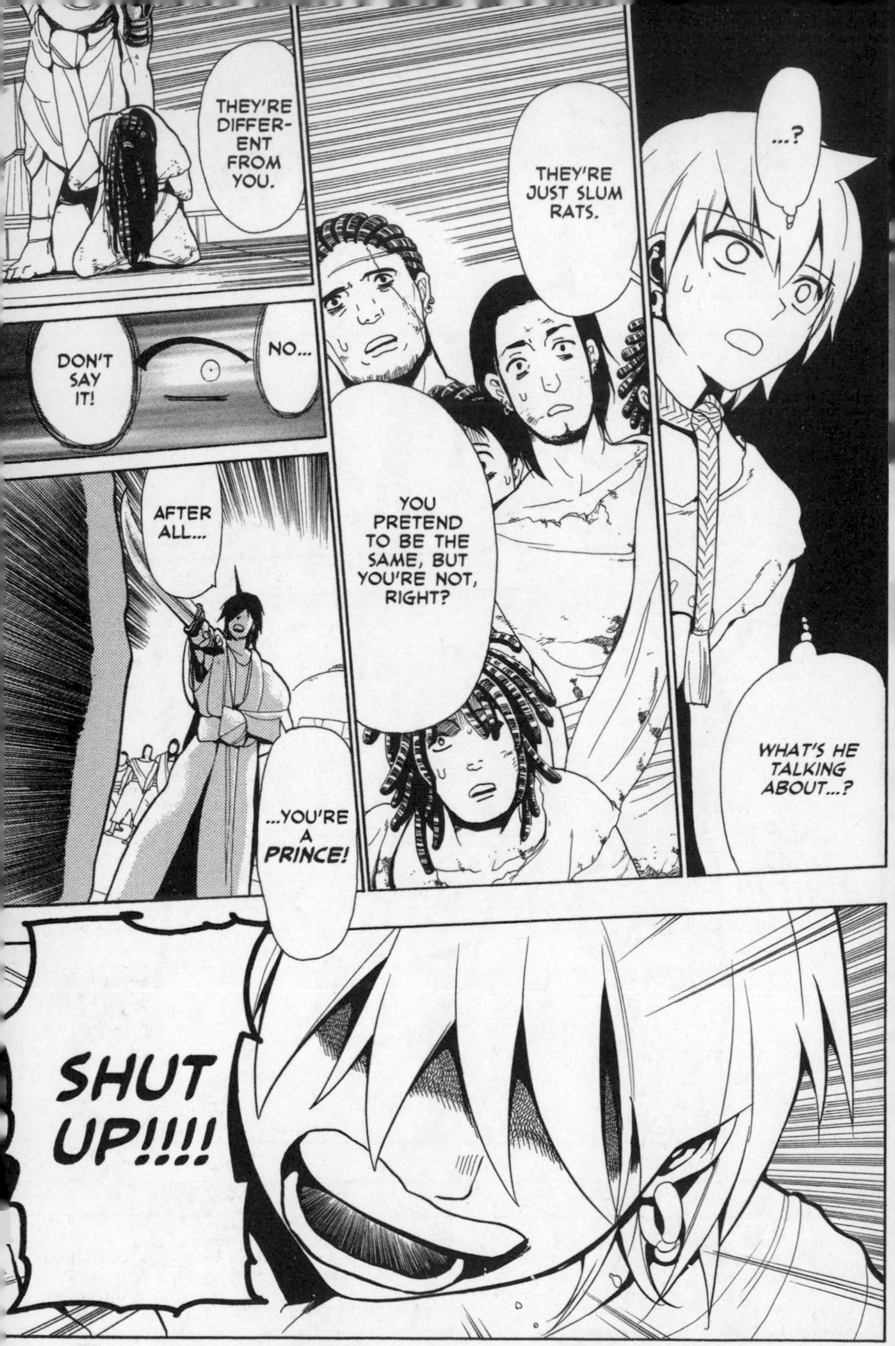
...?
WHAT'S HE TALKING ABOUT...?
THEY'RE JUST SLUM RATS.
YOU PRETEND TO BE THE SAME, BUT YOU'RE NOT, RIGHT?
THEY'RE DIFFER-ENT FROM YOU.
NO...
DON'T SAY IT!
AFTER ALL...
...YOU'RE A PRINCE!
SHUT UP!!!!

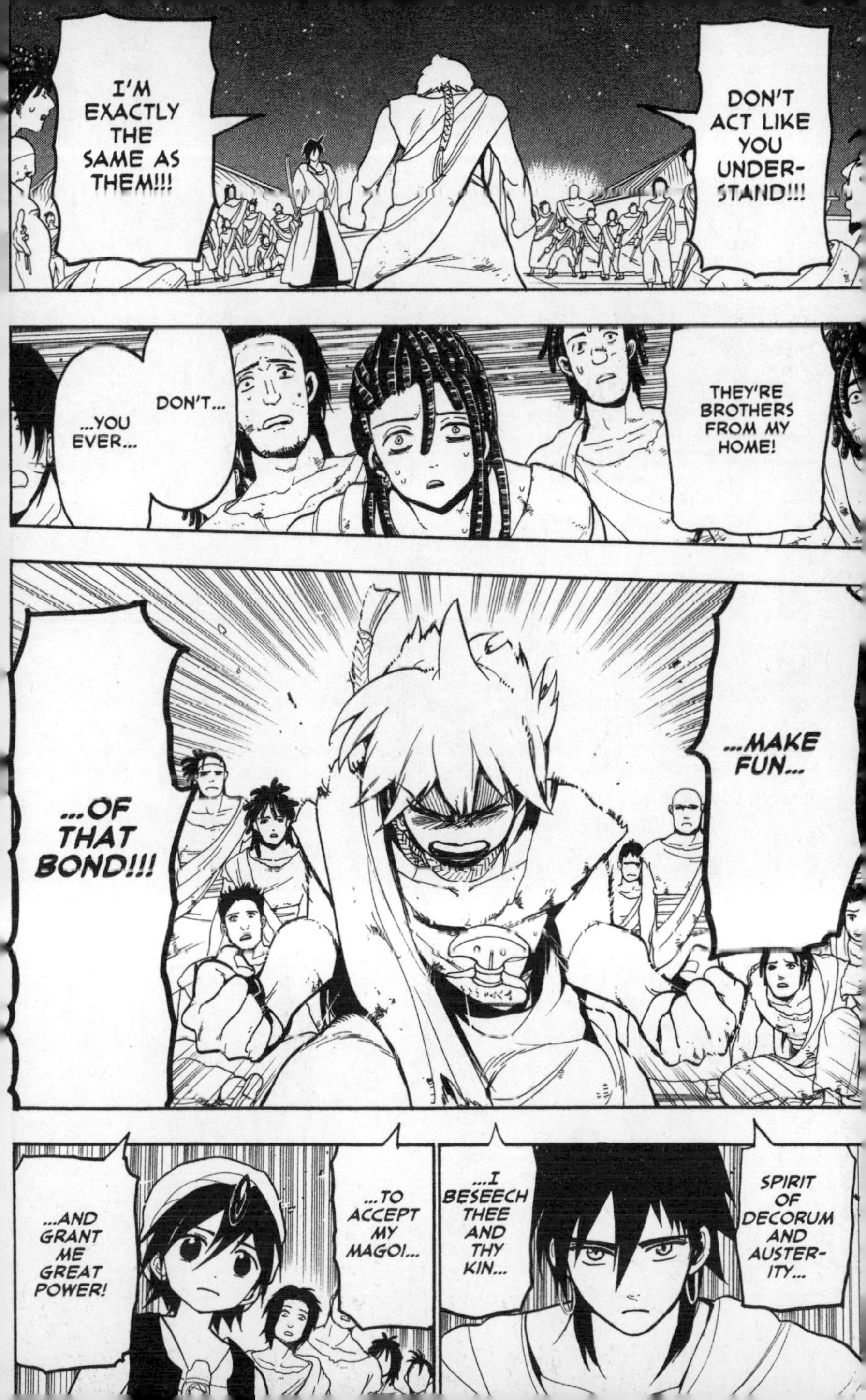
DON'T ACT LIKE YOU UNDER-STAND!!!
I'M EXACTLY THE SAME AS THEM!!!
THEY'RE BROTHERS FROM MY HOME!
DON'T...
...YOU EVER...
...MAKE FUN...
...OF THAT BOND!!!
SPIRIT OF DECORUM AND AUSTER-ITY...
...I BESEECH THEE AND THY KIN...
...TO ACCEPT MY MAGOI...
...AND GRANT ME GREAT POWER!

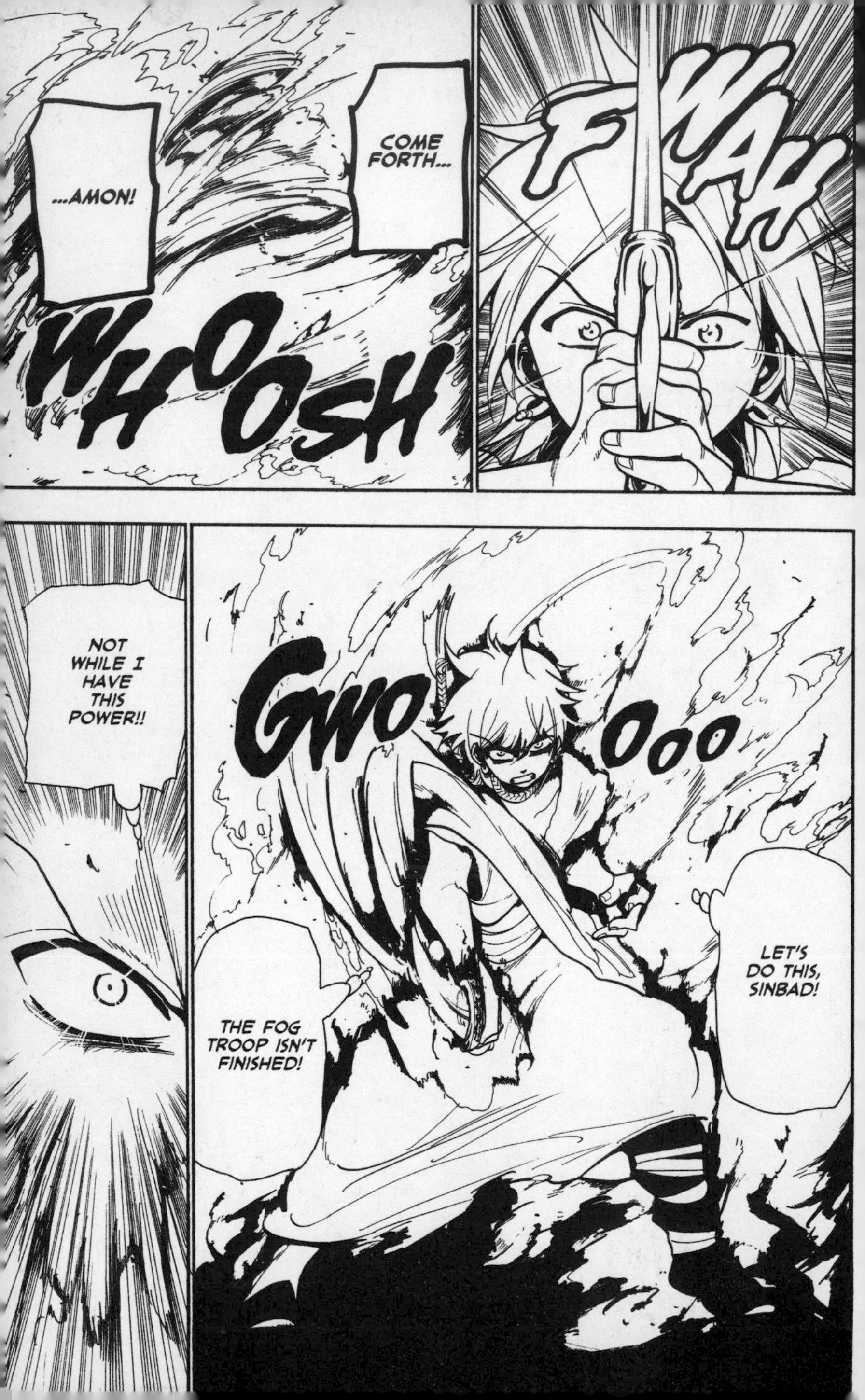
FWAH
COME FORTH...
...AMON!
WHOOSH
GWOOOO
LET'S DO THIS, SINBAD!
THE FOG TROOP ISN'T FINISHED!
NOT WHILE I HAVE THIS POWER!!

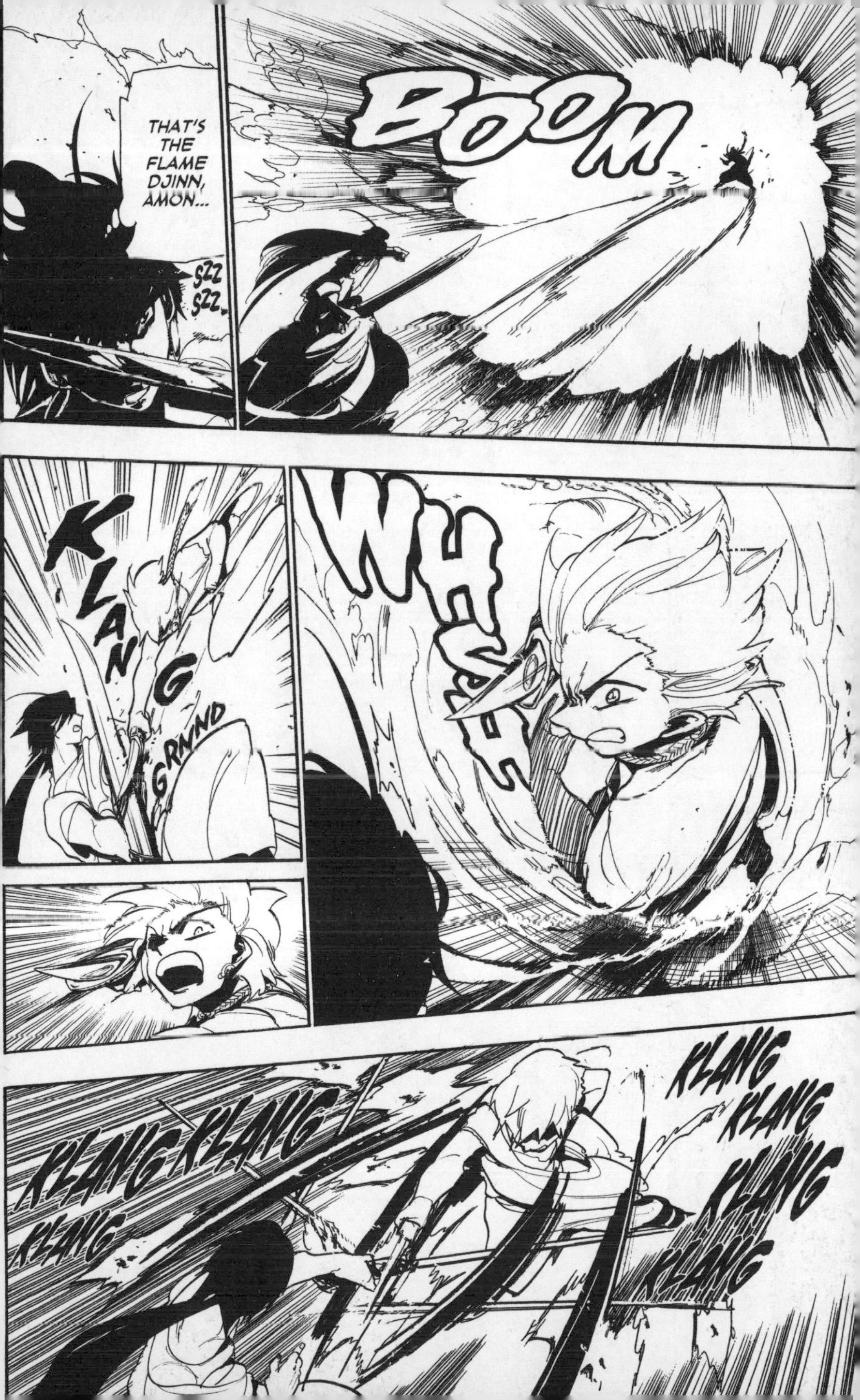
BOOM
THAT'S THE FLAME DJINN, AMON...
SZZ SZZ
KLANG
GRNND
KLANG
KLANG
KLANG
KLANG
KLANG KLANG
KLANG

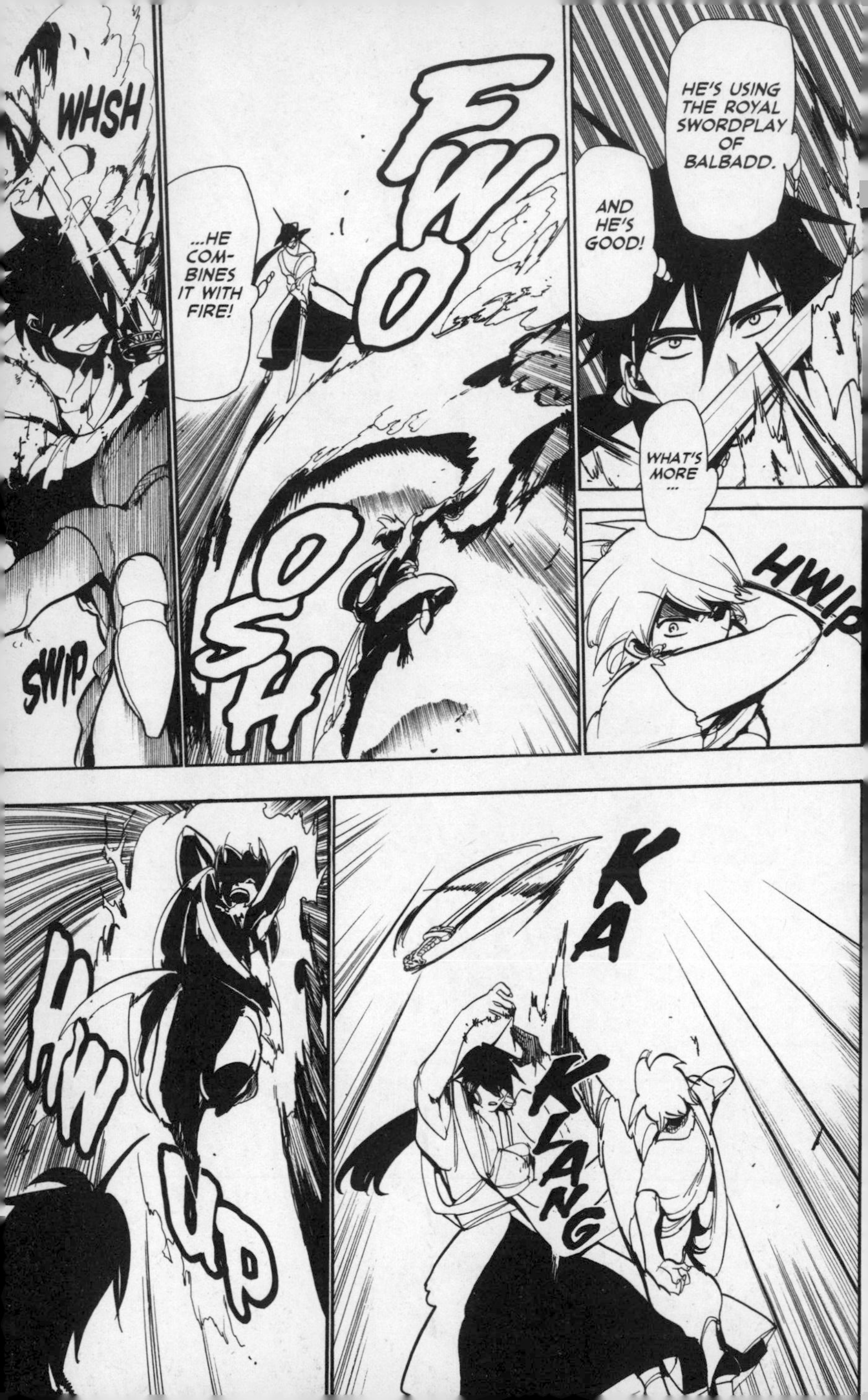
HE'S USING THE ROYAL SWORDPLAY OF BALBADD.
AND HE'S GOOD!
WHAT'S MORE ...
HWIP
FWOOOSH
...HE COMBINES IT WITH FIRE!
WHSH
SWIP
KA
KLANG
HWUP

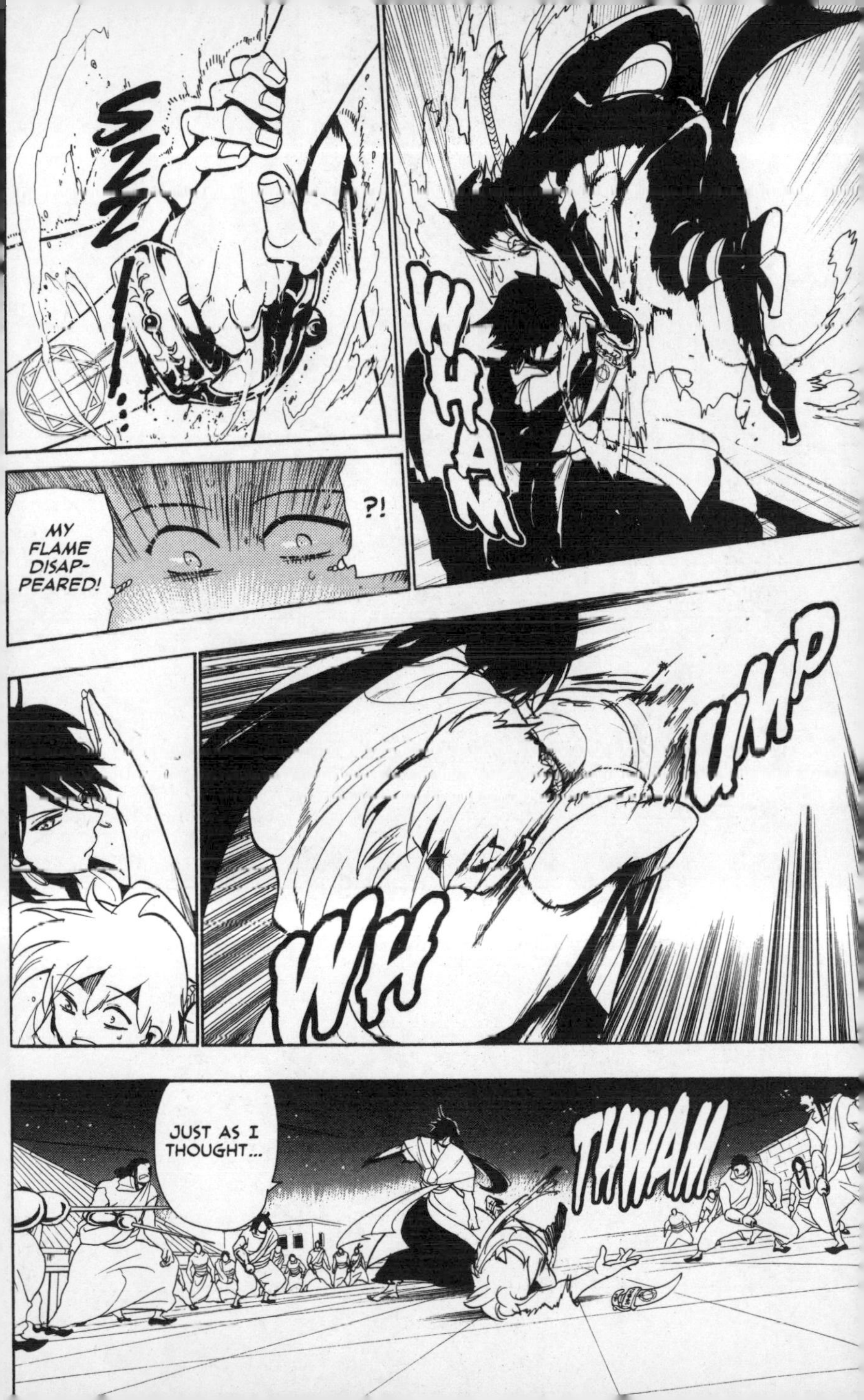
WHAM
SZZZ...
?!
MY FLAME DISAPPEARED!
WHUMP
THWAM
JUST AS I THOUGHT...

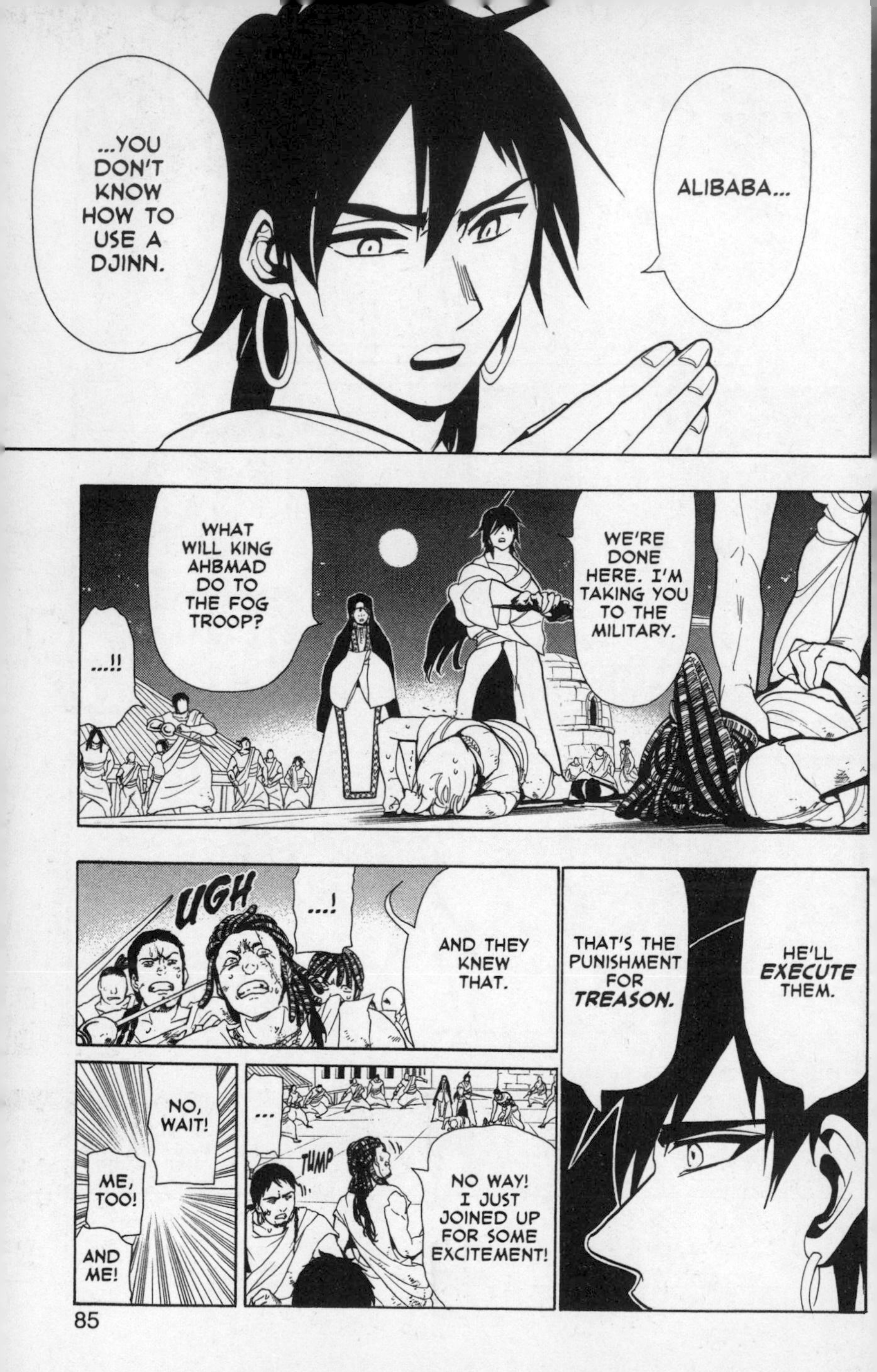
ALIBABA...
...YOU DON'T KNOW HOW TO USE A DJINN.
WE'RE DONE HERE. I'M TAKING YOU TO THE MILITARY.
WHAT WILL KING AHBMAD DO TO THE FOG TROOP?
...!!
HE'LL EXECUTE THEM.
THAT'S THE PUNISHMENT FOR TREASON.
AND THEY KNEW THAT.
...!
UGH
NO WAY! I JUST JOINED UP FOR SOME EXCITEMENT!
TUMP
...
NO, WAIT!
ME, TOO!
AND ME!

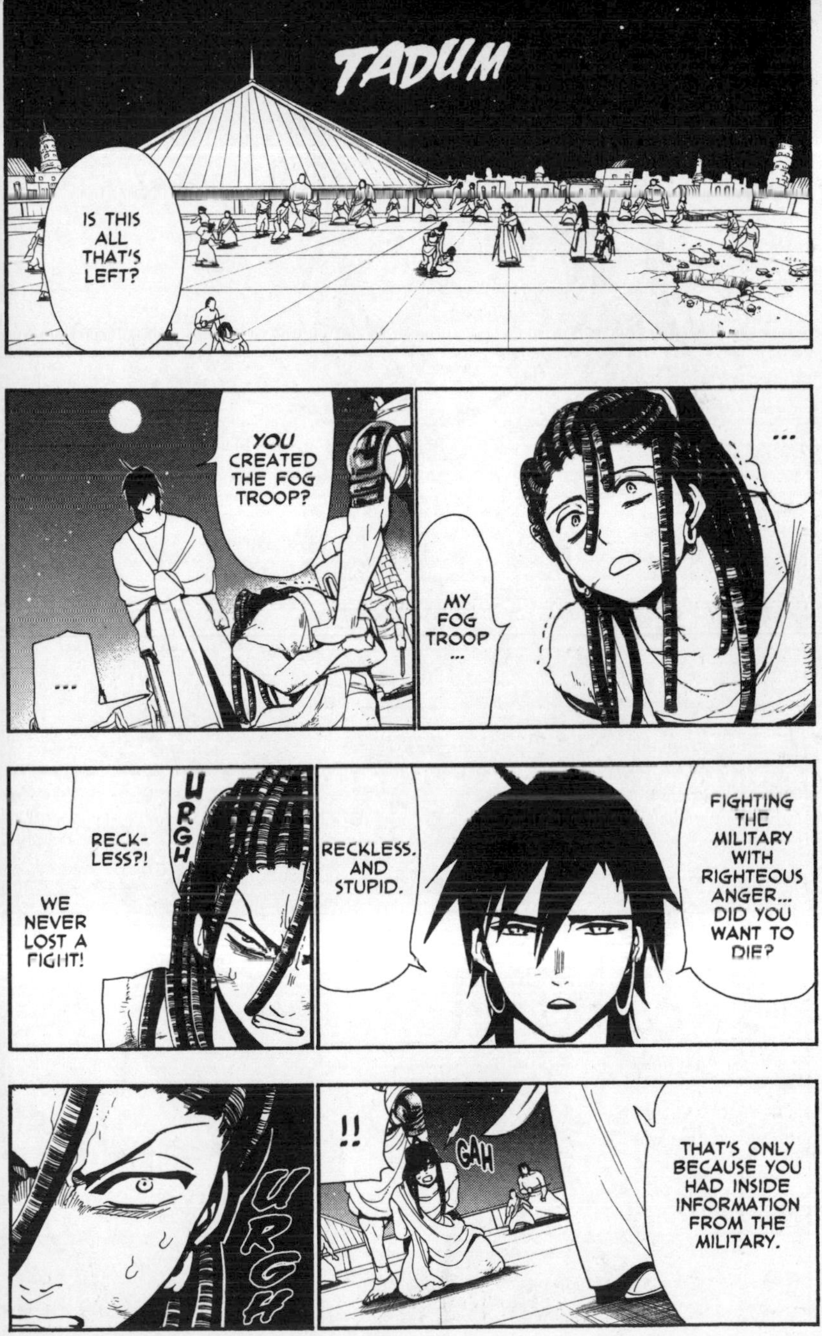
TADUM
IS THIS ALL THAT'S LEFT?
...
MY FOG TROOP ...
YOU CREATED THE FOG TROOP?
...
FIGHTING THE MILITARY WITH RIGHTEOUS ANGER... DID YOU WANT TO DIE?
RECKLESS. AND STUPID.
URGH
RECK-LESS?!
WE NEVER LOST A FIGHT!
THAT'S ONLY BECAUSE YOU HAD INSIDE INFORMATION FROM THE MILITARY.
GAH
!!
URGH

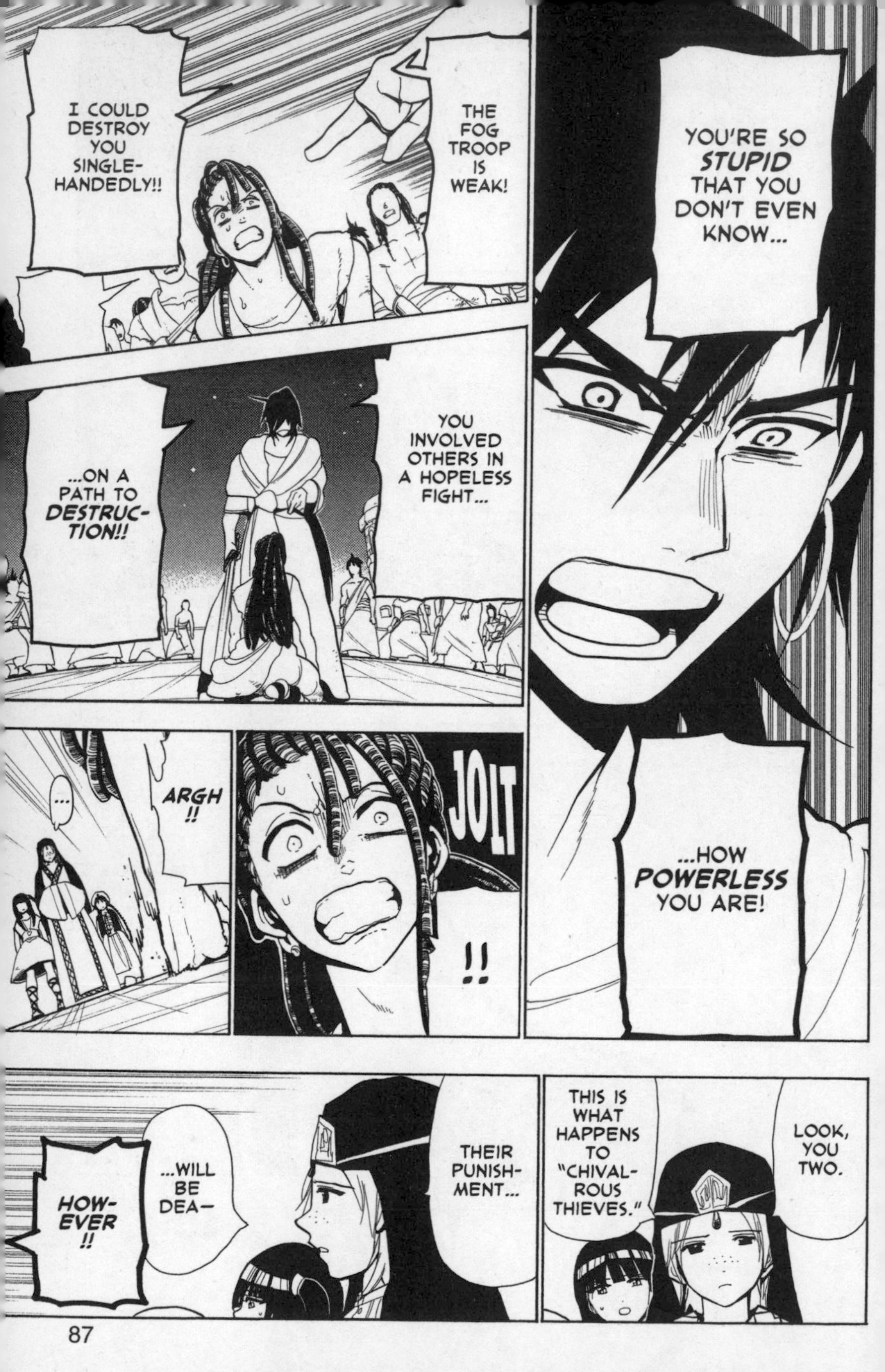

YOU'RE SO STUPID THAT YOU DON'T EVEN KNOW...
...HOW POWERLESS YOU ARE!
THE FOG TROOP IS WEAK!
I COULD DESTROY YOU SINGLE-HANDEDLY!!
YOU INVOLVED OTHERS IN A HOPELESS FIGHT...
...ON A PATH TO DESTRUCTION!!
JOLT
!!
ARGH!!
...
LOOK, YOU TWO.
THIS IS WHAT HAPPENS TO "CHIVALROUS THIEVES."
THEIR PUNISHMENT...
...WILL BE DEA—
HOWEVER!!

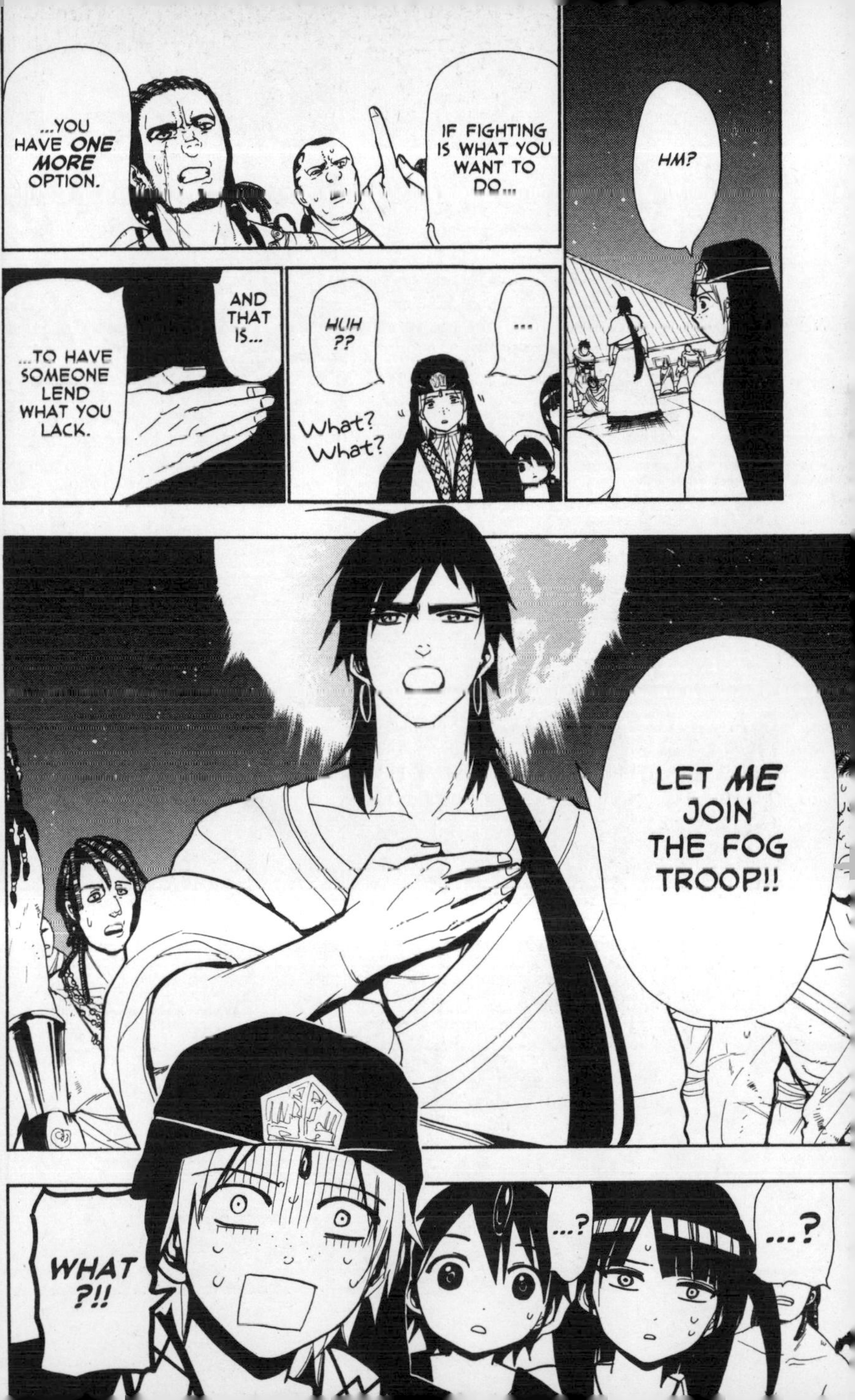
HM?
IF FIGHTING IS WHAT YOU WANT TO DO...
...YOU HAVE ONE MORE OPTION.
...
HUH ??
What? What?
AND THAT IS...
...TO HAVE SOMEONE LEND WHAT YOU LACK.
LET ME JOIN THE FOG TROOP!!
...?
...?
WHAT ?!!

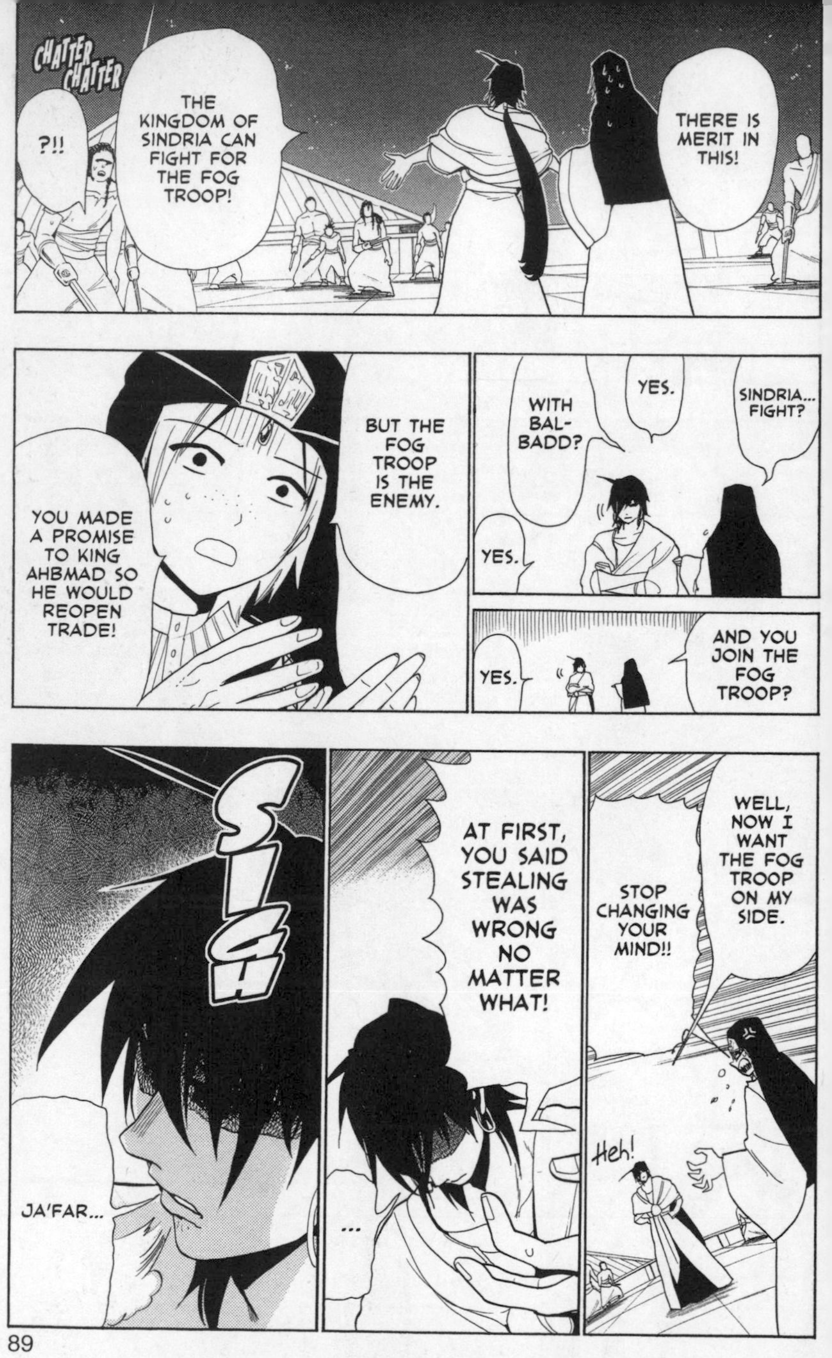
THERE IS MERIT IN THIS!
THE KINGDOM OF SINDRIA CAN FIGHT FOR THE FOG TROOP!
CHATTER CHATTER
?!!
SINDRIA... FIGHT?
YES.
WITH BAL-BADD?
YES.
AND YOU JOIN THE FOG TROOP?
YES.
BUT THE FOG TROOP IS THE ENEMY.
YOU MADE A PROMISE TO KING AHBMAD SO HE WOULD REOPEN TRADE!
WELL, NOW I WANT THE FOG TROOP ON MY SIDE.
STOP CHANGING YOUR MIND!!
Heh!
AT FIRST, YOU SAID STEALING WAS WRONG NO MATTER WHAT!
...
SIGH
JA'FAR...

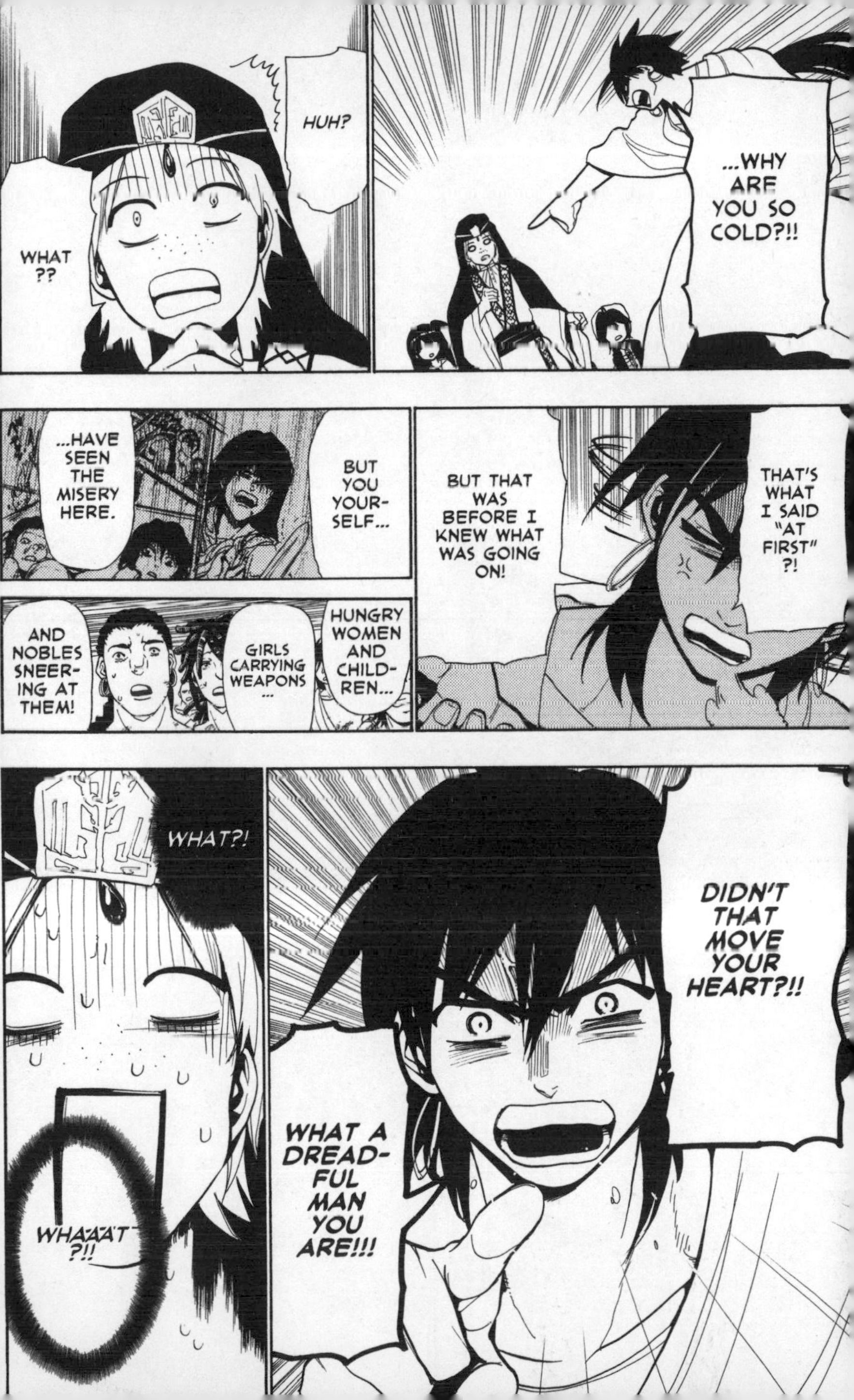
...WHY ARE YOU SO COLD?!!
HUH?
WHAT ??
THAT'S WHAT I SAID "AT FIRST" ?!
BUT THAT WAS BEFORE I KNEW WHAT WAS GOING ON!
BUT YOU YOURSELF...
...HAVE SEEN THE MISERY HERE.
HUNGRY WOMEN AND CHILDREN...
GIRLS CARRYING WEAPONS ...
AND NOBLES SNEERING AT THEM!
DIDN'T THAT MOVE YOUR HEART?!!
WHAT A DREADFUL MAN YOU ARE!!!
WHAT?!
WHAÄÄT ?!!

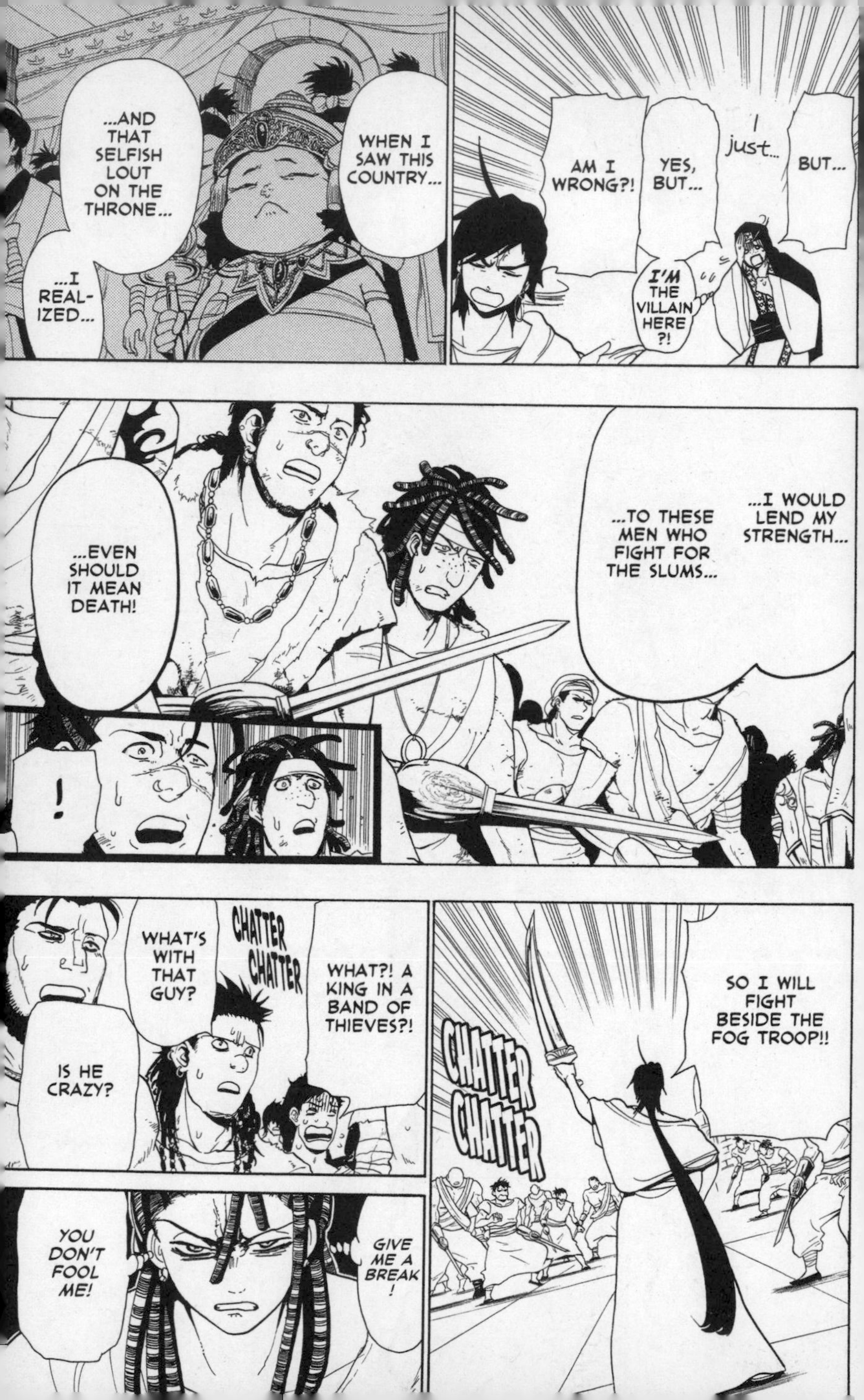
BUT...
I just...
YES, BUT...
AM I WRONG?!
I'M THE VILLAIN HERE?!
WHEN I SAW THIS COUNTRY...
...AND THAT SELFISH LOUT ON THE THRONE...
...I REALIZED...
...I WOULD LEND MY STRENGTH...
...TO THESE MEN WHO FIGHT FOR THE SLUMS...
...EVEN SHOULD IT MEAN DEATH!
!
SO I WILL FIGHT BESIDE THE FOG TROOP!!
CHATTER CHATTER
WHAT?! A KING IN A BAND OF THIEVES?!
CHATTER CHATTER
WHAT'S WITH THAT GUY?
IS HE CRAZY?
GIVE ME A BREAK!
YOU DON'T FOOL ME!

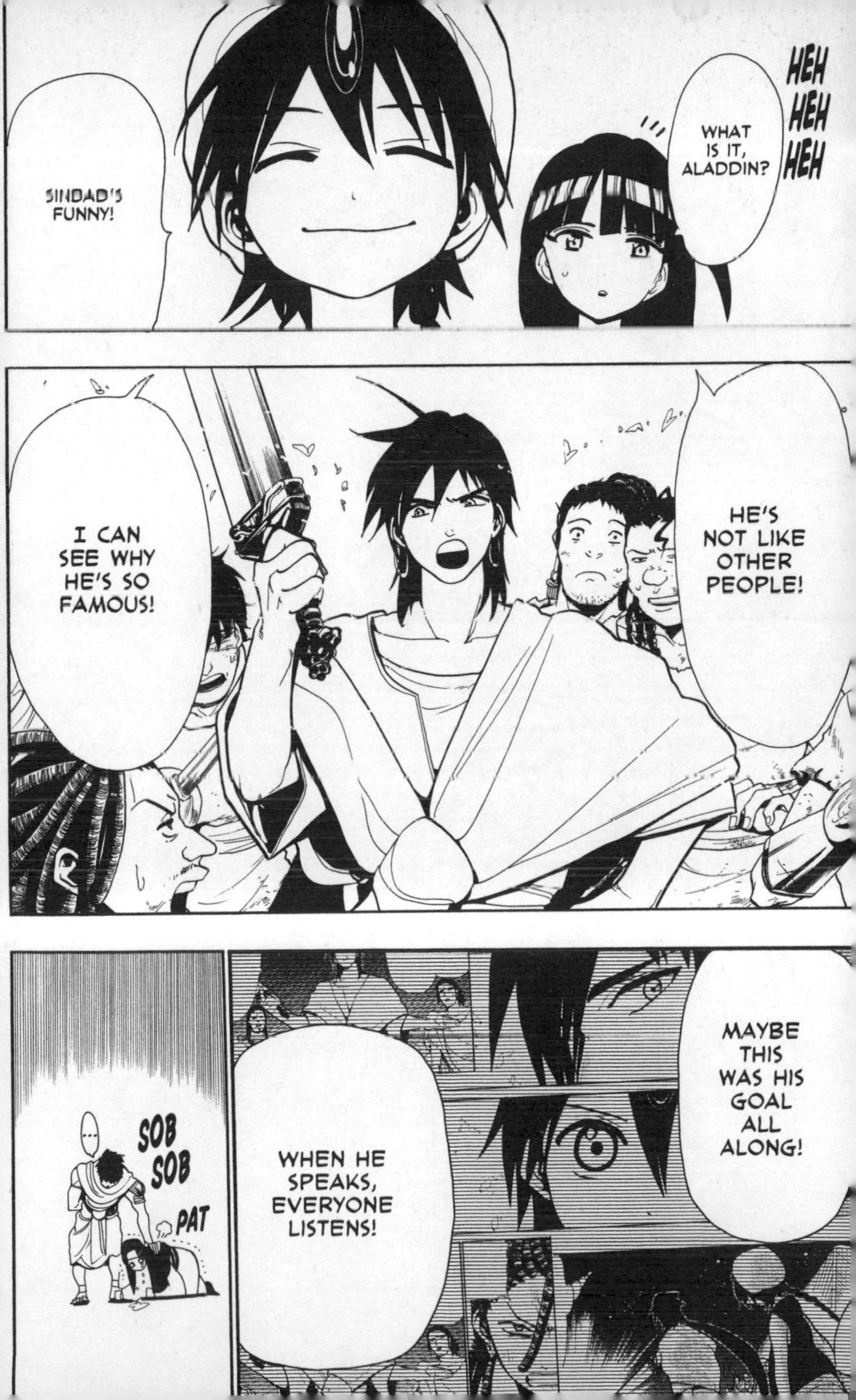
HEH HEH HEH
WHAT IS IT, ALADDIN?
SINDAD'S FUNNY!
HE'S NOT LIKE OTHER PEOPLE!
I CAN SEE WHY HE'S SO FAMOUS!
MAYBE THIS WAS HIS GOAL ALL ALONG!
WHEN HE SPEAKS, EVERYONE LISTENS!
...
SOB SOB
PAT

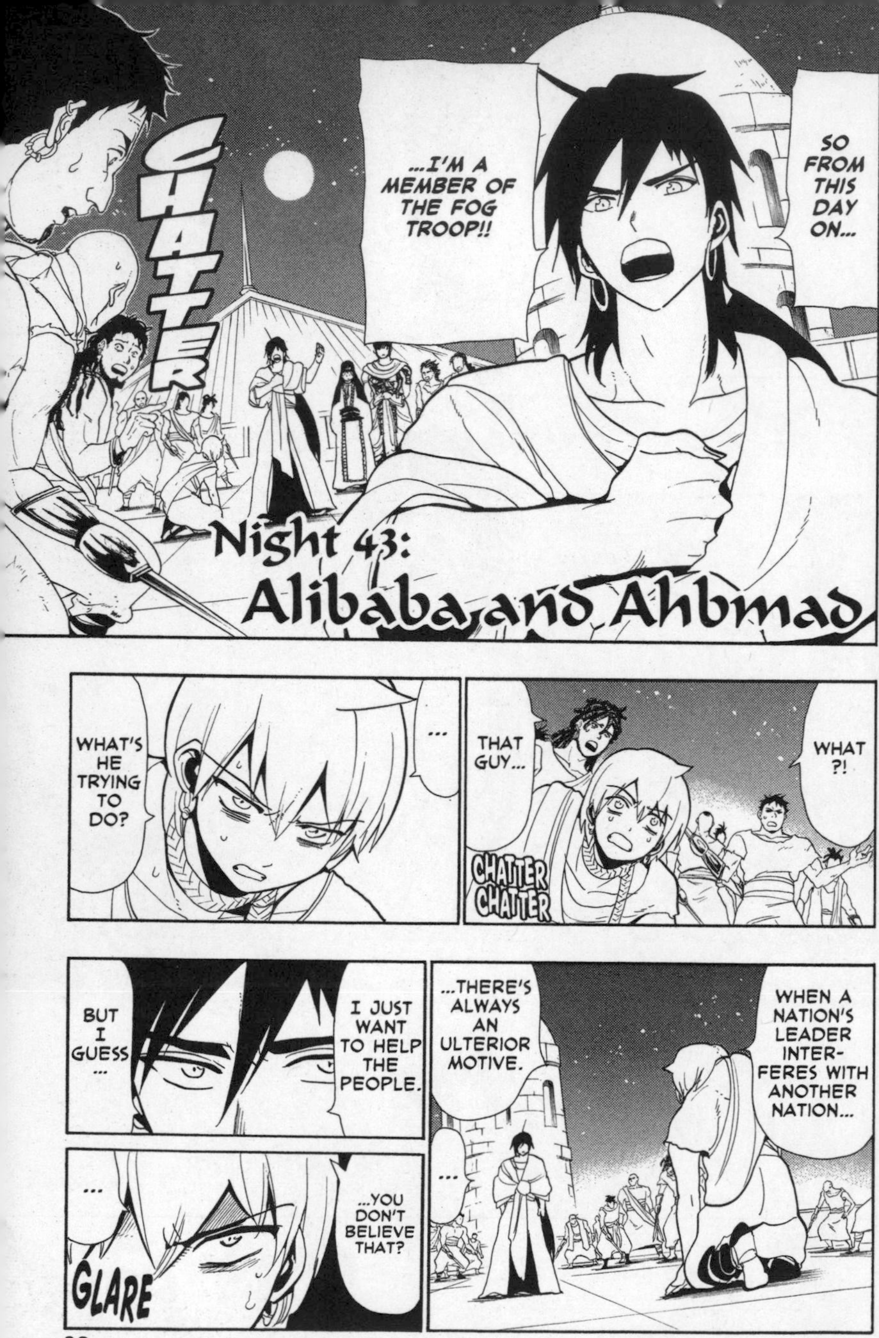
SO FROM THIS DAY ON...
...I'M A MEMBER OF THE FOG TROOP!!
CHATTER
Night 43: Alibaba and Ahbmad
WHAT?!
THAT GUY...
CHATTER CHATTER
...
WHAT'S HE TRYING TO DO?
WHEN A NATION'S LEADER INTERFERES WITH ANOTHER NATION...
...THERE'S ALWAYS AN ULTERIOR MOTIVE.
...
I JUST WANT TO HELP THE PEOPLE.
BUT I GUESS...
...YOU DON'T BELIEVE THAT?
...
GLARE

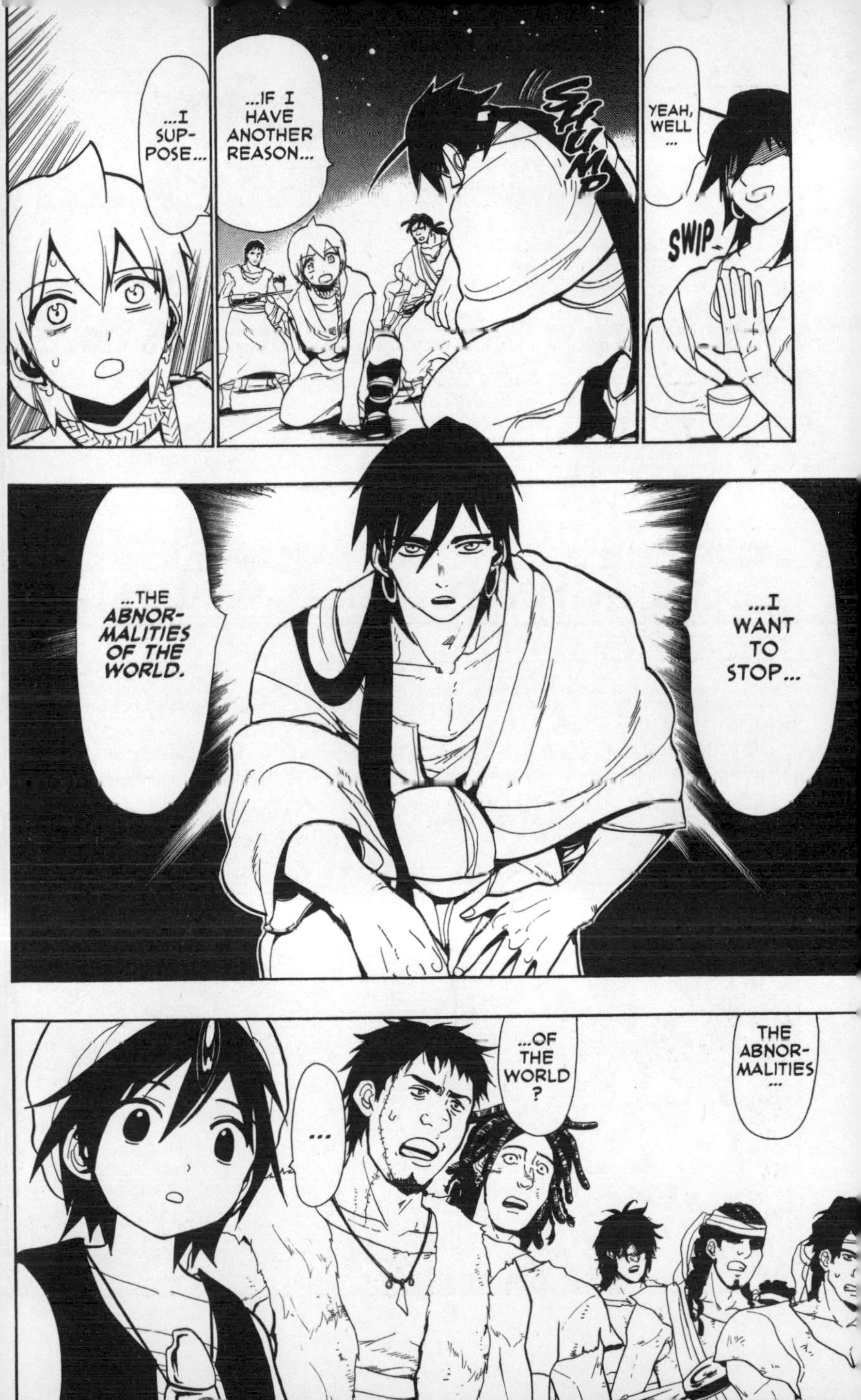
YEAH, WELL ...
SWIP
SHUMP
...IF I HAVE ANOTHER REASON...
...I SUP-POSE...
...I WANT TO STOP...
...THE ABNOR-MALITIES OF THE WORLD.
THE ABNOR-MALITIES ...
...OF THE WORLD ?
...

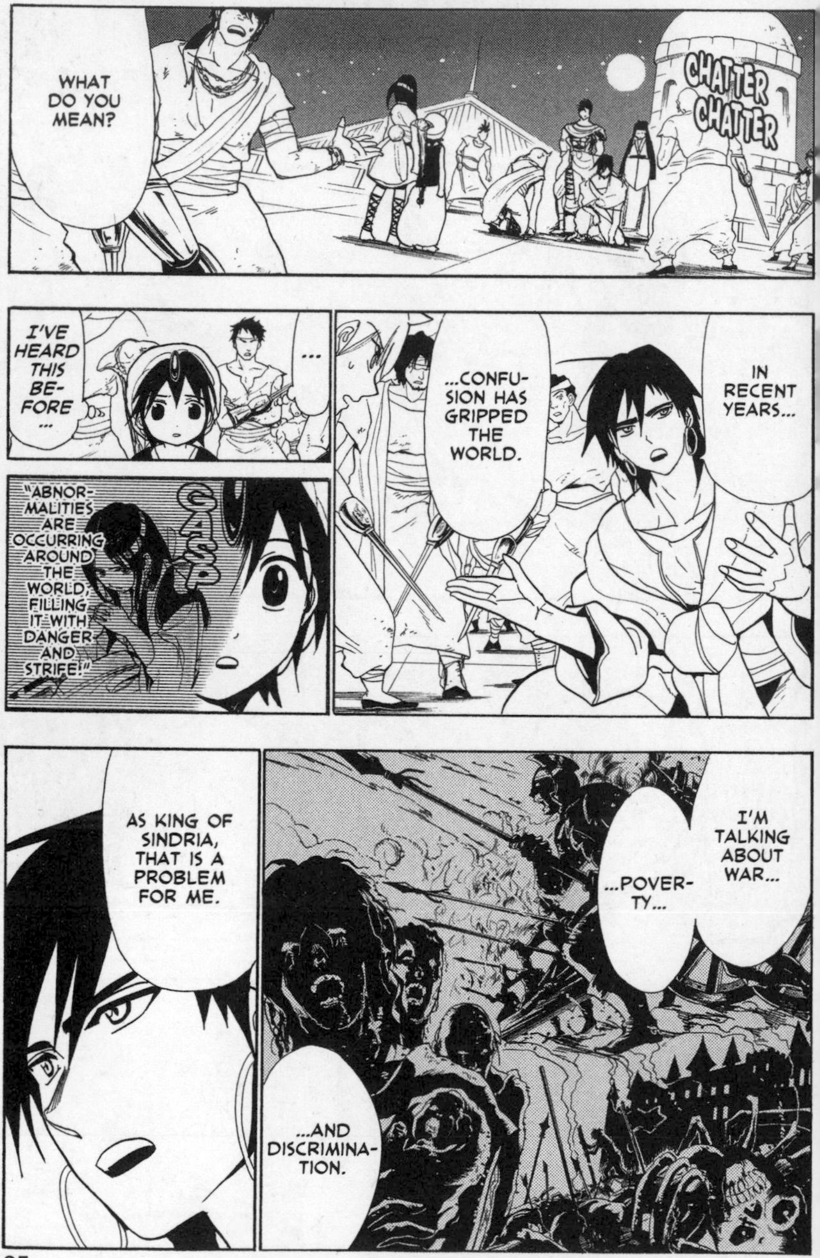
CHATTER CHATTER
WHAT DO YOU MEAN?
IN RECENT YEARS...
...CONFUSION HAS GRIPPED THE WORLD.
...
I'VE HEARD THIS BEFORE...
GASP
"ABNORMALITIES ARE OCCURRING AROUND THE WORLD, FILLING IT WITH DANGER AND STRIFE!"
I'M TALKING ABOUT WAR...
...POVERTY...
...AND DISCRIMINATION.
AS KING OF SINDRIA, THAT IS A PROBLEM FOR ME.

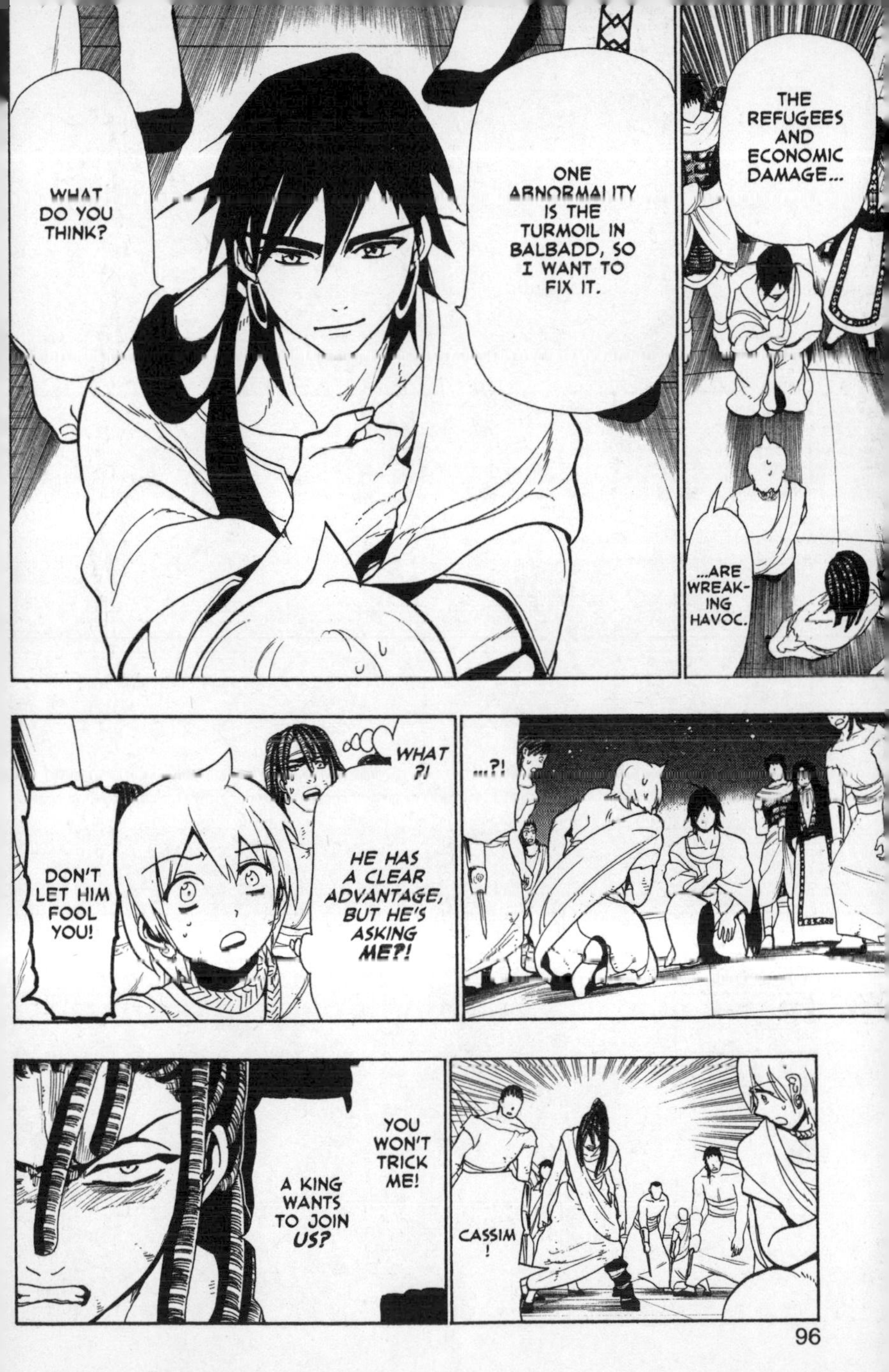
THE REFUGEES AND ECONOMIC DAMAGE...
...ARE WREAKING HAVOC.
ONE ABNORMALITY IS THE TURMOIL IN BALBADD, SO I WANT TO FIX IT.
WHAT DO YOU THINK?
...?!
WHAT ?!
HE HAS A CLEAR ADVANTAGE, BUT HE'S ASKING *ME*?!
DON'T LET HIM FOOL YOU!
CASSIM !
YOU WON'T TRICK ME!
A KING WANTS TO JOIN *US*?

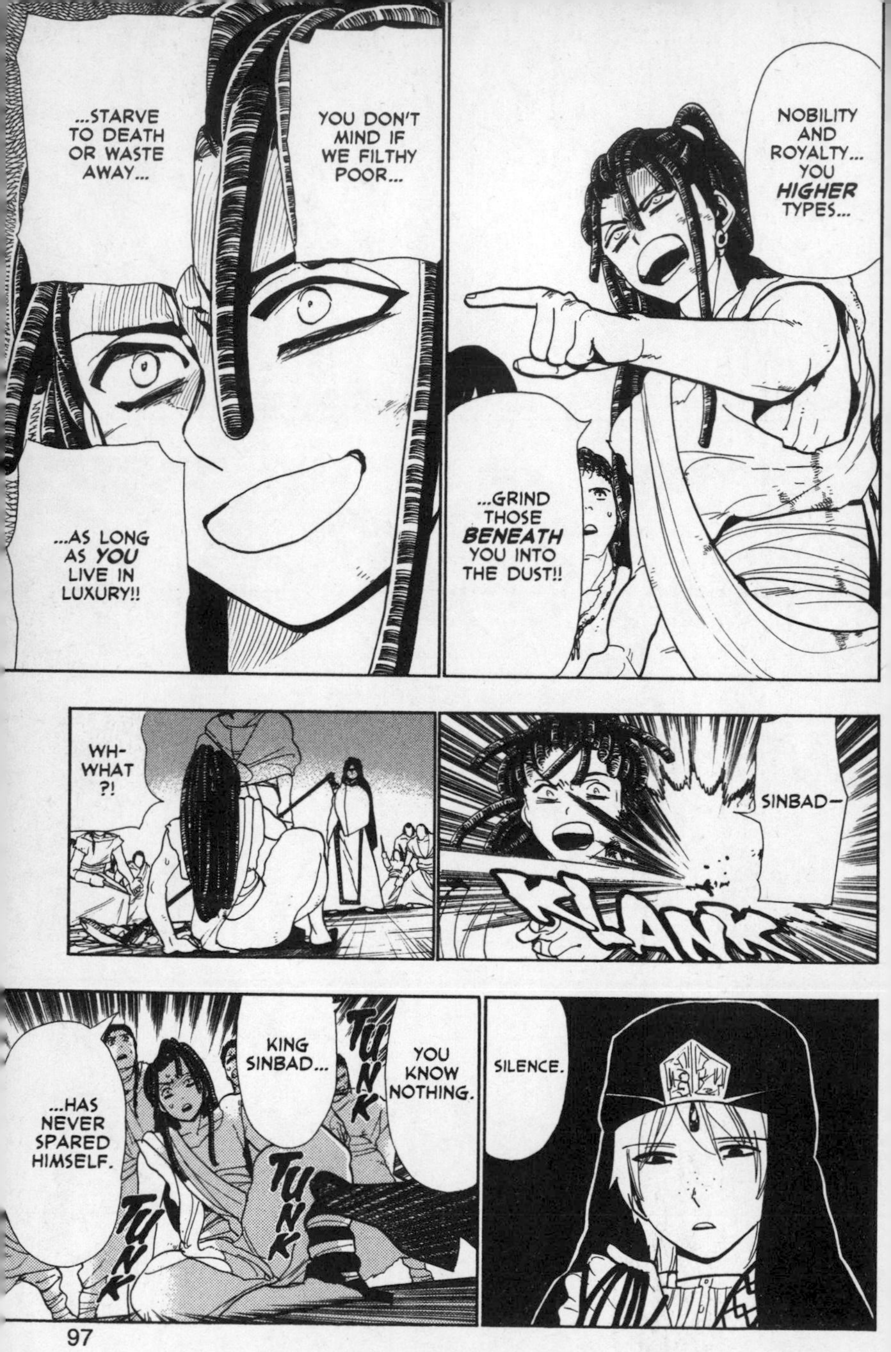
NOBILITY AND ROYALTY... YOU *HIGHER* TYPES...
...GRIND THOSE *BENEATH* YOU INTO THE DUST!!
YOU DON'T MIND IF WE FILTHY POOR...
...STARVE TO DEATH OR WASTE AWAY...
...AS LONG AS *YOU* LIVE IN LUXURY!!
SINBAD—
KLANK
WH-WHAT?!
SILENCE.
YOU KNOW NOTHING.
TUNK
KING SINBAD...
TUNK
TUNK
...HAS NEVER SPARED HIMSELF.

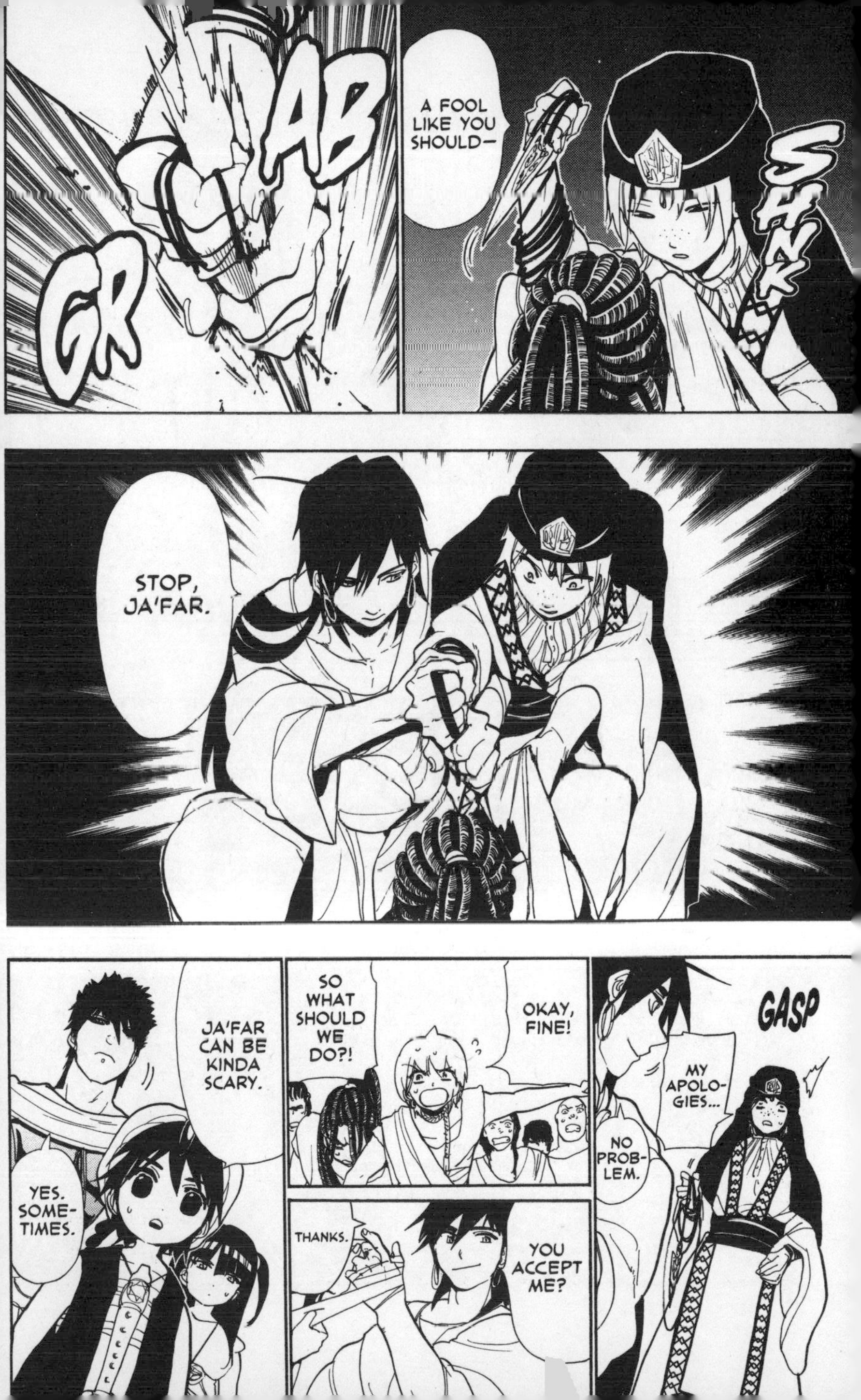
A FOOL LIKE YOU SHOULD—
SHNK
GRAB
STOP, JA'FAR.
GASP
MY APOLOGIES...
NO PROBLEM.
OKAY, FINE!
SO WHAT SHOULD WE DO?!
YOU ACCEPT ME?
THANKS.
JA'FAR CAN BE KINDA SCARY.
YES. SOMETIMES.

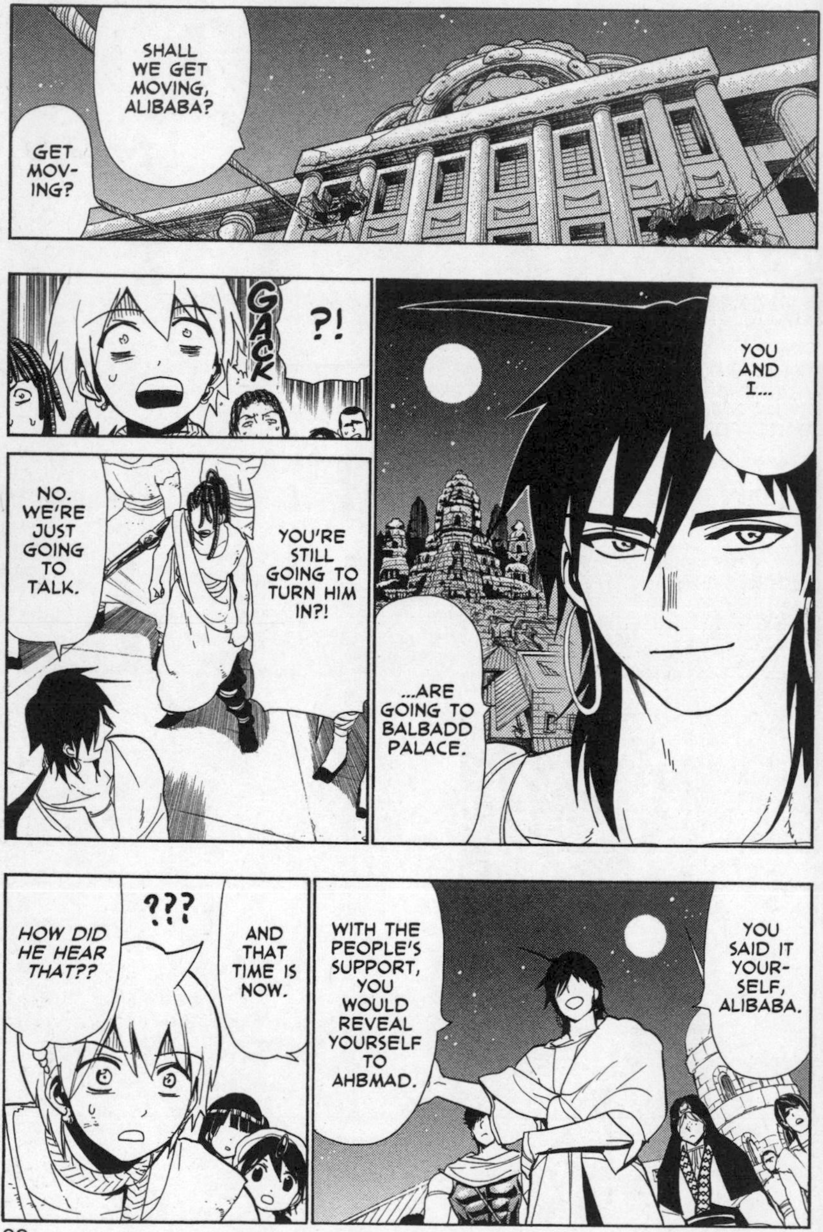
SHALL WE GET MOVING, ALIBABA?
GET MOVING?
YOU AND I...
...ARE GOING TO BALBADD PALACE.
?!
GACK
YOU'RE STILL GOING TO TURN HIM IN?!
NO. WE'RE JUST GOING TO TALK.
YOU SAID IT YOURSELF, ALIBABA.
WITH THE PEOPLE'S SUPPORT, YOU WOULD REVEAL YOURSELF TO AHBMAD.
AND THAT TIME IS NOW.
???
*HOW DID HE HEAR THAT??*

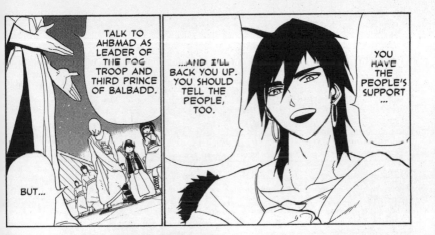

YOU HAVE THE PEOPLE'S SUPPORT ...
...AND I'LL BACK YOU UP. YOU SHOULD TELL THE PEOPLE, TOO.
TALK TO AHBMAD AS LEADER OF THE FOG TROOP AND THIRD PRINCE OF BALBADD.
BUT...
ARE YOU SCARED THEY WON'T ACCEPT YOU AS PRINCE?
...
DON'T WORRY. YOU'RE A PRINCE.
I KNEW YOUR FATHER, AND HE TOLD ME.
WHAT?!
YOU'RE A LOT LIKE HIM.
WITHOUT A DOUBT, YOU ARE A PRINCE OF BALBADD.
AND THAT MEANS ...
...YOU BEAR A GREAT RESPONSI-BILITY.

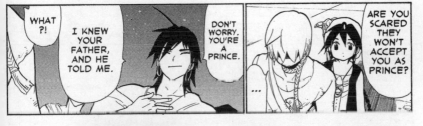

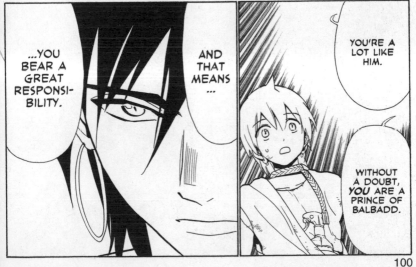

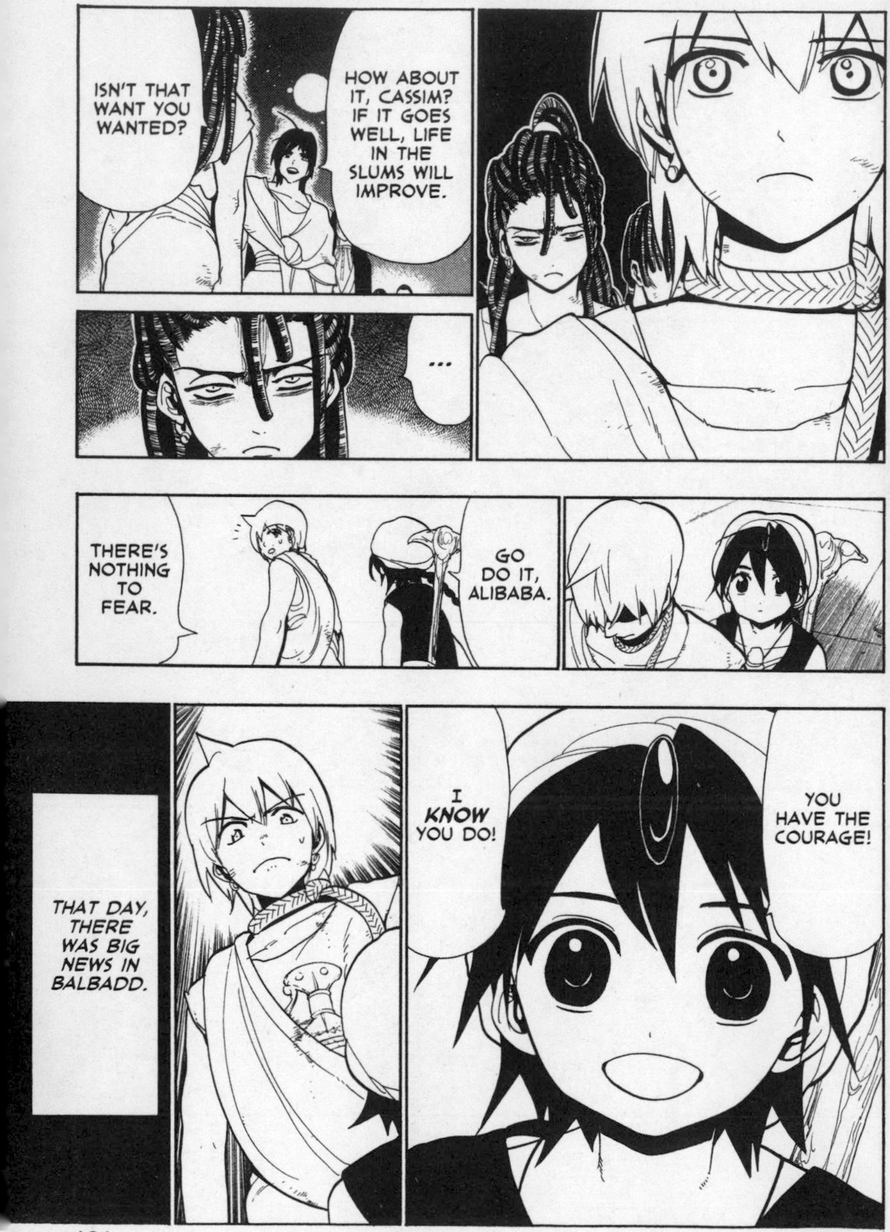
HOW ABOUT IT, CASSIM? IF IT GOES WELL, LIFE IN THE SLUMS WILL IMPROVE.
ISN'T THAT WANT YOU WANTED?
...
GO DO IT, ALIBABA.
THERE'S NOTHING TO FEAR.
YOU HAVE THE COURAGE!
I *KNOW* YOU DO!
THAT DAY, THERE WAS BIG NEWS IN BALBADD.

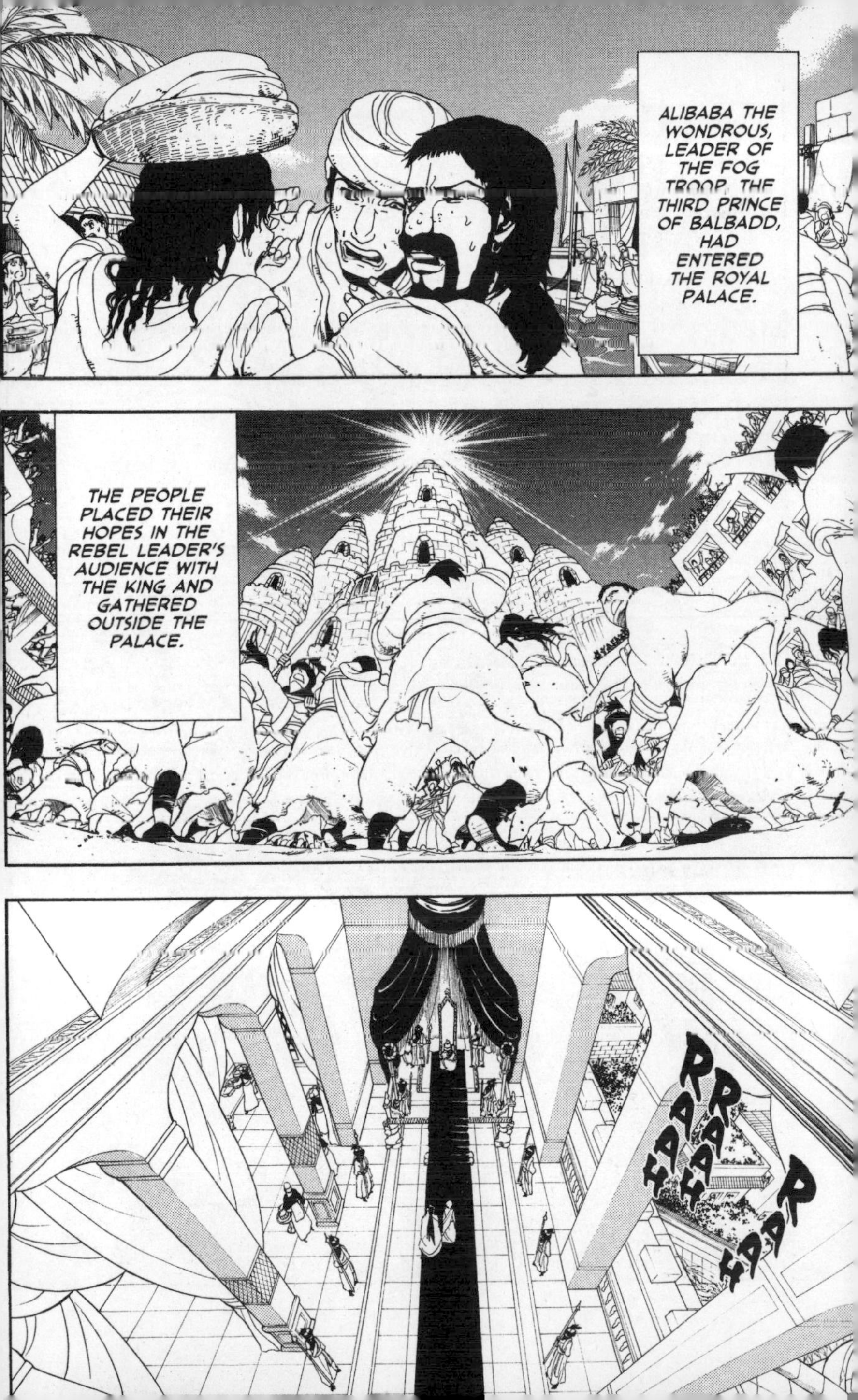
ALIBABA THE WONDROUS, LEADER OF THE FOG TROOP, THE THIRD PRINCE OF BALBADD, HAD ENTERED THE ROYAL PALACE.
THE PEOPLE PLACED THEIR HOPES IN THE REBEL LEADER'S AUDIENCE WITH THE KING AND GATHERED OUTSIDE THE PALACE.

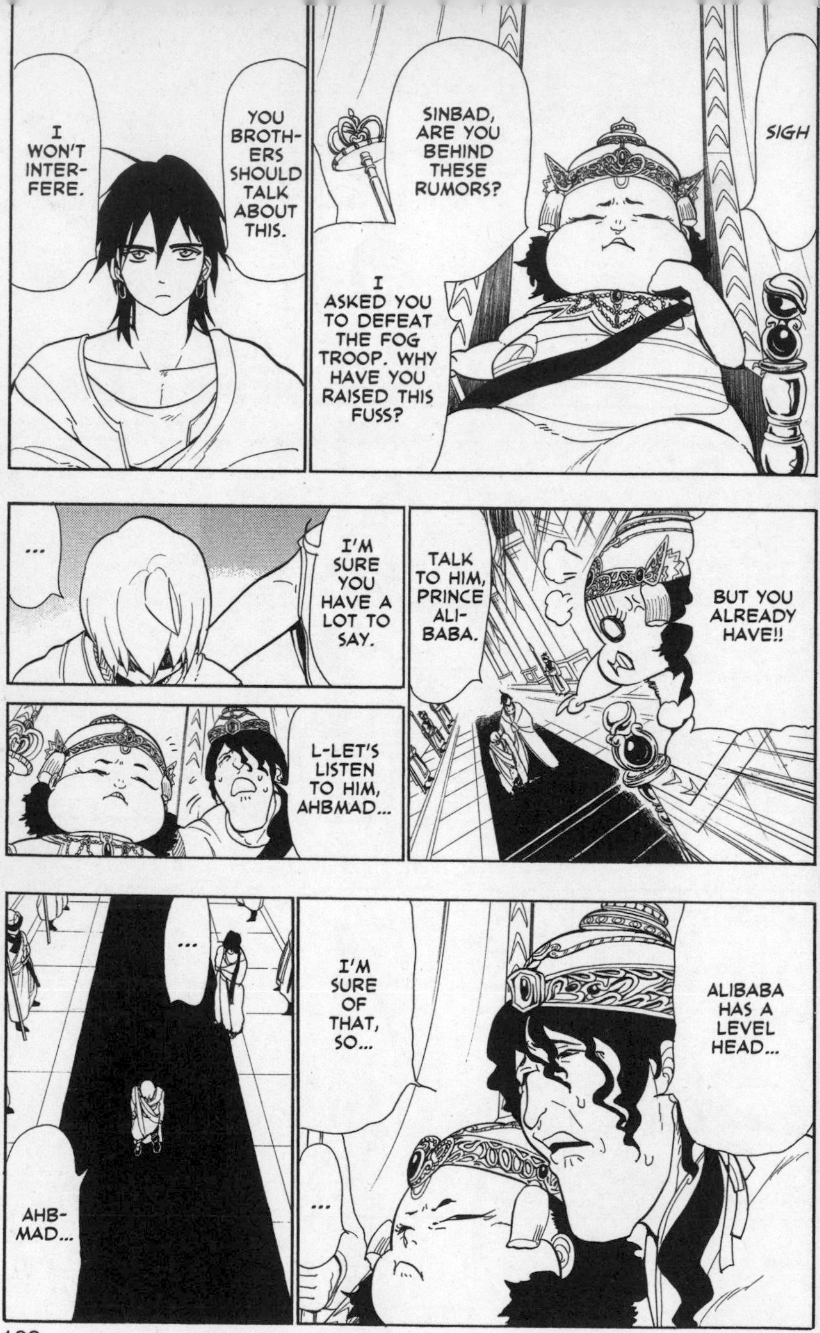
SIGH
SINBAD, ARE YOU BEHIND THESE RUMORS?
I ASKED YOU TO DEFEAT THE FOG TROOP. WHY HAVE YOU RAISED THIS FUSS?
YOU BROTHERS SHOULD TALK ABOUT THIS.
I WON'T INTERFERE.
BUT YOU ALREADY HAVE!!
TALK TO HIM, PRINCE ALIBABA.
I'M SURE YOU HAVE A LOT TO SAY.
...
L-LET'S LISTEN TO HIM, AHBMAD...
ALIBABA HAS A LEVEL HEAD...
I'M SURE OF THAT, SO...
...
...
AHBMAD...

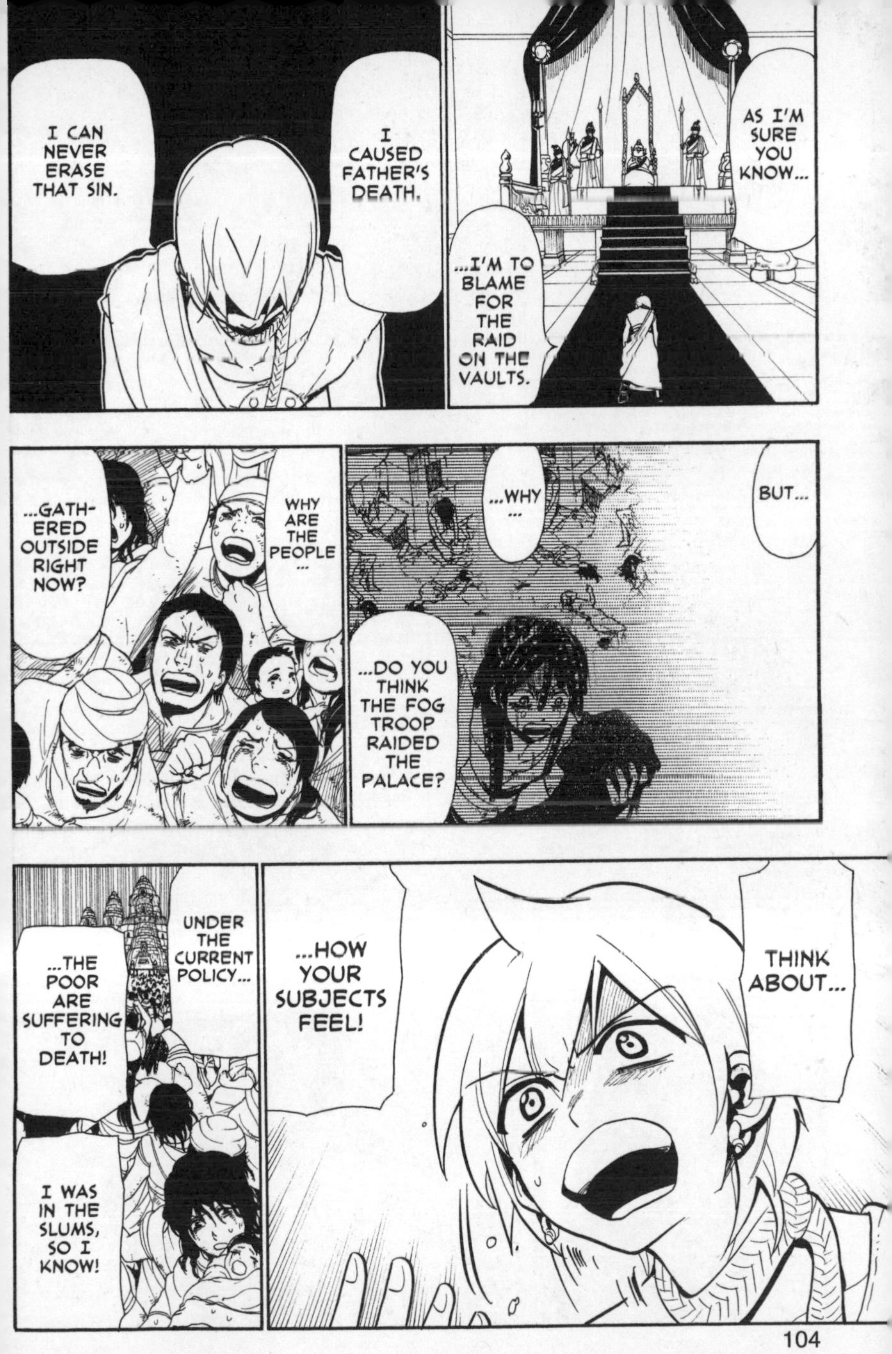
AS I'M SURE YOU KNOW...
...I'M TO BLAME FOR THE RAID ON THE VAULTS.
I CAUSED FATHER'S DEATH.
I CAN NEVER ERASE THAT SIN.
BUT...
...WHY...
...DO YOU THINK THE FOG TROOP RAIDED THE PALACE?
WHY ARE THE PEOPLE...
...GATH-ERED OUTSIDE RIGHT NOW?
THINK ABOUT...
...HOW YOUR SUBJECTS FEEL!
UNDER THE CURRENT POLICY...
...THE POOR ARE SUFFERING TO DEATH!
I WAS IN THE SLUMS, SO I KNOW!

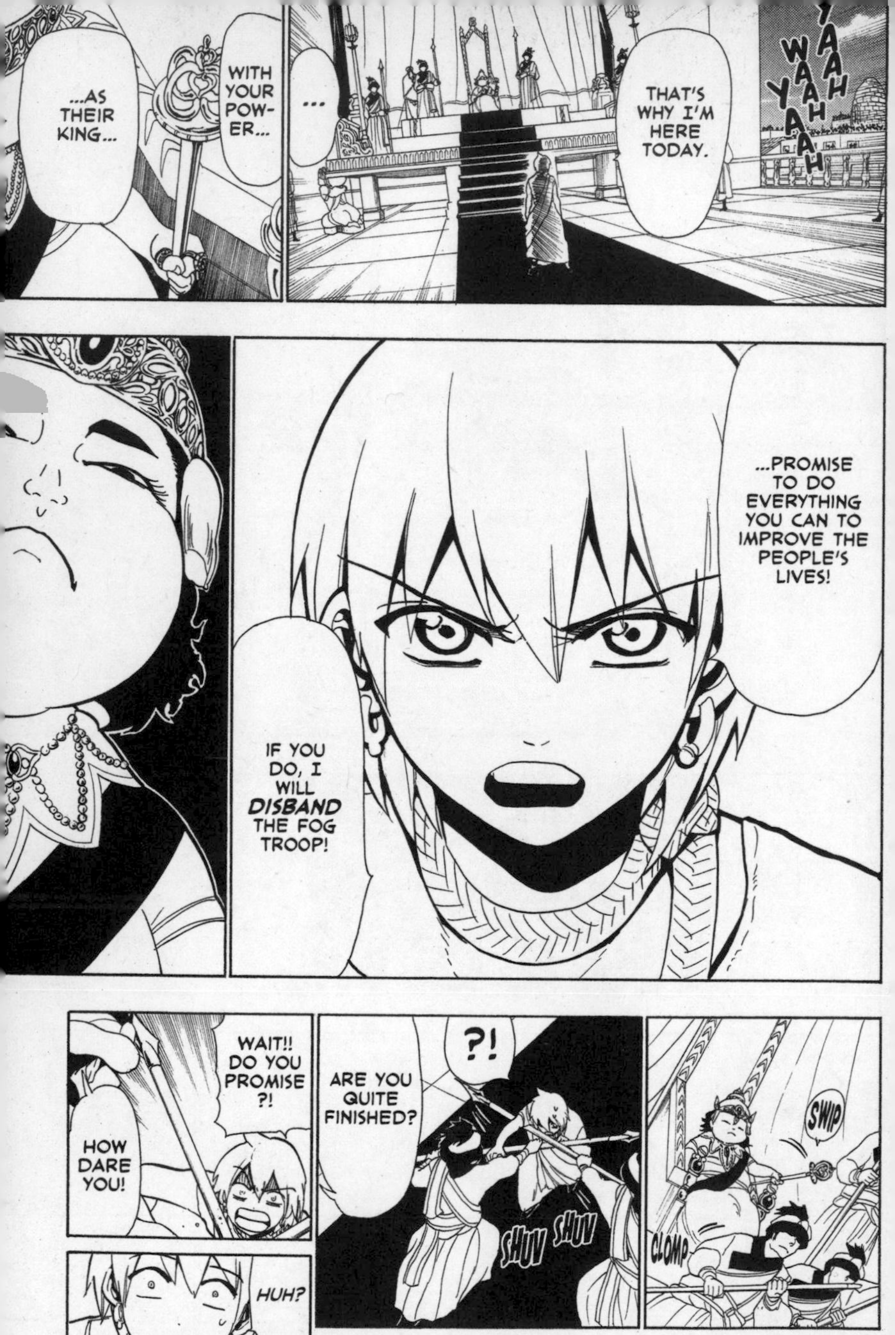
YAAH
WAAH
YAAAH
THAT'S WHY I'M HERE TODAY.
...
WITH YOUR POW-ER...
...AS THEIR KING...
...PROMISE TO DO EVERYTHING YOU CAN TO IMPROVE THE PEOPLE'S LIVES!
IF YOU DO, I WILL *DISBAND* THE FOG TROOP!
SWIP
CLOMP
?!
ARE YOU QUITE FINISHED?
SHUV SHUV
WAIT!! DO YOU PROMISE ?!
HOW DARE YOU!
HUH?

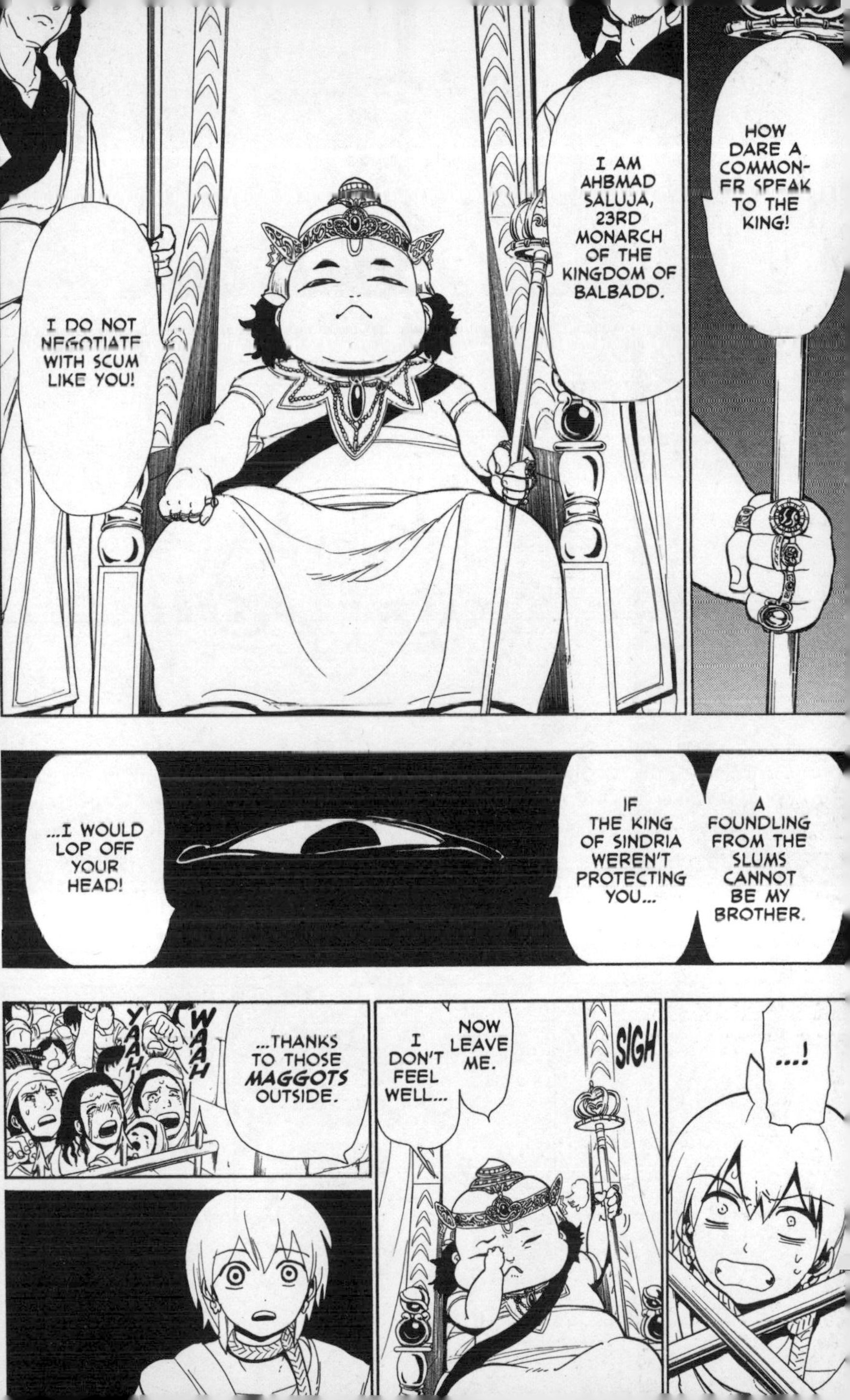
HOW DARE A COMMONER SPEAK TO THE KING!
I AM AHBMAD SALUJA, 23RD MONARCH OF THE KINGDOM OF BALBADD.
I DO NOT NEGOTIATE WITH SCUM LIKE YOU!
A FOUNDLING FROM THE SLUMS CANNOT BE MY BROTHER.
IF THE KING OF SINDRIA WEREN'T PROTECTING YOU...
...I WOULD LOP OFF YOUR HEAD!
...!
SIGH
NOW LEAVE ME.
I DON'T FEEL WELL...
...THANKS TO THOSE *MAGGOTS* OUTSIDE.
WAAH
YAAH

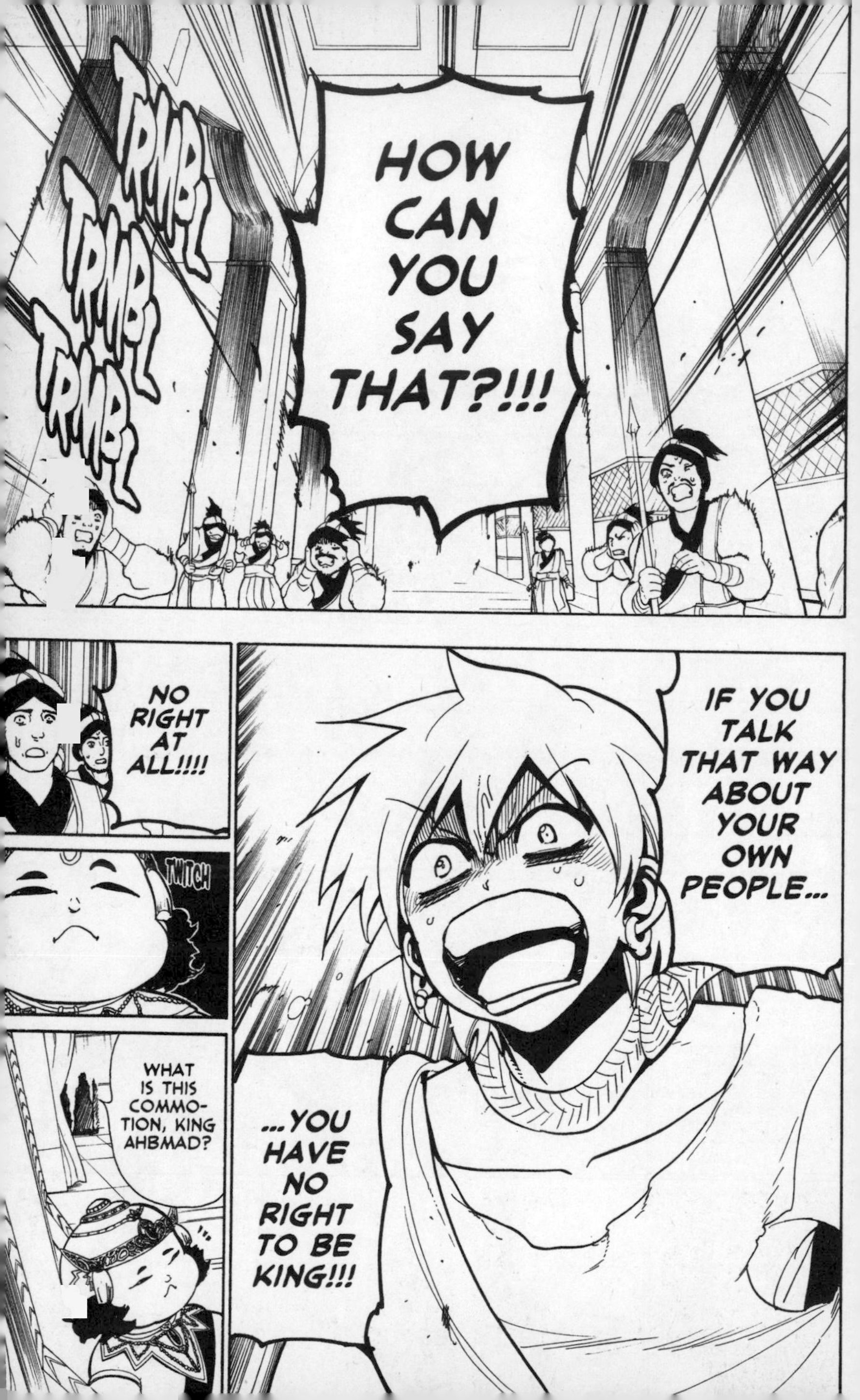
HOW CAN YOU SAY THAT?!!!
TRMBL TRMBL TRMBL
IF YOU TALK THAT WAY ABOUT YOUR OWN PEOPLE...
...YOU HAVE NO RIGHT TO BE KING!!!
NO RIGHT AT ALL!!!!
TWITCH
WHAT IS THIS COMMOTION, KING AHBMAD?

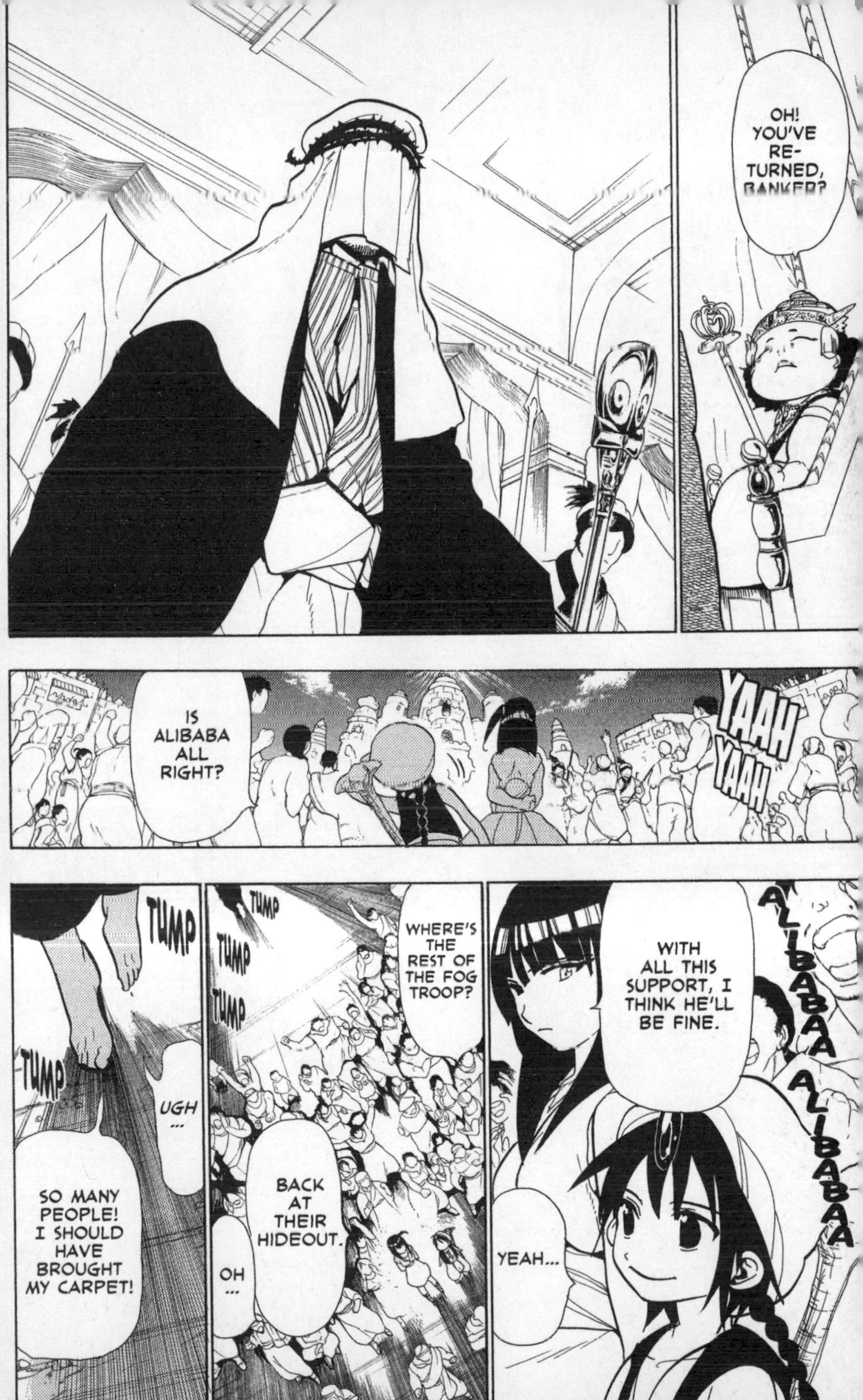
OH! YOU'VE RE-TURNED, BANKER?
YAAH
YAAH
IS ALIBABA ALL RIGHT?
ALIBABA ALIBABA
WITH ALL THIS SUPPORT, I THINK HE'LL BE FINE.
YEAH...
TUMP
TUMP
TUMP
WHERE'S THE REST OF THE FOG TROOP?
BACK AT THEIR HIDEOUT.
OH...
TUMP
TUMP
UGH...
SO MANY PEOPLE! I SHOULD HAVE BROUGHT MY CARPET!

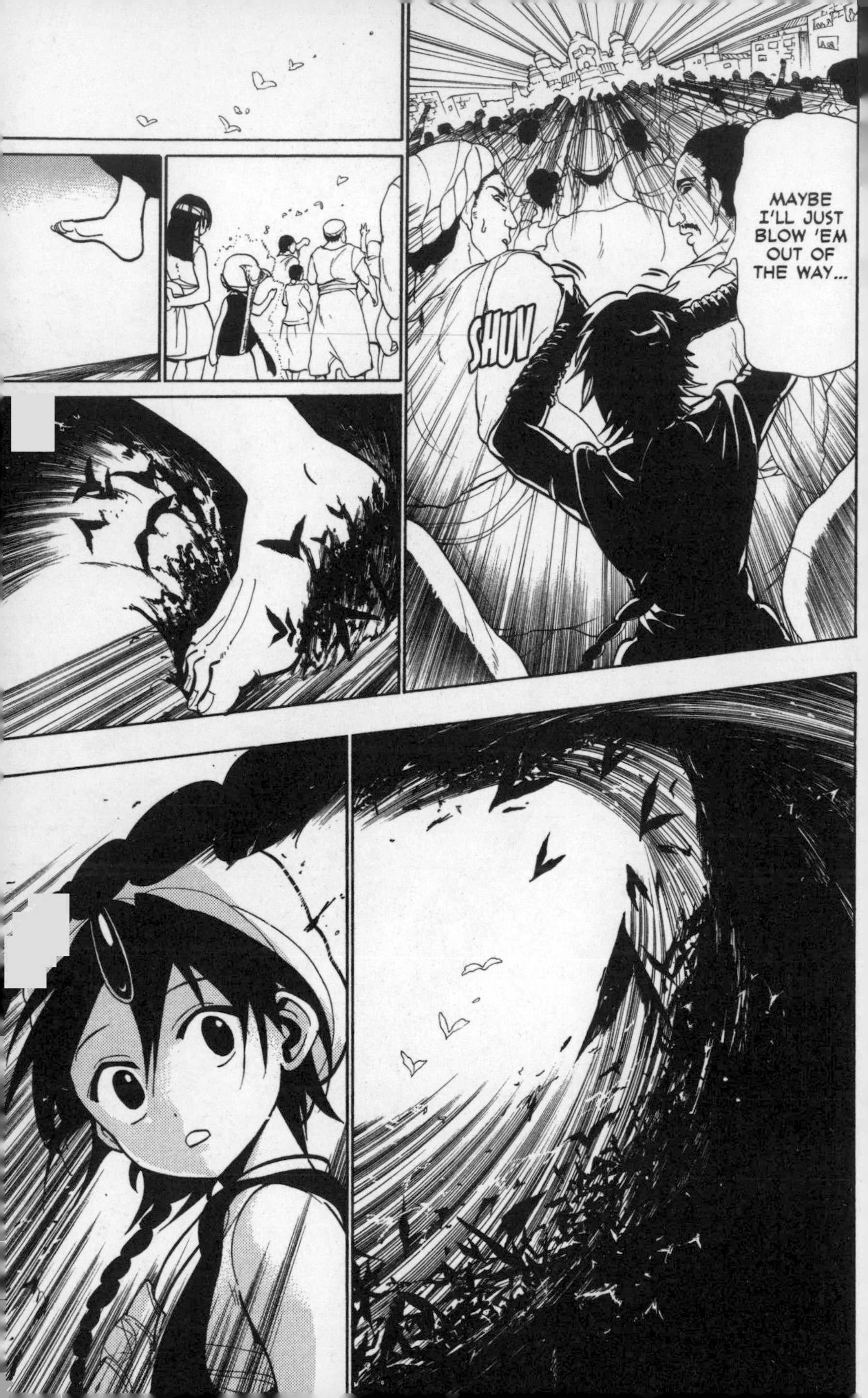
MAYBE I'LL JUST BLOW 'EM OUT OF THE WAY...
SHUV

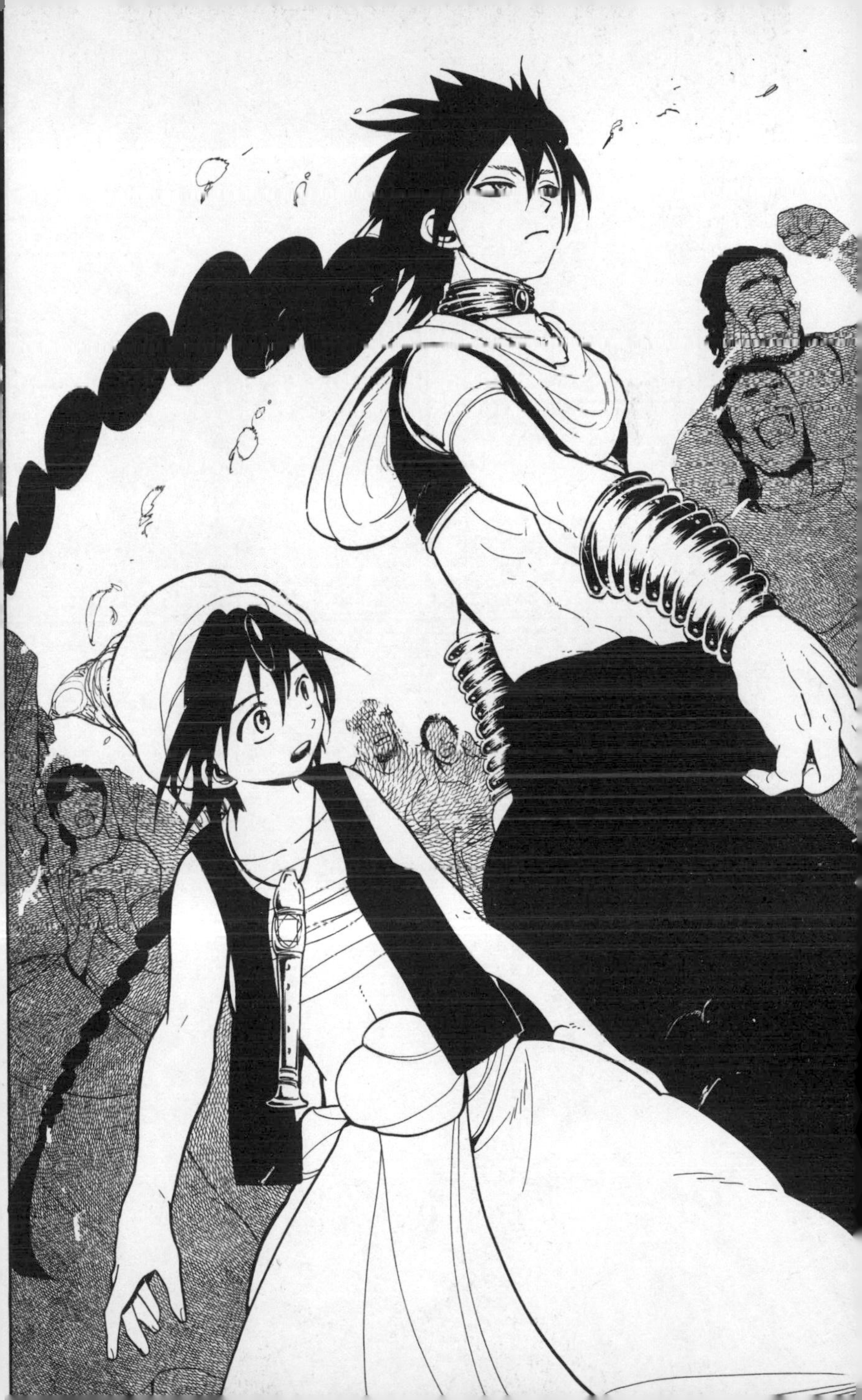

# Night 44: Black Sun

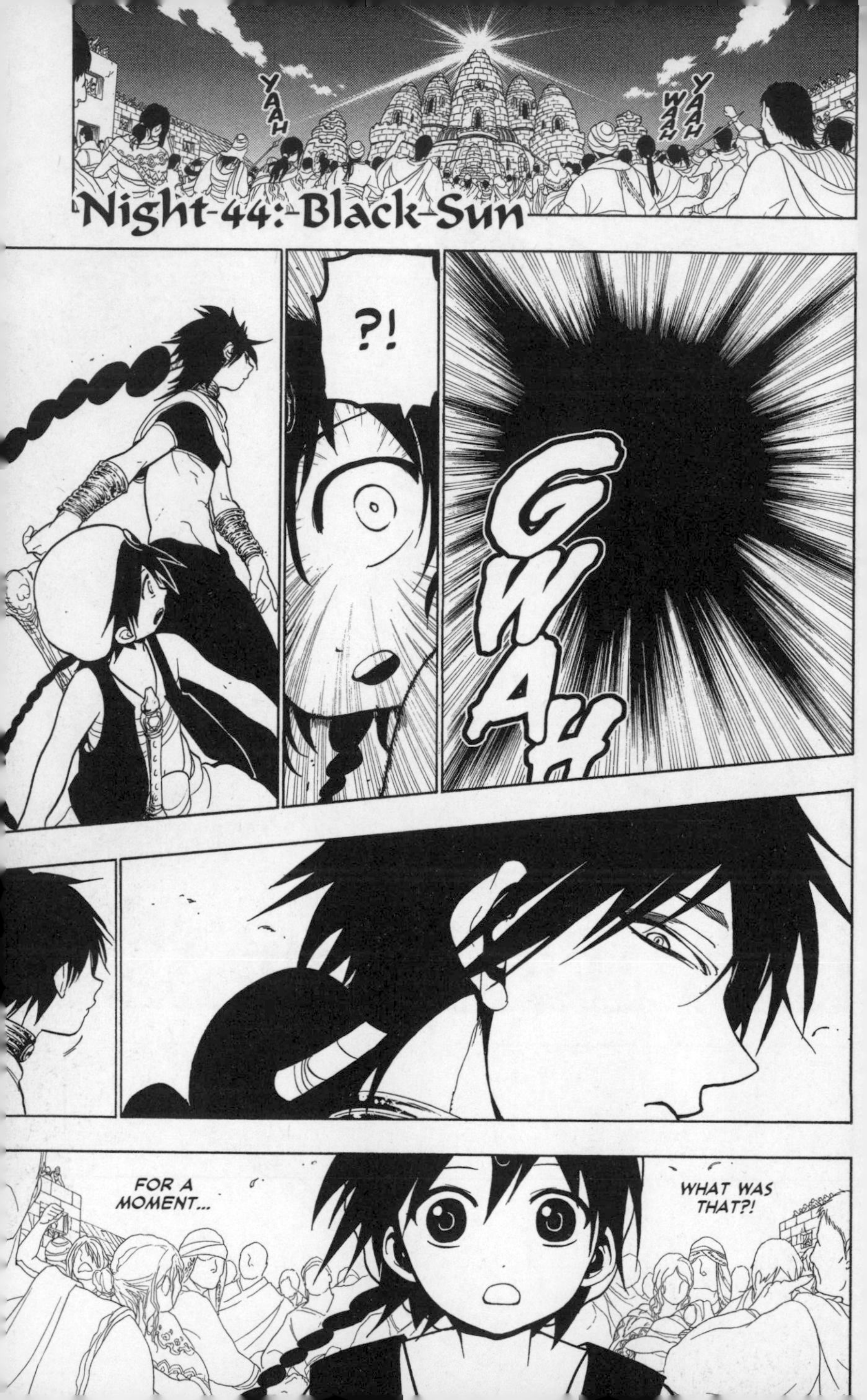
YAAH
WAAH
YAAH
GWAH
?!
WHAT WAS THAT?!
FOR A MOMENT...

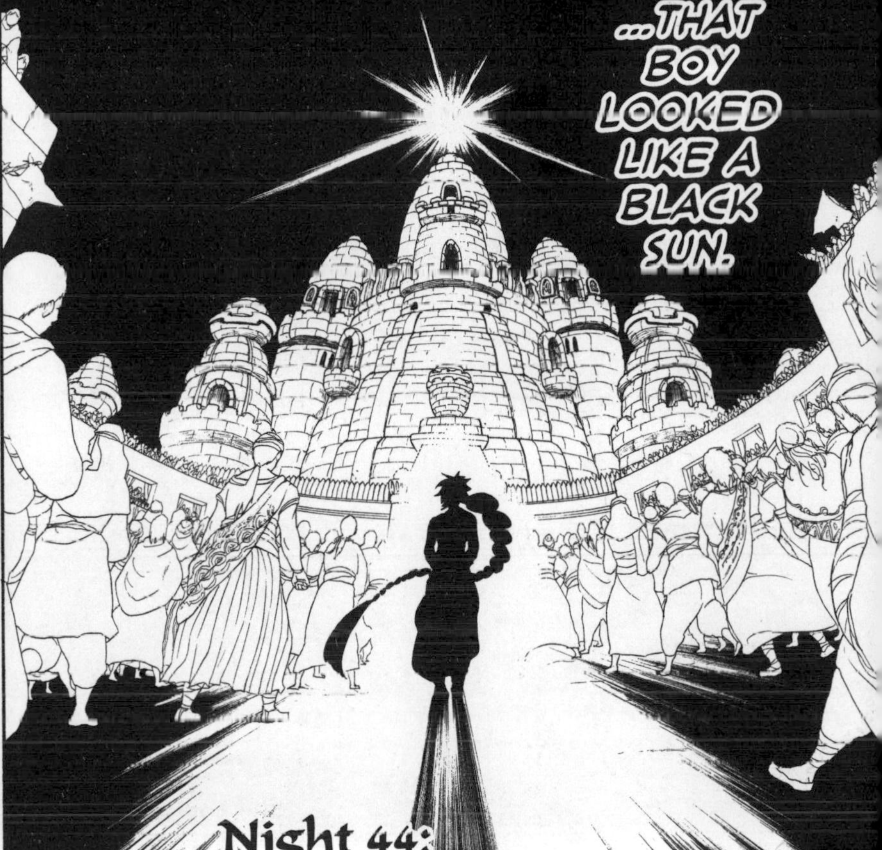
...THAT BOY LOOKED LIKE A BLACK SUN.

# Night 44: Black Sun

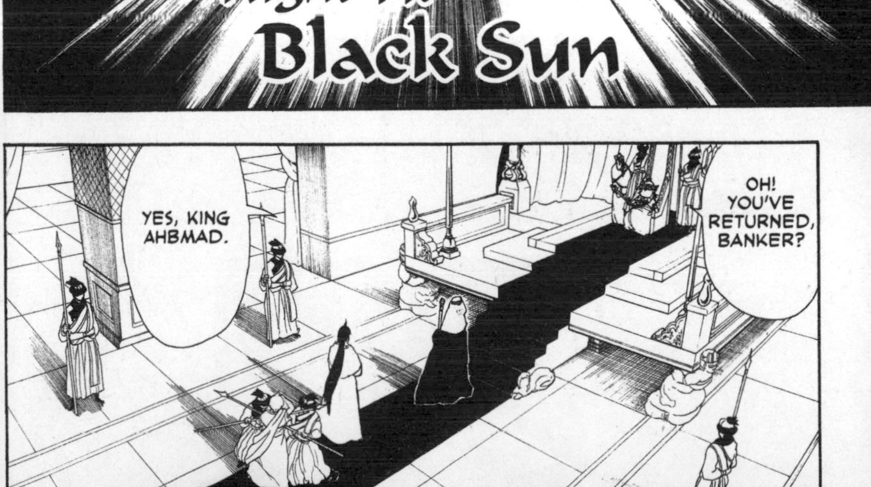
OH! YOU'VE RETURNED, BANKER?
YES, KING AHBMAD.

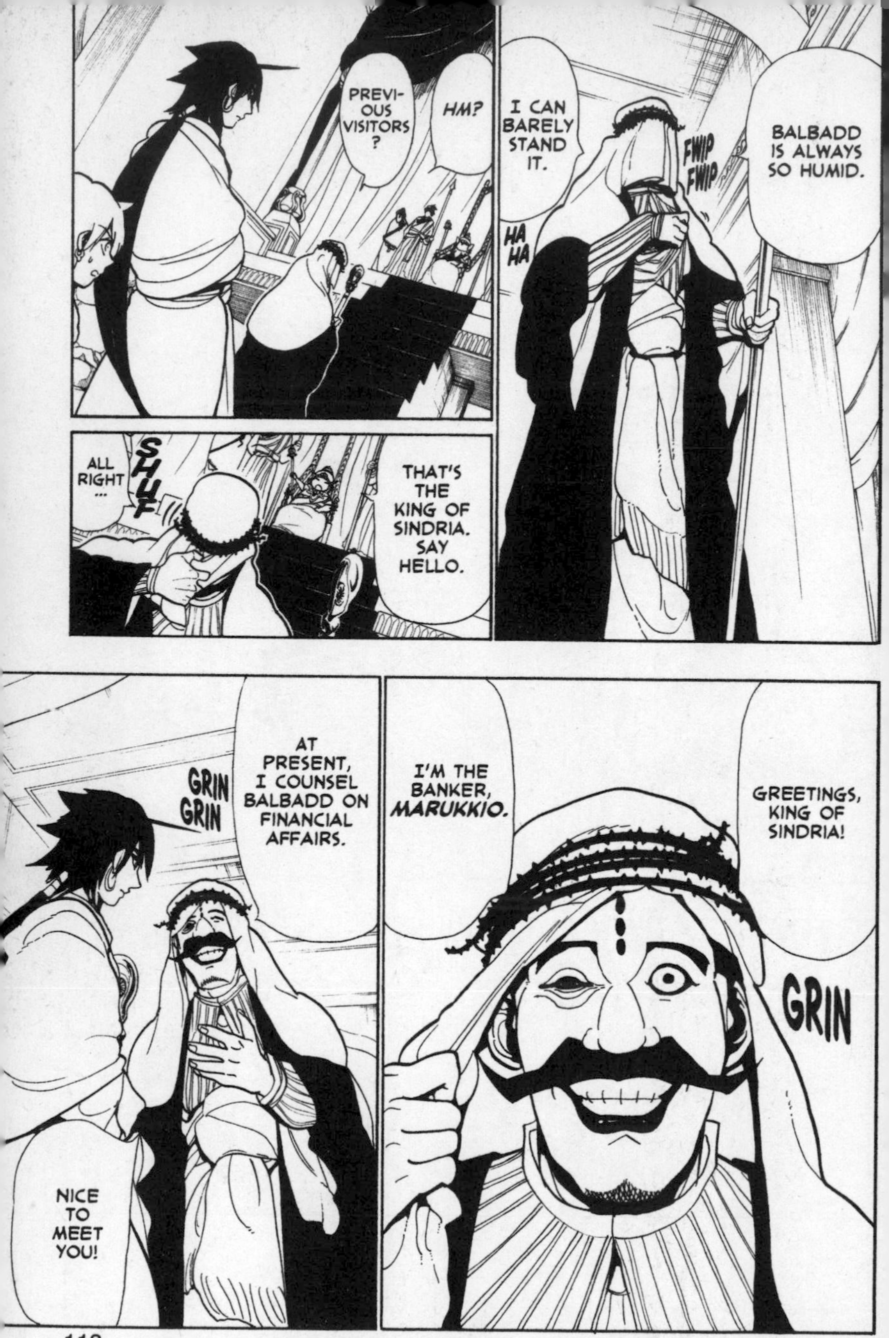

BALBADD IS ALWAYS SO HUMID.
FWIP FWIP
I CAN BARELY STAND IT.
HA HA
HM?
PREVIOUS VISITORS?
THAT'S THE KING OF SINDRIA. SAY HELLO.
SHUF
ALL RIGHT...
GREETINGS, KING OF SINDRIA!
GRIN
I'M THE BANKER, *MARUKKIO.*
AT PRESENT, I COUNSEL BALBADD ON FINANCIAL AFFAIRS.
GRIN GRIN
NICE TO MEET YOU!

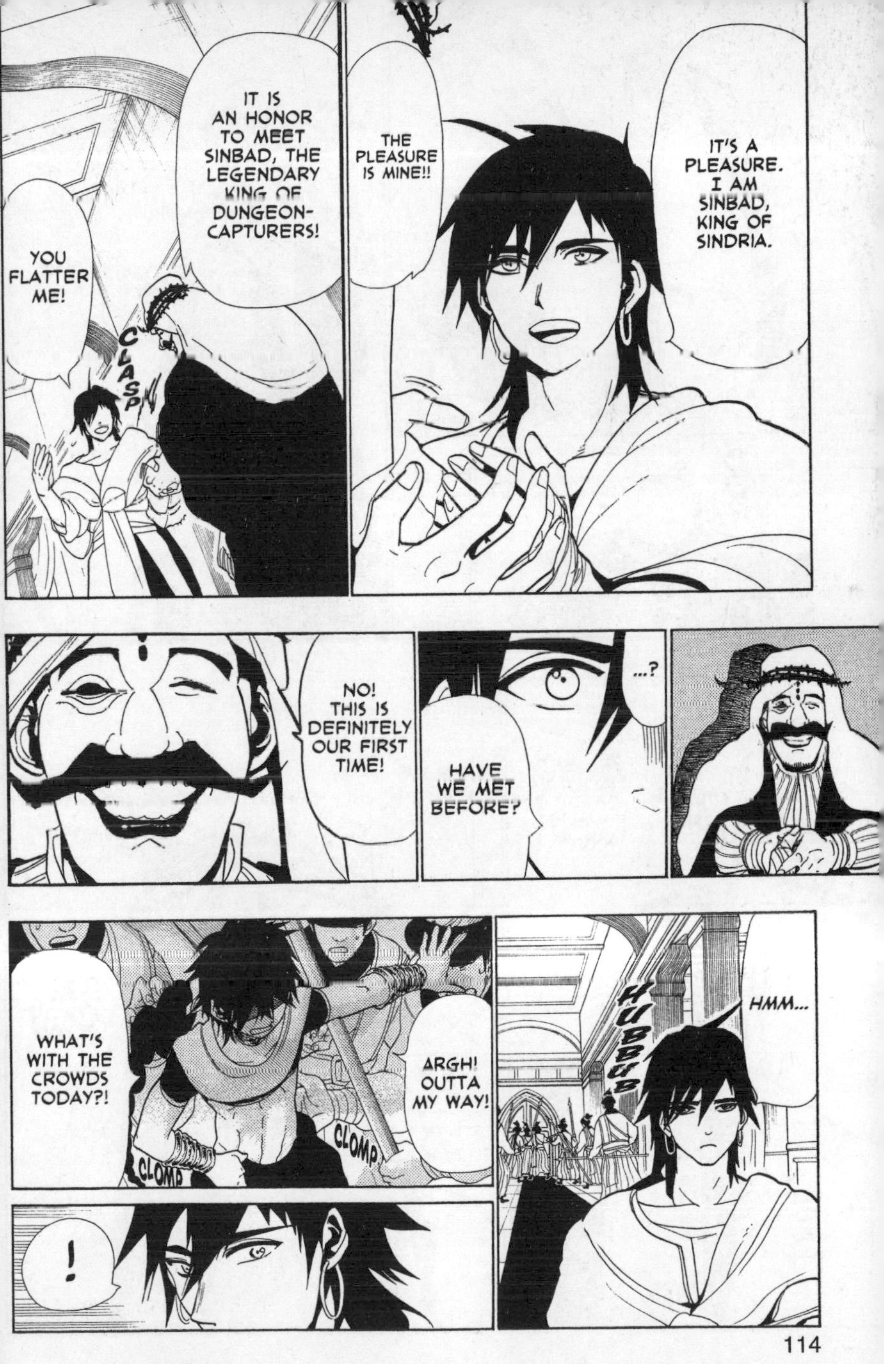
IT'S A PLEASURE. I AM SINBAD, KING OF SINDRIA.
THE PLEASURE IS MINE!!
IT IS AN HONOR TO MEET SINBAD, THE LEGENDARY KING OF DUNGEON-CAPTURERS!
CLASP
YOU FLATTER ME!
...?
HAVE WE MET BEFORE?
NO! THIS IS DEFINITELY OUR FIRST TIME!
HMM...
HUBBUB
ARGH! OUTTA MY WAY!
WHAT'S WITH THE CROWDS TODAY?!
CLOMP
CLOMP
!

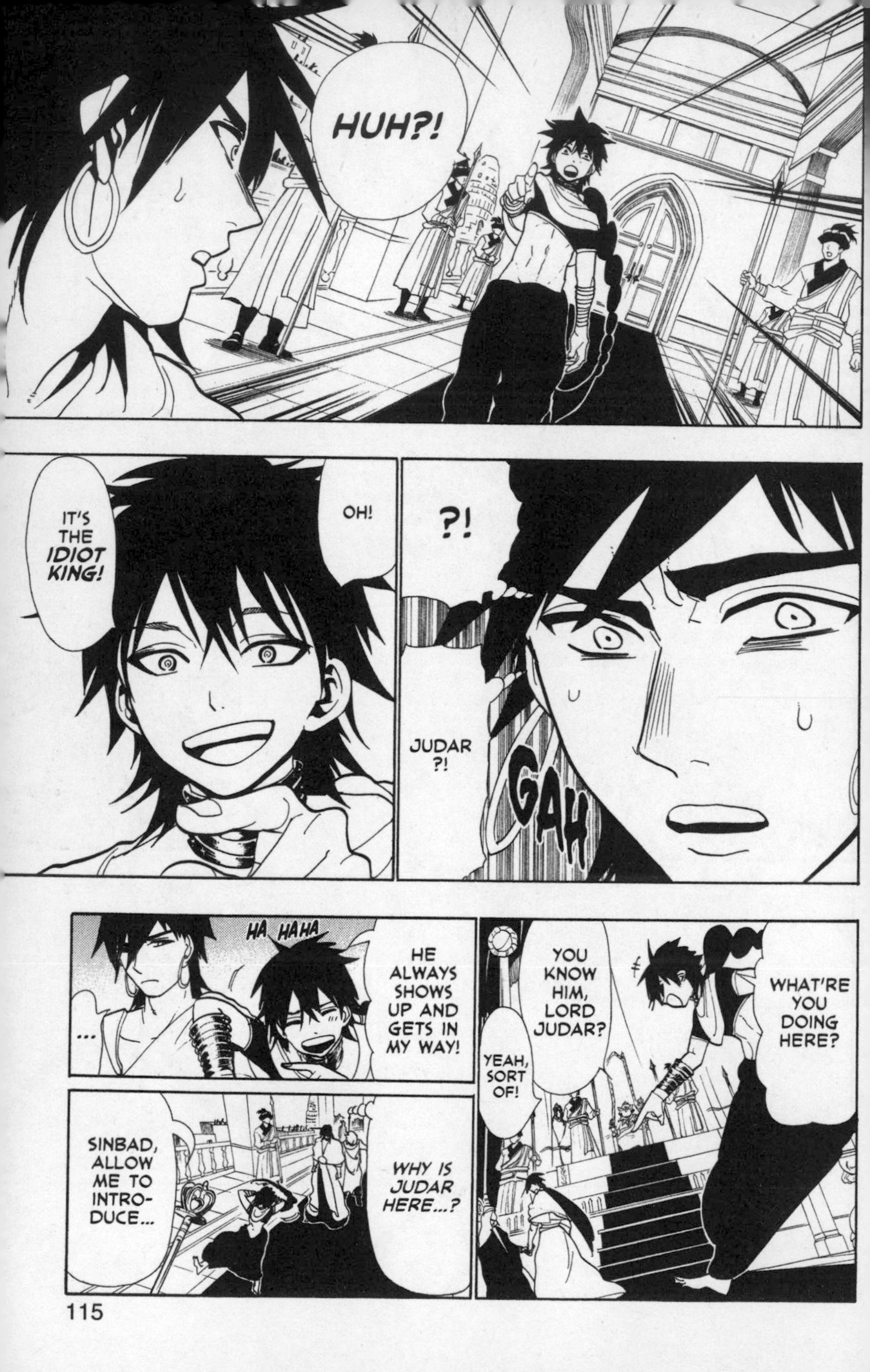
HUH?!
?!
JUDAR ?!
GAH
OH!
IT'S THE IDIOT KING!
WHAT'RE YOU DOING HERE?
YOU KNOW HIM, LORD JUDAR?
YEAH, SORT OF!
HA HAHA
HE ALWAYS SHOWS UP AND GETS IN MY WAY!
...
WHY IS JUDAR HERE...?
SINBAD, ALLOW ME TO INTRODUCE...

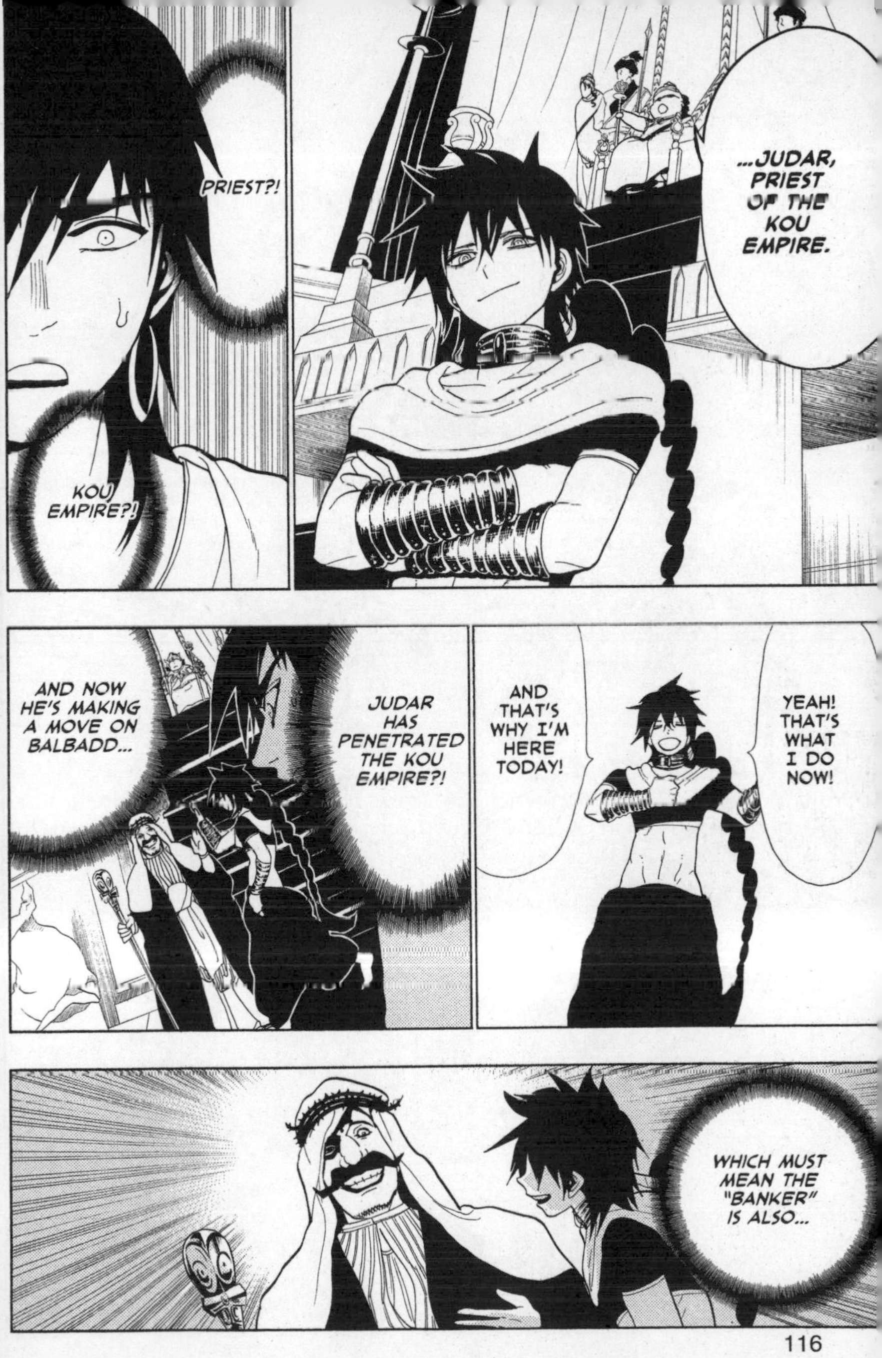
...JUDAR, PRIEST OF THE KOU EMPIRE.
PRIEST?!
KOU EMPIRE?!
YEAH! THAT'S WHAT I DO NOW!
AND THAT'S WHY I'M HERE TODAY!
JUDAR HAS PENETRATED THE KOU EMPIRE?!
AND NOW HE'S MAKING A MOVE ON BALBADD...
WHICH MUST MEAN THE "BANKER" IS ALSO...

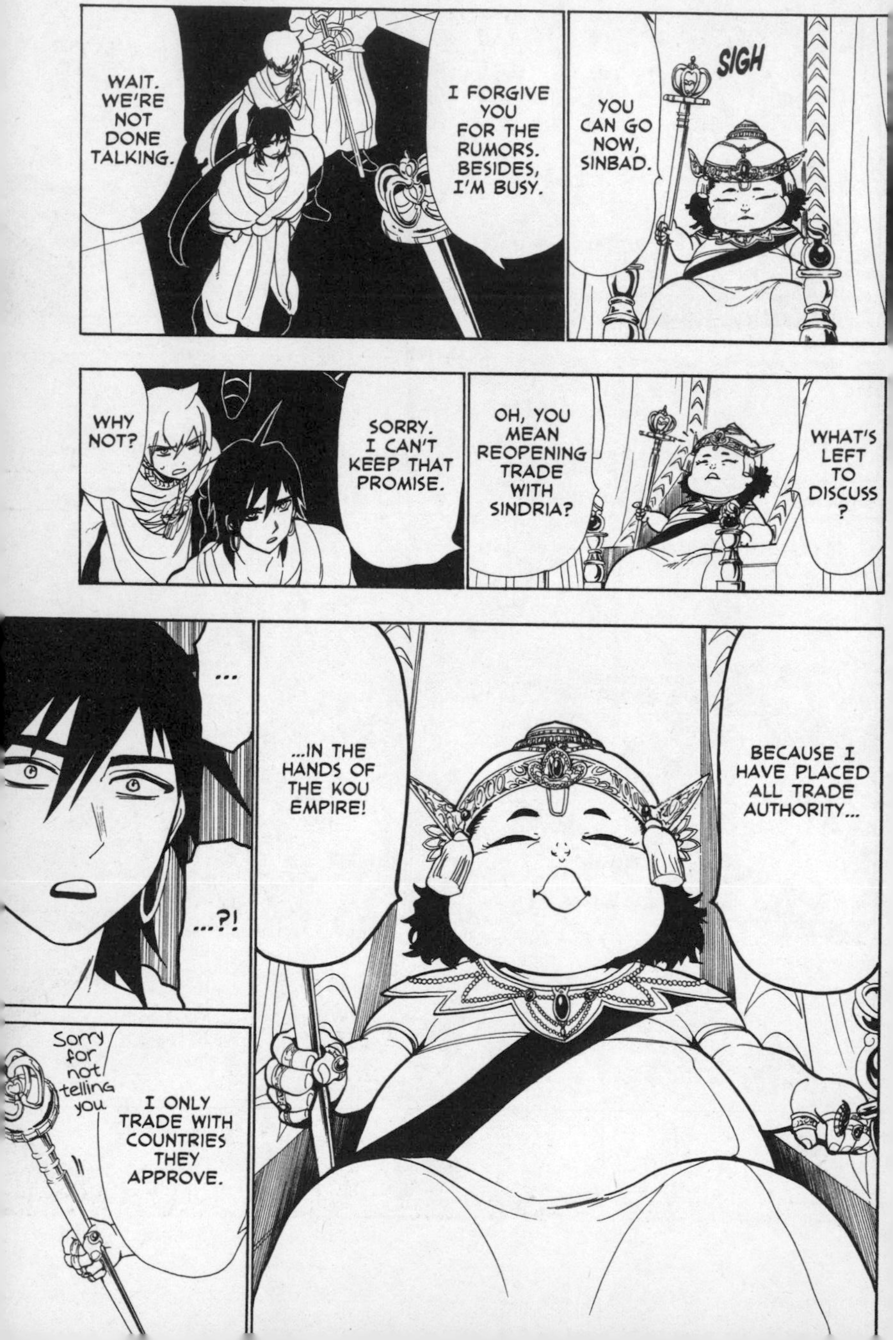
SIGH
YOU CAN GO NOW, SINBAD.
I FORGIVE YOU FOR THE RUMORS. BESIDES, I'M BUSY.
WAIT. WE'RE NOT DONE TALKING.
WHAT'S LEFT TO DISCUSS?
OH, YOU MEAN REOPENING TRADE WITH SINDRIA?
SORRY. I CAN'T KEEP THAT PROMISE.
WHY NOT?
BECAUSE I HAVE PLACED ALL TRADE AUTHORITY...
...IN THE HANDS OF THE KOU EMPIRE!
...
...?!
I ONLY TRADE WITH COUNTRIES THEY APPROVE.
Sorry for not telling you

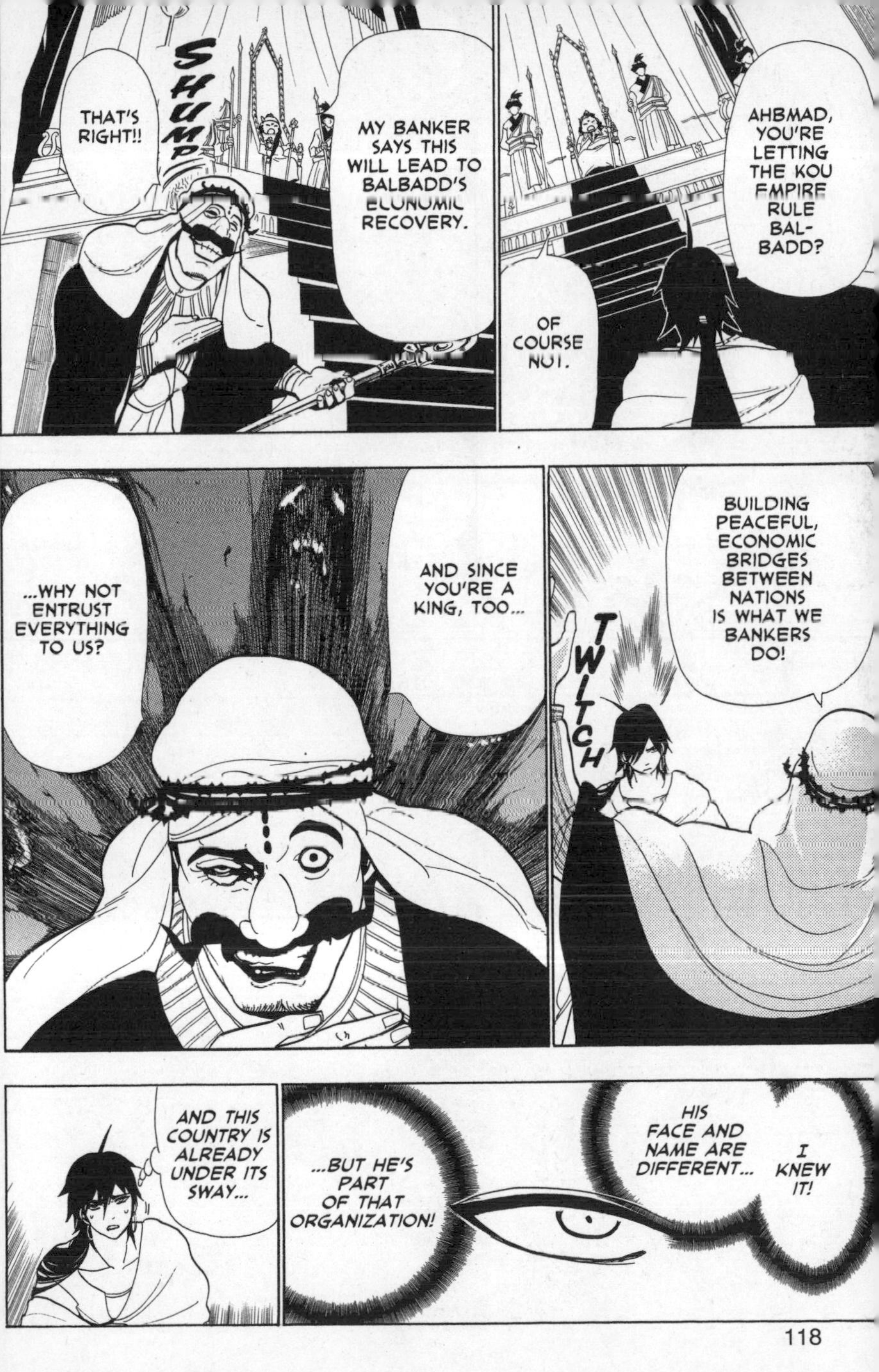
AHBMAD, YOU'RE LETTING THE KOU EMPIRE RULE BAL-BADD?
OF COURSE NOT.
MY BANKER SAYS THIS WILL LEAD TO BALBADD'S ECONOMIC RECOVERY.
SHUMP
THAT'S RIGHT!!
BUILDING PEACEFUL, ECONOMIC BRIDGES BETWEEN NATIONS IS WHAT WE BANKERS DO!
TWITCH
AND SINCE YOU'RE A KING, TOO...
...WHY NOT ENTRUST EVERYTHING TO US?
I KNEW IT!
HIS FACE AND NAME ARE DIFFERENT...
...BUT HE'S PART OF THAT ORGANIZATION!
AND THIS COUNTRY IS ALREADY UNDER ITS SWAY...

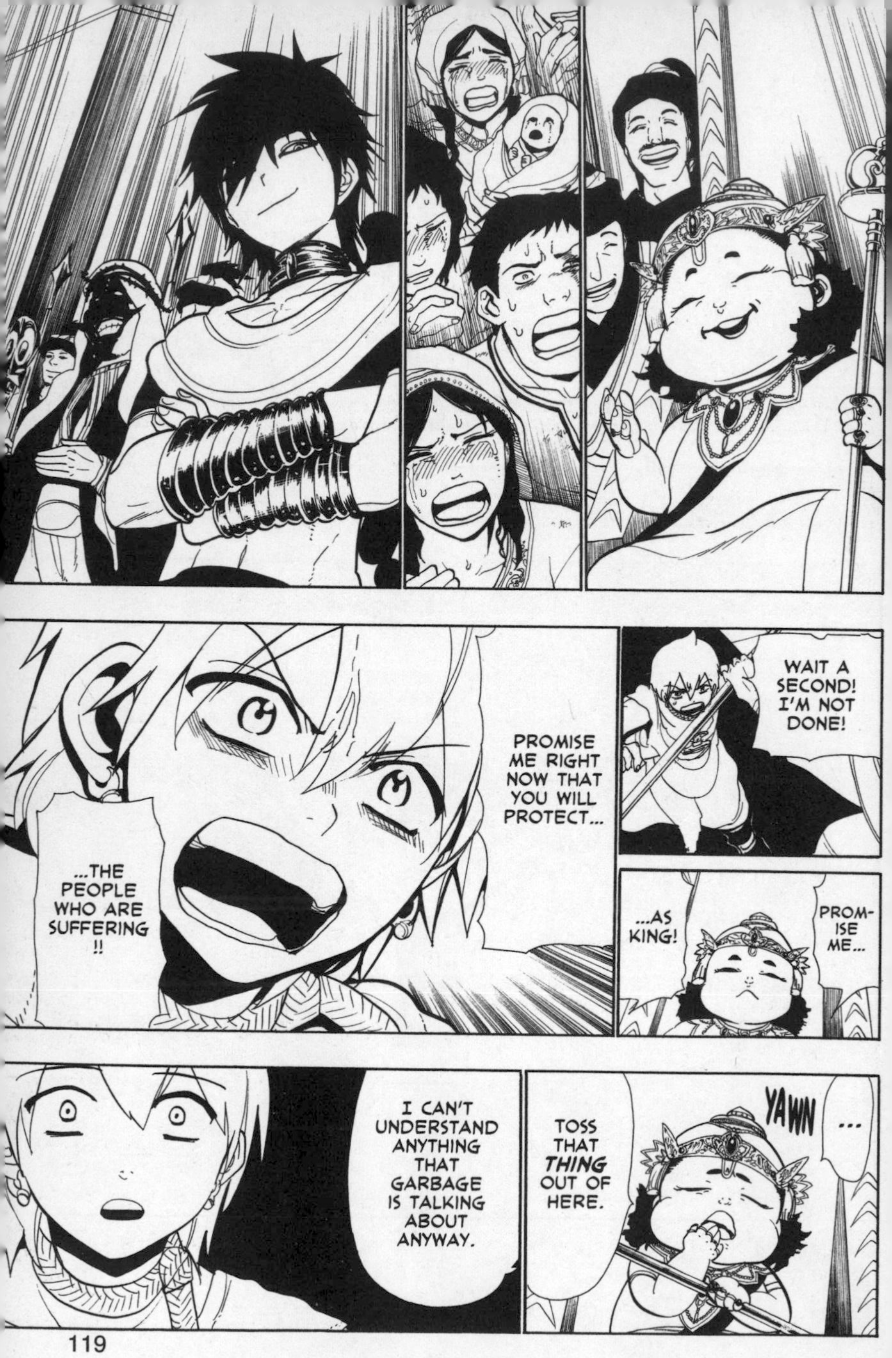
WAIT A SECOND! I'M NOT DONE!
PROM-ISE ME...
...AS KING!
PROMISE ME RIGHT NOW THAT YOU WILL PROTECT...
...THE PEOPLE WHO ARE SUFFERING!!
...
YAWN
TOSS THAT *THING* OUT OF HERE.
I CAN'T UNDERSTAND ANYTHING THAT GARBAGE IS TALKING ABOUT ANYWAY.

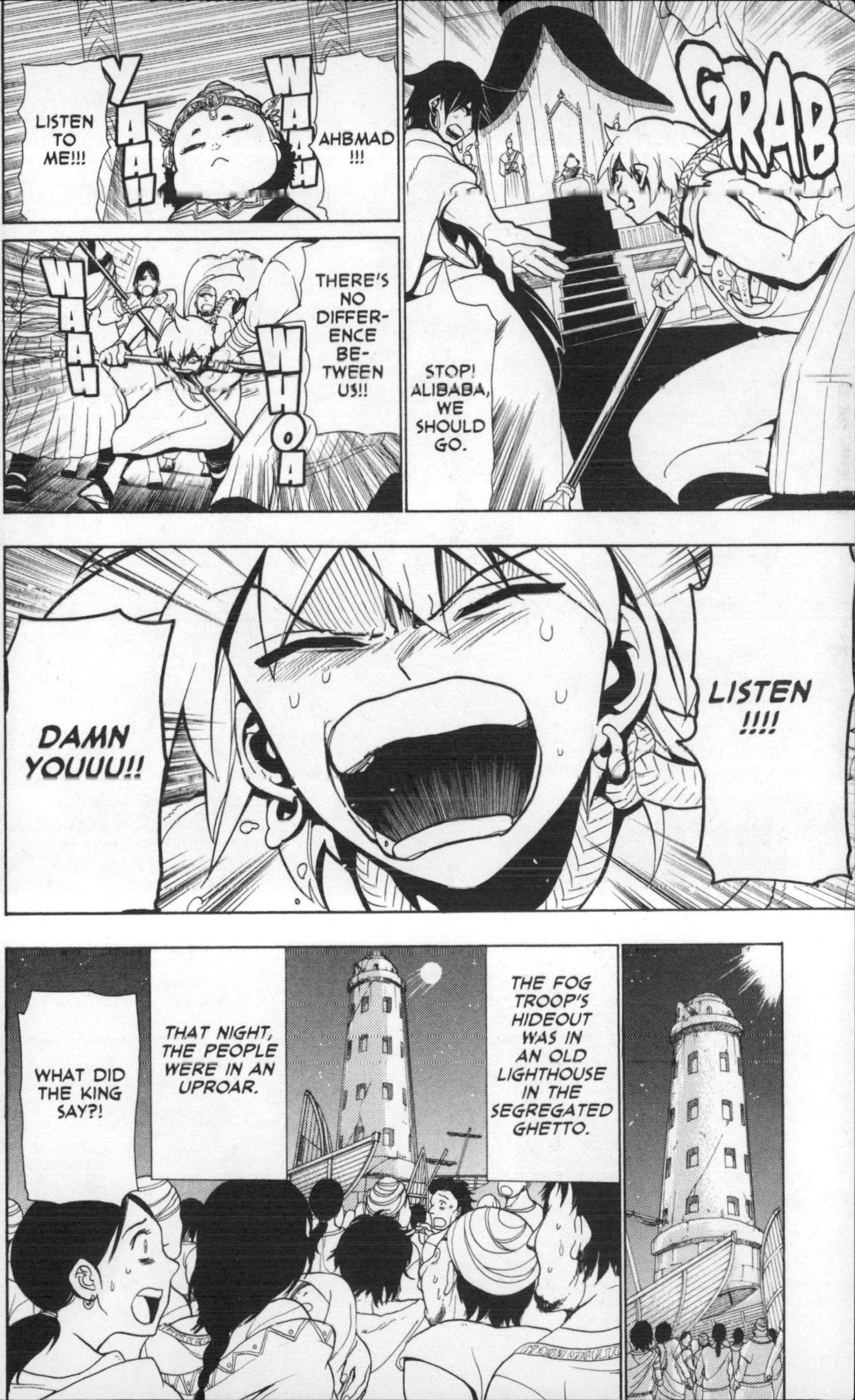
GRAB
STOP! ALIBABA, WE SHOULD GO.
AHBMAD!!!
WAAAH
YAAAH
LISTEN TO ME!!!
THERE'S NO DIFFERENCE BETWEEN US!!
WHOA
WAAAH
LISTEN!!!!
DAMN YOUUU!!
THE FOG TROOP'S HIDEOUT WAS IN AN OLD LIGHTHOUSE IN THE SEGREGATED GHETTO.
THAT NIGHT, THE PEOPLE WERE IN AN UPROAR.
WHAT DID THE KING SAY?!

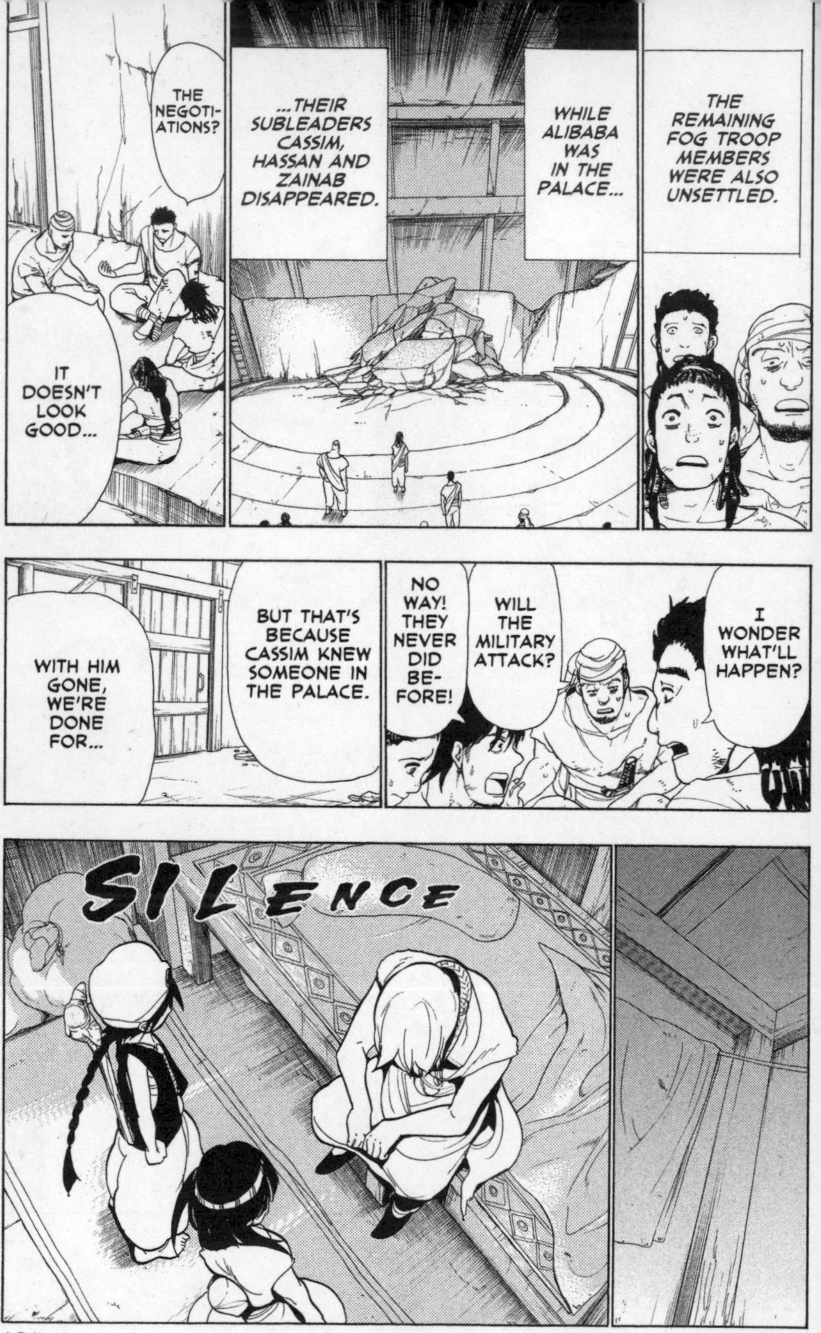
THE REMAINING FOG TROOP MEMBERS WERE ALSO UNSETTLED.
WHILE ALIBABA WAS IN THE PALACE...
...THEIR SUBLEADERS CASSIM, HASSAN AND ZAINAB DISAPPEARED.
THE NEGOTI-ATIONS?
IT DOESN'T LOOK GOOD...
I WONDER WHAT'LL HAPPEN?
WILL THE MILITARY ATTACK?
NO WAY! THEY NEVER DID BE-FORE!
BUT THAT'S BECAUSE CASSIM KNEW SOMEONE IN THE PALACE.
WITH HIM GONE, WE'RE DONE FOR...
SILENCE

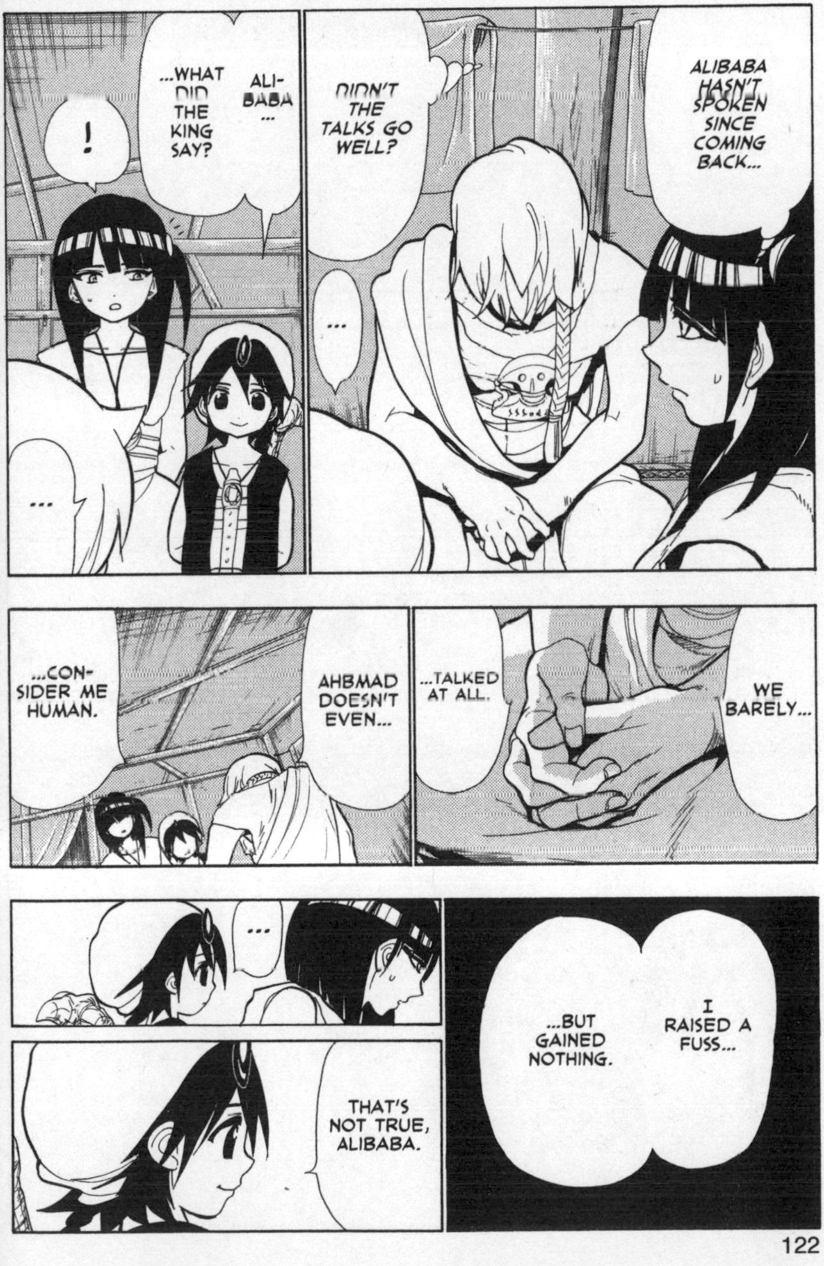

ALIBABA HASN'T SPOKEN SINCE COMING BACK...
DIDN'T THE TALKS GO WELL?
...
ALI-BABA...
...WHAT DID THE KING SAY?
!
...
WE BARELY...
...TALKED AT ALL.
AHBMAD DOESN'T EVEN...
...CON-SIDER ME HUMAN.
I RAISED A FUSS...
...BUT GAINED NOTHING.
...
THAT'S NOT TRUE, ALIBABA.

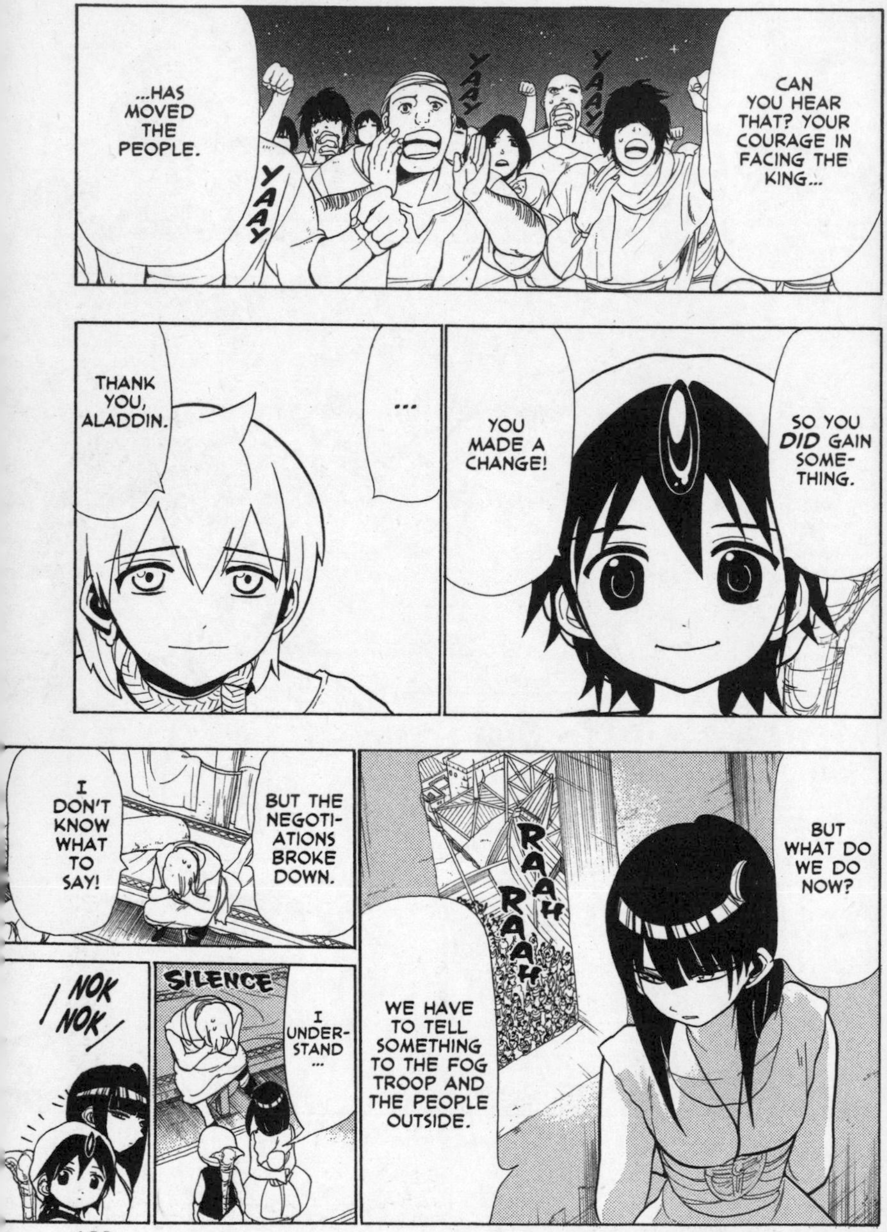
CAN YOU HEAR THAT? YOUR COURAGE IN FACING THE KING...
YAAY
YAAY
YAAY
...HAS MOVED THE PEOPLE.
SO YOU *DID* GAIN SOMETHING.
YOU MADE A CHANGE!
...
THANK YOU, ALADDIN.
BUT WHAT DO WE DO NOW?
RAAH
RAAH
WE HAVE TO TELL SOMETHING TO THE FOG TROOP AND THE PEOPLE OUTSIDE.
BUT THE NEGOTIATIONS BROKE DOWN.
I DON'T KNOW WHAT TO SAY!
SILENCE
I UNDERSTAND...
NOK NOK

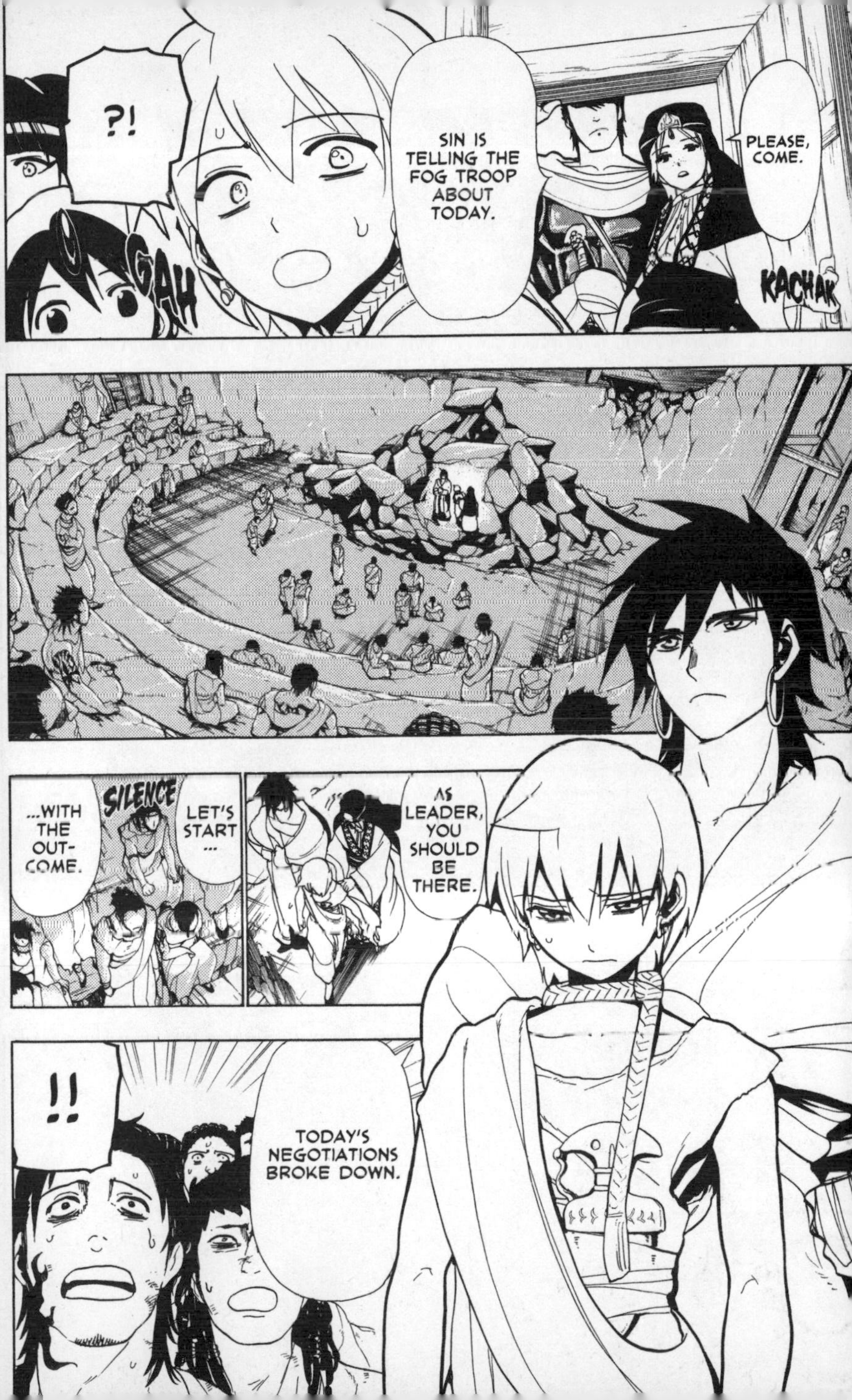
PLEASE, COME.
KACHAK
SIN IS TELLING THE FOG TROOP ABOUT TODAY.
?!
GAH
AS LEADER, YOU SHOULD BE THERE.
LET'S START ...
SILENCE
...WITH THE OUT-COME.
TODAY'S NEGOTIATIONS BROKE DOWN.
!!

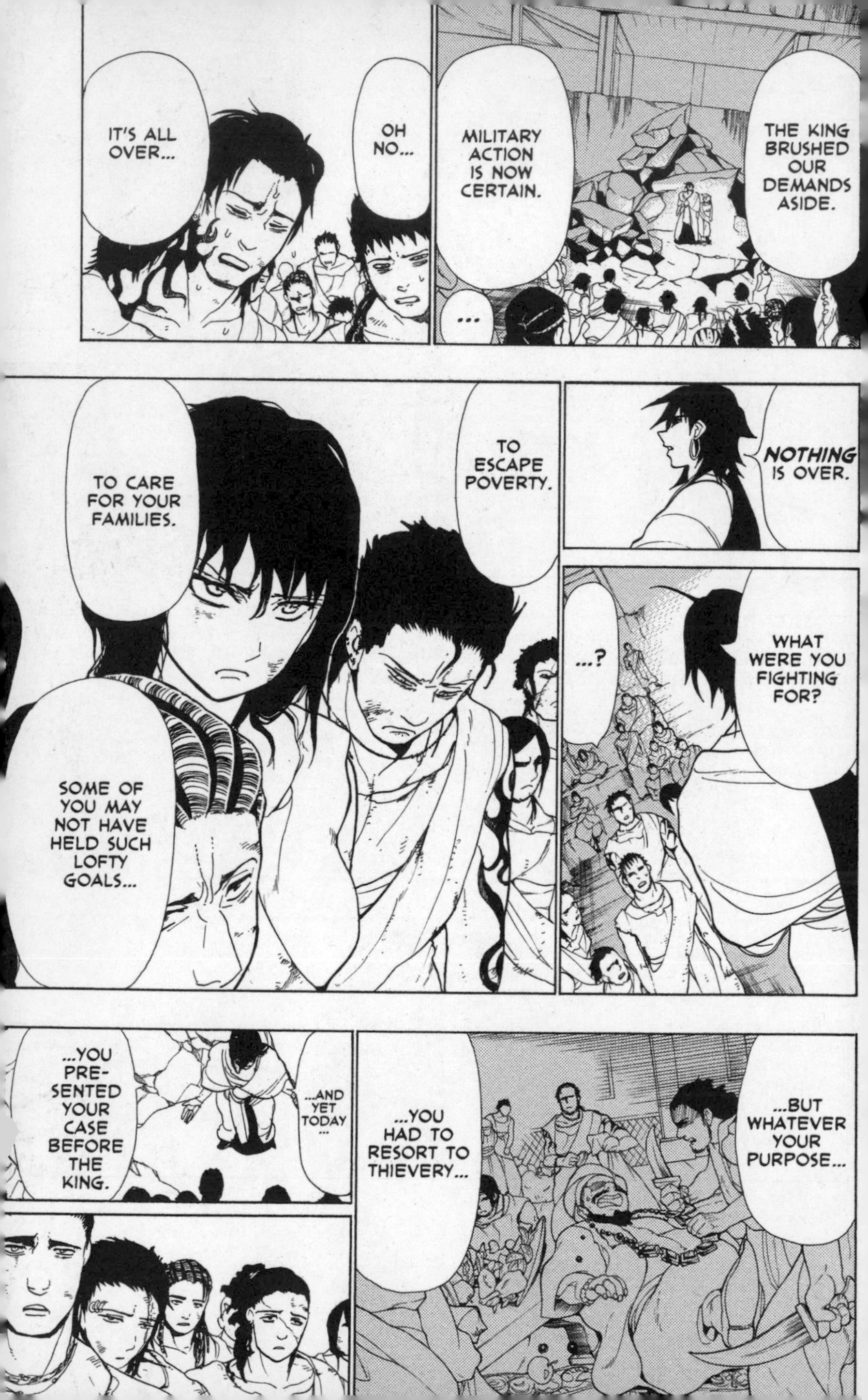
THE KING BRUSHED OUR DEMANDS ASIDE.
MILITARY ACTION IS NOW CERTAIN.
...
OH NO...
IT'S ALL OVER...
*NOTHING* IS OVER.
WHAT WERE YOU FIGHTING FOR?
...?
TO ESCAPE POVERTY.
TO CARE FOR YOUR FAMILIES.
SOME OF YOU MAY NOT HAVE HELD SUCH LOFTY GOALS...
...BUT WHATEVER YOUR PURPOSE...
...YOU HAD TO RESORT TO THIEVERY...
...AND YET TODAY...
...YOU PRE-SENTED YOUR CASE BEFORE THE KING.

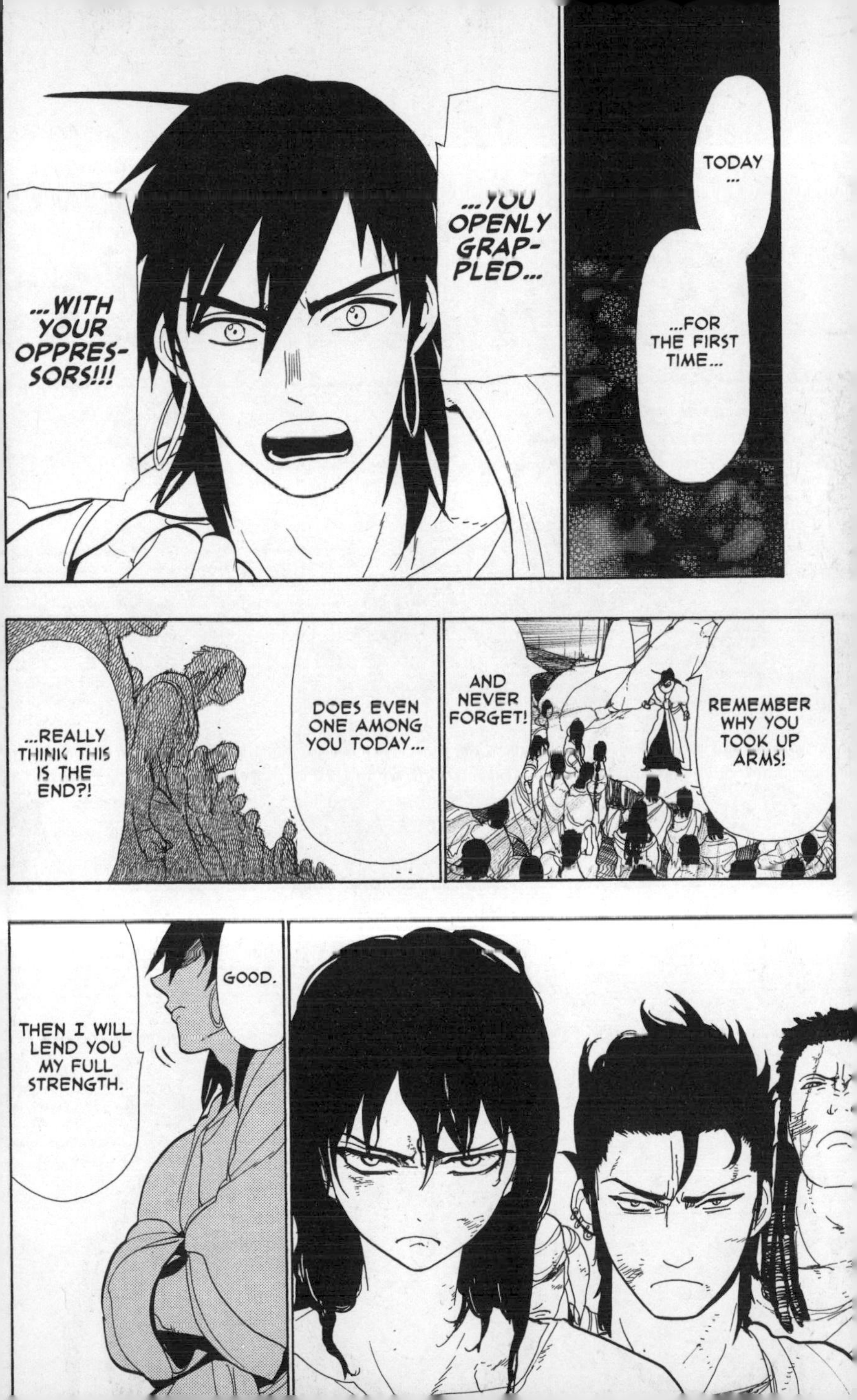
TODAY ...
...FOR THE FIRST TIME...
...YOU OPENLY GRAP-PLED...
...WITH YOUR OPPRES-SORS!!!
REMEMBER WHY YOU TOOK UP ARMS!
AND NEVER FORGET!
DOES EVEN ONE AMONG YOU TODAY...
...REALLY THINK THIS IS THE END?!
GOOD.
THEN I WILL LEND YOU MY FULL STRENGTH.

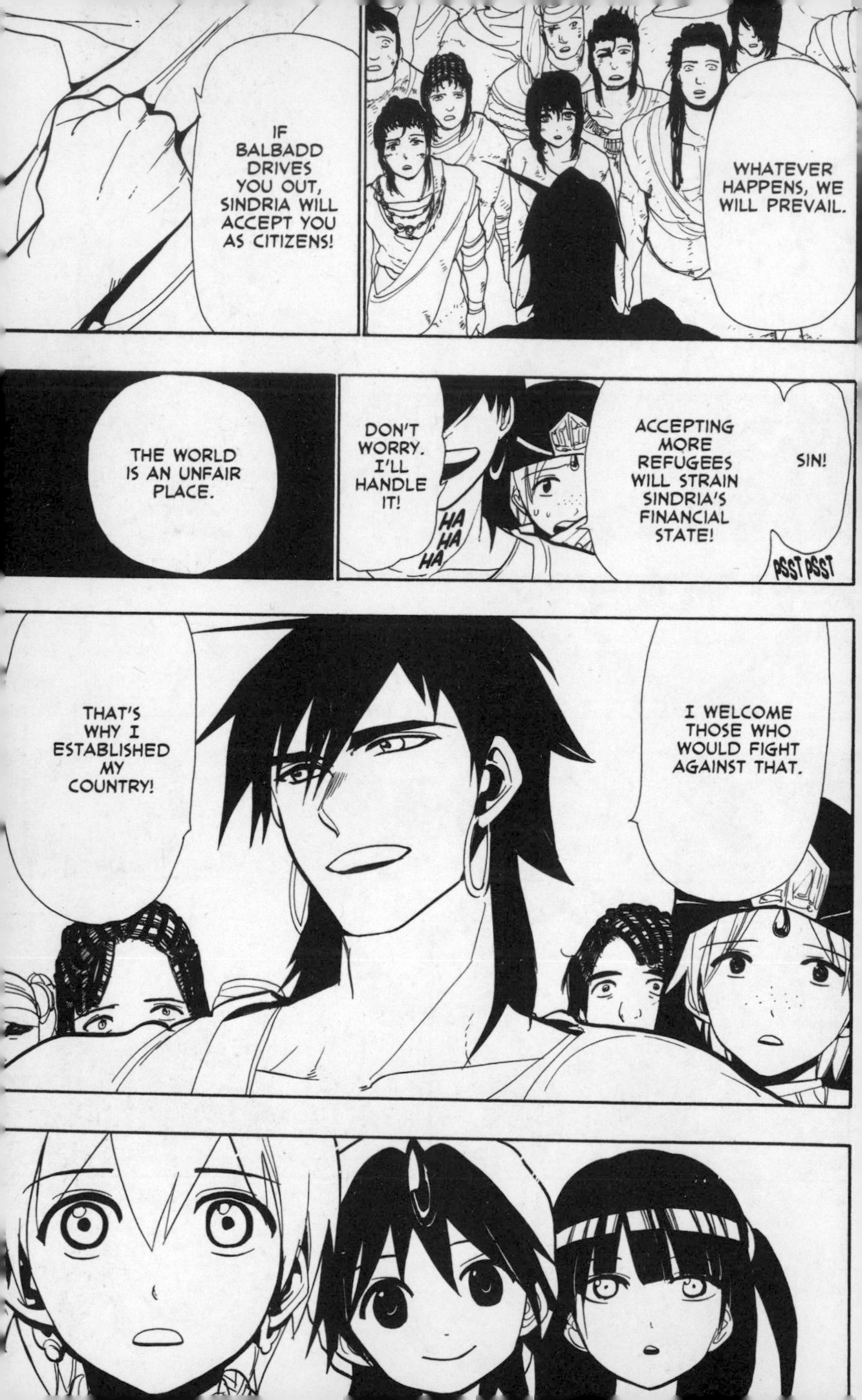
WHATEVER HAPPENS, WE WILL PREVAIL.
IF BALBADD DRIVES YOU OUT, SINDRIA WILL ACCEPT YOU AS CITIZENS!
SIN!
ACCEPTING MORE REFUGEES WILL STRAIN SINDRIA'S FINANCIAL STATE!
PSST PSST
DON'T WORRY. I'LL HANDLE IT!
HA HA HA
THE WORLD IS AN UNFAIR PLACE.
I WELCOME THOSE WHO WOULD FIGHT AGAINST THAT.
THAT'S WHY I ESTABLISHED MY COUNTRY!

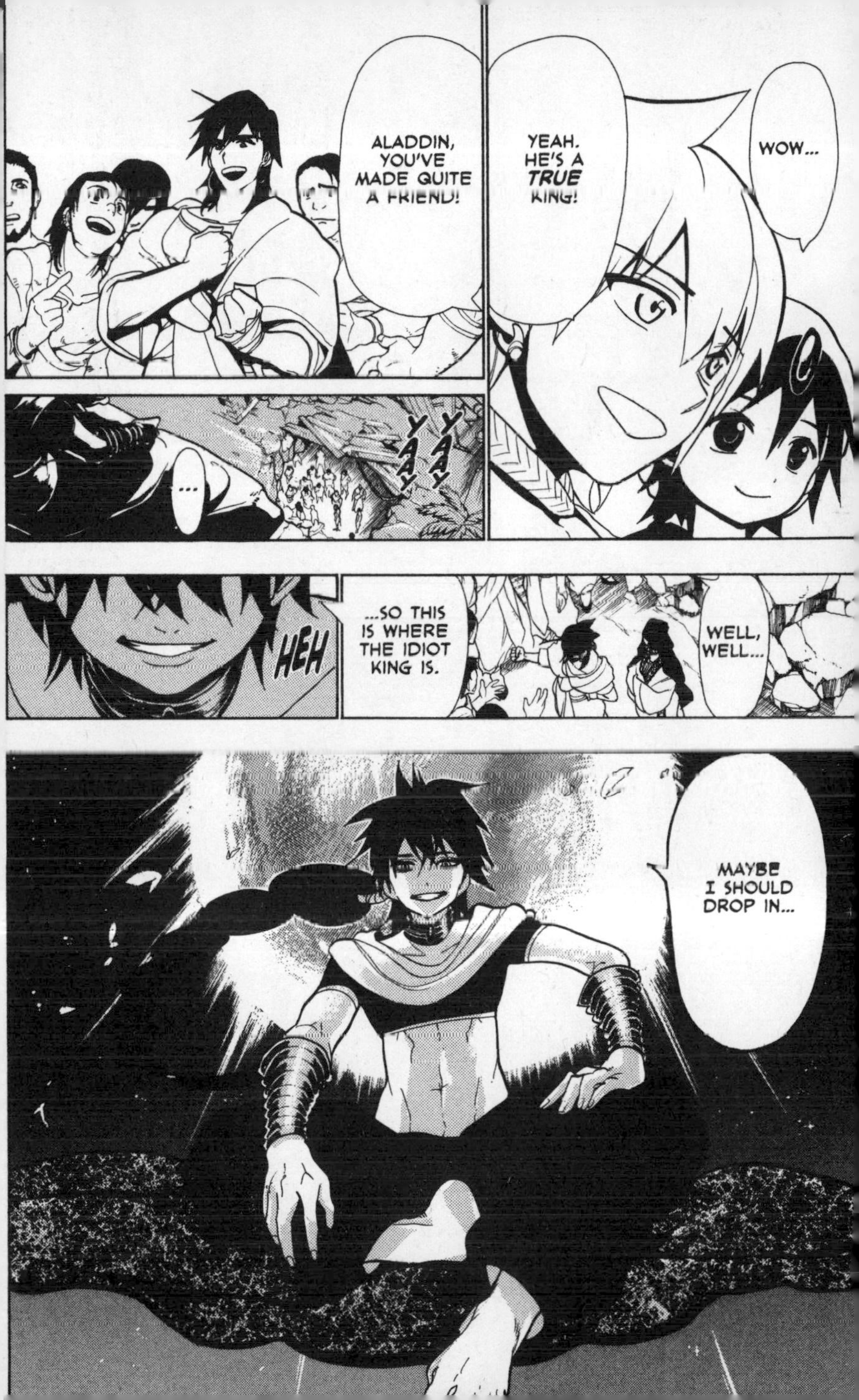
WOW...
YEAH. HE'S A TRUE KING!
ALADDIN, YOU'VE MADE QUITE A FRIEND!
YAAY YAAY
...
WELL, WELL...
...SO THIS IS WHERE THE IDIOT KING IS.
HEH
MAYBE I SHOULD DROP IN...

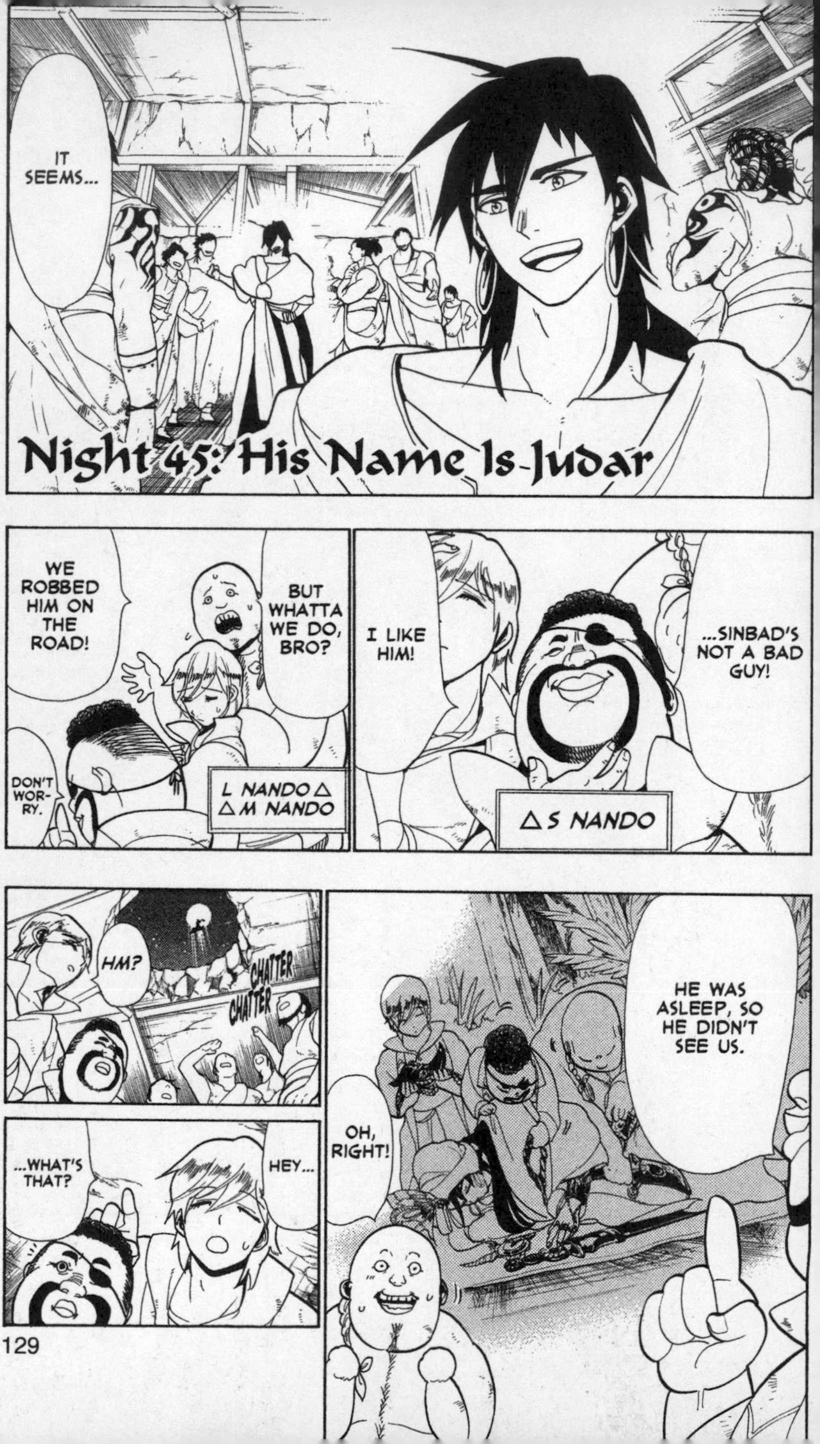
IT SEEMS...
Night 45: His Name Is Judar
...SINBAD'S NOT A BAD GUY!
I LIKE HIM!
△S NANDO
BUT WHATTA WE DO, BRO?
WE ROBBED HIM ON THE ROAD!
DON'T WOR-RY.
L NANDO△
△M NANDO
HE WAS ASLEEP, SO HE DIDN'T SEE US.
OH, RIGHT!
HM?
CHATTER
CHATTER
HEY...
...WHAT'S THAT?

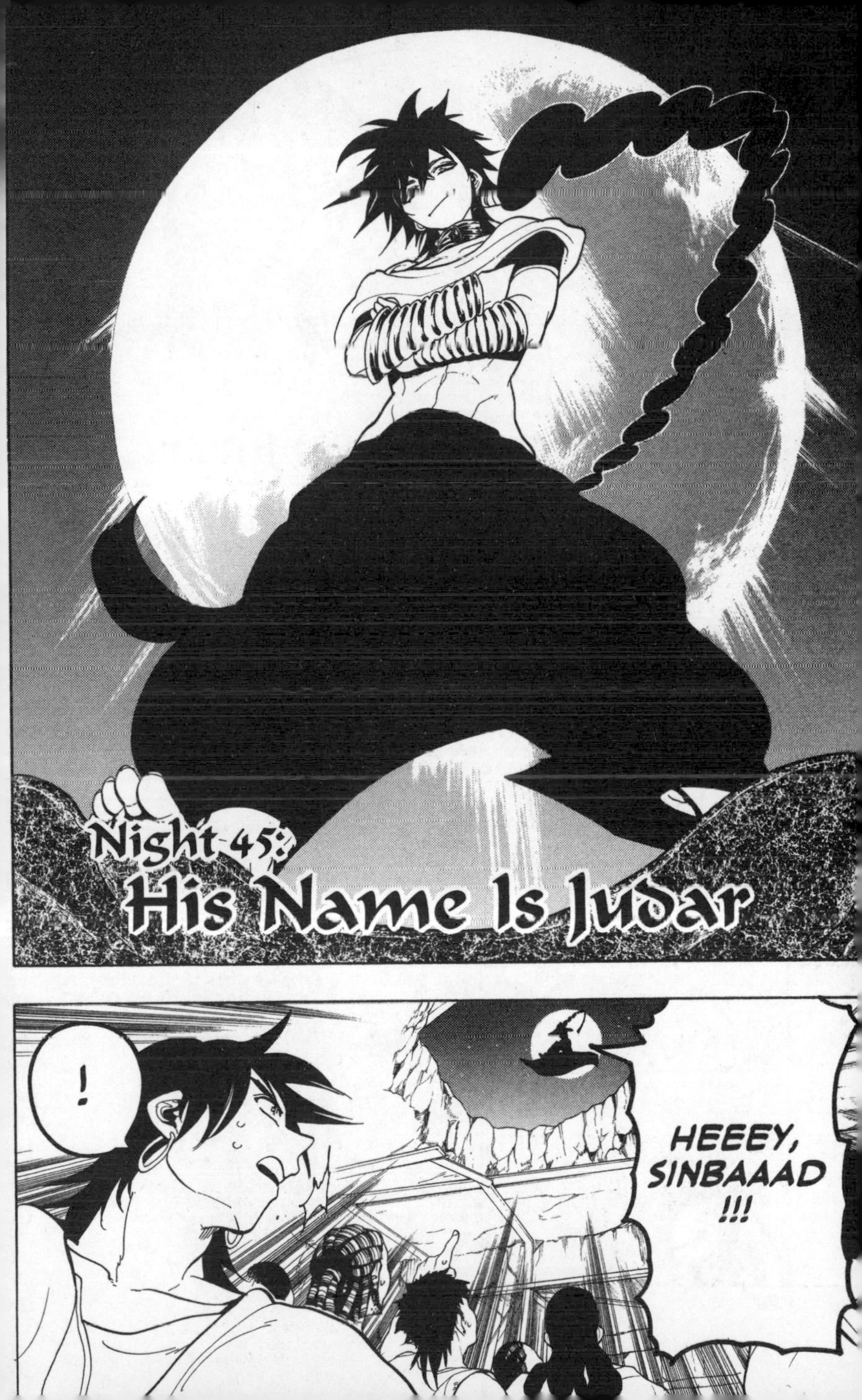
Night 45:
His Name Is Judar
HEEEY, SINBAAAD !!!
!

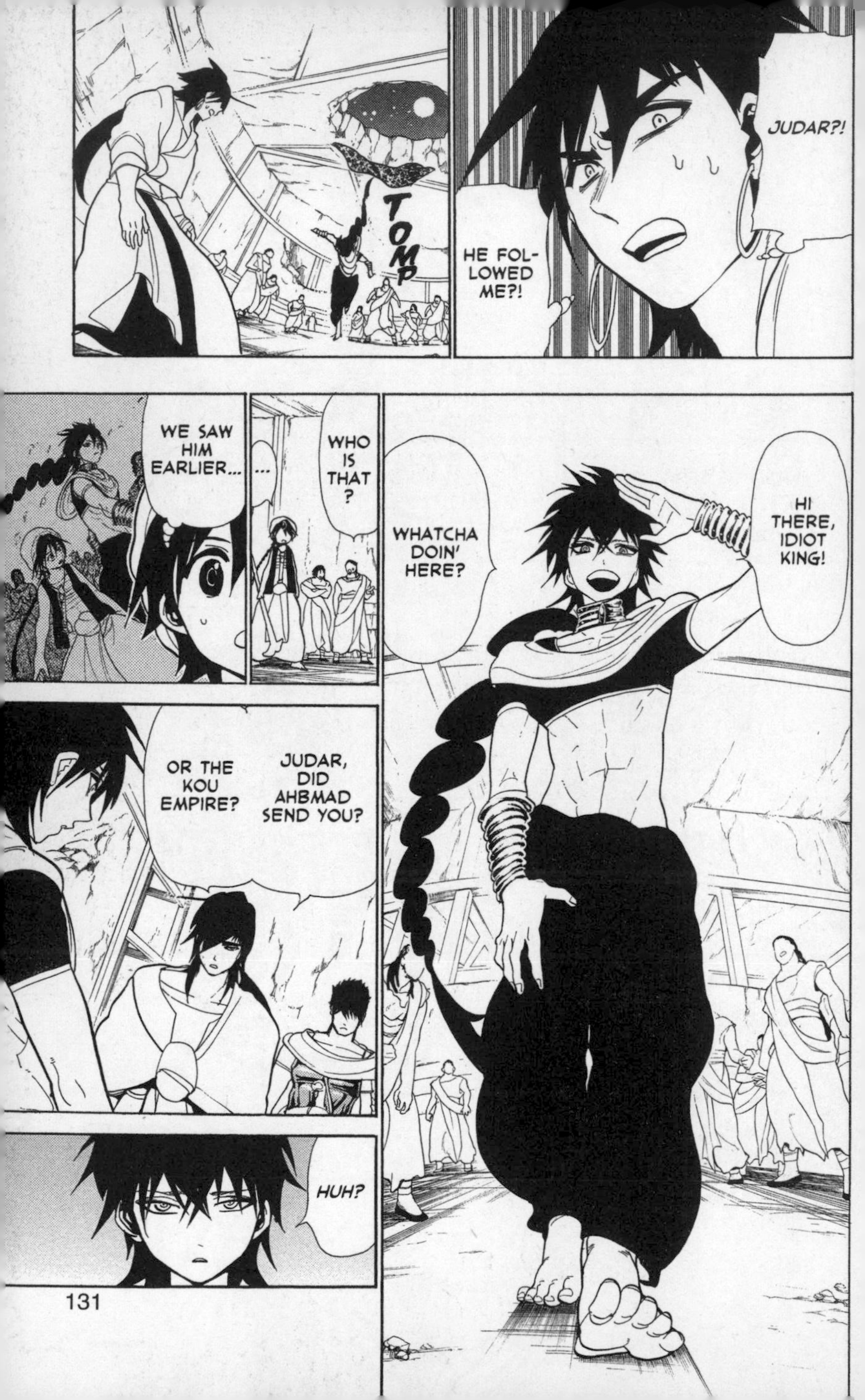
JUDAR?!
HE FOL-LOWED ME?!
TOMP
HI THERE, IDIOT KING!
WHATCHA DOIN' HERE?
WHO IS THAT?
...
WE SAW HIM EARLIER...
JUDAR, DID AHBMAD SEND YOU?
OR THE KOU EMPIRE?
HUH?

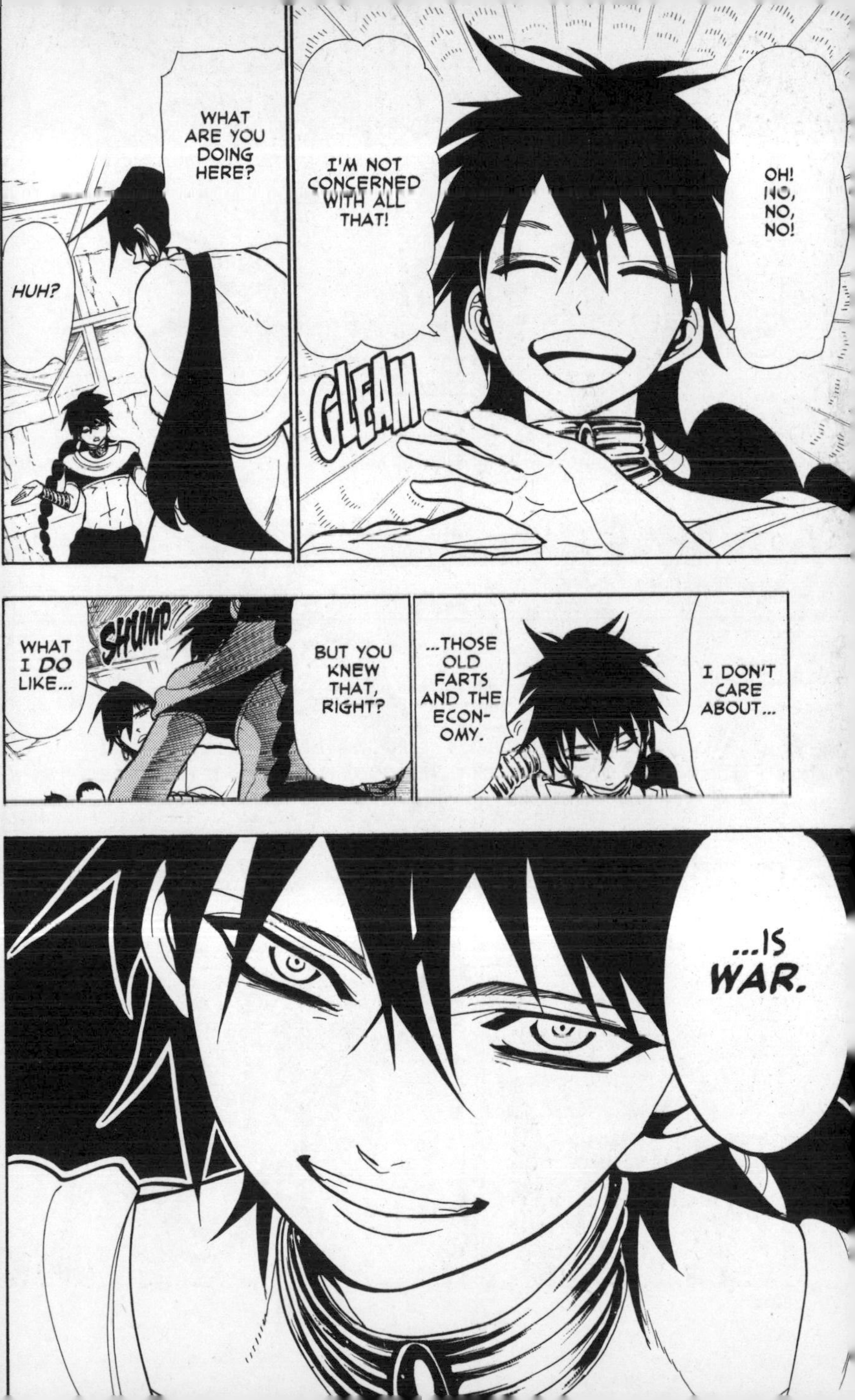
OH! NO, NO, NO!
I'M NOT CONCERNED WITH ALL THAT!
GLEAM
WHAT ARE YOU DOING HERE?
HUH?
I DON'T CARE ABOUT...
...THOSE OLD FARTS AND THE ECONOMY.
BUT YOU KNEW THAT, RIGHT?
SHUMP
WHAT I DO LIKE...
...IS WAR.

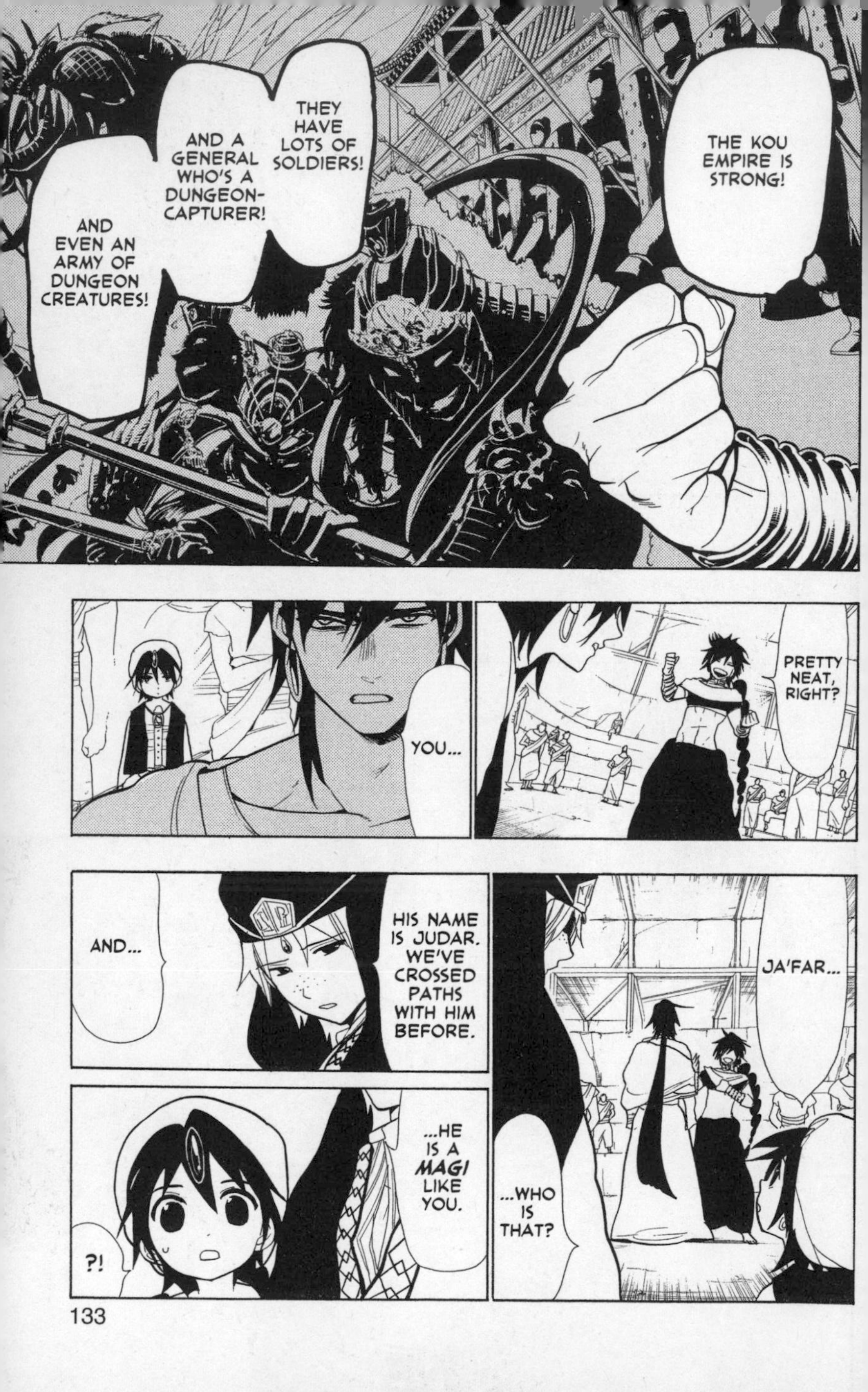
THE KOU EMPIRE IS STRONG!
THEY HAVE LOTS OF SOLDIERS!
AND A GENERAL WHO'S A DUNGEON-CAPTURER!
AND EVEN AN ARMY OF DUNGEON CREATURES!
PRETTY NEAT, RIGHT?
YOU...
JA'FAR...
...WHO IS THAT?
HIS NAME IS JUDAR. WE'VE CROSSED PATHS WITH HIM BEFORE.
AND...
...HE IS A *MAGI* LIKE YOU.
?!

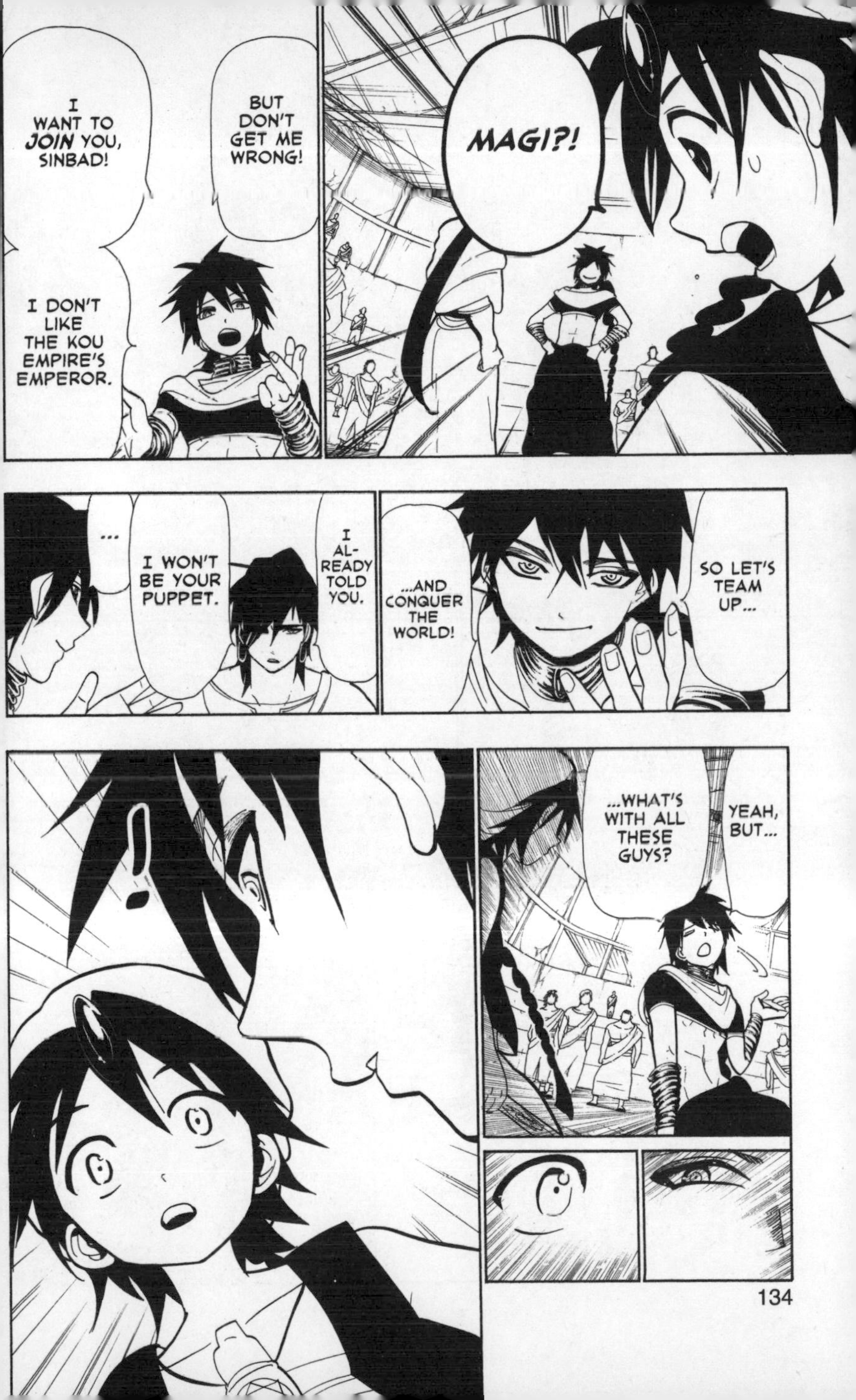
MAGI?!
BUT DON'T GET ME WRONG!
I WANT TO JOIN YOU, SINBAD!
I DON'T LIKE THE KOU EMPIRE'S EMPEROR.
SO LET'S TEAM UP...
...AND CONQUER THE WORLD!
I ALREADY TOLD YOU.
I WON'T BE YOUR PUPPET.
...
YEAH, BUT...
...WHAT'S WITH ALL THESE GUYS?

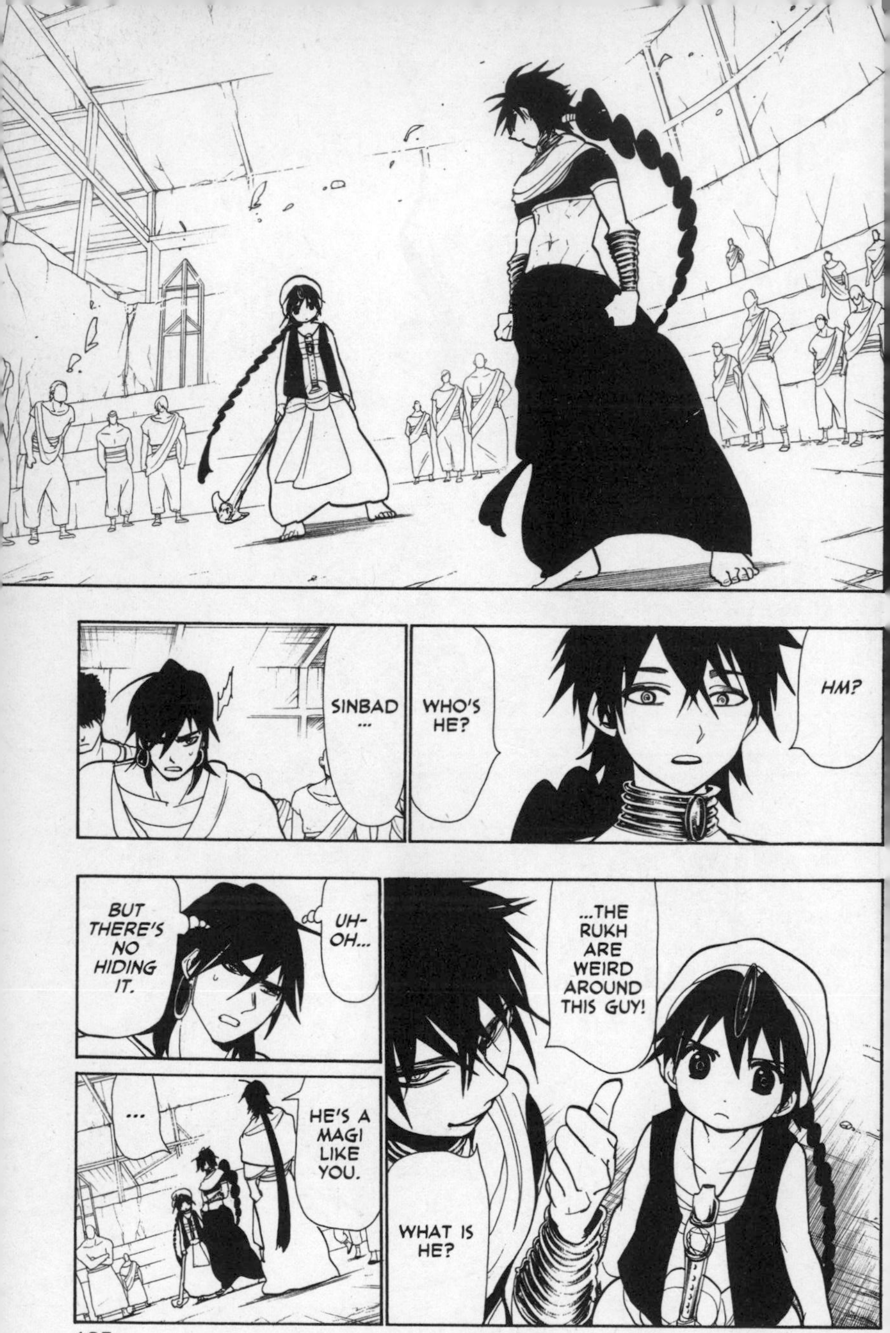
HM?
WHO'S HE?
SINBAD...
...THE RUKH ARE WEIRD AROUND THIS GUY!
WHAT IS HE?
UH-OH...
BUT THERE'S NO HIDING IT.
HE'S A MAGI LIKE YOU.
...

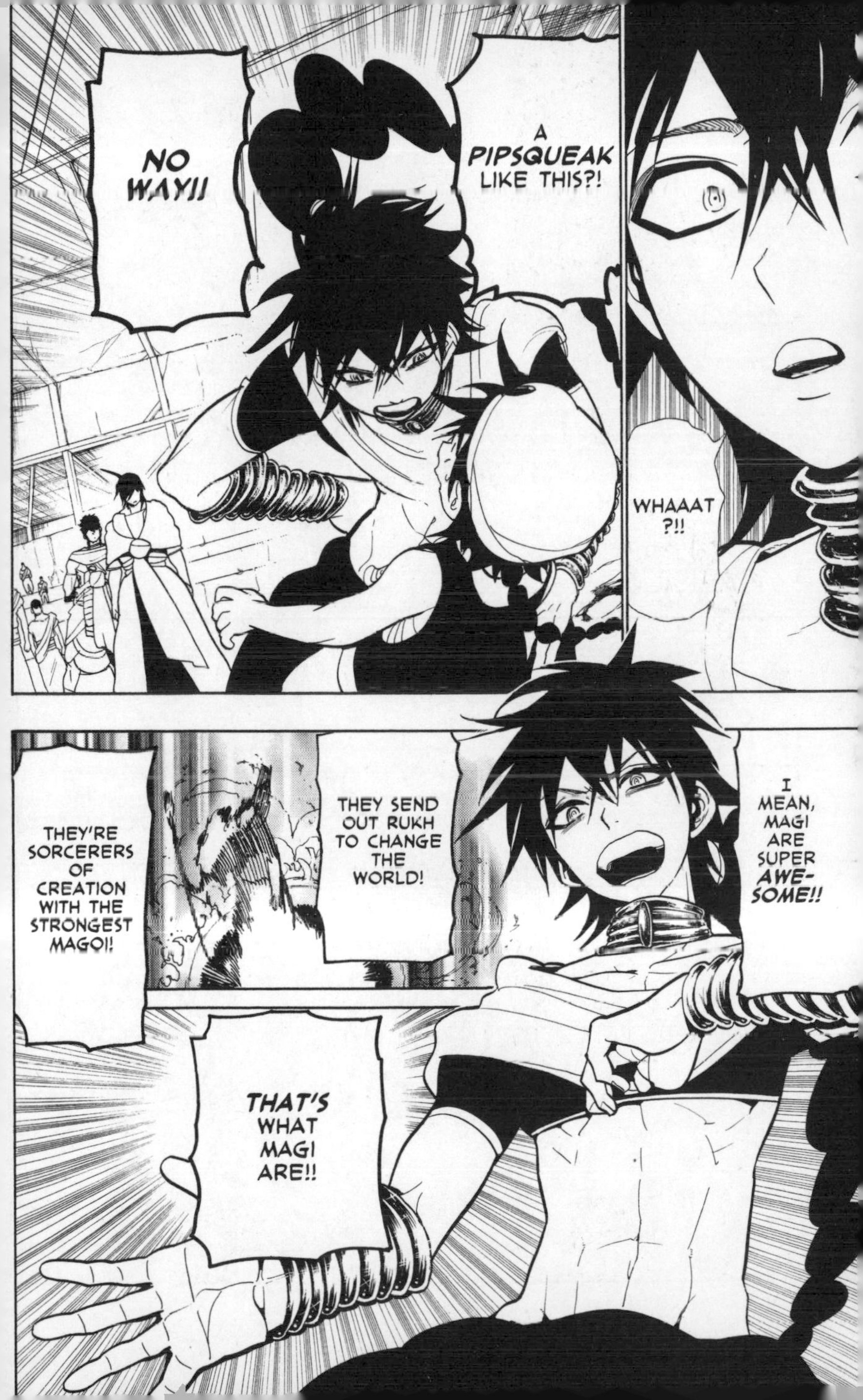
WHAAAT?!!
A PIPSQUEAK LIKE THIS?!
NO WAY!!
I MEAN, MAGI ARE SUPER AWESOME!!
THEY SEND OUT RUKH TO CHANGE THE WORLD!
THEY'RE SORCERERS OF CREATION WITH THE STRONGEST MAGOI!
THAT'S WHAT MAGI ARE!!

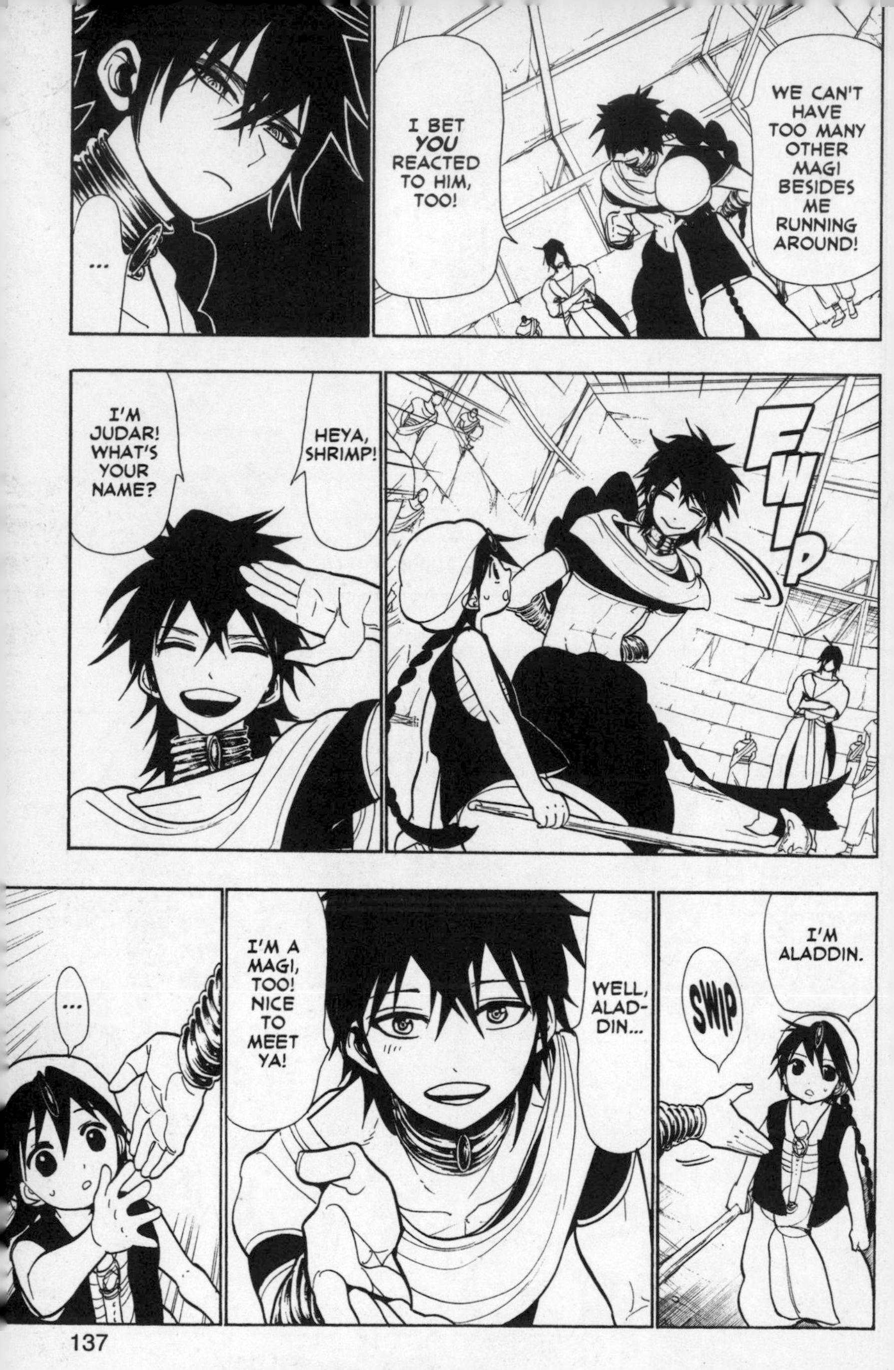
WE CAN'T HAVE TOO MANY OTHER MAGI BESIDES ME RUNNING AROUND!
I BET *YOU* REACTED TO HIM, TOO!
...
FWIP
HEYA, SHRIMP!
I'M JUDAR! WHAT'S YOUR NAME?
I'M ALADDIN.
SWIP
WELL, ALAD-DIN...
I'M A MAGI, TOO! NICE TO MEET YA!
...

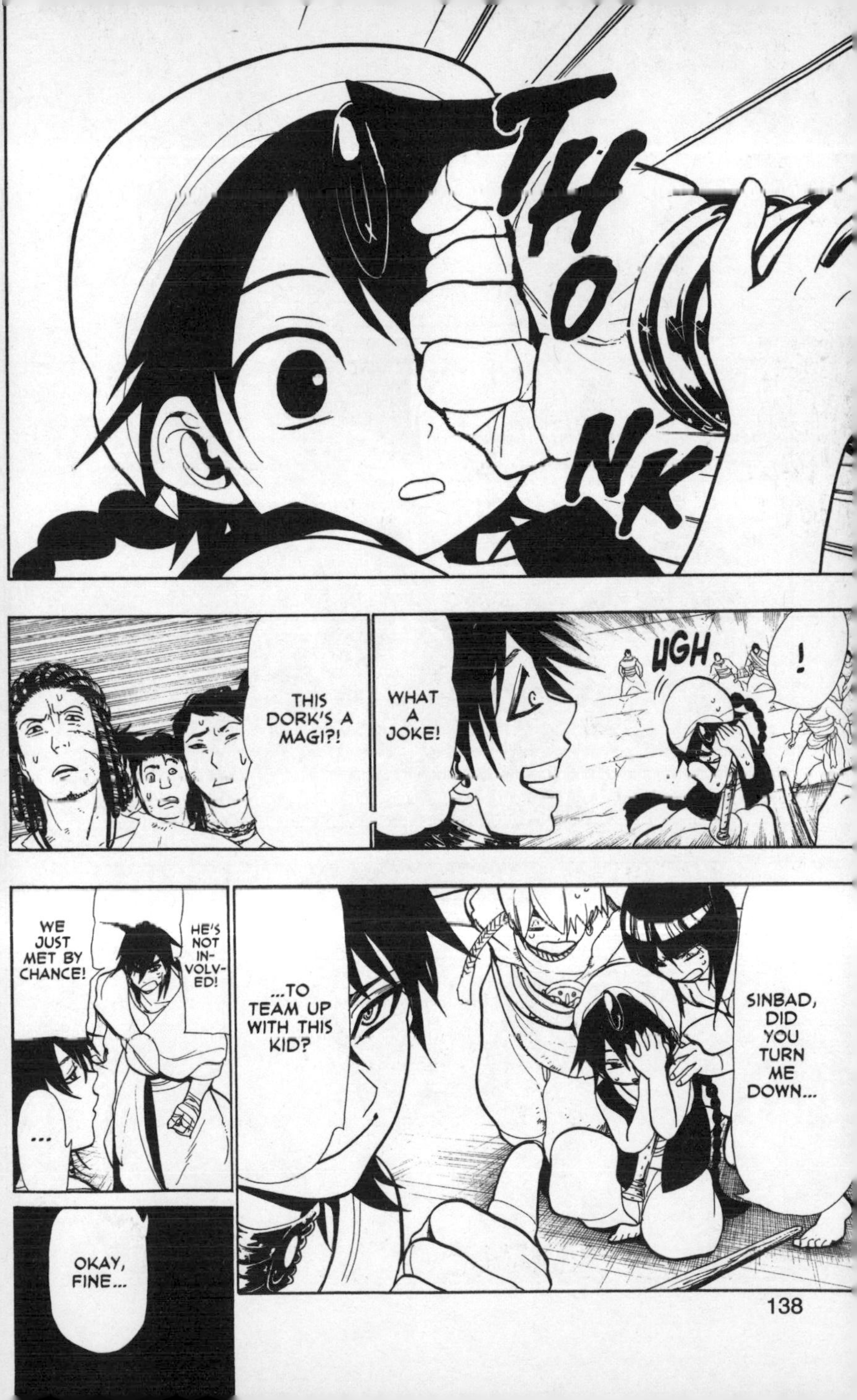
THONK
!
UGH
WHAT A JOKE!
THIS DORK'S A MAGI?!
SINBAD, DID YOU TURN ME DOWN...
...TO TEAM UP WITH THIS KID?
HE'S NOT INVOLVED!
WE JUST MET BY CHANCE!
...
OKAY, FINE...

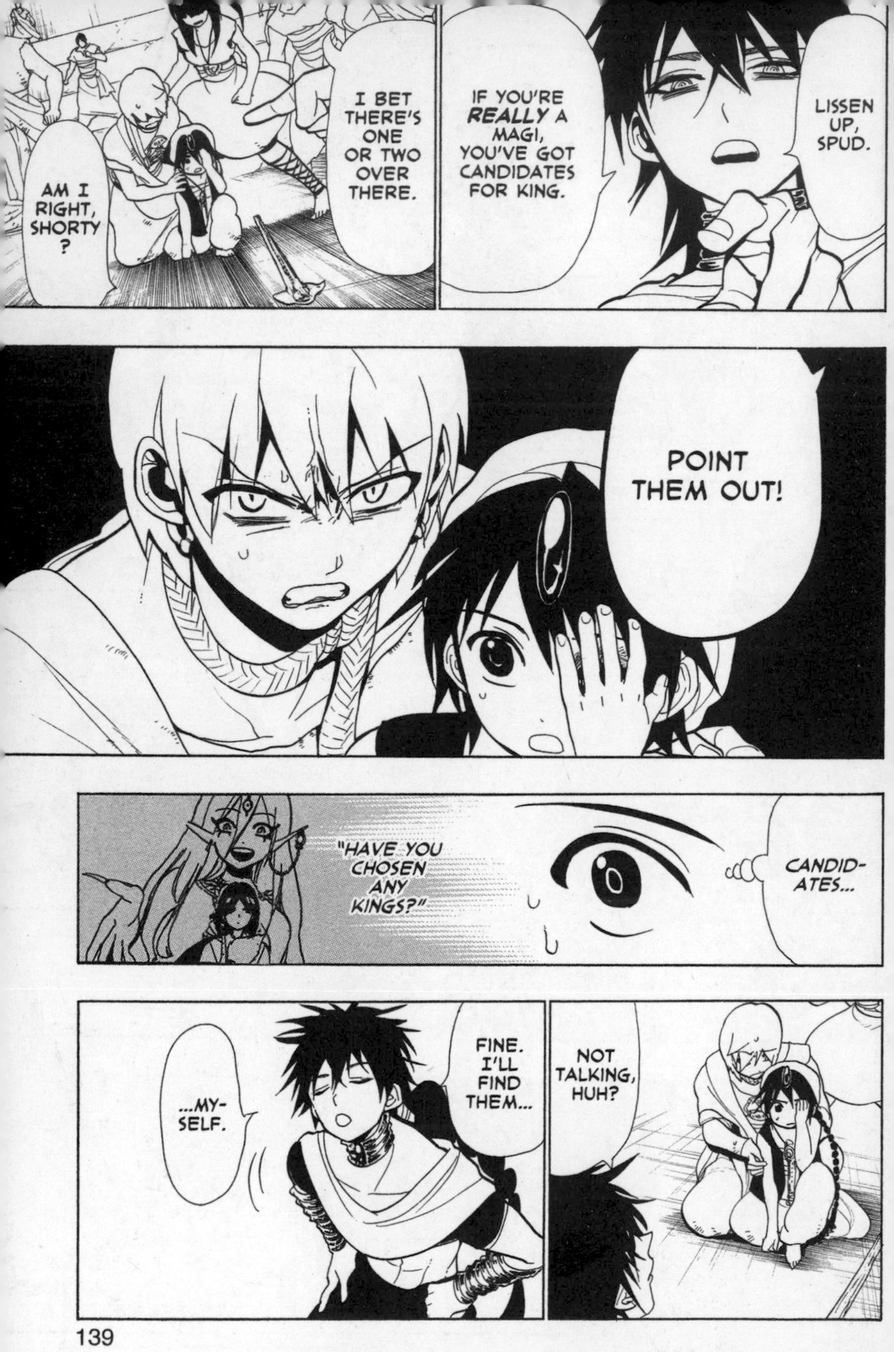
LISSEN UP, SPUD.
IF YOU'RE *REALLY* A MAGI, YOU'VE GOT CANDIDATES FOR KING.
I BET THERE'S ONE OR TWO OVER THERE.
AM I RIGHT, SHORTY?
POINT THEM OUT!
CANDID-ATES...
"HAVE YOU CHOSEN ANY KINGS?"
NOT TALKING, HUH?
FINE. I'LL FIND THEM...
...MY-SELF.

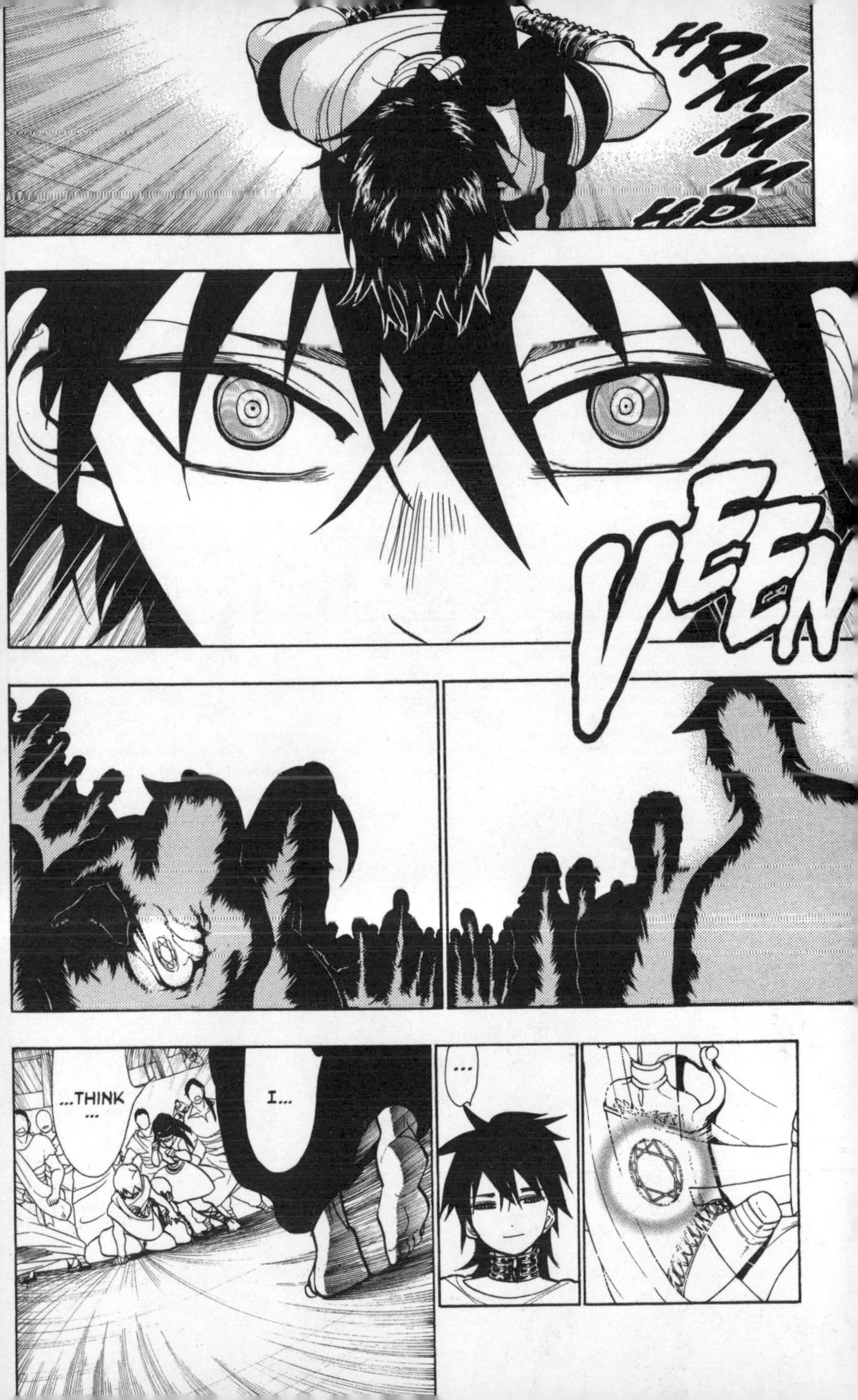
HRMMMHP
VEEN
...
I...
...THINK
...

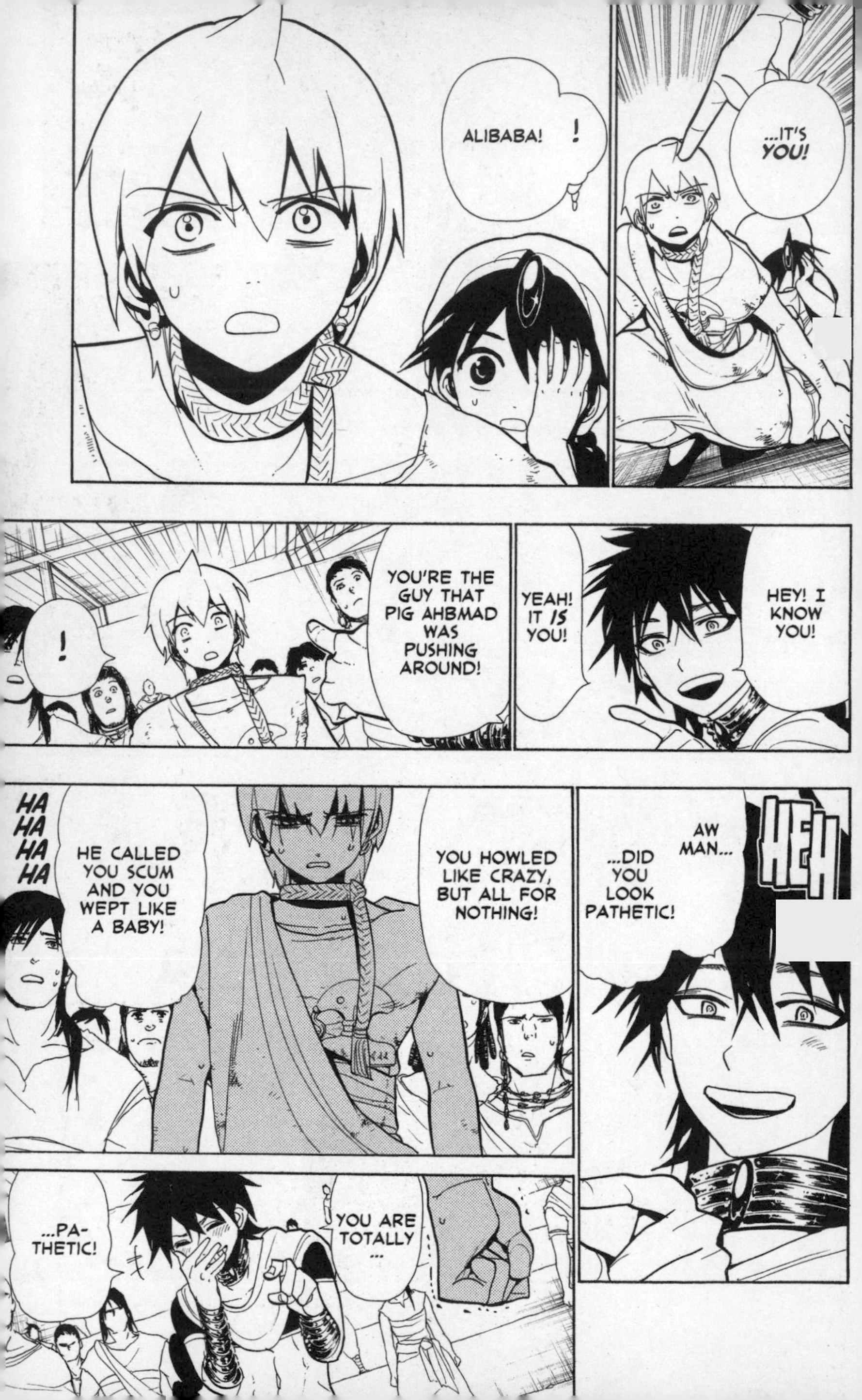
...IT'S YOU!
ALIBABA!
!
HEY! I KNOW YOU!
YEAH! IT IS YOU!
YOU'RE THE GUY THAT PIG AHBMAD WAS PUSHING AROUND!
!
HEH
AW MAN...
...DID YOU LOOK PATHETIC!
YOU HOWLED LIKE CRAZY, BUT ALL FOR NOTHING!
HE CALLED YOU SCUM AND YOU WEPT LIKE A BABY!
HA HA HA HA
YOU ARE TOTALLY ...
...PA-THETIC!

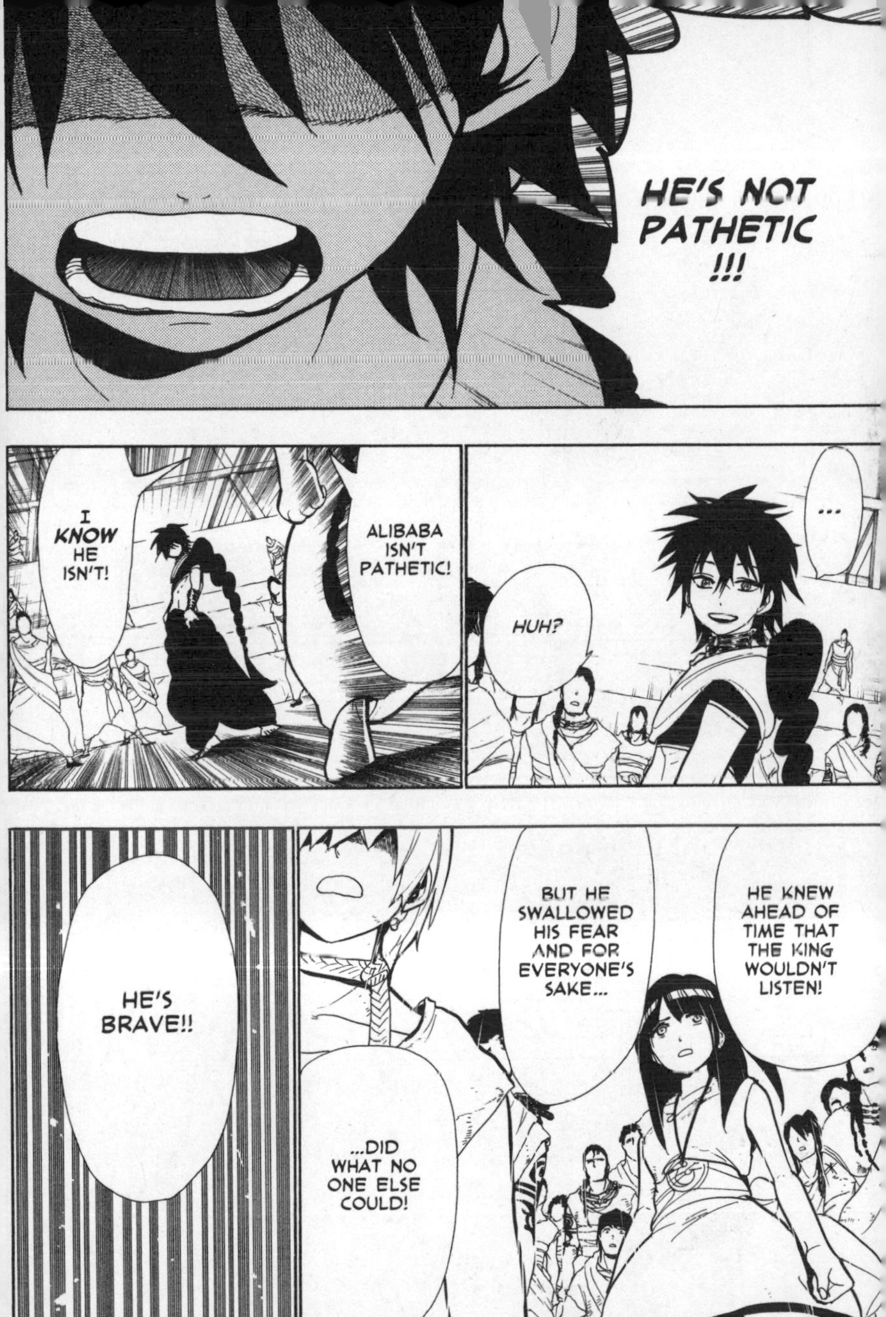
HE'S NOT PATHETIC !!!
...
HUH?
ALIBABA ISN'T PATHETIC!
I KNOW HE ISN'T!
HE KNEW AHEAD OF TIME THAT THE KING WOULDN'T LISTEN!
BUT HE SWALLOWED HIS FEAR AND FOR EVERYONE'S SAKE...
...DID WHAT NO ONE ELSE COULD!
HE'S BRAVE!!

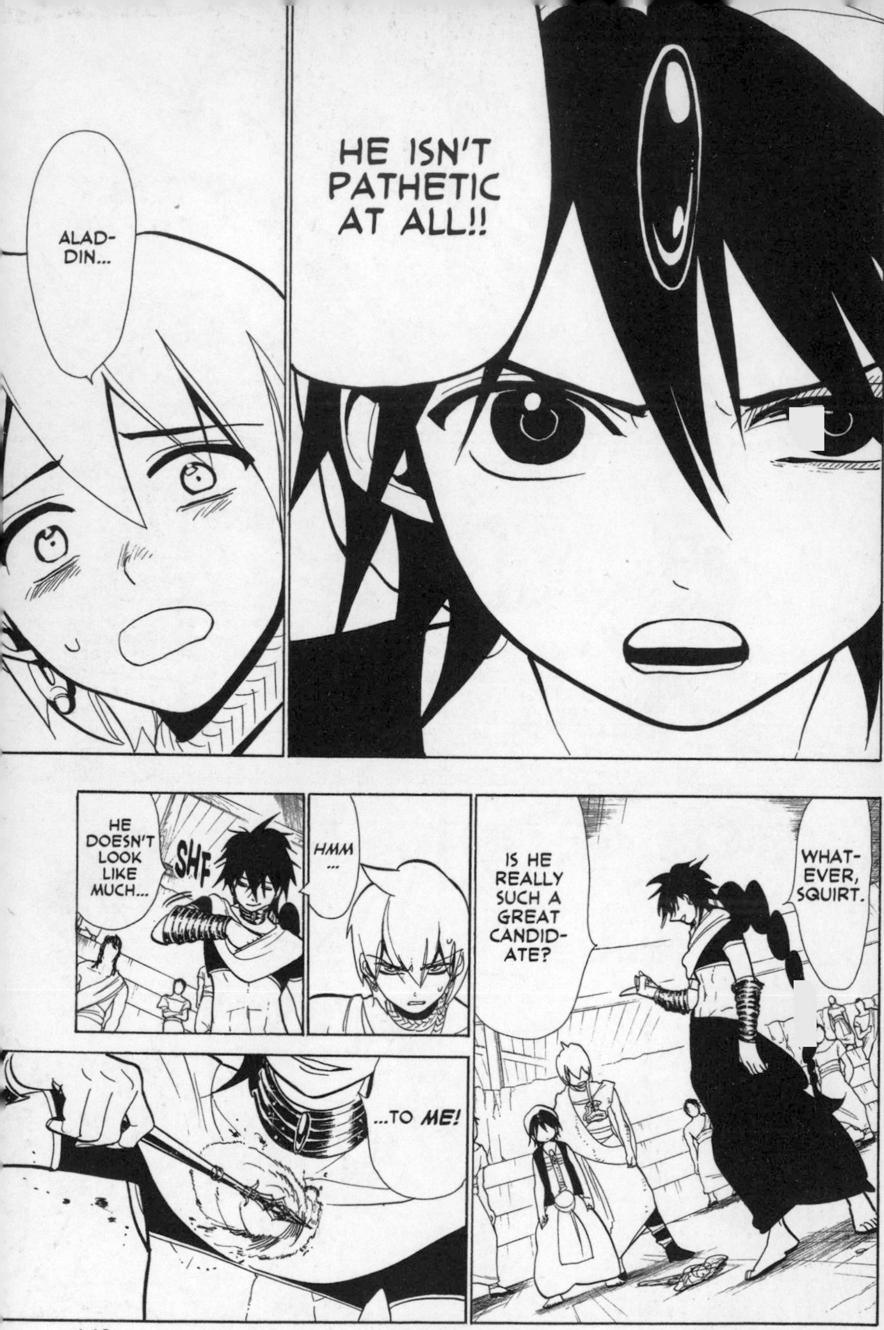
HE ISN'T PATHETIC AT ALL!!
ALAD-DIN...
WHAT-EVER, SQUIRT.
IS HE REALLY SUCH A GREAT CANDID-ATE?
HMM ...
HE DOESN'T LOOK LIKE MUCH...
SHF
...TO ME!

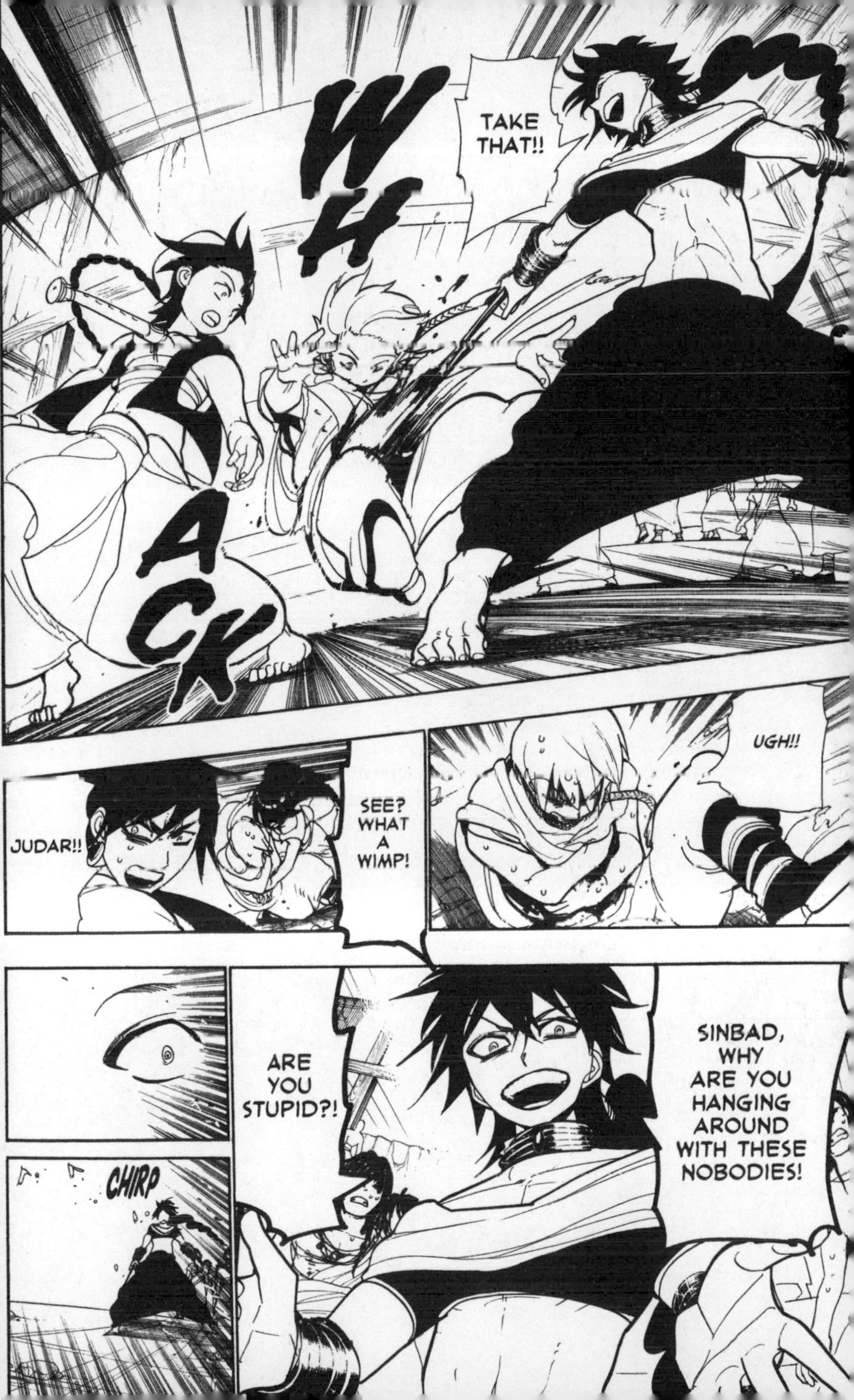
TAKE THAT!!
WHACK
UGH!!
SEE? WHAT A WIMP!
JUDAR!!
SINBAD, WHY ARE YOU HANGING AROUND WITH THESE NOBODIES!
ARE YOU STUPID?!
CHIRP

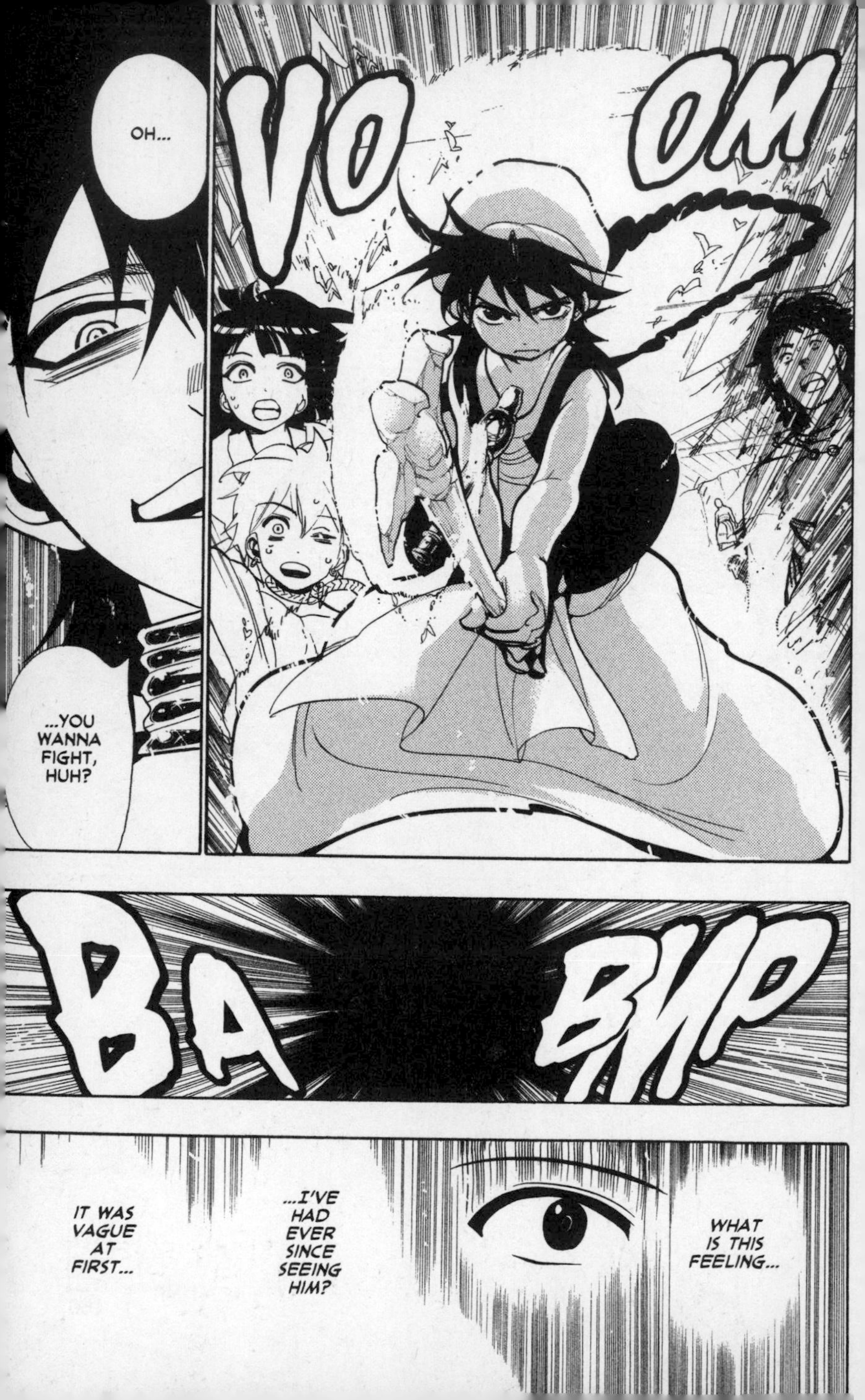
VO OM
OH...
...YOU WANNA FIGHT, HUH?
BA BMP
WHAT IS THIS FEELING...
...I'VE HAD EVER SINCE SEEING HIM?
IT WAS VAGUE AT FIRST...

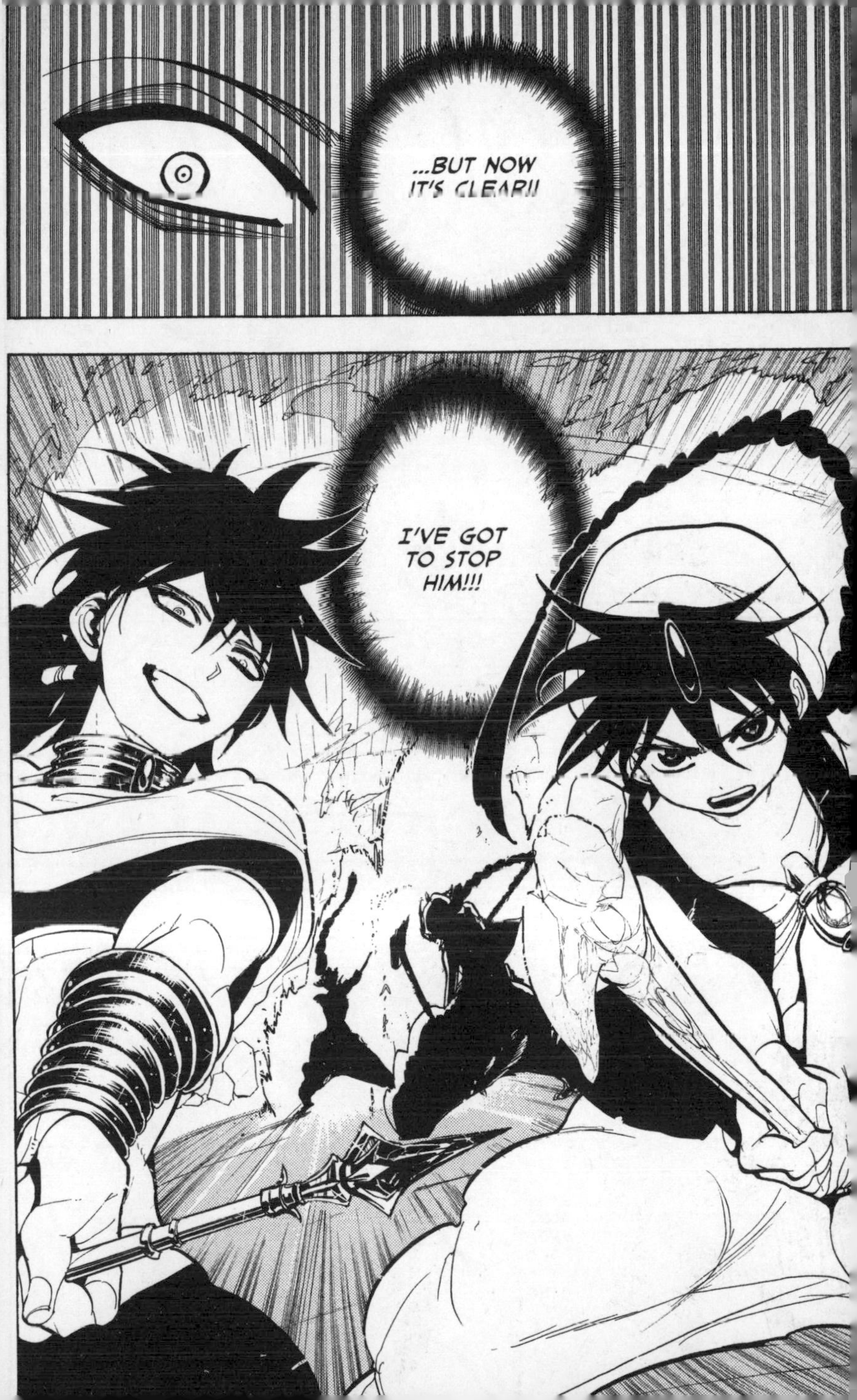
...BUT NOW IT'S CLEAR!!
I'VE GOT TO STOP HIM!!!

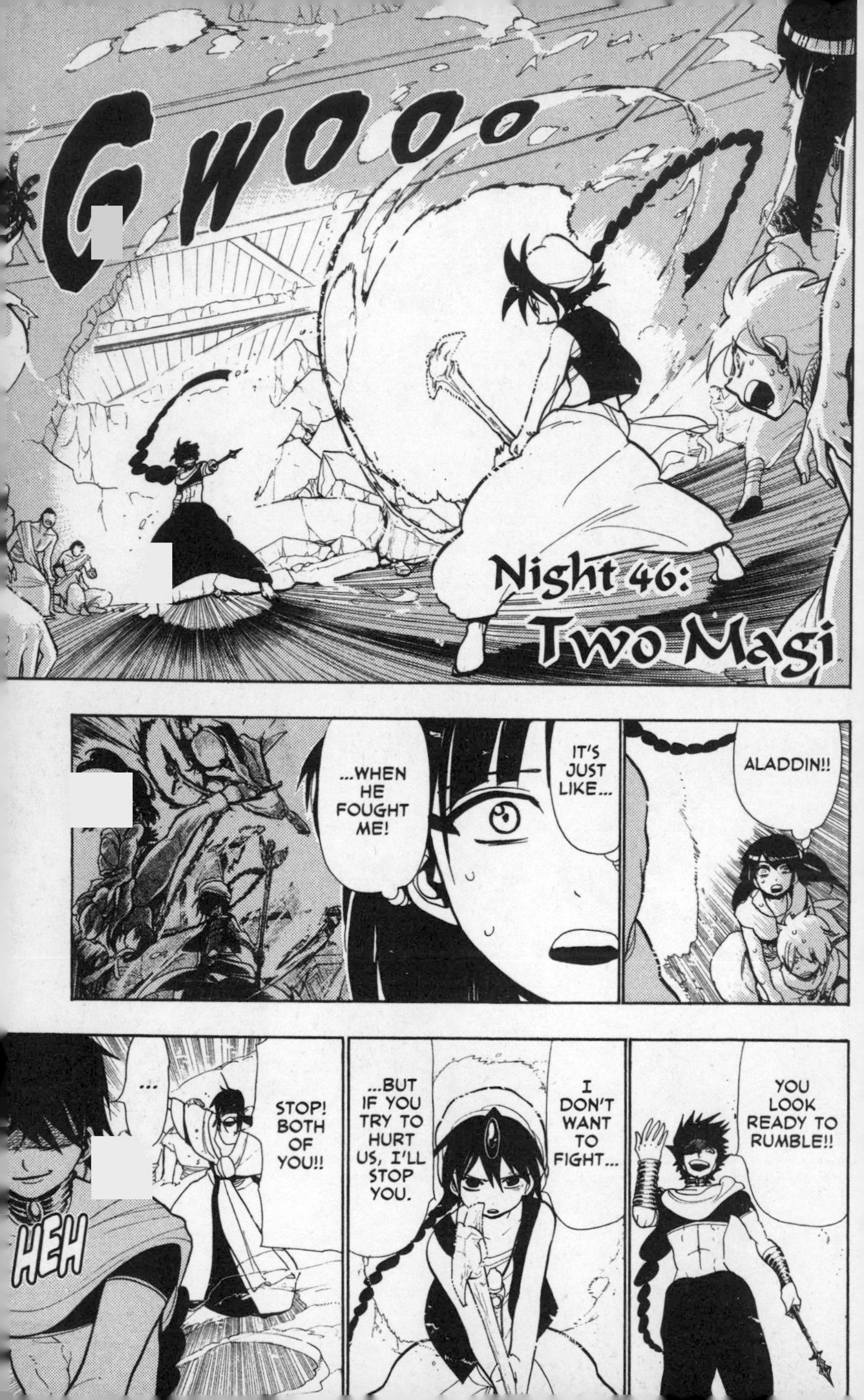
GWOOO
Night 46:
Two Magi
ALADDIN!!
IT'S JUST LIKE...
...WHEN HE FOUGHT ME!
YOU LOOK READY TO RUMBLE!!
I DON'T WANT TO FIGHT...
...BUT IF YOU TRY TO HURT US, I'LL STOP YOU.
STOP! BOTH OF YOU!!
...
HEH

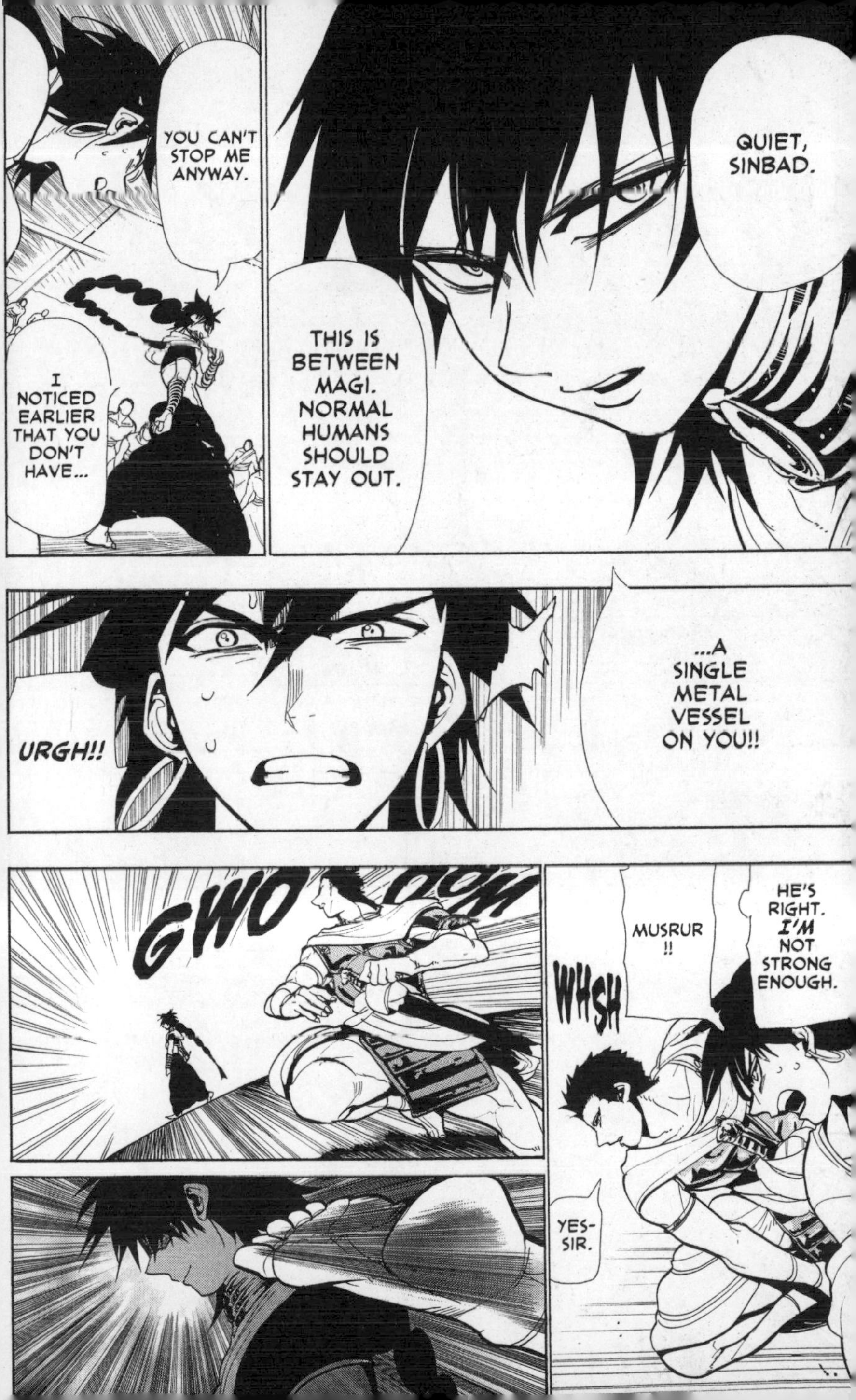
QUIET, SINBAD.
THIS IS BETWEEN MAGI. NORMAL HUMANS SHOULD STAY OUT.
YOU CAN'T STOP ME ANYWAY.
I NOTICED EARLIER THAT YOU DON'T HAVE...
...A SINGLE METAL VESSEL ON YOU!!
URGH!!
HE'S RIGHT. I'M NOT STRONG ENOUGH.
MUSRUR !!
WHSH
YES-SIR.
GWOOOM

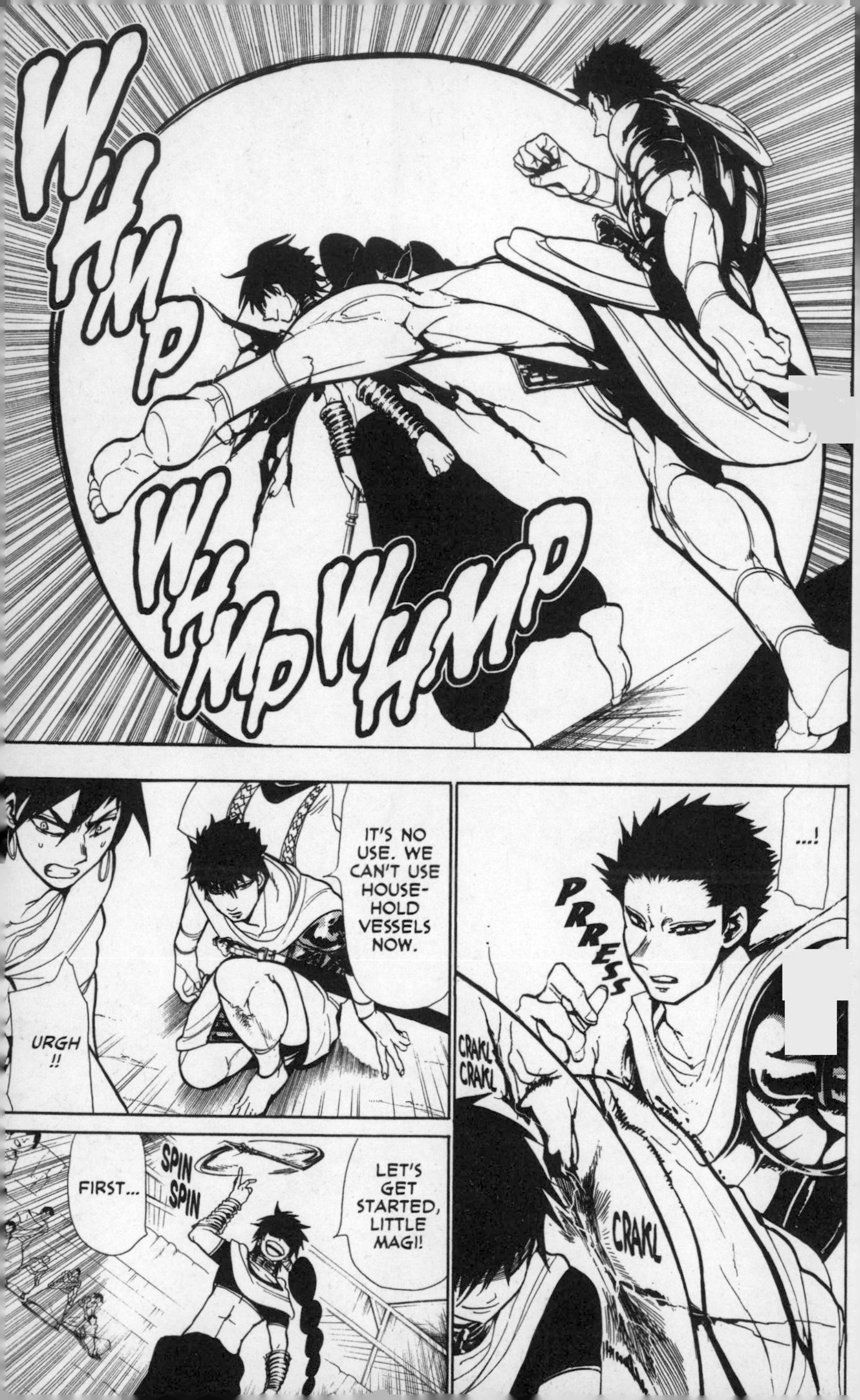
WHAMP
WHAMP
WHAMP
...!
PRRESS
CRAKL CRAKL
CRAKL
IT'S NO USE. WE CAN'T USE HOUSE-HOLD VESSELS NOW.
URGH !!
LET'S GET STARTED, LITTLE MAGI!
SPIN SPIN
FIRST...

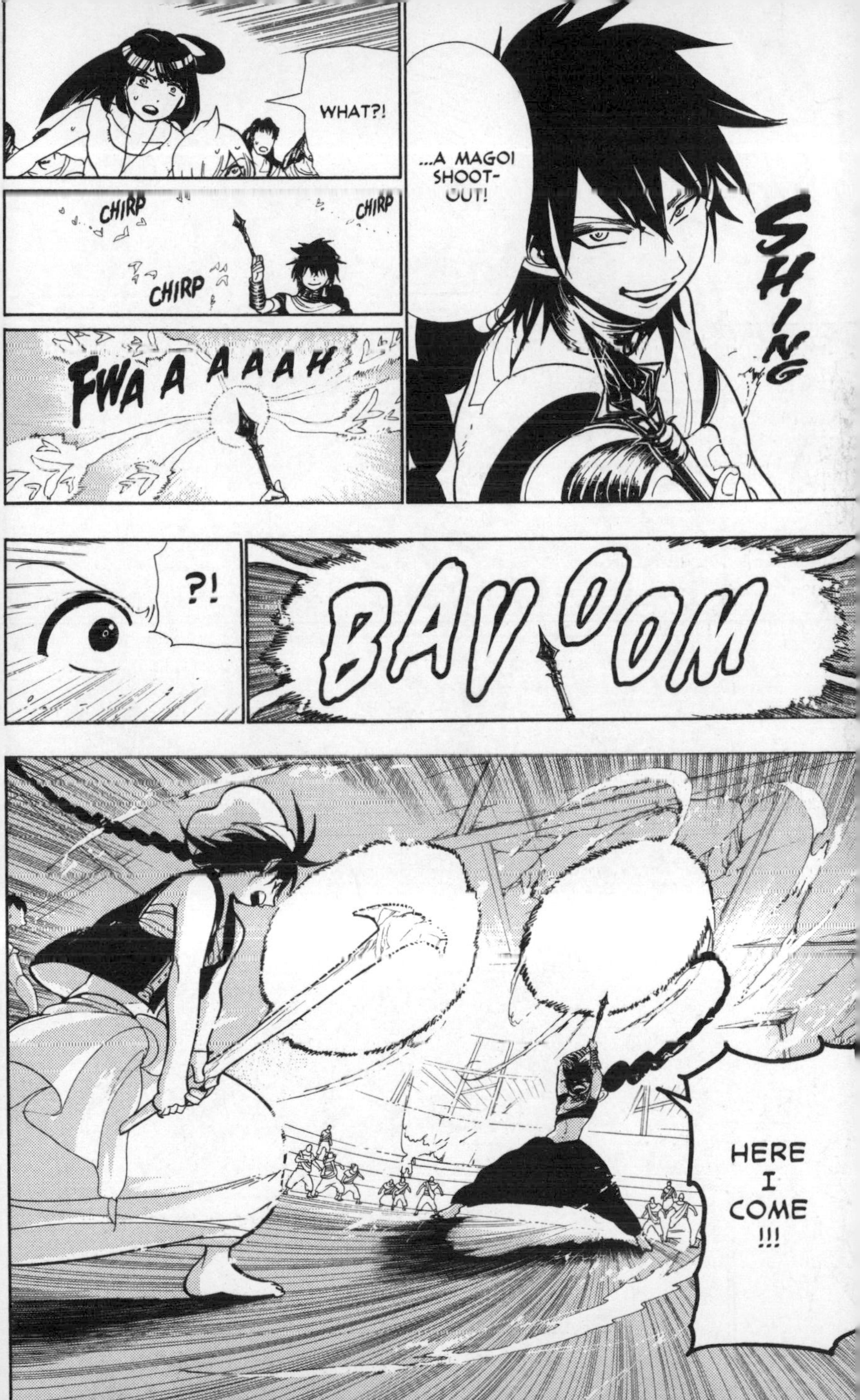
...A MAGOI SHOOT-OUT!
SHING
WHAT?!
CHIRP
CHIRP
CHIRP
FWA A A A A H
BAVOOM
?!
HERE I COME!!!

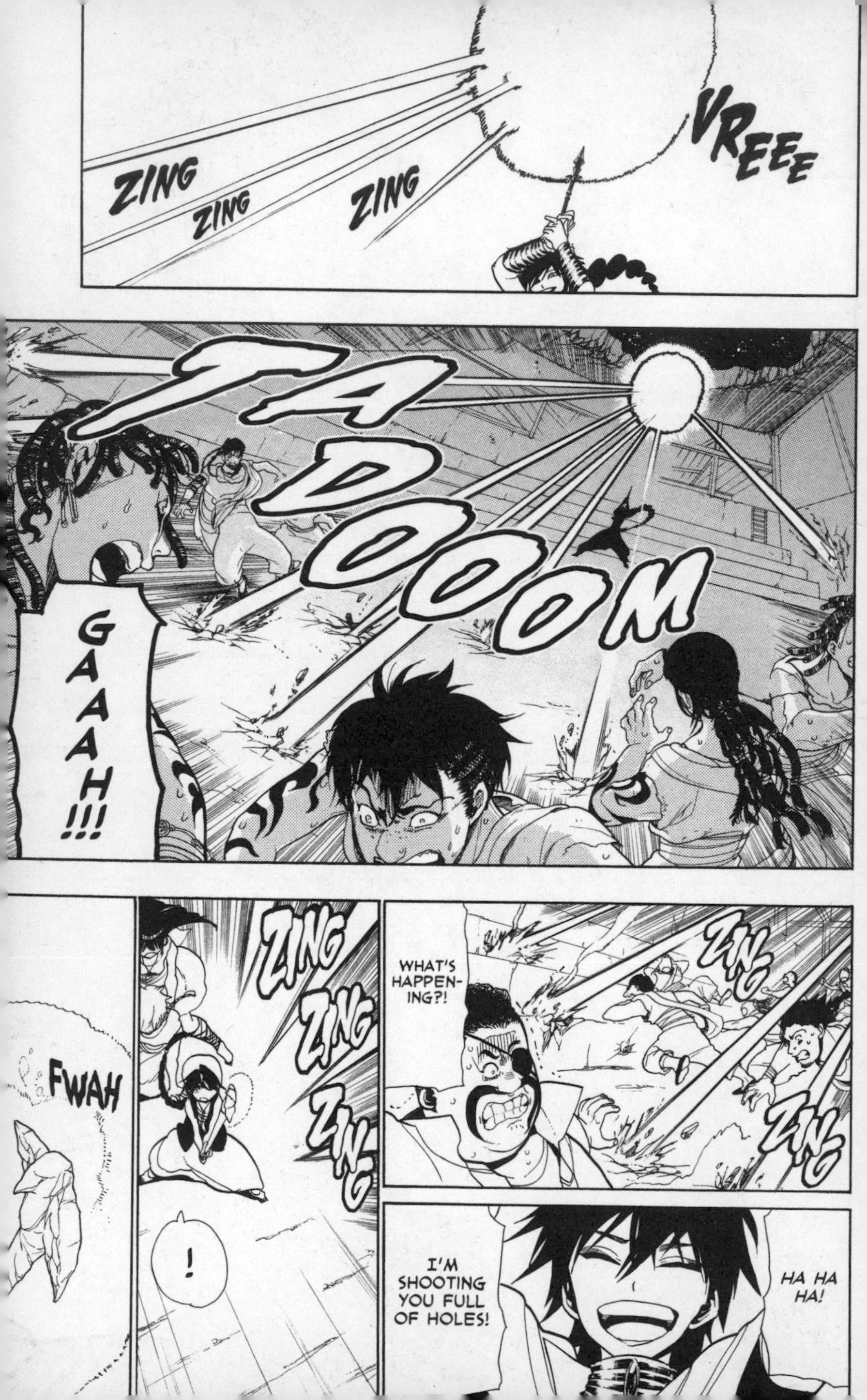
VREEE
ZING
ZING
ZING
TA
DOOOM
GAAAH!!!
WHAT'S HAPPEN-ING?!
ZING
ZING
HA HA HA!
I'M SHOOTING YOU FULL OF HOLES!
ZING
ZING
ZING
!
FWAH

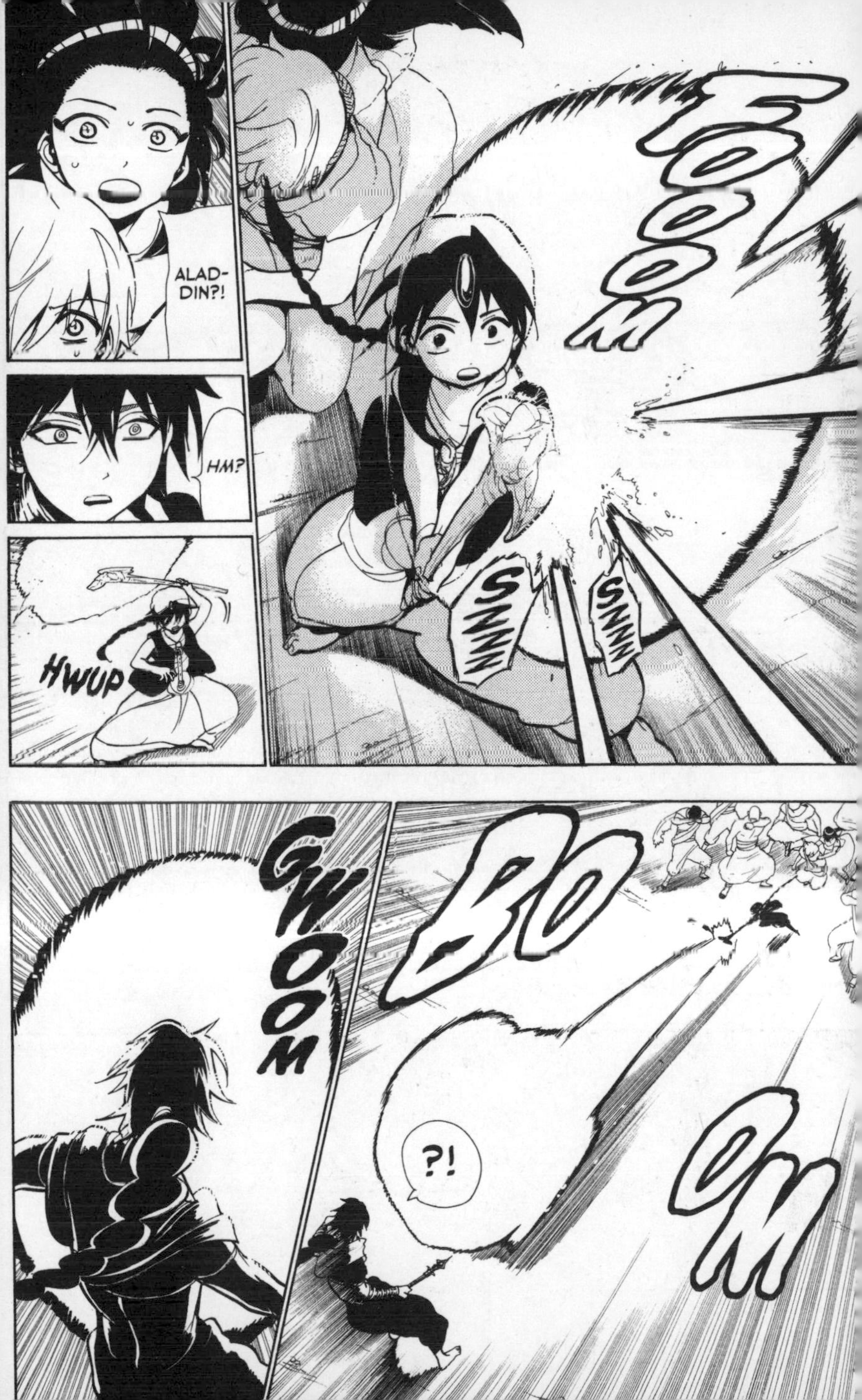
FOOOOOM
SNNN
SNNN
ALAD-DIN?!
HM?
HWUP
BOOM
?!
GWOOOM

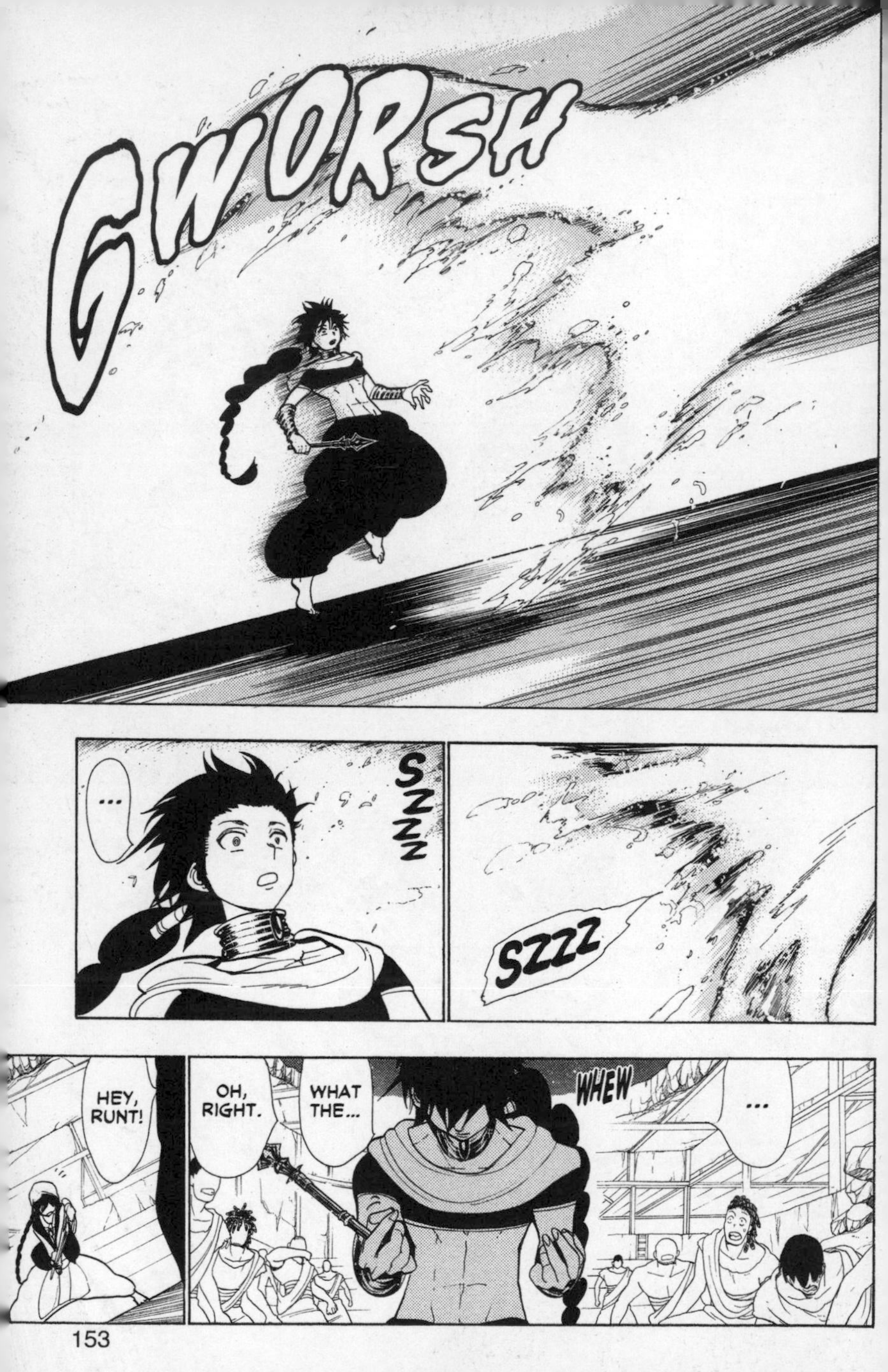
GWORSH
SZZZ
...
SZZZ
...
WHEW
WHAT THE...
OH, RIGHT.
HEY, RUNT!

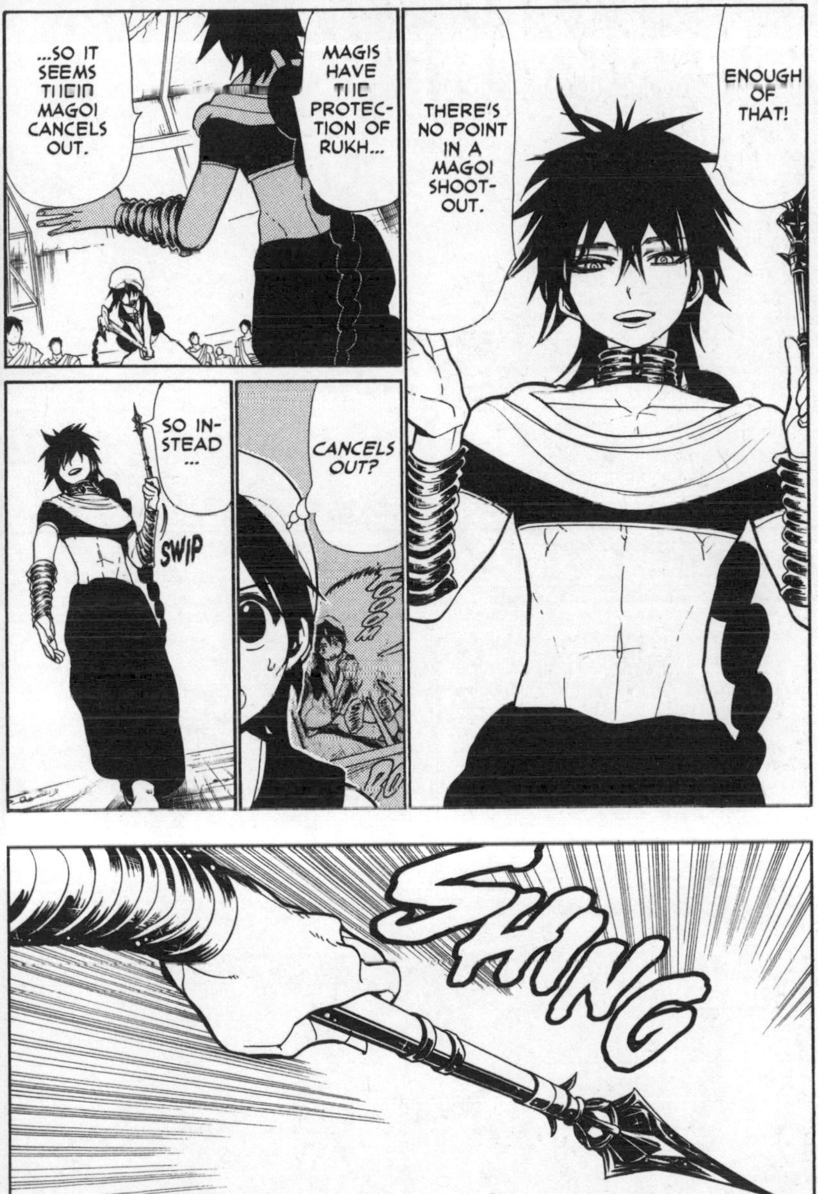

ENOUGH OF THAT!
THERE'S NO POINT IN A MAGOI SHOOT-OUT.
MAGIS HAVE THE PROTECTION OF RUKH...
...SO IT SEEMS THEIR MAGOI CANCELS OUT.
CANCELS OUT?
SO IN-STEAD ...
SWIP
SHING

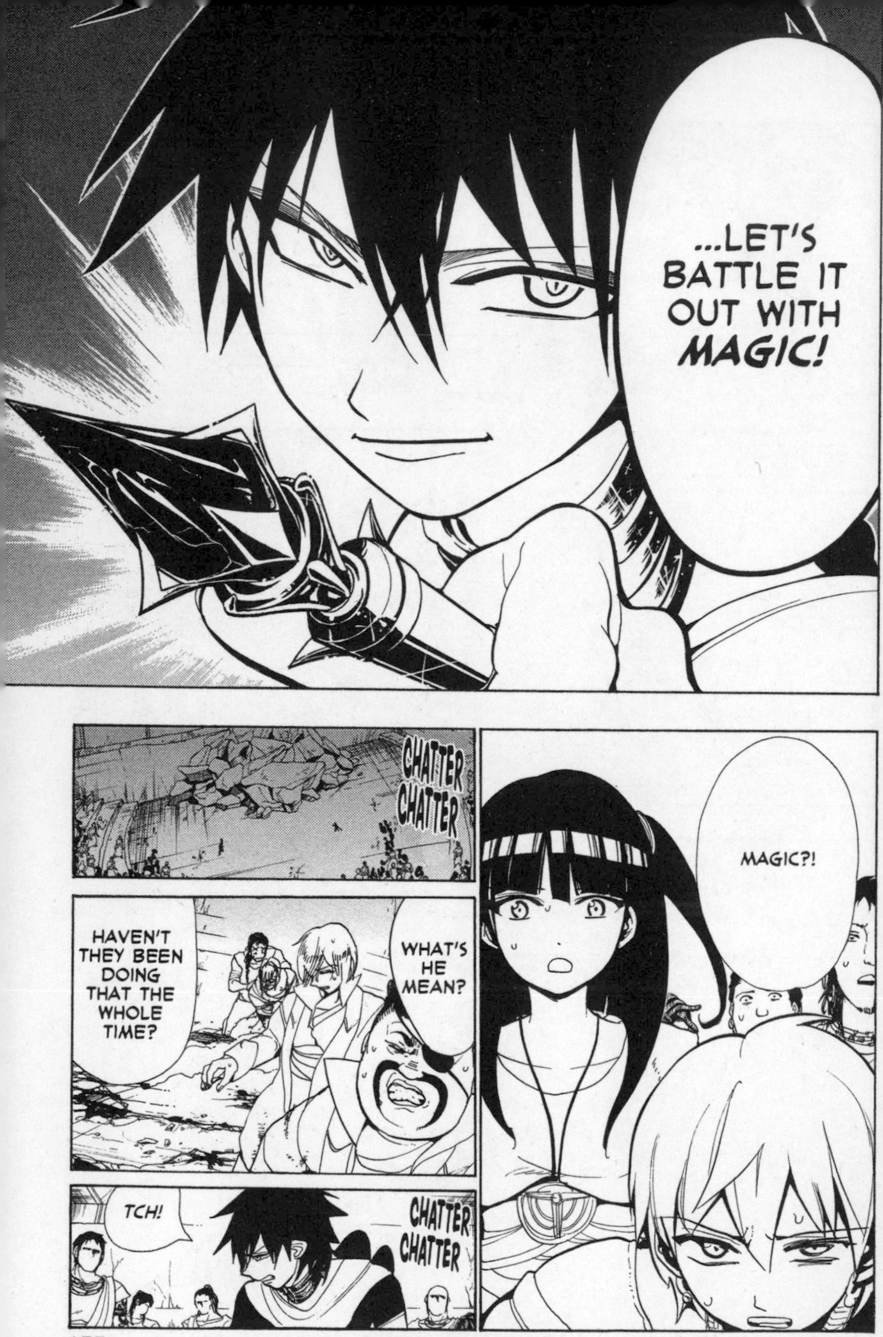
...LET'S BATTLE IT OUT WITH MAGIC!
MAGIC?!
CHATTER CHATTER
WHAT'S HE MEAN?
HAVEN'T THEY BEEN DOING THAT THE WHOLE TIME?
CHATTER CHATTER
TCH!

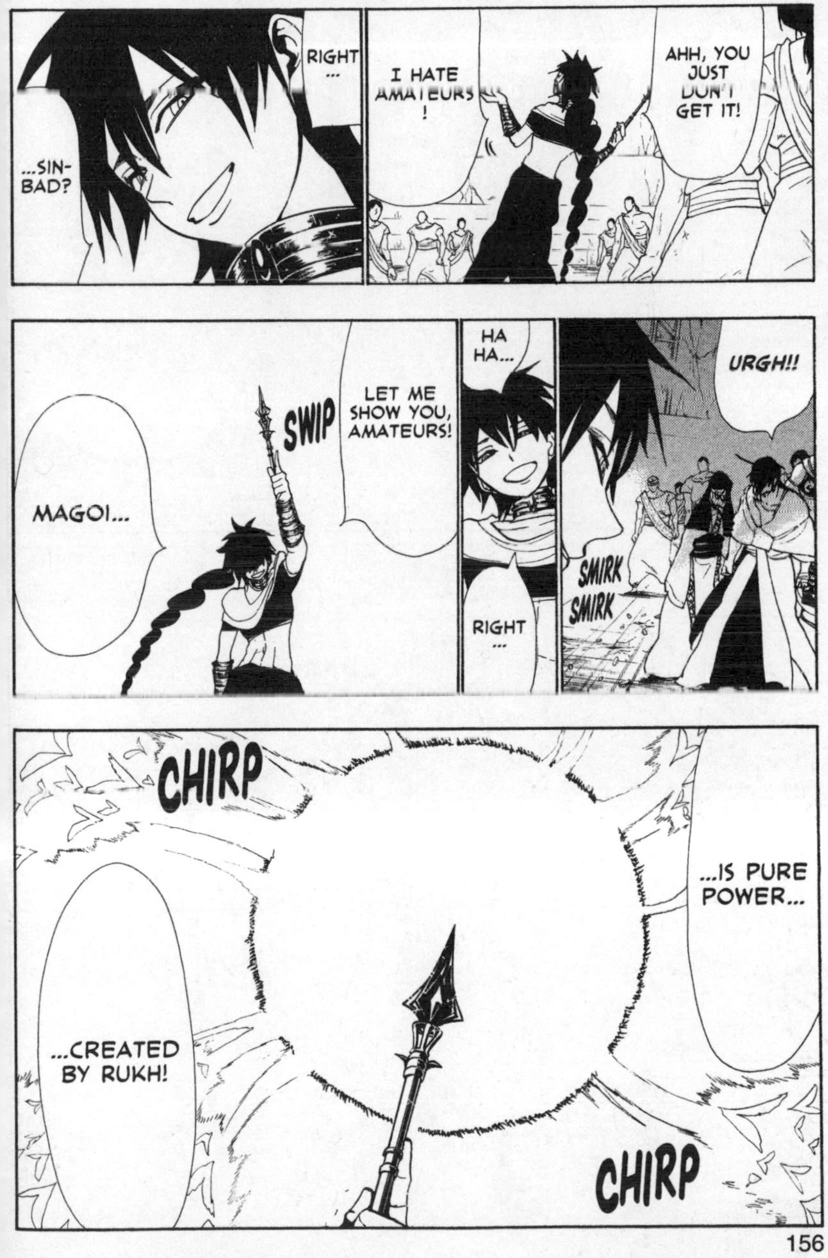
AHH, YOU JUST DON'T GET IT!
I HATE AMATEURS!
RIGHT...
...SIN-BAD?
URGH!!
SMIRK SMIRK
HA HA...
RIGHT...
LET ME SHOW YOU, AMATEURS!
SWIP
MAGOI...
CHIRP
...IS PURE POWER...
...CREATED BY RUKH!
CHIRP

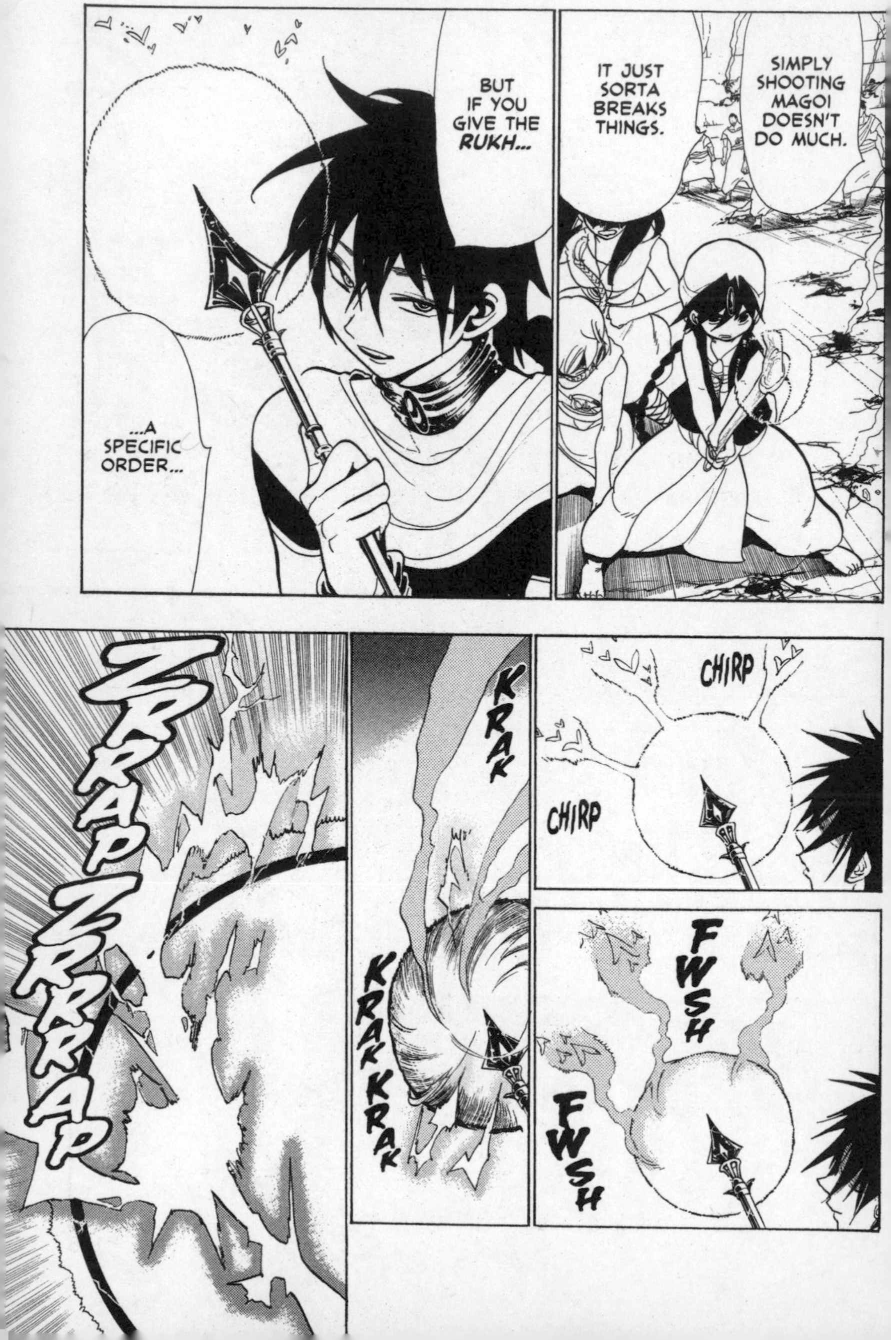
SIMPLY SHOOTING MAGOI DOESN'T DO MUCH.
IT JUST SORTA BREAKS THINGS.
BUT IF YOU GIVE THE *RUKH*...
...A SPECIFIC ORDER...
CHIRP
CHIRP
FWSH
FWSH
KRAK
KRAKKRAK
ZRRAP
ZRRAP

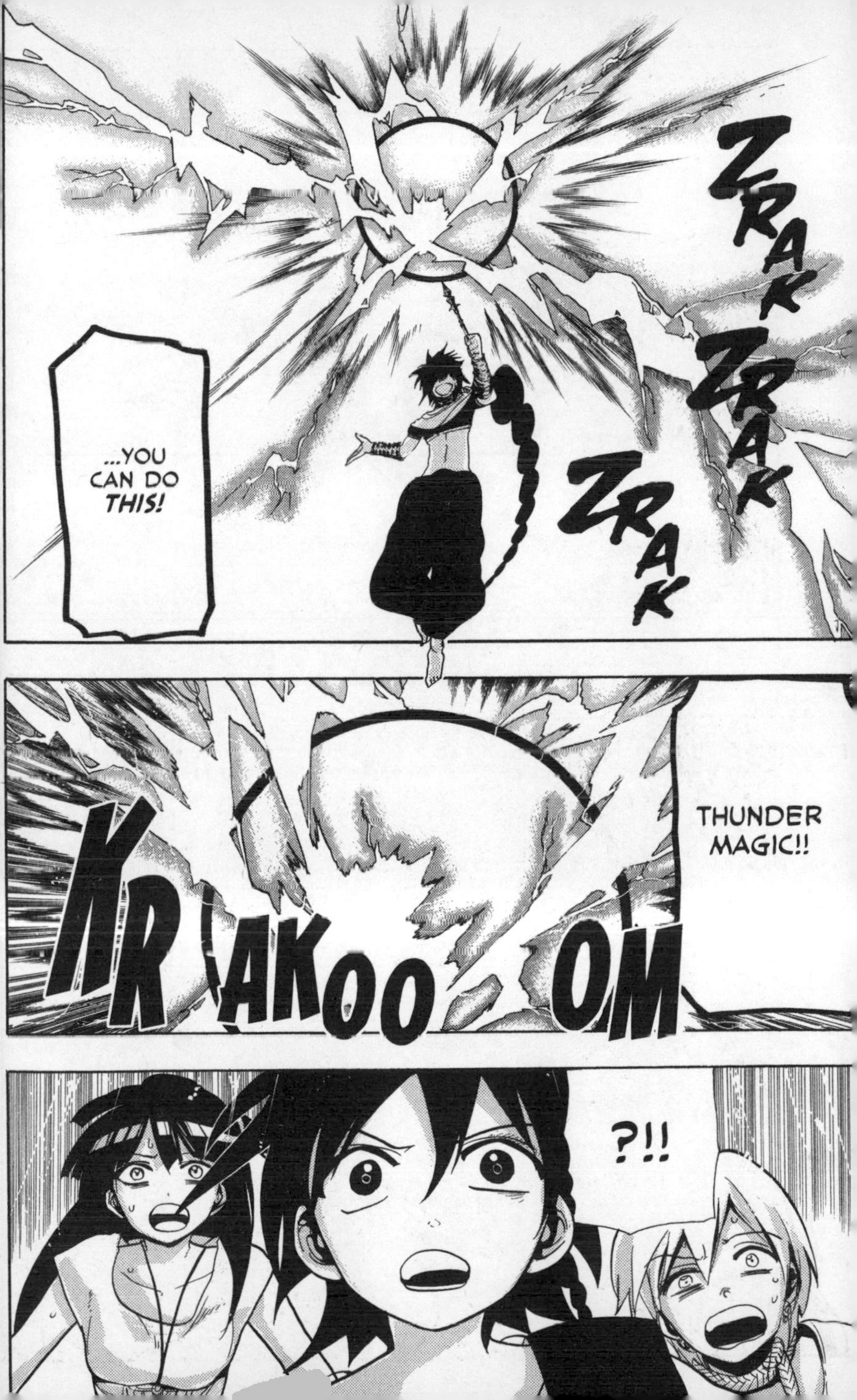
ZRAK ZRAK ZRAK
...YOU CAN DO THIS!
THUNDER MAGIC!!
KRAKOOOM
?!!

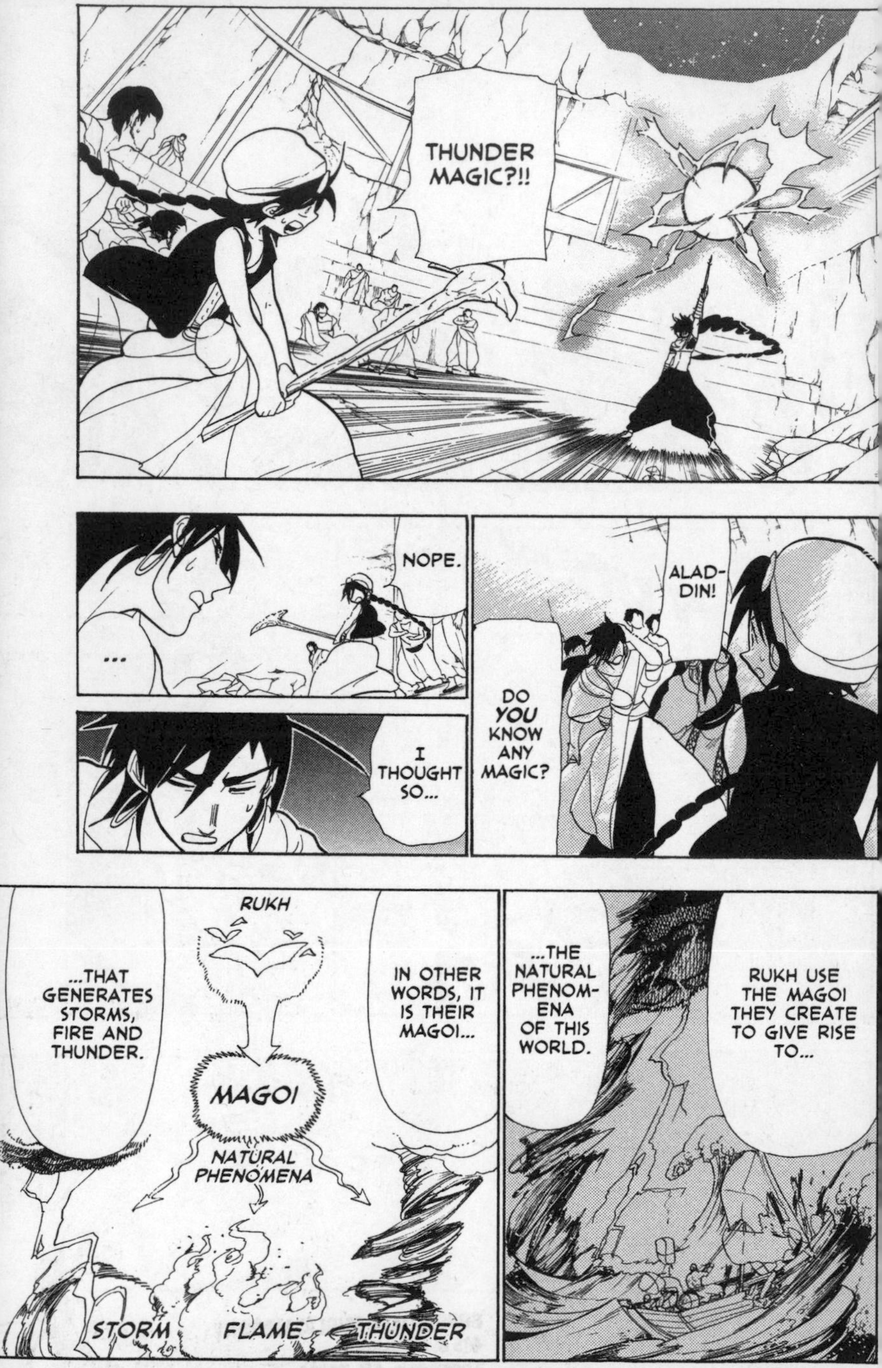
THUNDER MAGIC?!!
ALAD-DIN!
DO YOU KNOW ANY MAGIC?
NOPE.
...
I THOUGHT SO...
RUKH USE THE MAGOI THEY CREATE TO GIVE RISE TO...
...THE NATURAL PHENOMENA OF THIS WORLD.
IN OTHER WORDS, IT IS THEIR MAGOI...
RUKH
MAGOI
NATURAL PHENOMENA
STORM
FLAME
THUNDER
...THAT GENERATES STORMS, FIRE AND THUNDER.

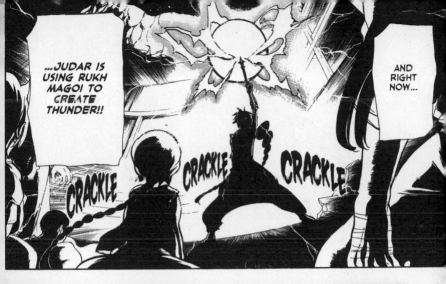

...JUDAR IS USING RUKH MAGOI TO CREATE THUNDER!!

CRACKLE

CRACKLE

CRACKLE

AND RIGHT NOW...

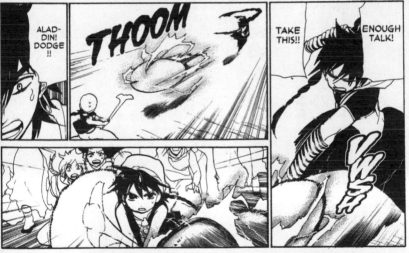

ALAD-DIN! DODGE!!

THOOM

TAKE THIS!!

ENOUGH TALK!

VWSH

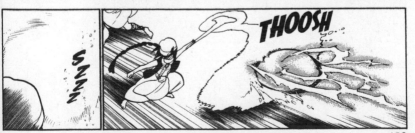

SZZZ

THOOSH

160

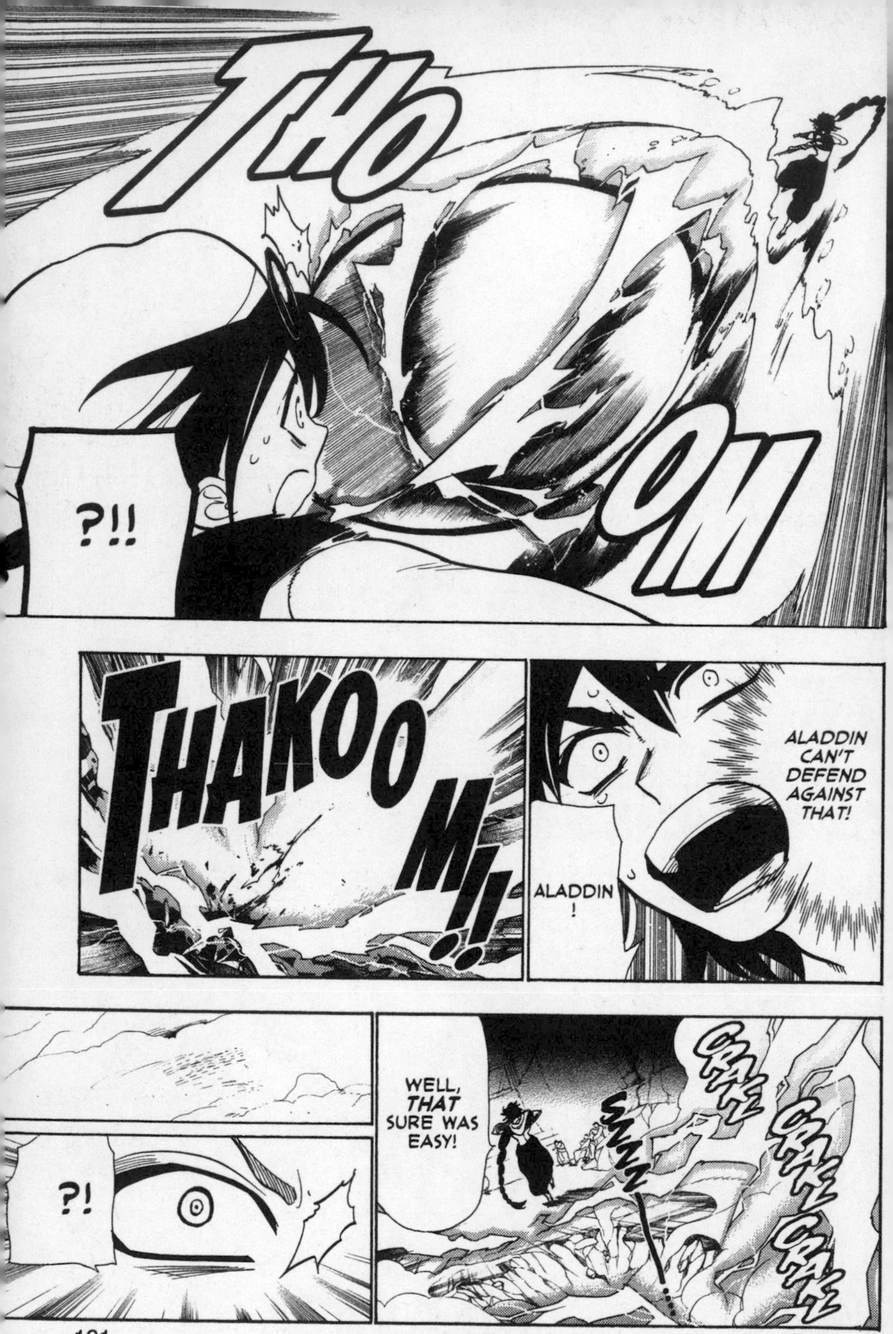
THO
OM
?!!
ALADDIN CAN'T DEFEND AGAINST THAT!
ALADDIN!
THAKOOM!!
CRAK
CRAK CRAK CRAK
SWNNN—...
WELL, *THAT* SURE WAS EASY!
?!

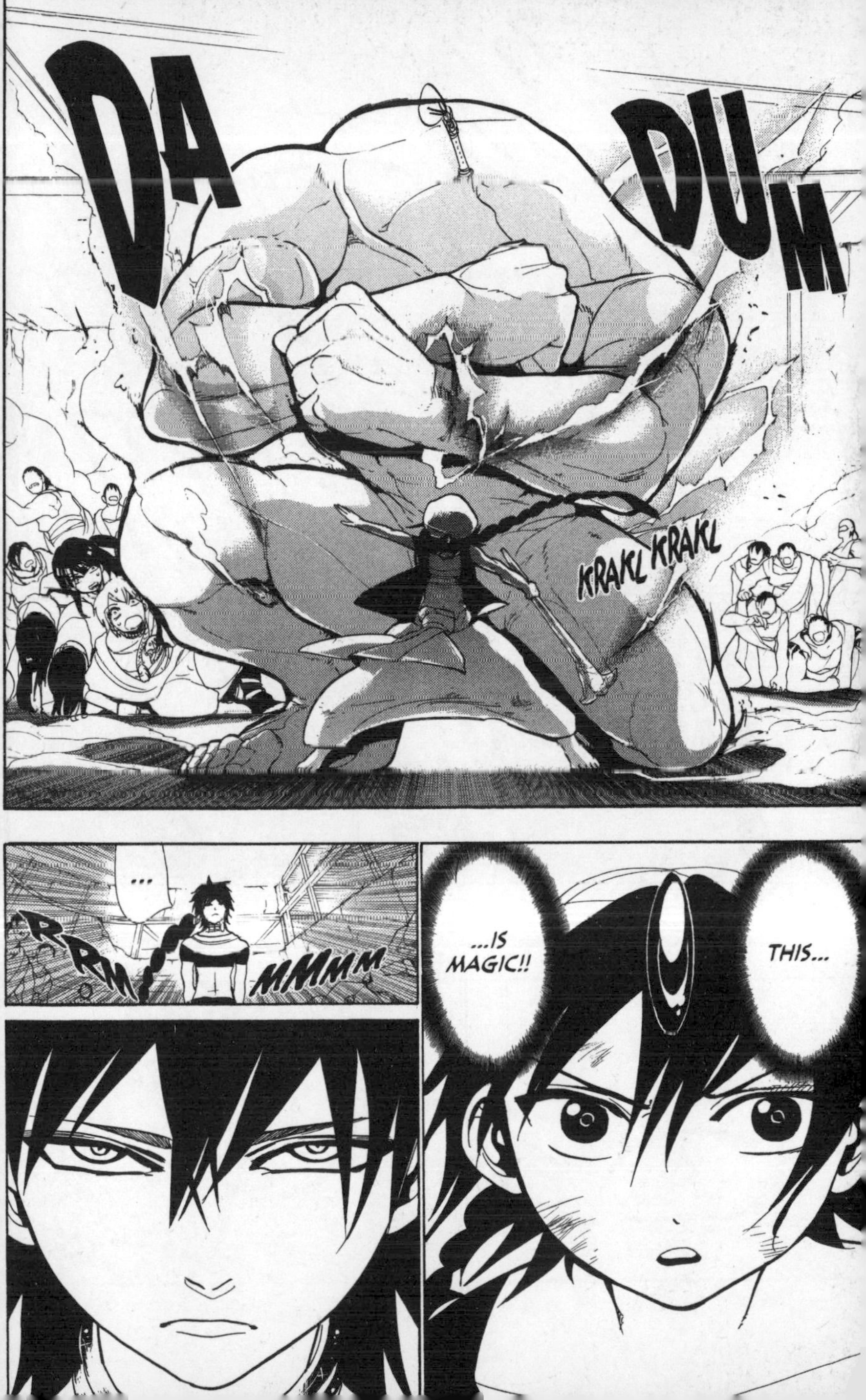
DA DUM
KRAKL KRAKL
THIS...
...IS MAGIC!!
...
RRRM MMMM

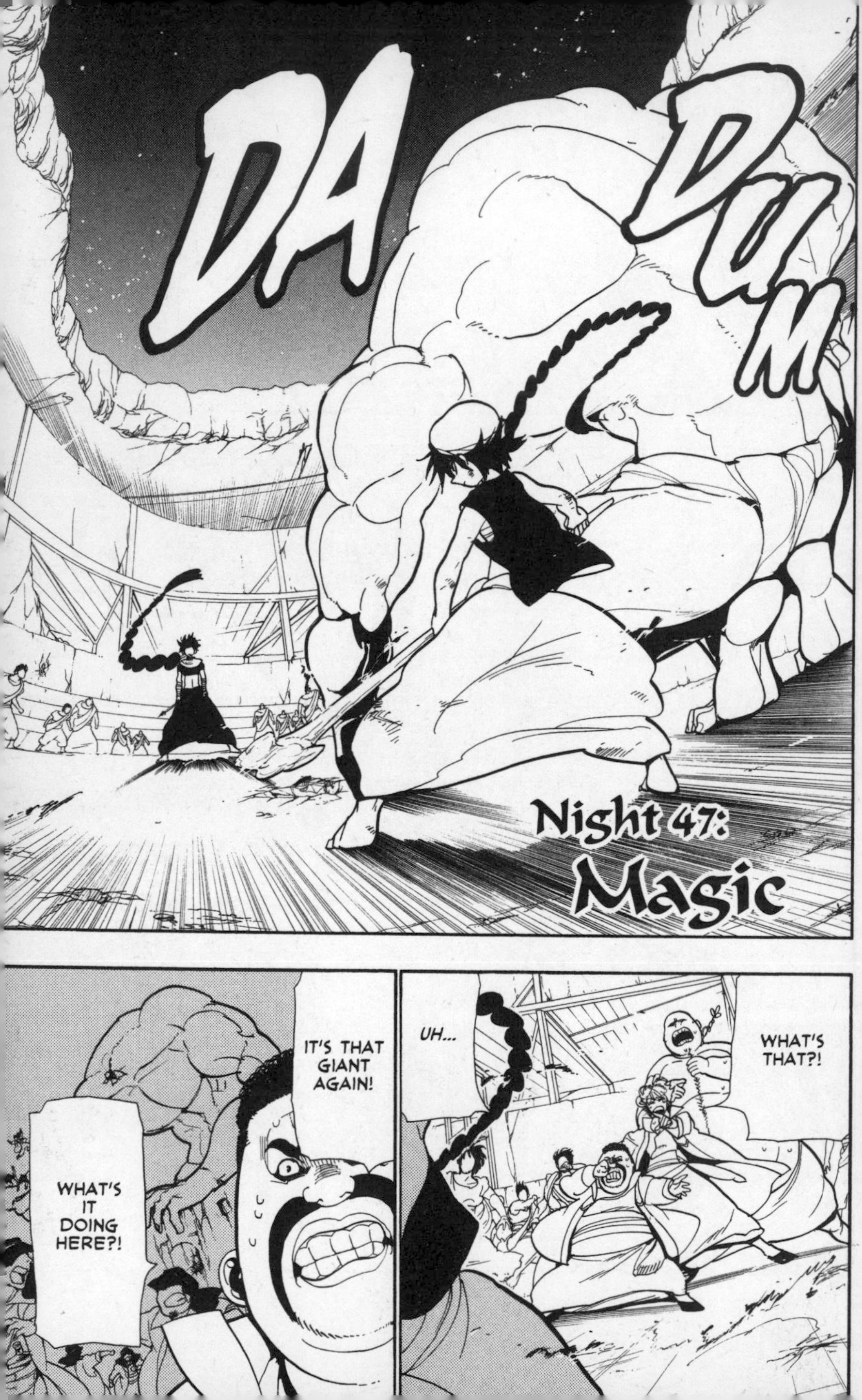
DA DUM
Night 47: Magic
WHAT'S THAT?!
UH...
IT'S THAT GIANT AGAIN!
WHAT'S IT DOING HERE?!

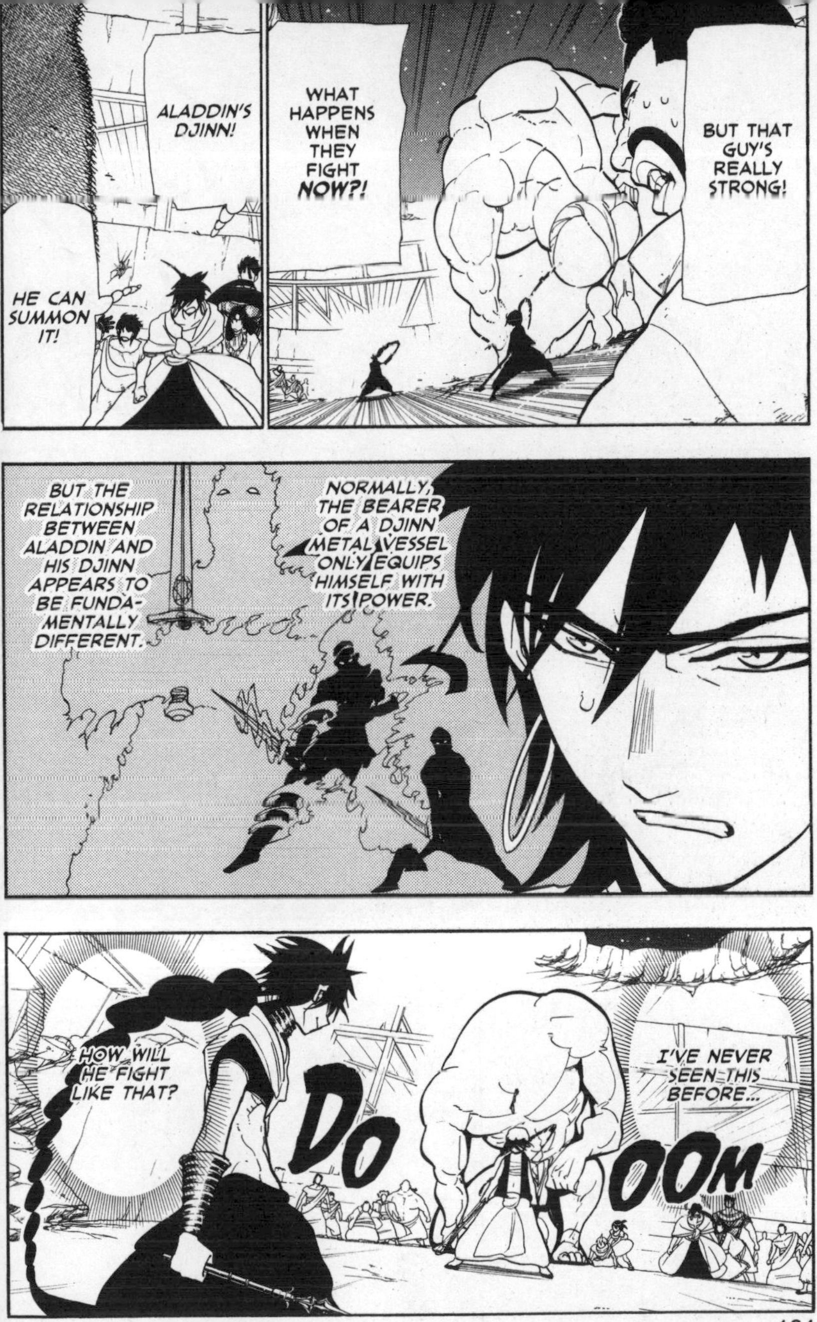
BUT THAT GUY'S REALLY STRONG!
WHAT HAPPENS WHEN THEY FIGHT NOW?!
ALADDIN'S DJINN!
HE CAN SUMMON IT!
NORMALLY, THE BEARER OF A DJINN METAL VESSEL ONLY EQUIPS HIMSELF WITH ITS POWER.
BUT THE RELATIONSHIP BETWEEN ALADDIN AND HIS DJINN APPEARS TO BE FUNDA-MENTALLY DIFFERENT.
I'VE NEVER SEEN THIS BEFORE...
DOOOM
HOW WILL HE FIGHT LIKE THAT?

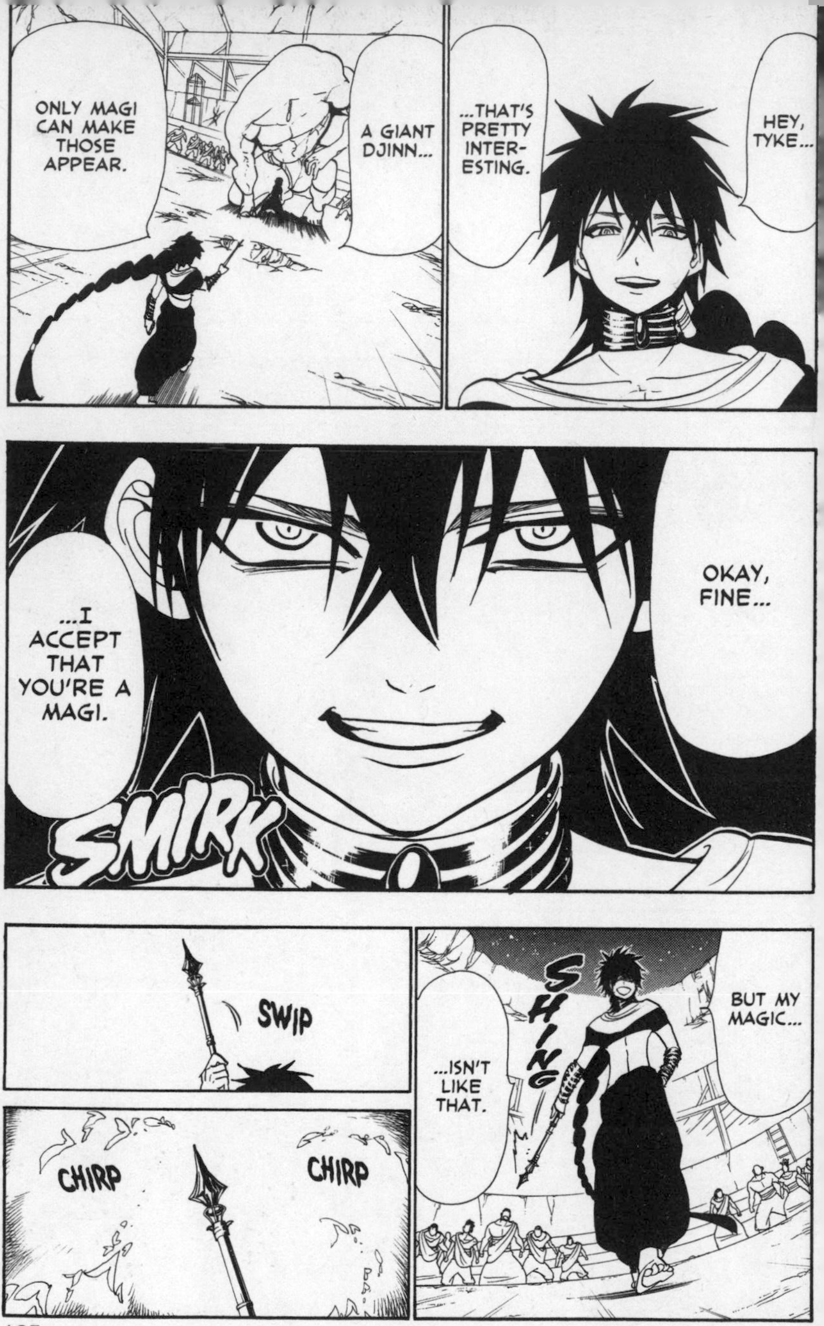
HEY, TYKE...
...THAT'S PRETTY INTERESTING.
A GIANT DJINN...
ONLY MAGI CAN MAKE THOSE APPEAR.
OKAY, FINE...
...I ACCEPT THAT YOU'RE A MAGI.
SMIRK
BUT MY MAGIC...
SHING
...ISN'T LIKE THAT.
SWIP
CHIRP
CHIRP

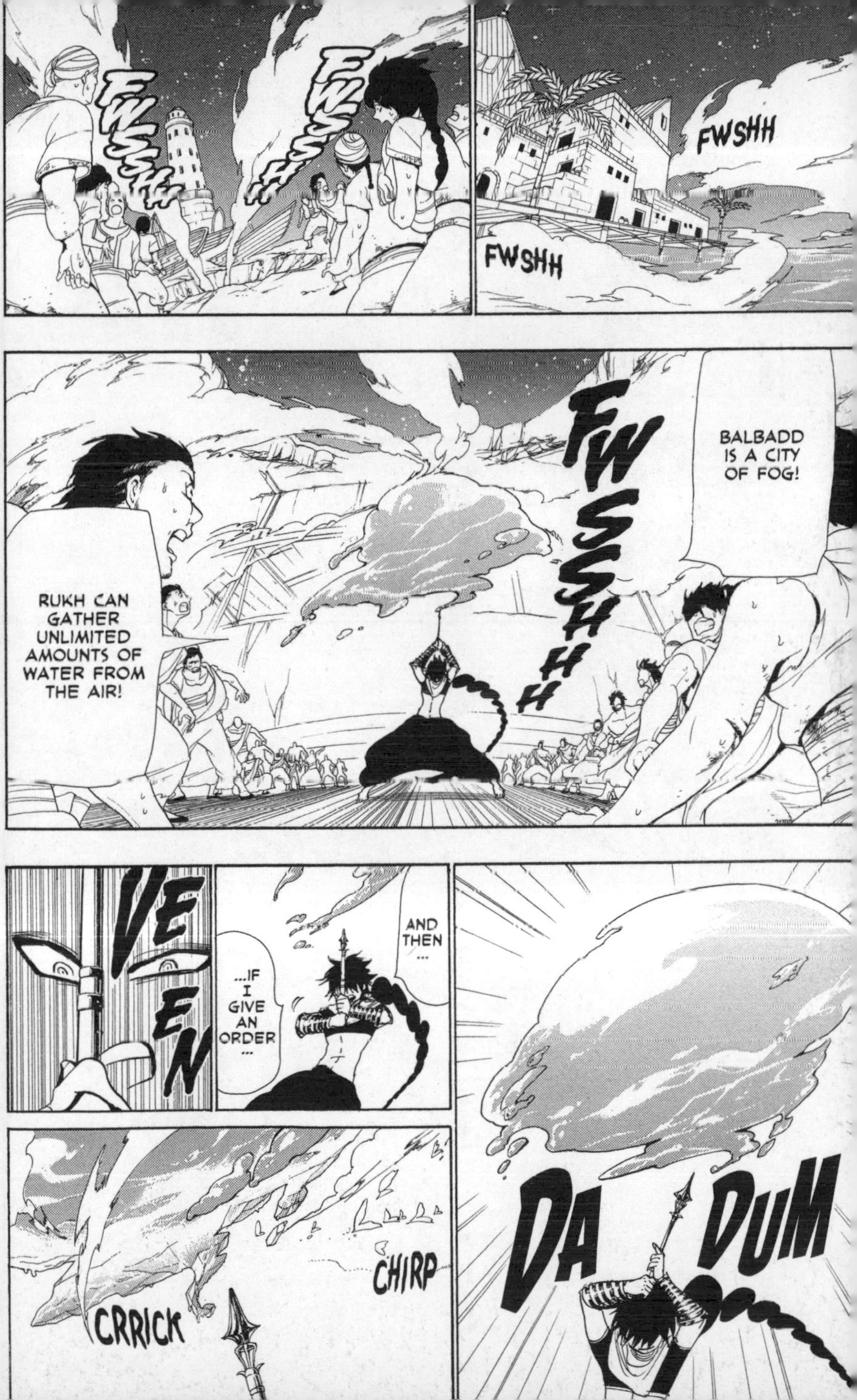
FWSHH
FWSHH
FWSSHH
FWSSHH
BALBADD IS A CITY OF FOG!
FWSSHHH
RUKH CAN GATHER UNLIMITED AMOUNTS OF WATER FROM THE AIR!
DA DUM
AND THEN ...
...IF I GIVE AN ORDER ...
VEEN
CHIRP
CRRICK

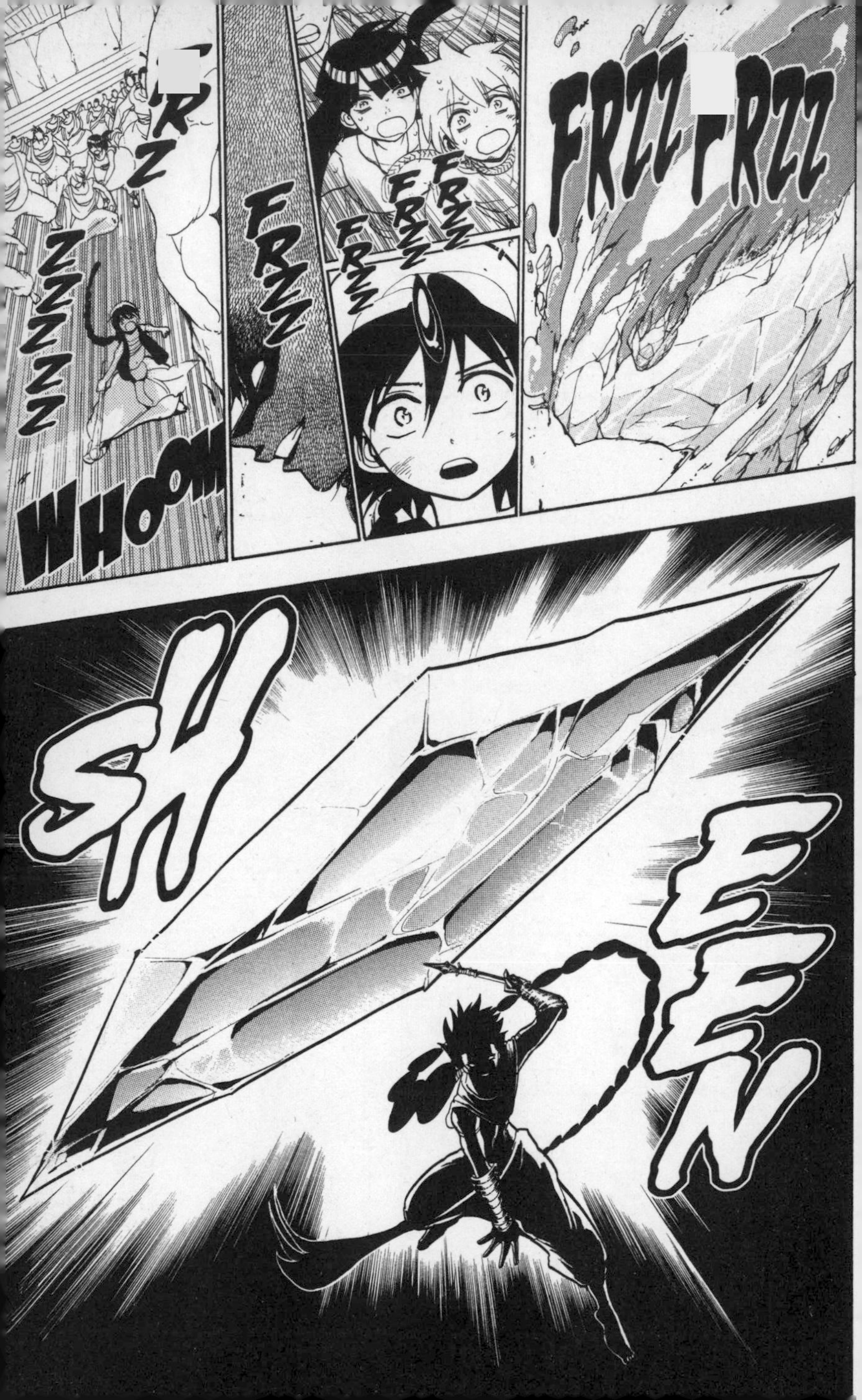
FRZZ RZZ
FRZZ
FRZZ
FRZZ
FRZZ
RZZ ZZZZZZZ
WHOOM
SHEEEN

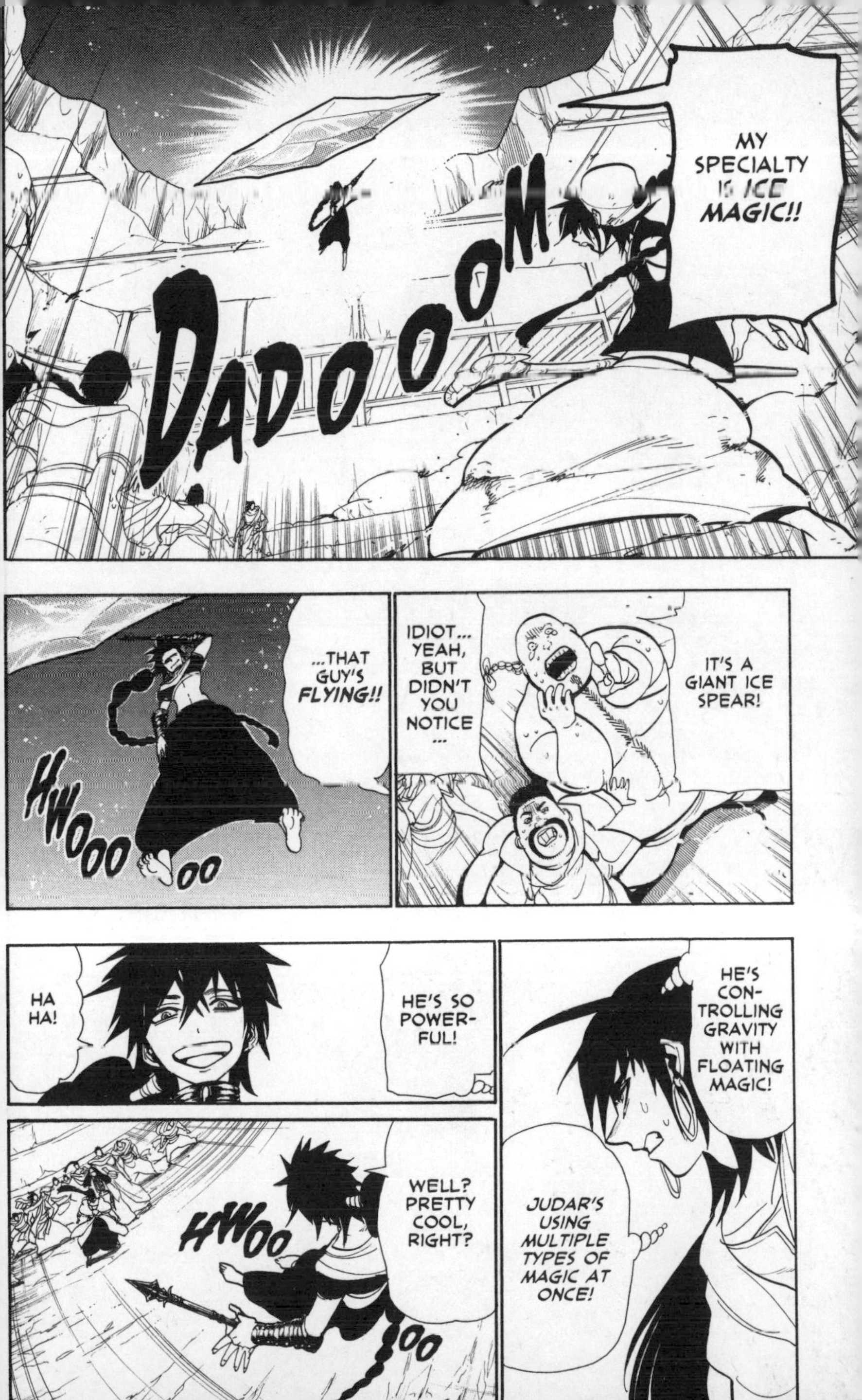
MY SPECIALTY IS ICE MAGIC!!
DADOOOOM
IT'S A GIANT ICE SPEAR!
IDIOT... YEAH, BUT DIDN'T YOU NOTICE...
...THAT GUY'S FLYING!!
HWOOOOOOO
HE'S CON-TROLLING GRAVITY WITH FLOATING MAGIC!
JUDAR'S USING MULTIPLE TYPES OF MAGIC AT ONCE!
HE'S SO POWER-FUL!
HA HA!
WELL? PRETTY COOL, RIGHT?
HWOOOO

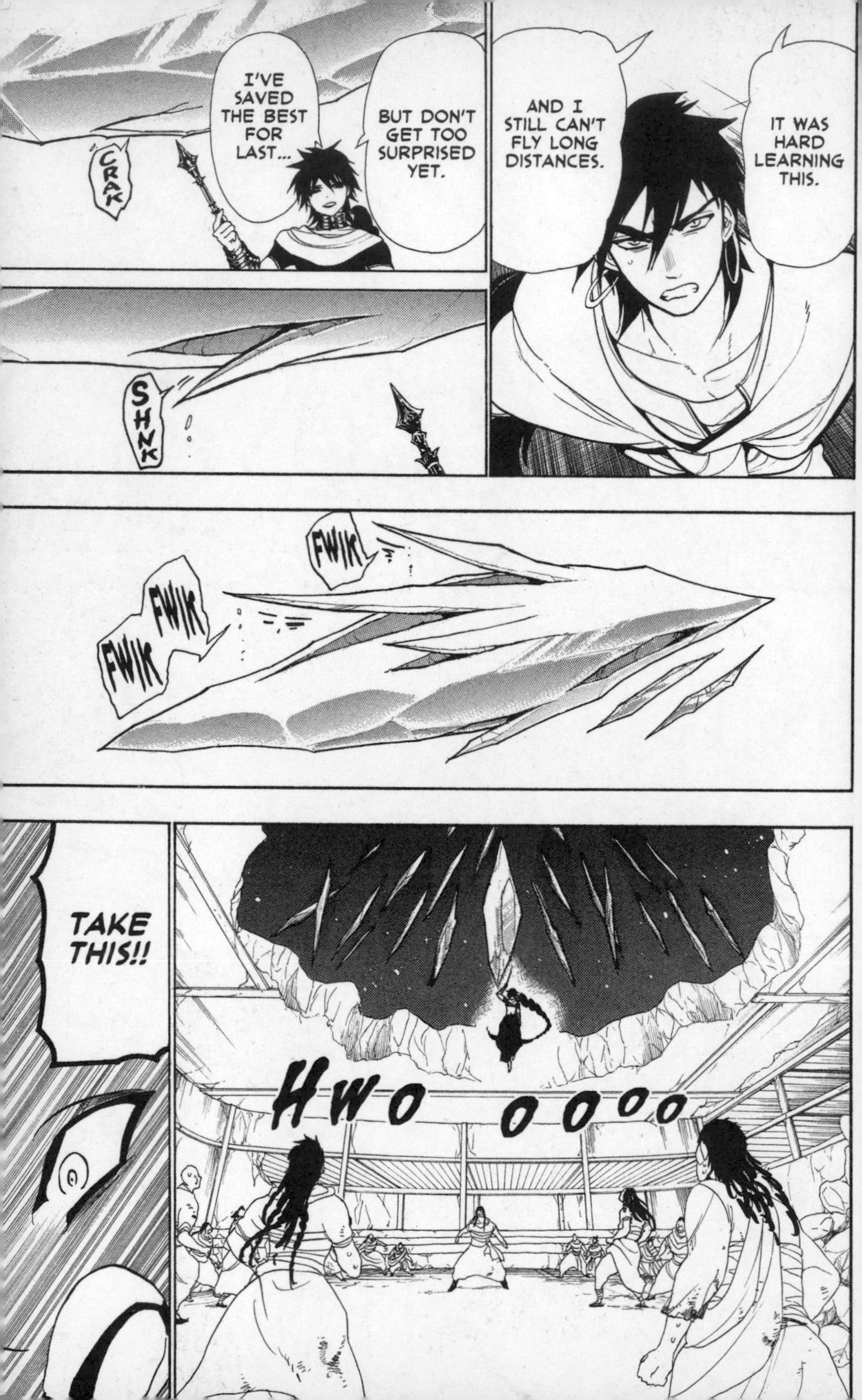

IT WAS HARD LEARNING THIS.
AND I STILL CAN'T FLY LONG DISTANCES.
BUT DON'T GET TOO SURPRISED YET.
I'VE SAVED THE BEST FOR LAST...
CRAK
SHNK
FWIK
FWIK
FWIK
HWOOOOO
TAKE THIS!!

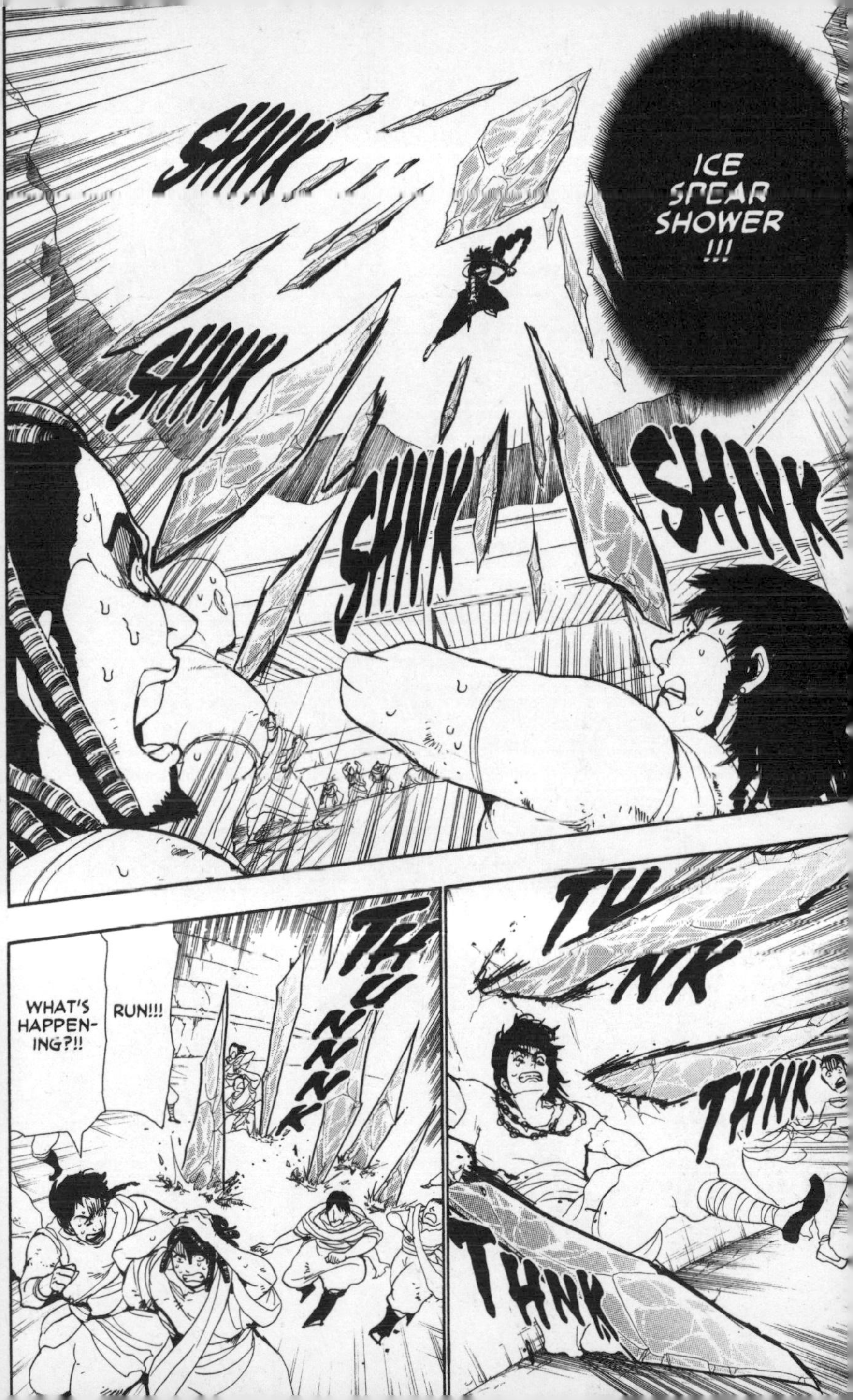
ICE SPEAR SHOWER!!!
SHINK
SHINK
SHINK
SHINK
THNK
THNK
THNK
THUNNNK
RUN!!!
WHAT'S HAPPEN-ING?!!

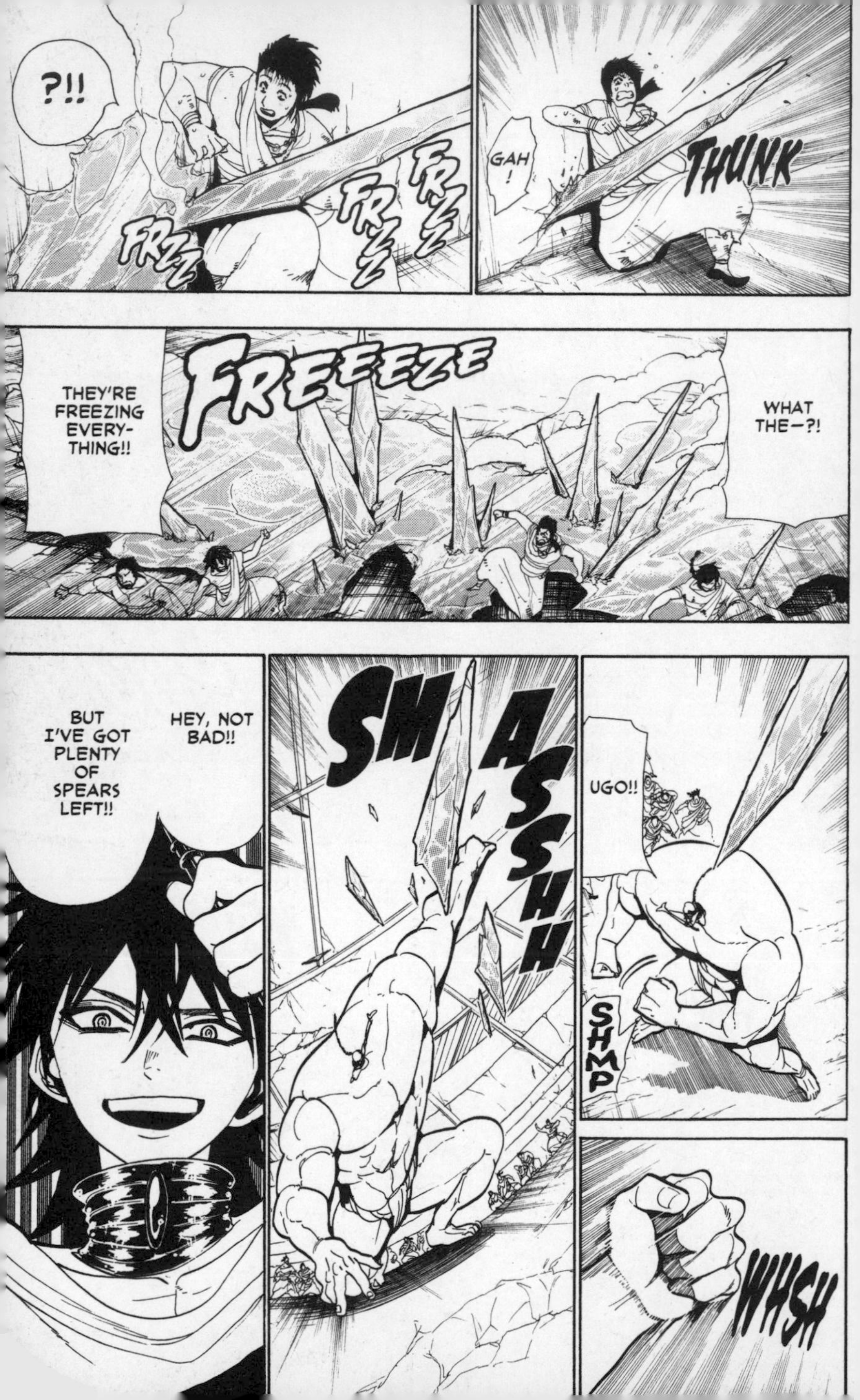
GAH!
THUNK
?!!
FRZZ
FRZZ
FRZZ
WHAT THE—?!
FREEEZE
THEY'RE FREEZING EVERY-THING!!
UGO!!
SHMP
WHSH
SMASHH
HEY, NOT BAD!!
BUT I'VE GOT PLENTY OF SPEARS LEFT!!

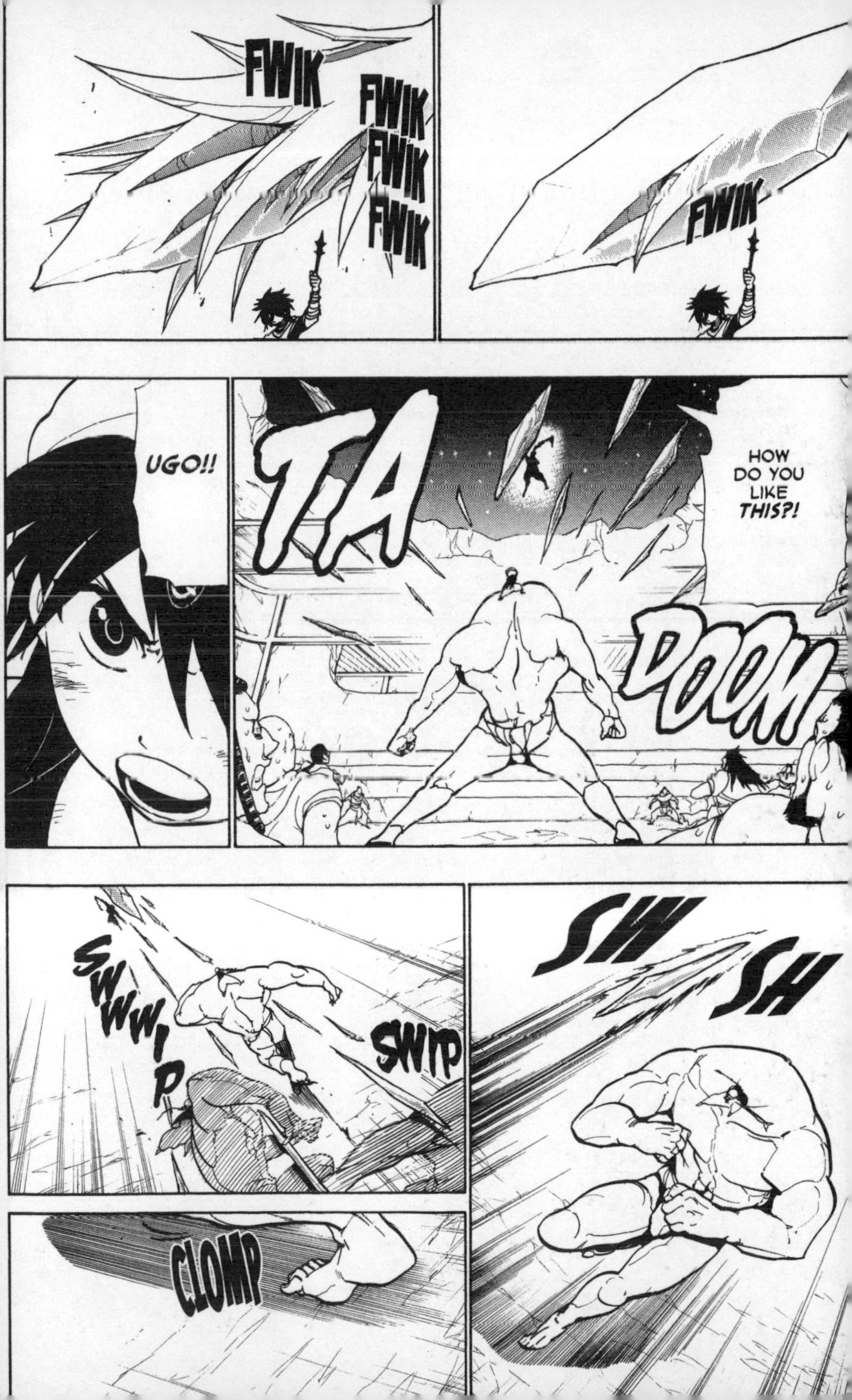
FWIK
FWIK
FWIK
FWIK
FWIK
HOW DO YOU LIKE THIS?!
DOOM
TA
UGO!!
SH
SH
SWIP
SWWWIP
CLOMP

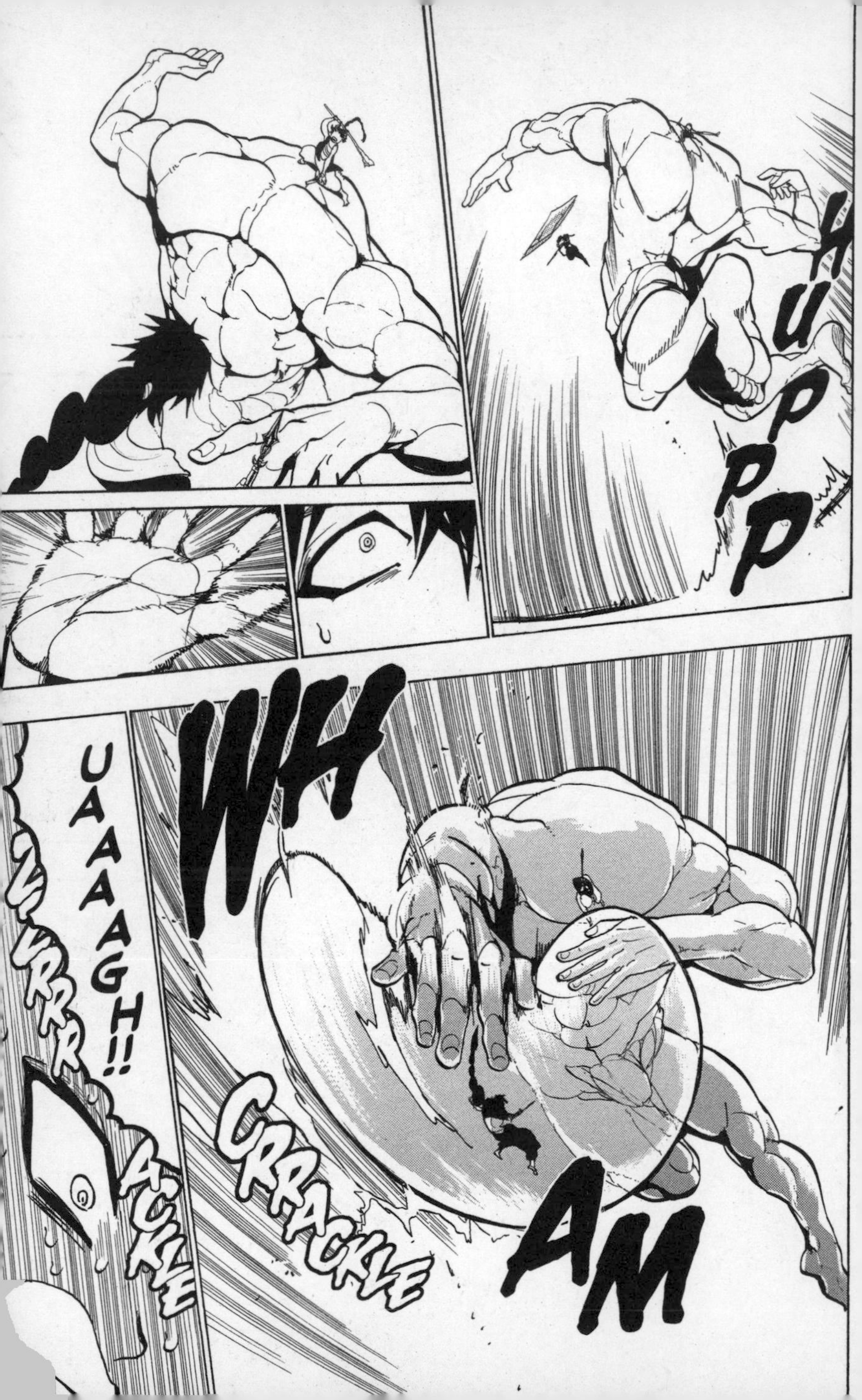
HUPPPP
WH
AM
CRRACKLE
UAAAAGH!!
VURRR
ACKLE

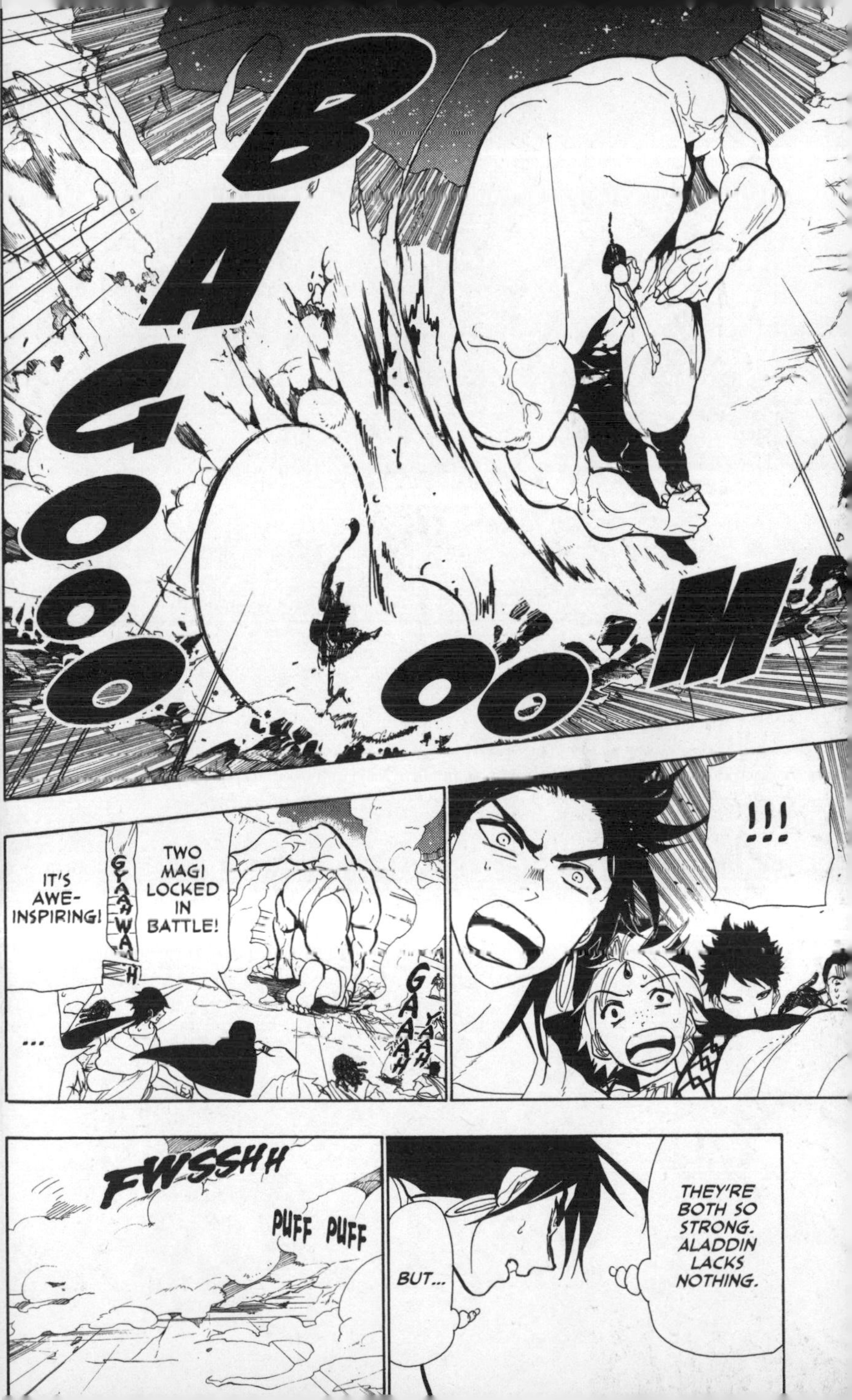

BAGOOOOOOM!!
!!!
TWO MAGI LOCKED IN BATTLE!
IT'S AWE-INSPIRING!
GYAAAH WAAH
GAAAH
YAAAH
...
THEY'RE BOTH SO STRONG. ALADDIN LACKS NOTHING.
BUT...
FWSSHH
PUFF PUFF

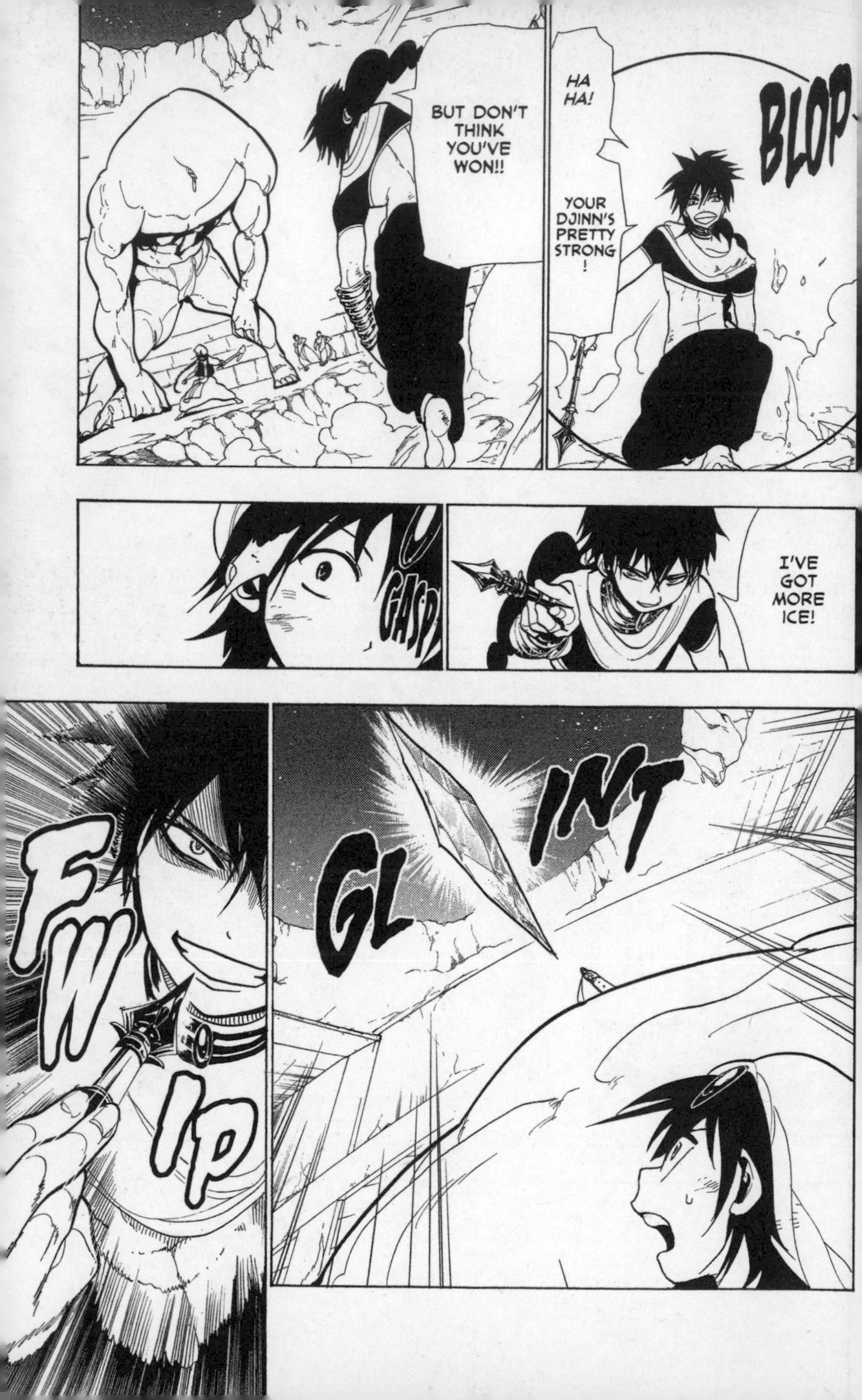
BLOP
HA HA!
YOUR DJINN'S PRETTY STRONG!
BUT DON'T THINK YOU'VE WON!!
I'VE GOT MORE ICE!
GASP
GL INT
FWIP

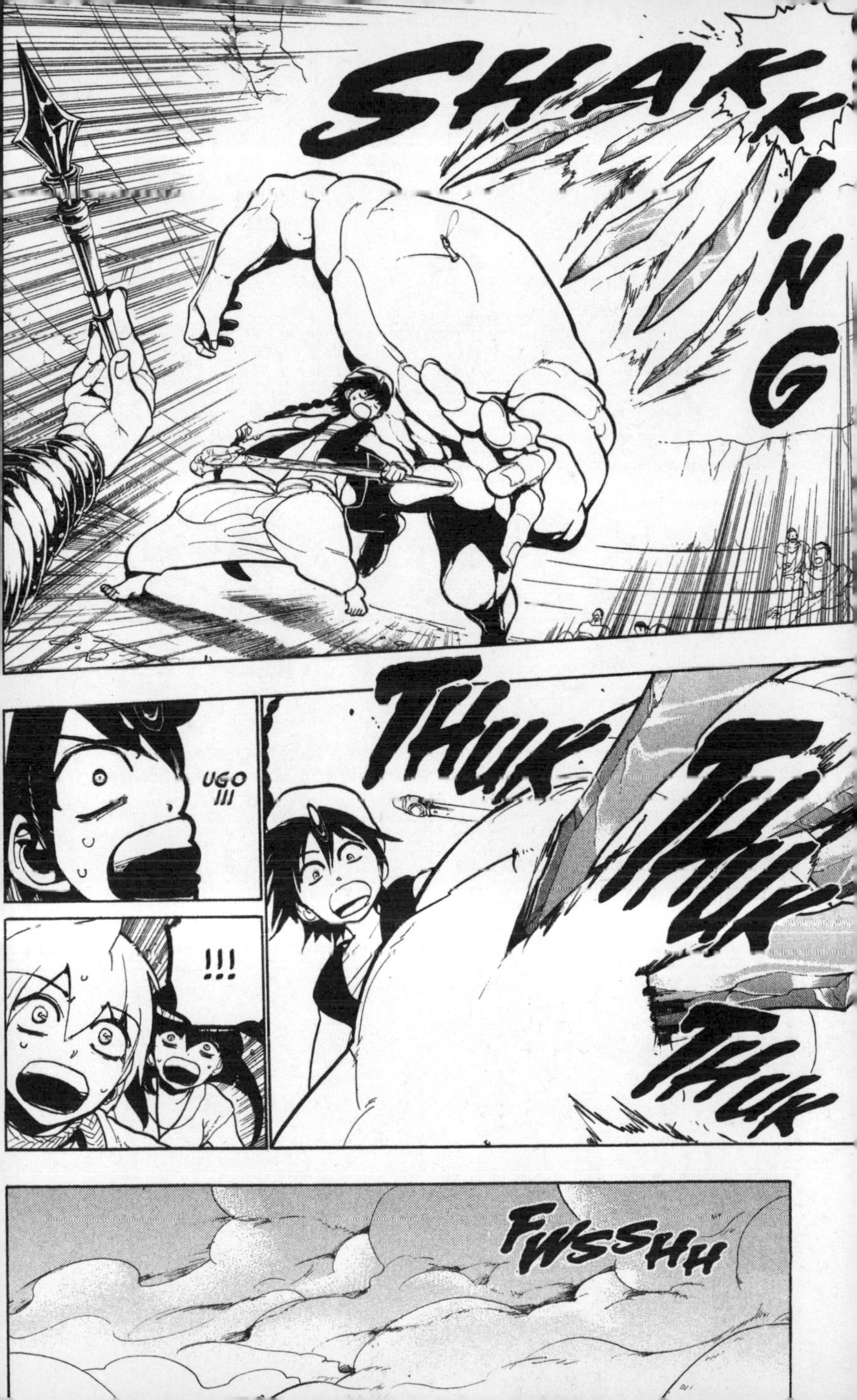
SHAKING
THUK THUK THUK
UGO !!!
!!!
FWSSHH

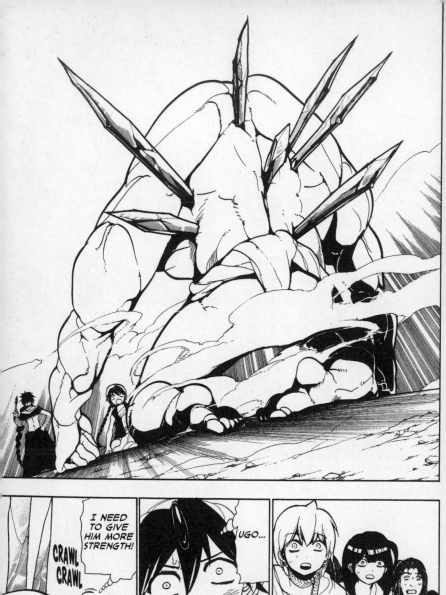

I NEED TO GIVE HIM MORE STRENGTH!

CRAWL CRAWL

AHHH...

UGO...

HE'S HURT!

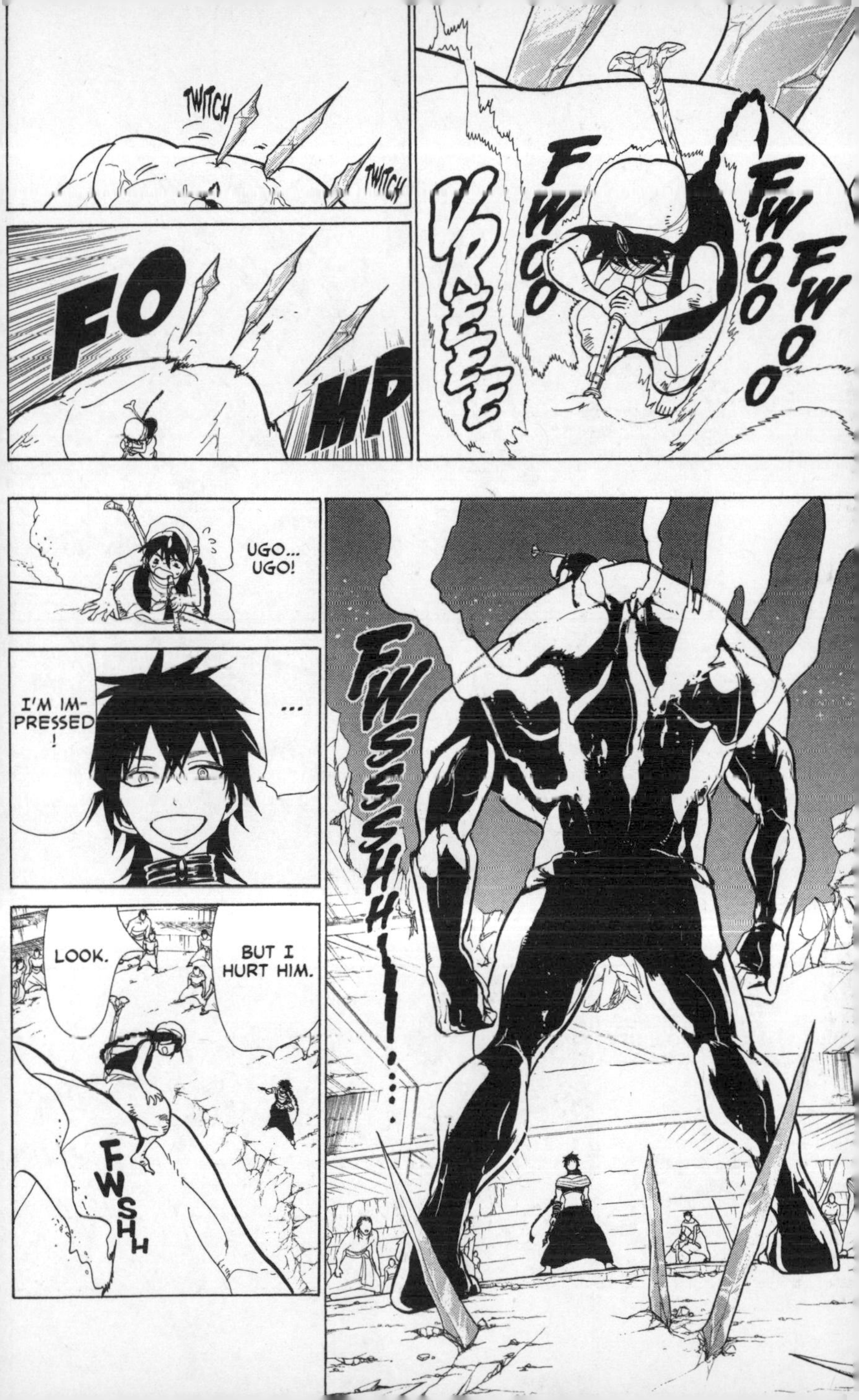
FWOO
FWOOO
FWOOO
VREEE
TWITCH
TWITCH
FO
MP
FWSSSHH!...
UGO... UGO!
...
I'M IM-PRESSED!
BUT I HURT HIM.
LOOK.
FWSHH

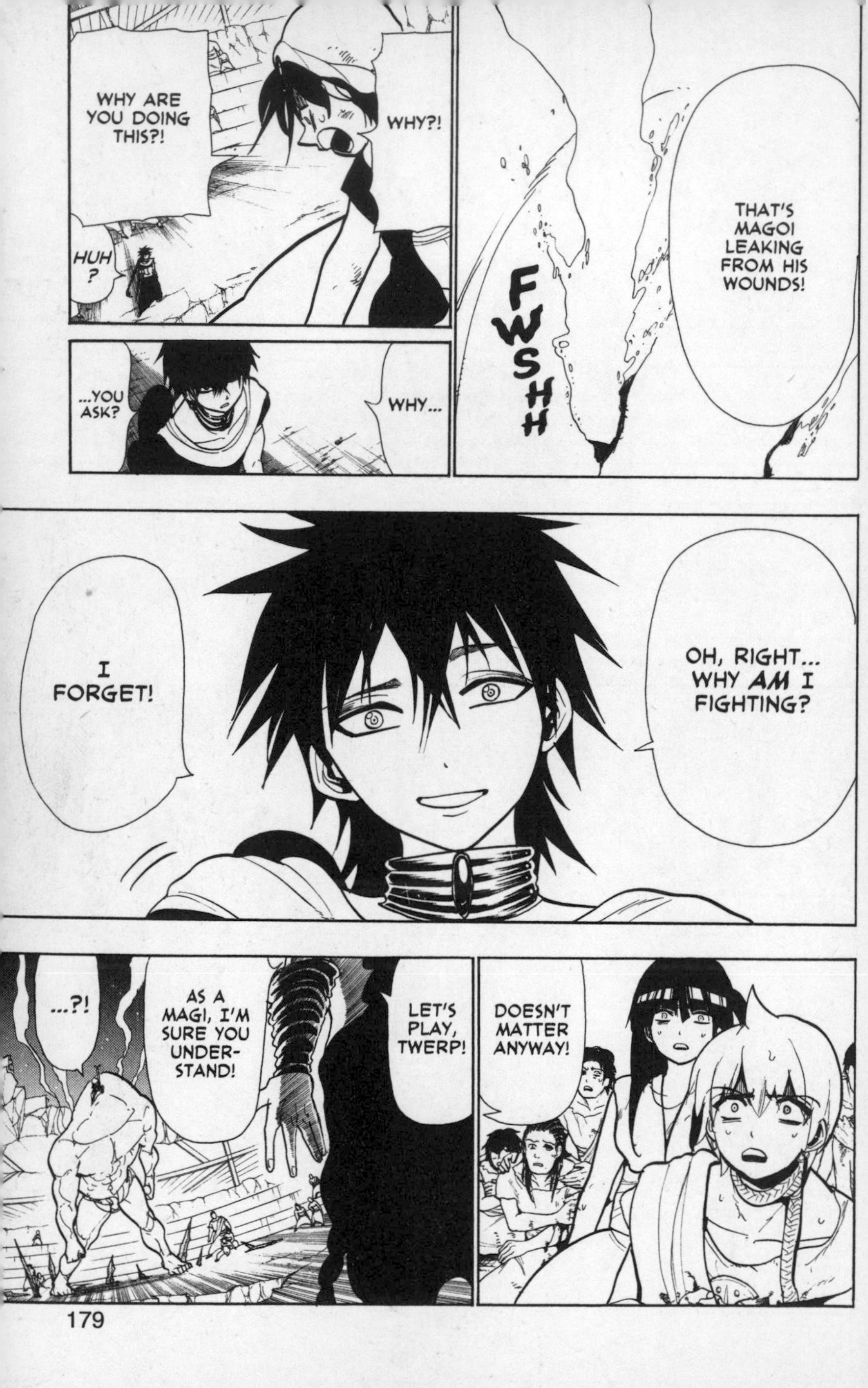
THAT'S MAGOI LEAKING FROM HIS WOUNDS!
FWSHH
WHY?!
WHY ARE YOU DOING THIS?!
HUH?
WHY...
...YOU ASK?
OH, RIGHT... WHY AM I FIGHTING?
I FORGET!
DOESN'T MATTER ANYWAY!
LET'S PLAY, TWERP!
AS A MAGI, I'M SURE YOU UNDER-STAND!
...?!

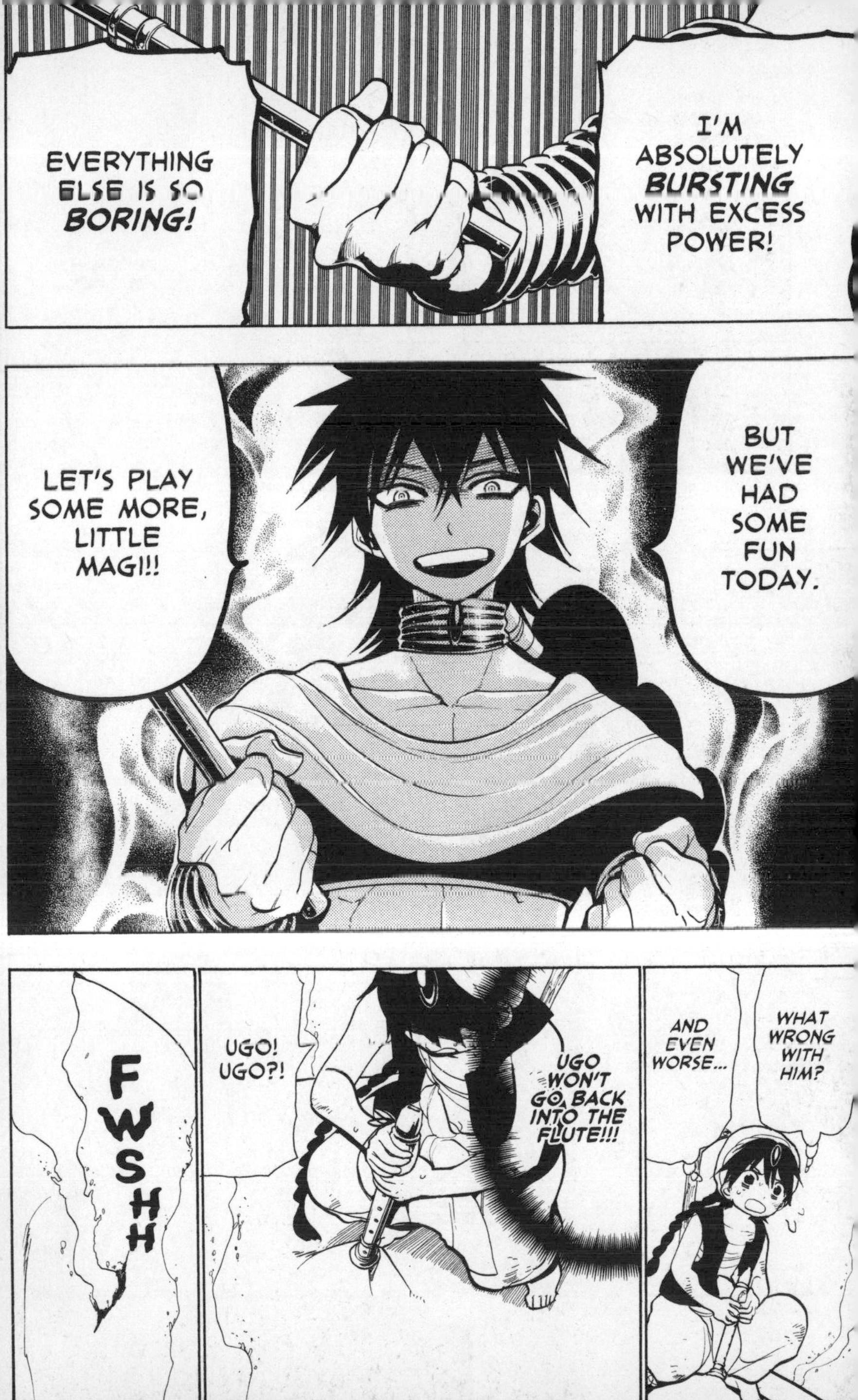
I'M ABSOLUTELY *BURSTING* WITH EXCESS POWER!
EVERYTHING ELSE IS SO *BORING!*
BUT WE'VE HAD SOME FUN TODAY.
LET'S PLAY SOME MORE, LITTLE MAGI!!!
WHAT WRONG WITH HIM?
AND EVEN WORSE...
UGO WON'T GO BACK INTO THE FLUTE!!!
UGO! UGO?!
FWSHH

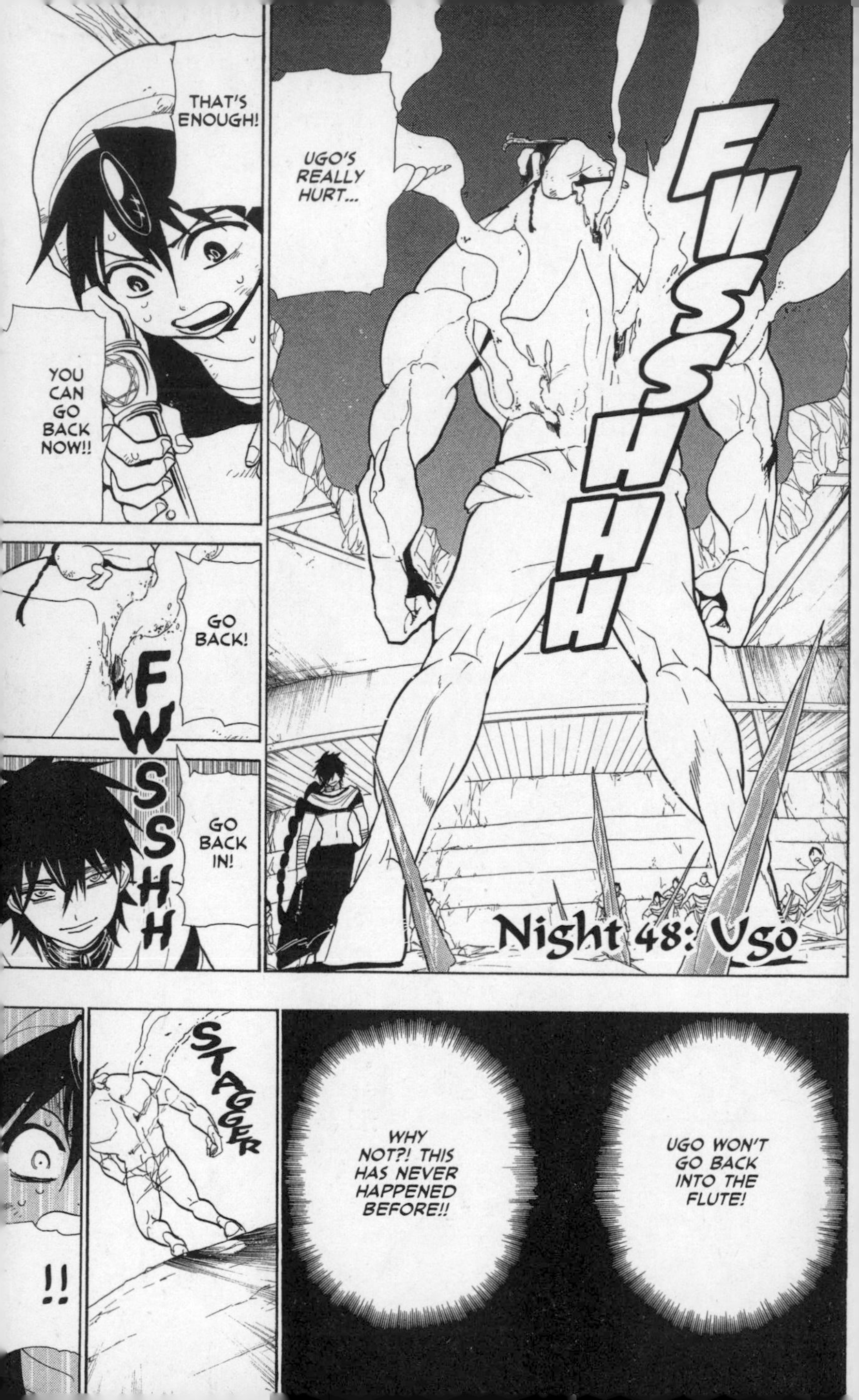
FWSSHHHH
UGO'S REALLY HURT...
Night 48: Ugo
THAT'S ENOUGH!
YOU CAN GO BACK NOW!!
GO BACK!
FWSSHH
GO BACK IN!
UGO WON'T GO BACK INTO THE FLUTE!
WHY NOT?! THIS HAS NEVER HAPPENED BEFORE!!
STAGGER
!!

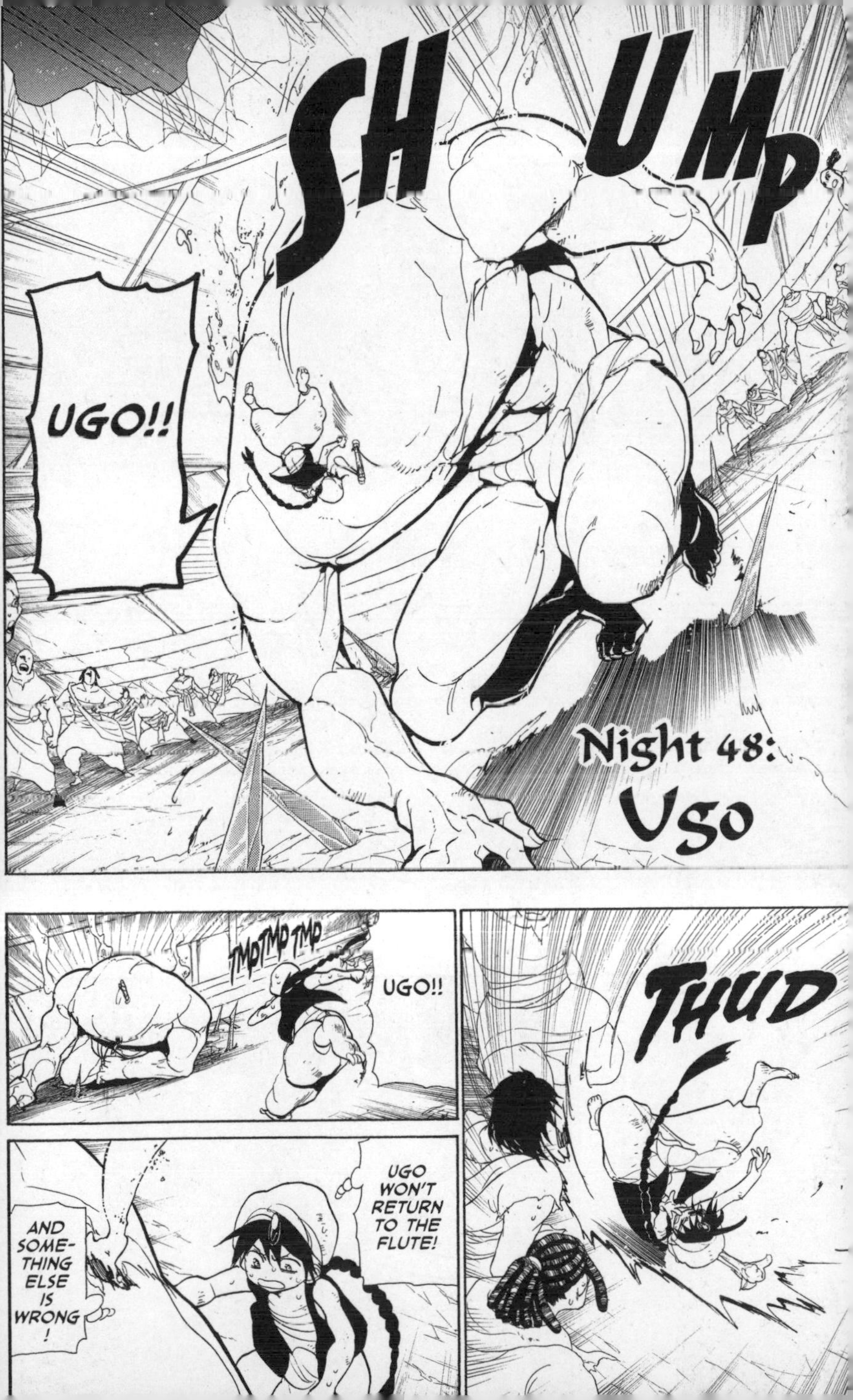
SHUMP
UGO!!
Night 48: Ugo
THUD
TMP TMP TMP
UGO!!
UGO WON'T RETURN TO THE FLUTE!
AND SOMETHING ELSE IS WRONG!

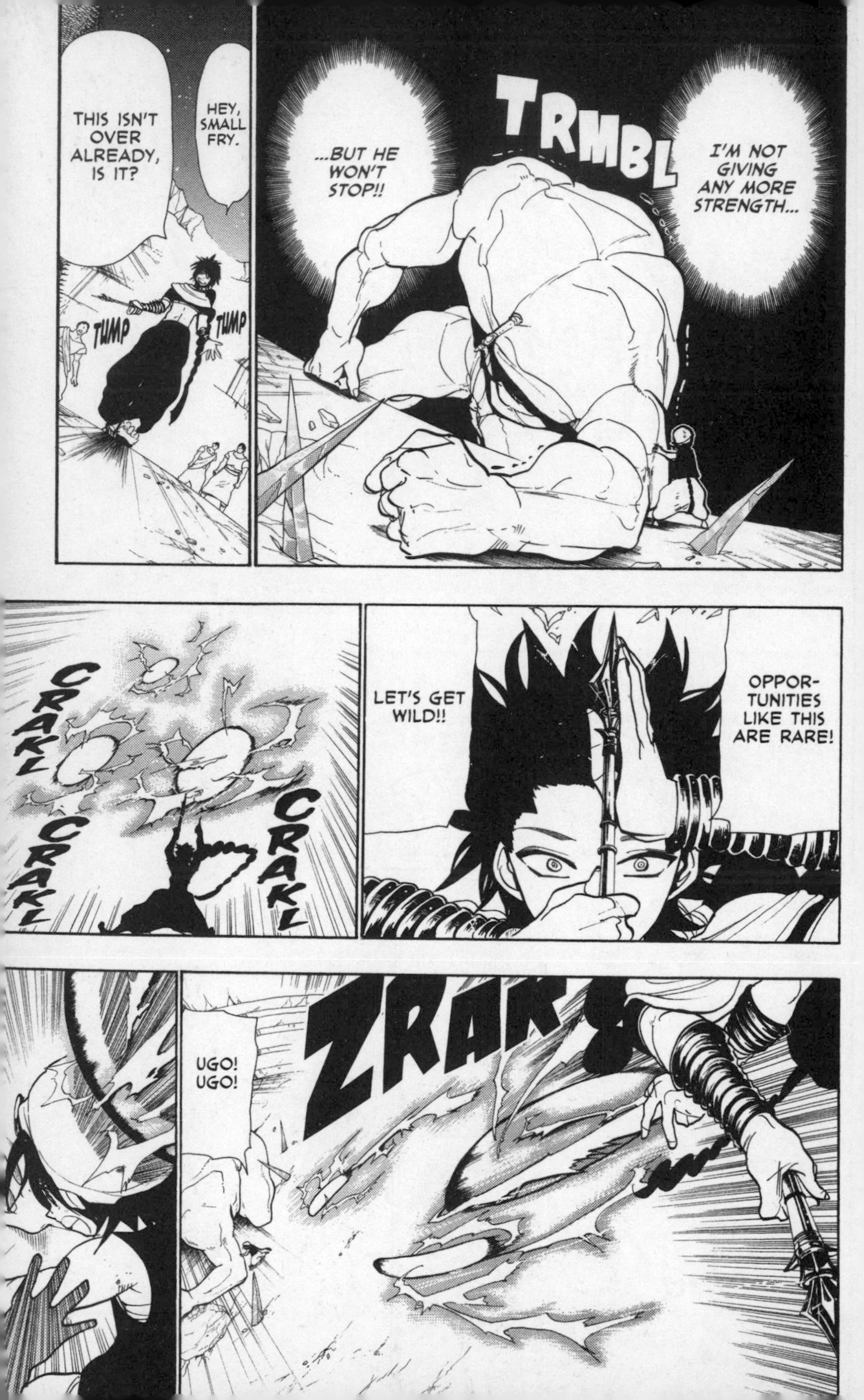
I'M NOT GIVING ANY MORE STRENGTH...
TRMBL
...BUT HE WON'T STOP!!
HEY, SMALL FRY.
THIS ISN'T OVER ALREADY, IS IT?
TUMP
TUMP
OPPOR-TUNITIES LIKE THIS ARE RARE!
LET'S GET WILD!!
CRAKL
CRAKL CRAKL
ZRAK
UGO! UGO!

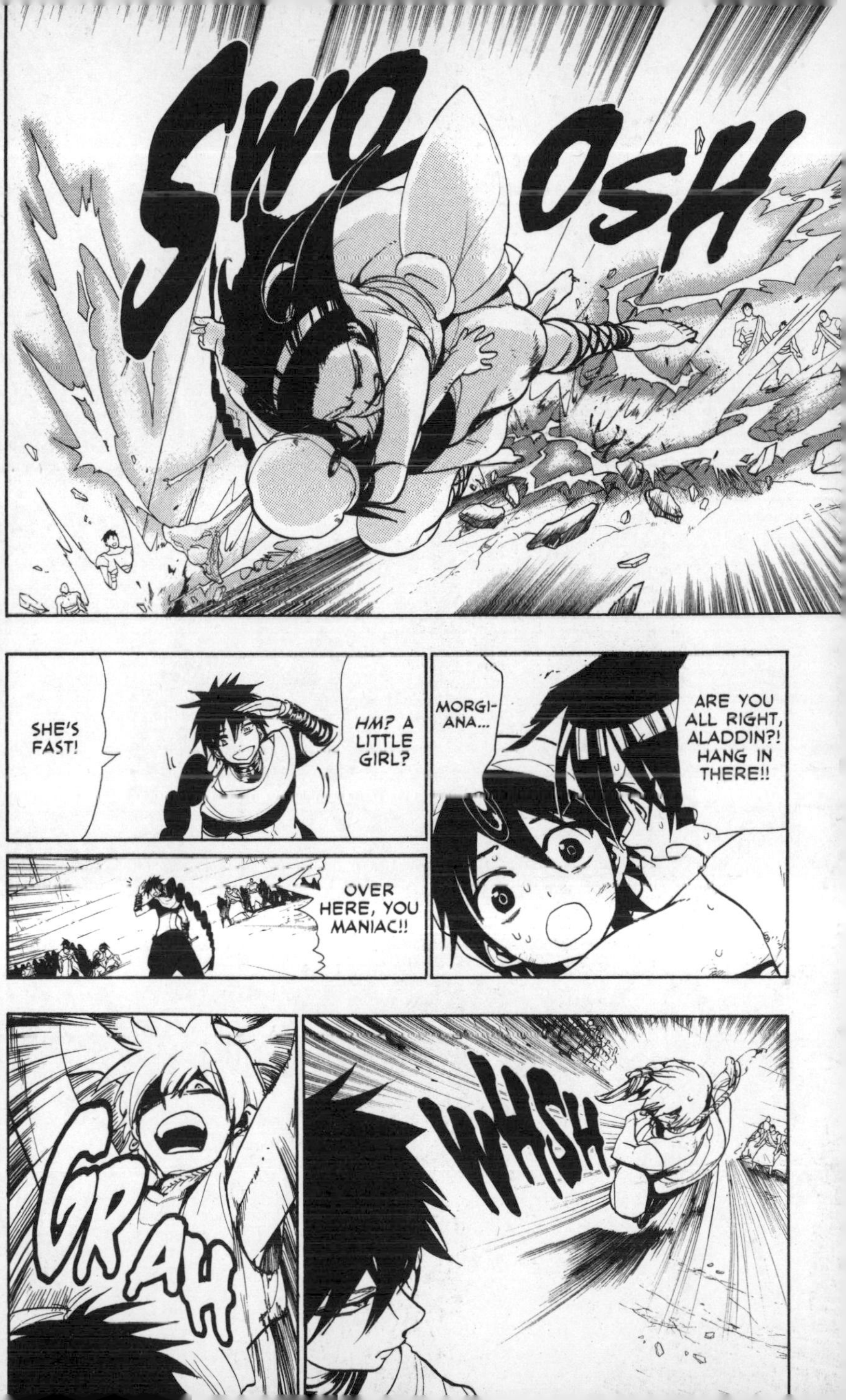
SWOOSH
ARE YOU ALL RIGHT, ALADDIN?! HANG IN THERE!!
MORGI-ANA...
HM? A LITTLE GIRL?
SHE'S FAST!
OVER HERE, YOU MANIAC!!
WHSH
GRAH

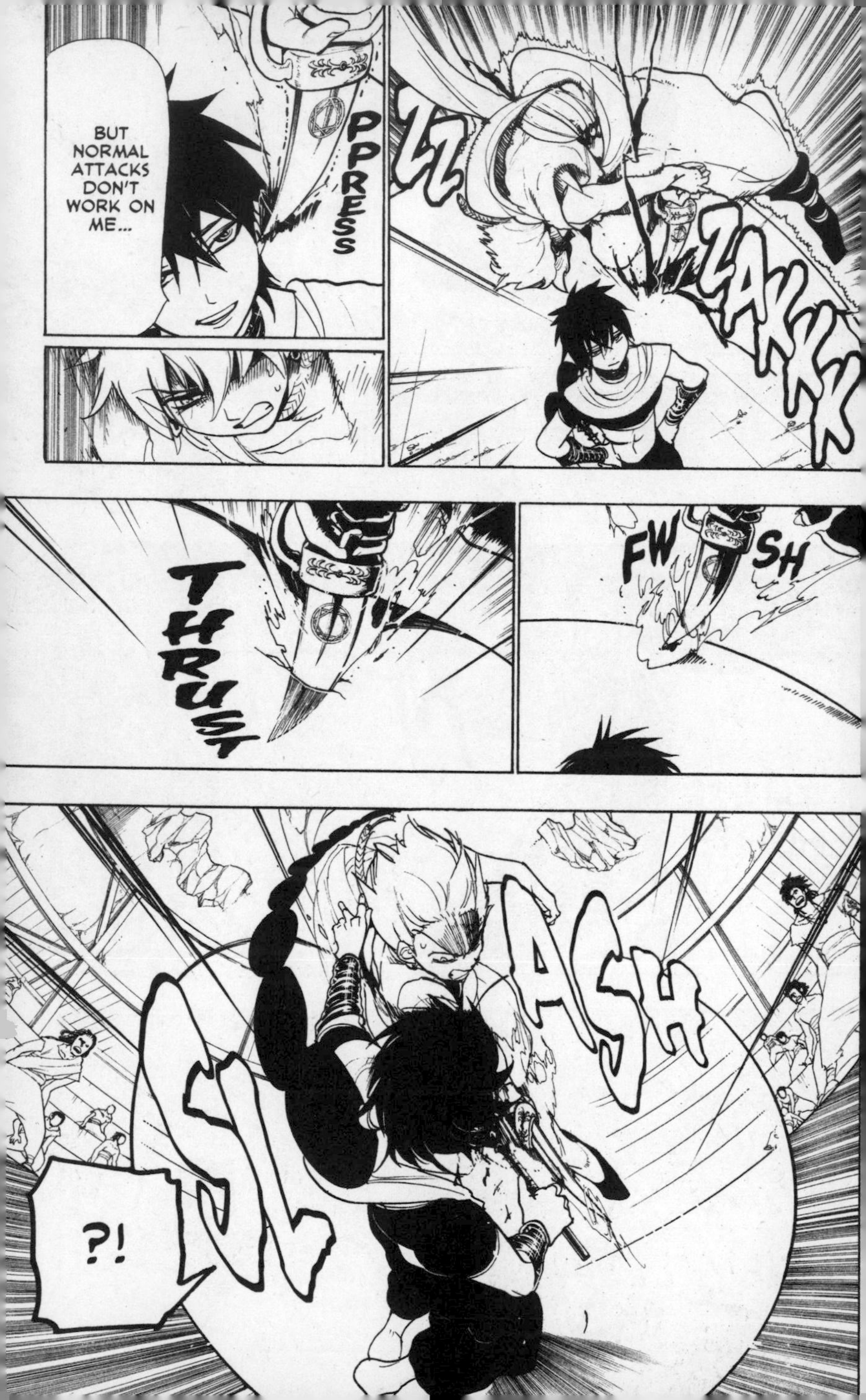
ZZ
ZAKKK
BUT NORMAL ATTACKS DON'T WORK ON ME...
PPRESS
FW SH
THRUST
SLASH
?!

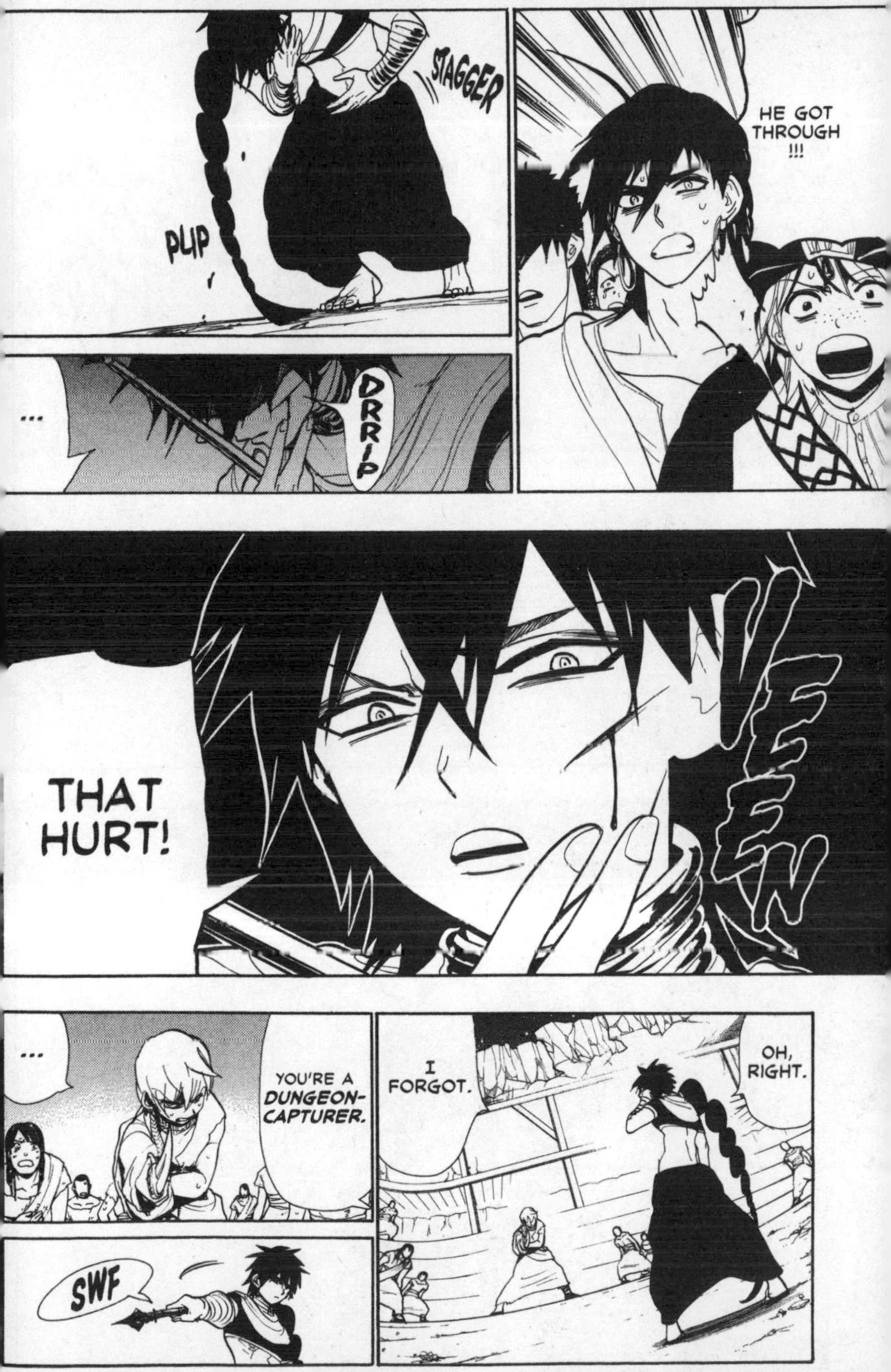
HE GOT THROUGH !!!
STAGGER
PLIP
DRRIP
...
THAT HURT!
OH, RIGHT.
I FORGOT.
YOU'RE A DUNGEON-CAPTURER.
...
SWF

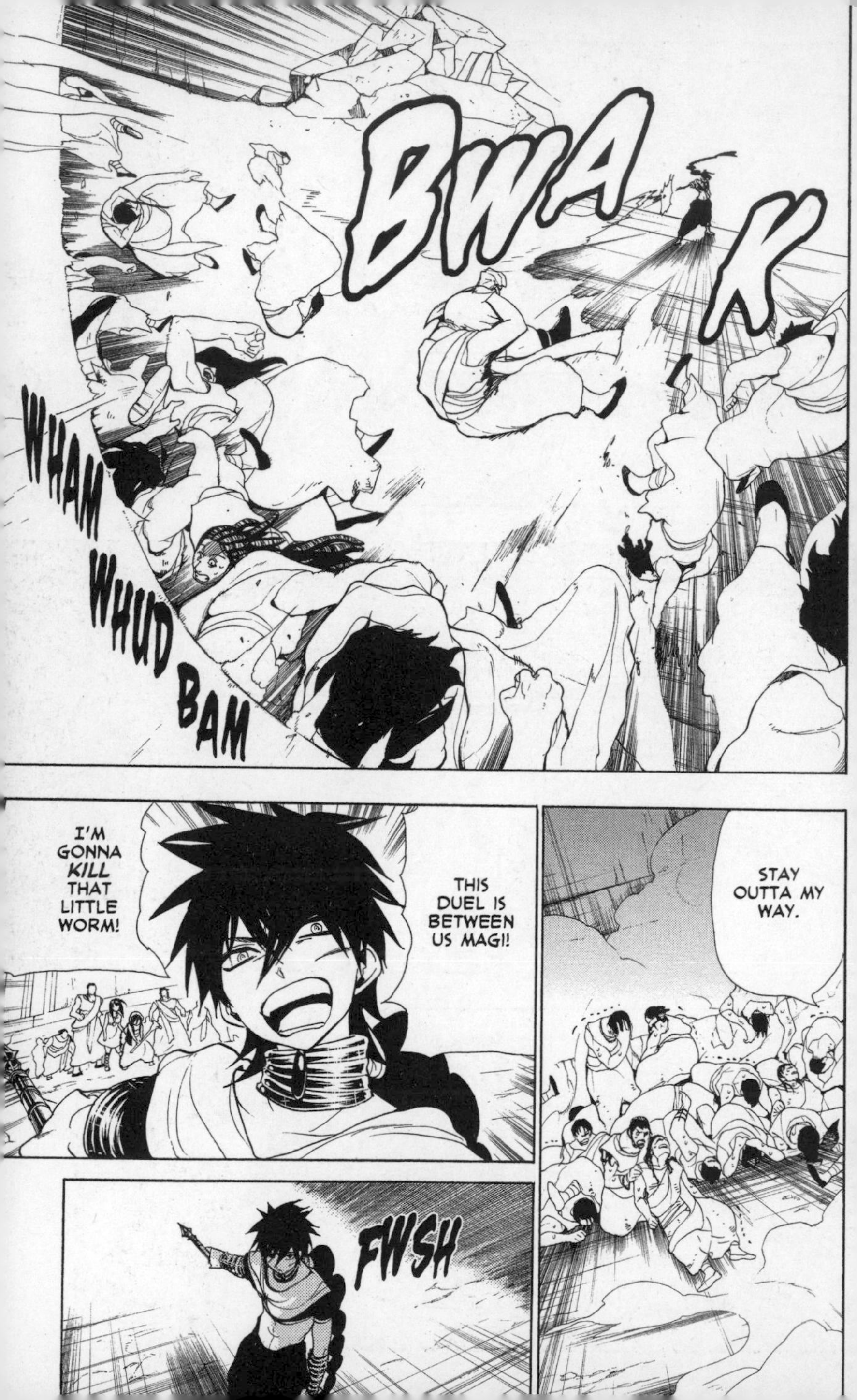
BWAK
WHAM
WHUD
BAM
STAY OUTTA MY WAY.
THIS DUEL IS BETWEEN US MAGI!
I'M GONNA *KILL* THAT LITTLE WORM!
FWSH

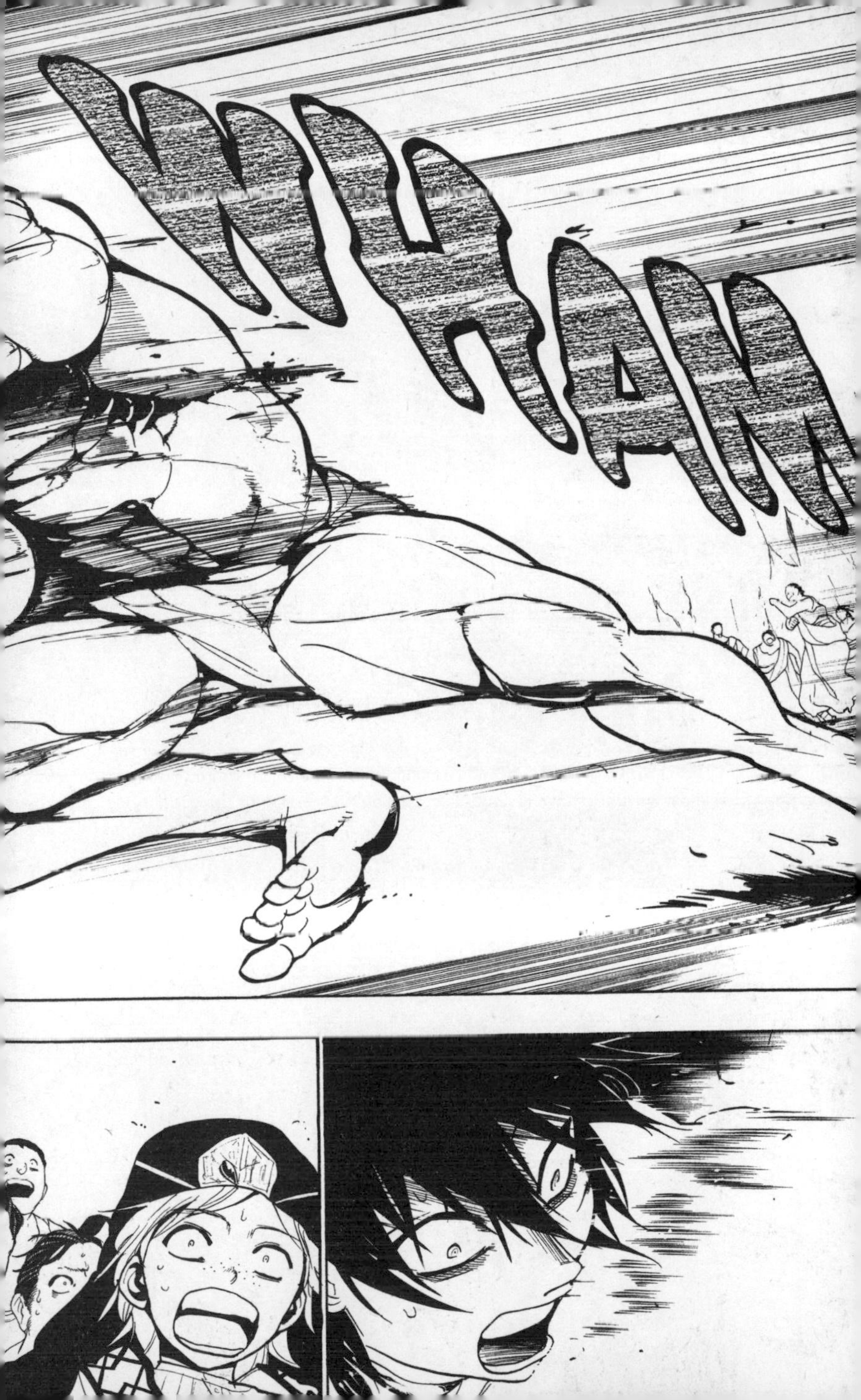
WHAM

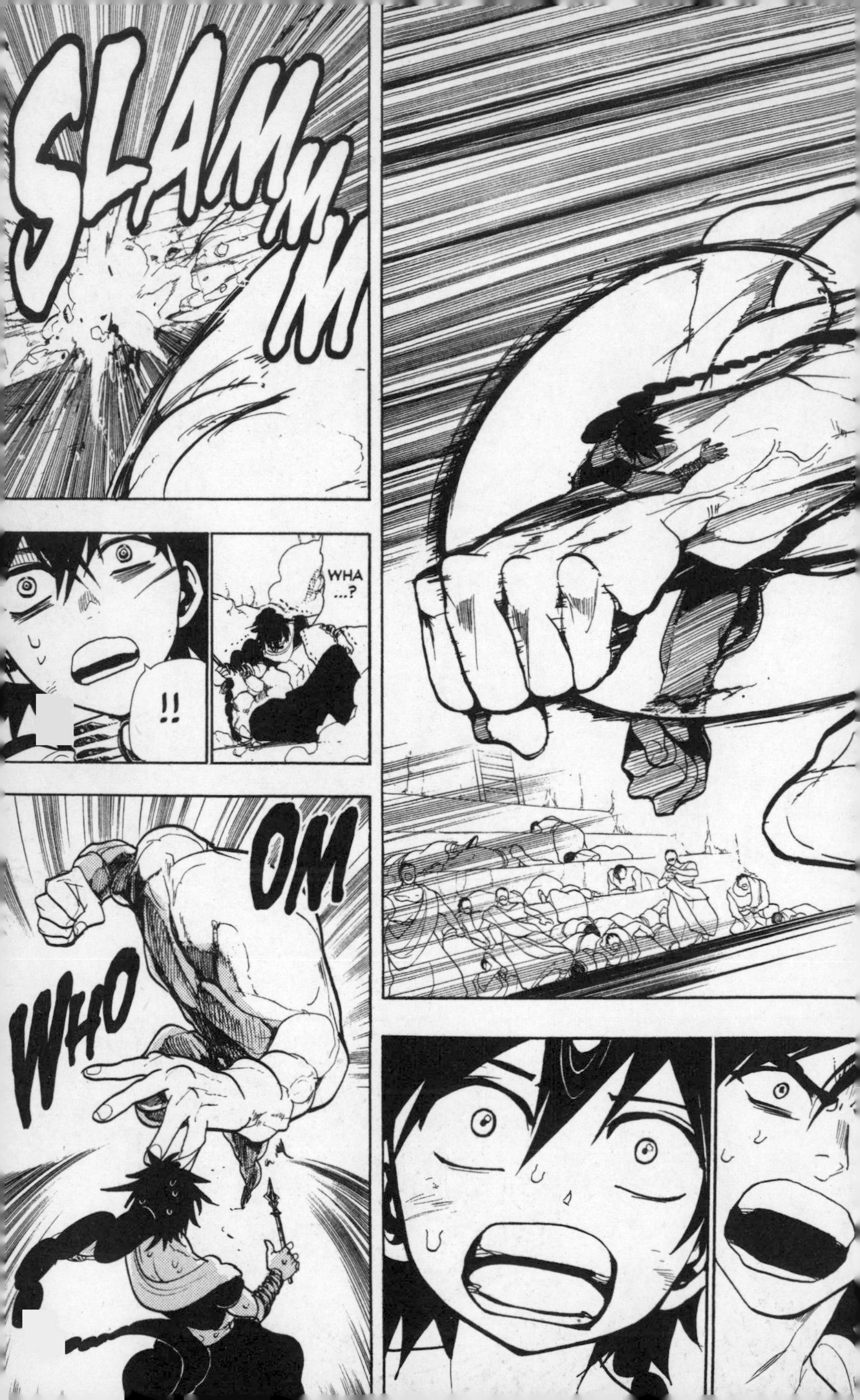
SLAMMM
WHA ...?
!!
WHO
OM

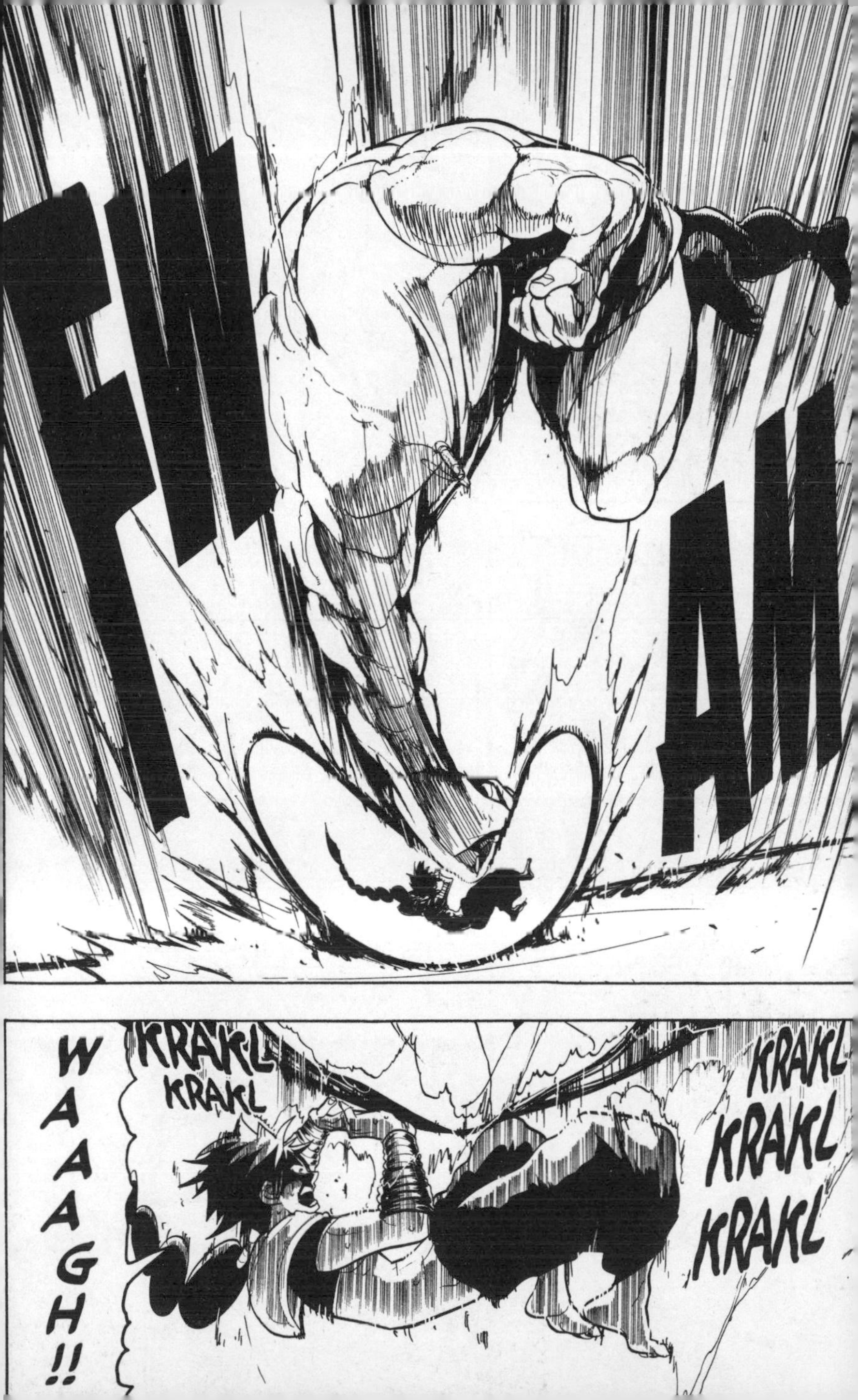
FWAM
KRAKL
KRAKL
KRAKL
KRAKL
KRAKL
WAAAGH!!

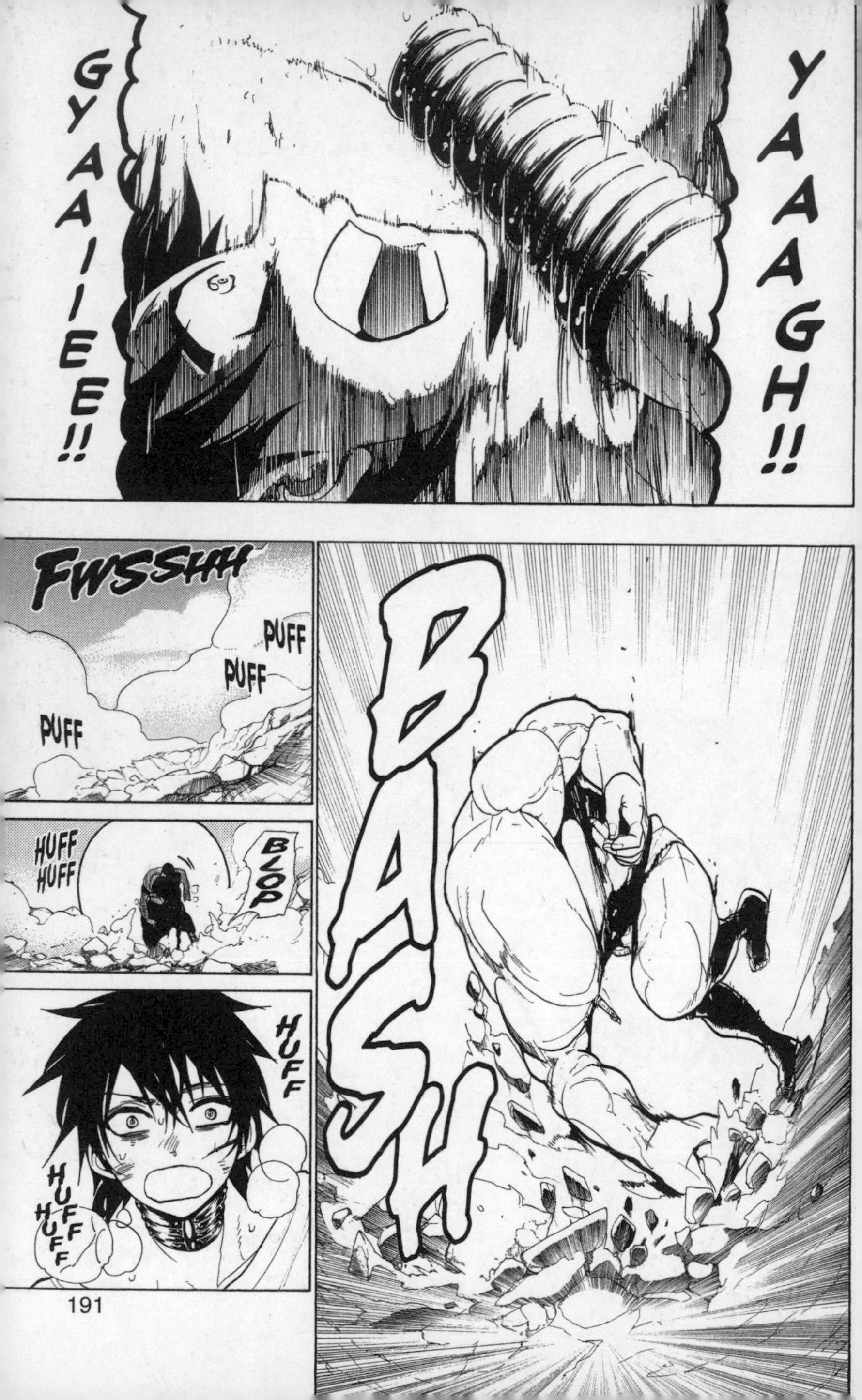
YAAAGH!!
GYAAIIEE!!
BASH
FWSSHH
PUFF
PUFF
PUFF
BLOP
HUFF HUFF
HUFF
HUFF HUFF HUFF

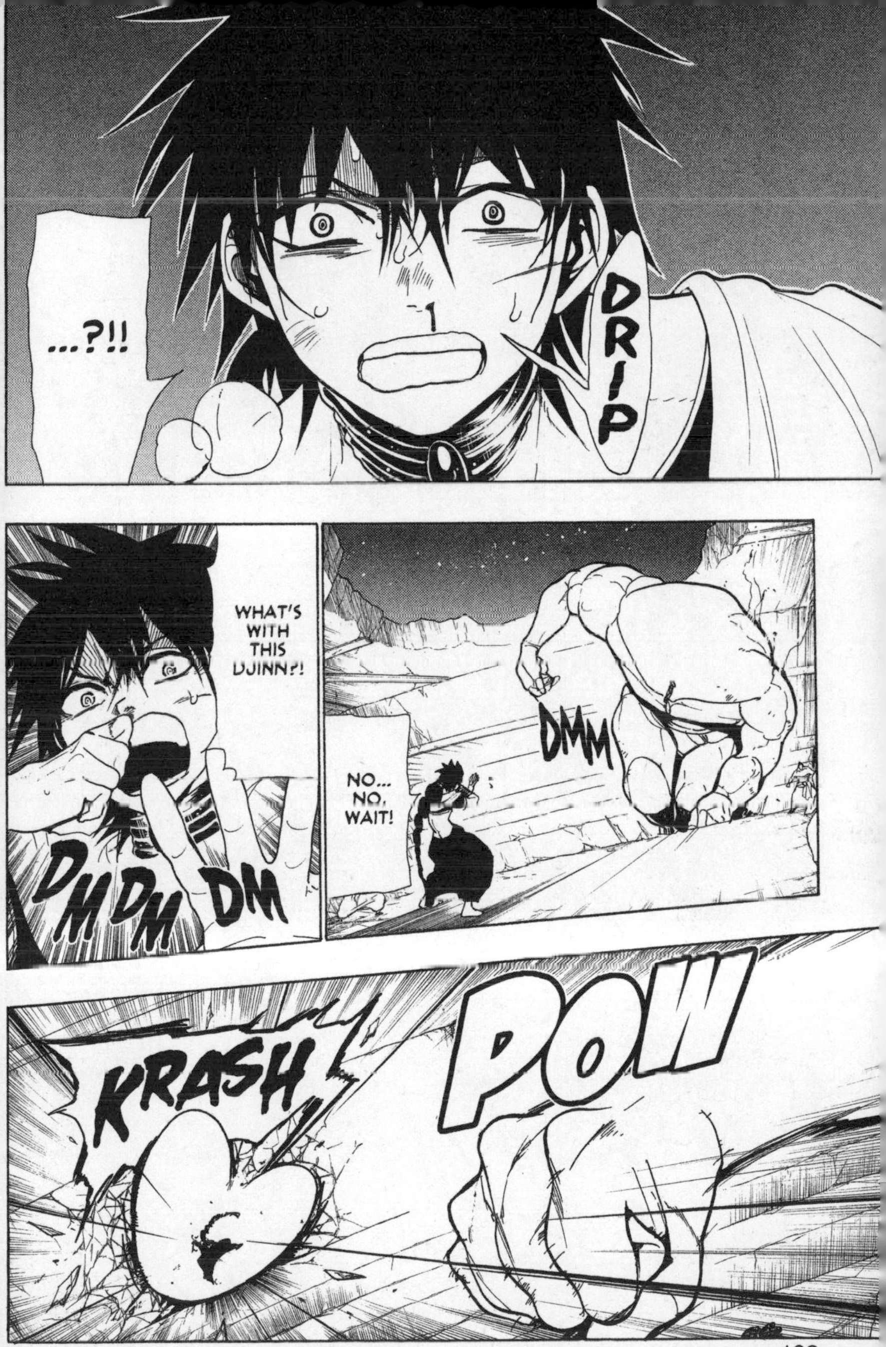
...?!!
DRIP
DMM
NO... NO, WAIT!
WHAT'S WITH THIS DJINN?!
DM DM DM
POW
KRASH

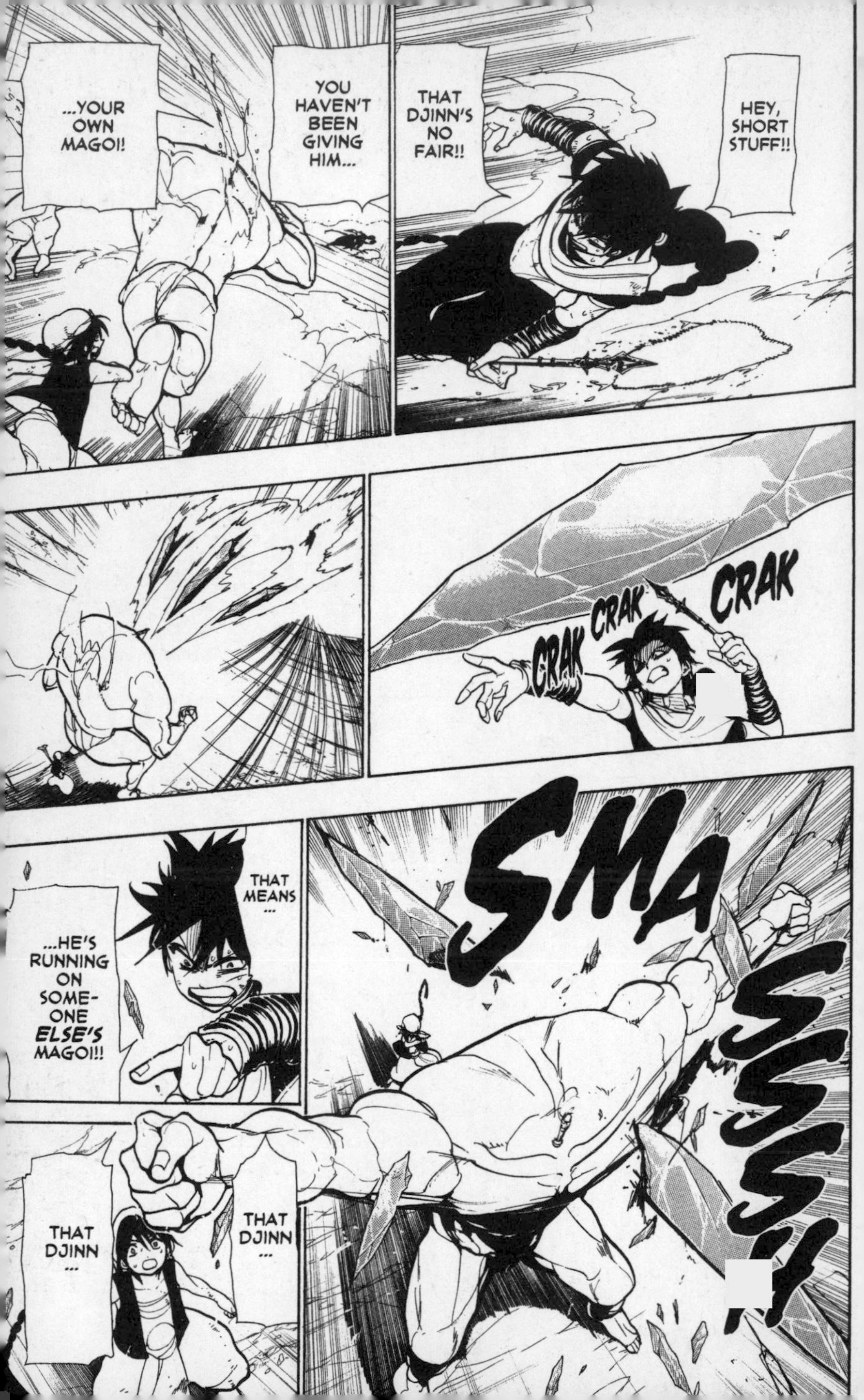

HEY, SHORT STUFF!!
THAT DJINN'S NO FAIR!!
YOU HAVEN'T BEEN GIVING HIM...
...YOUR OWN MAGOI!!
CRAK
CRAK
CRAK
SMASSSH!!
THAT MEANS...
...HE'S RUNNING ON SOME-ONE *ELSE'S* MAGOI!!
THAT DJINN...
THAT DJINN...

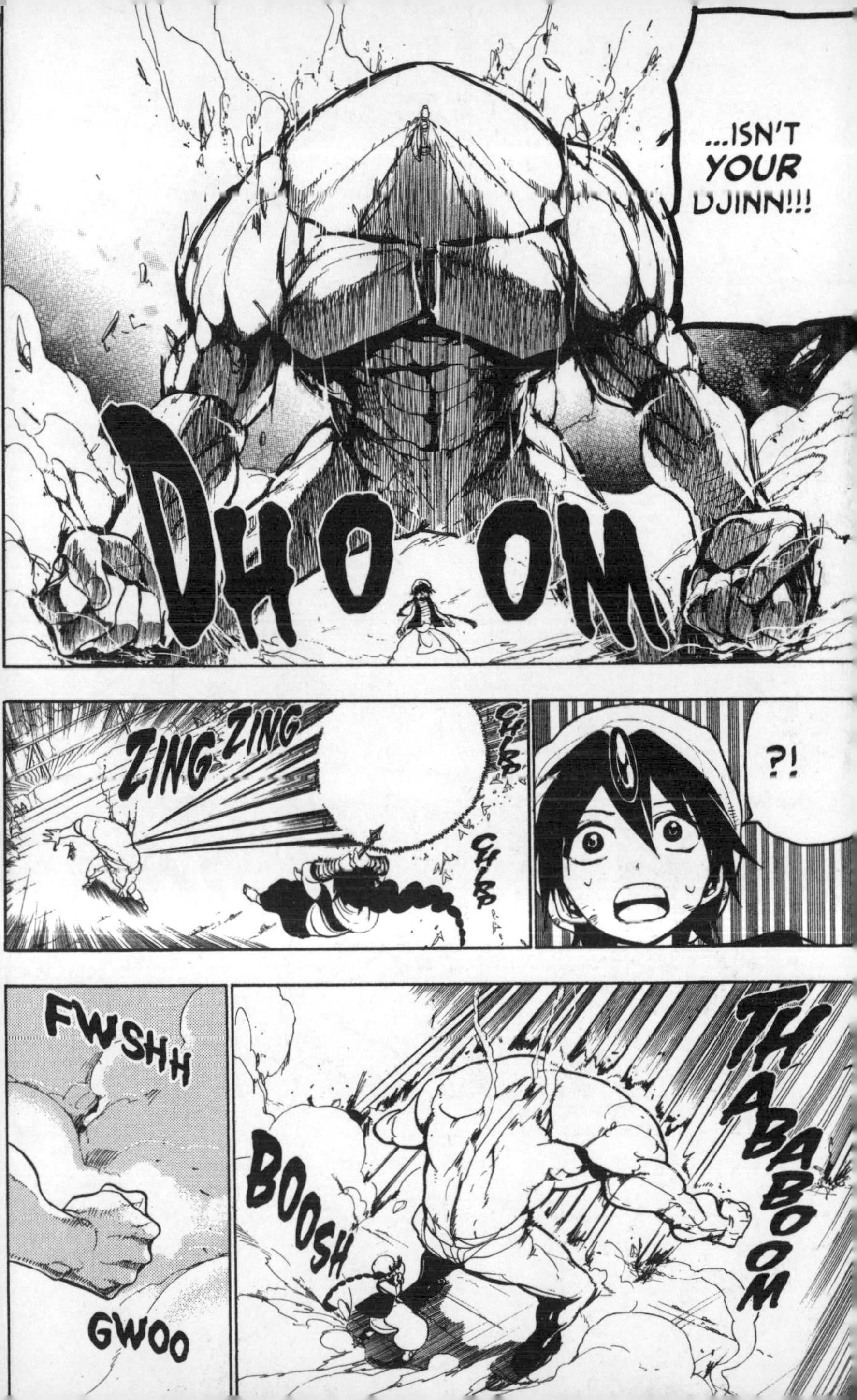
...ISN'T YOUR DJINN!!!
DHO OM
?!
ZING ZING
CHIRP
CHIRP
THABABOOM
BOOSH
FWSHH
GWOO

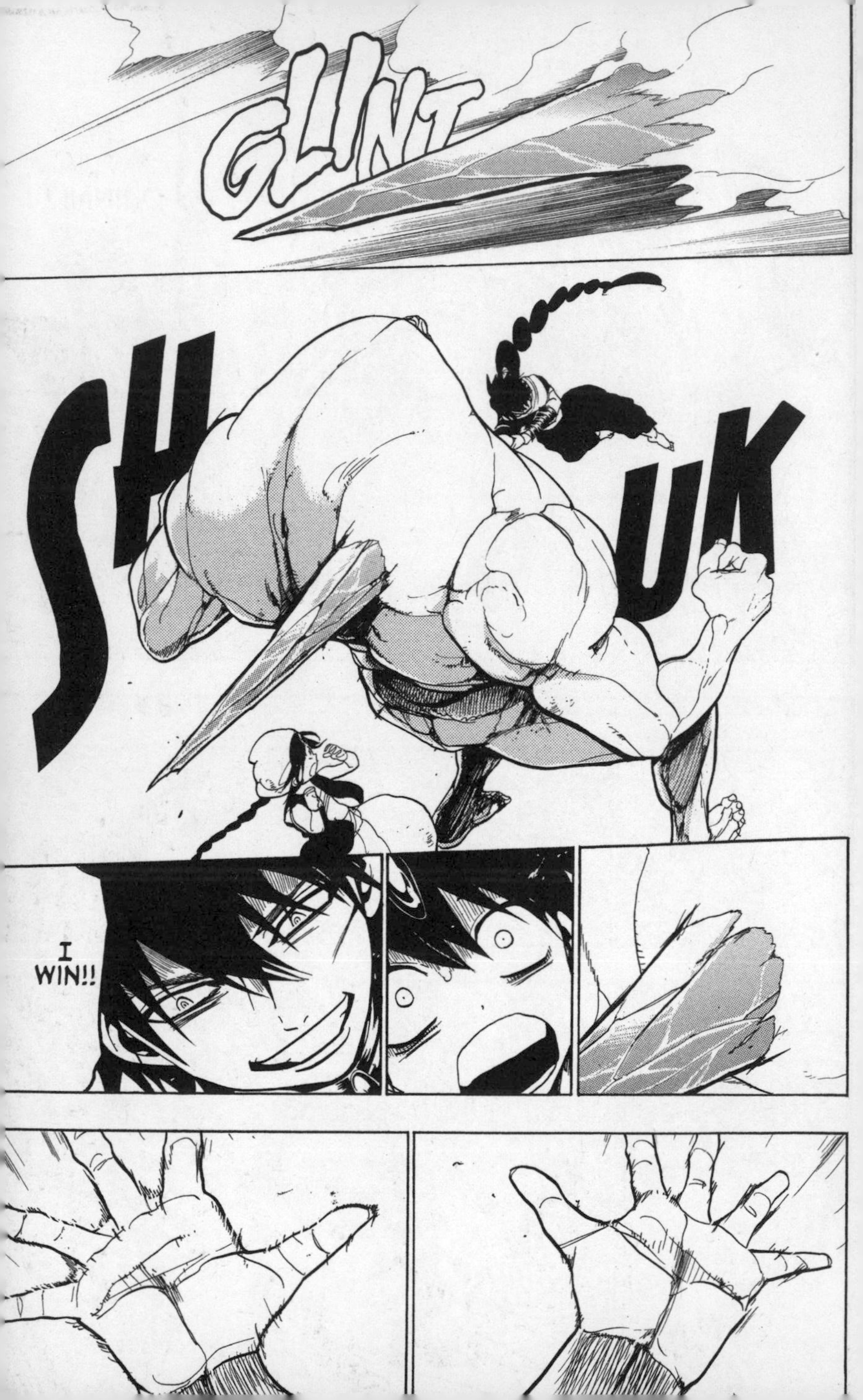
GLINT
SHUK
I WIN!!

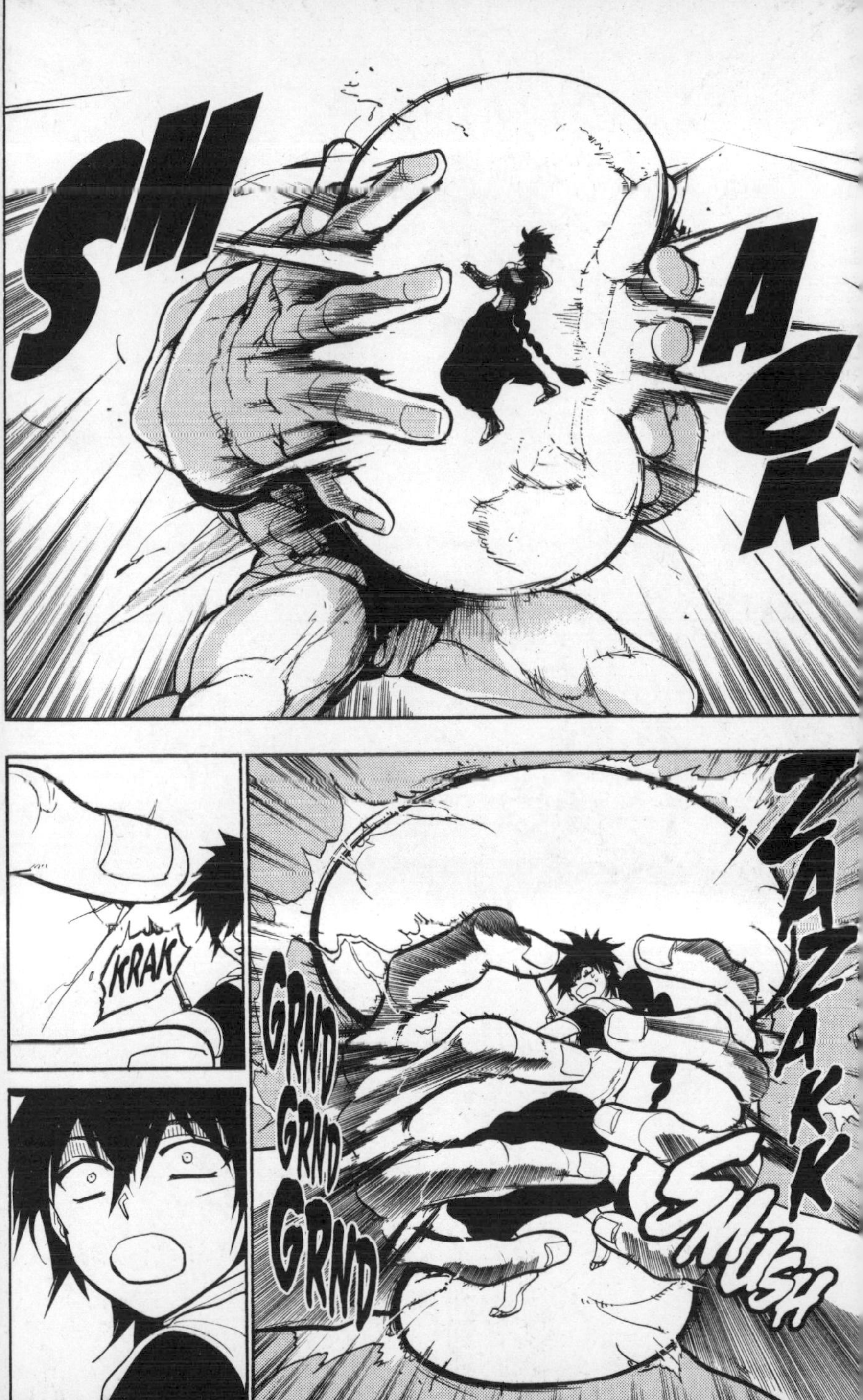
SMACK
ZAZAKK
SMUSH
GRND GRND GRND
KRAK

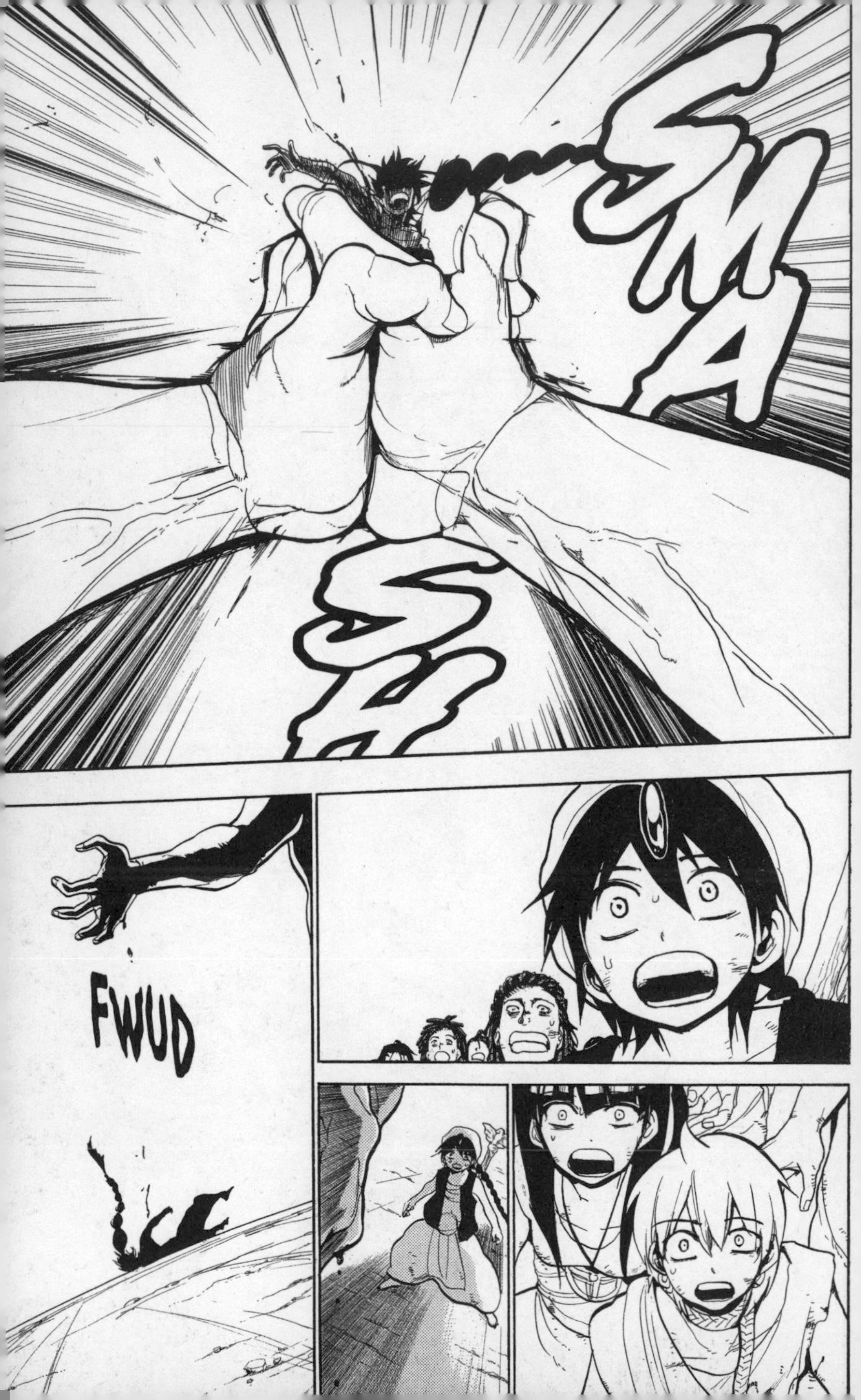
SMASH
FWUD

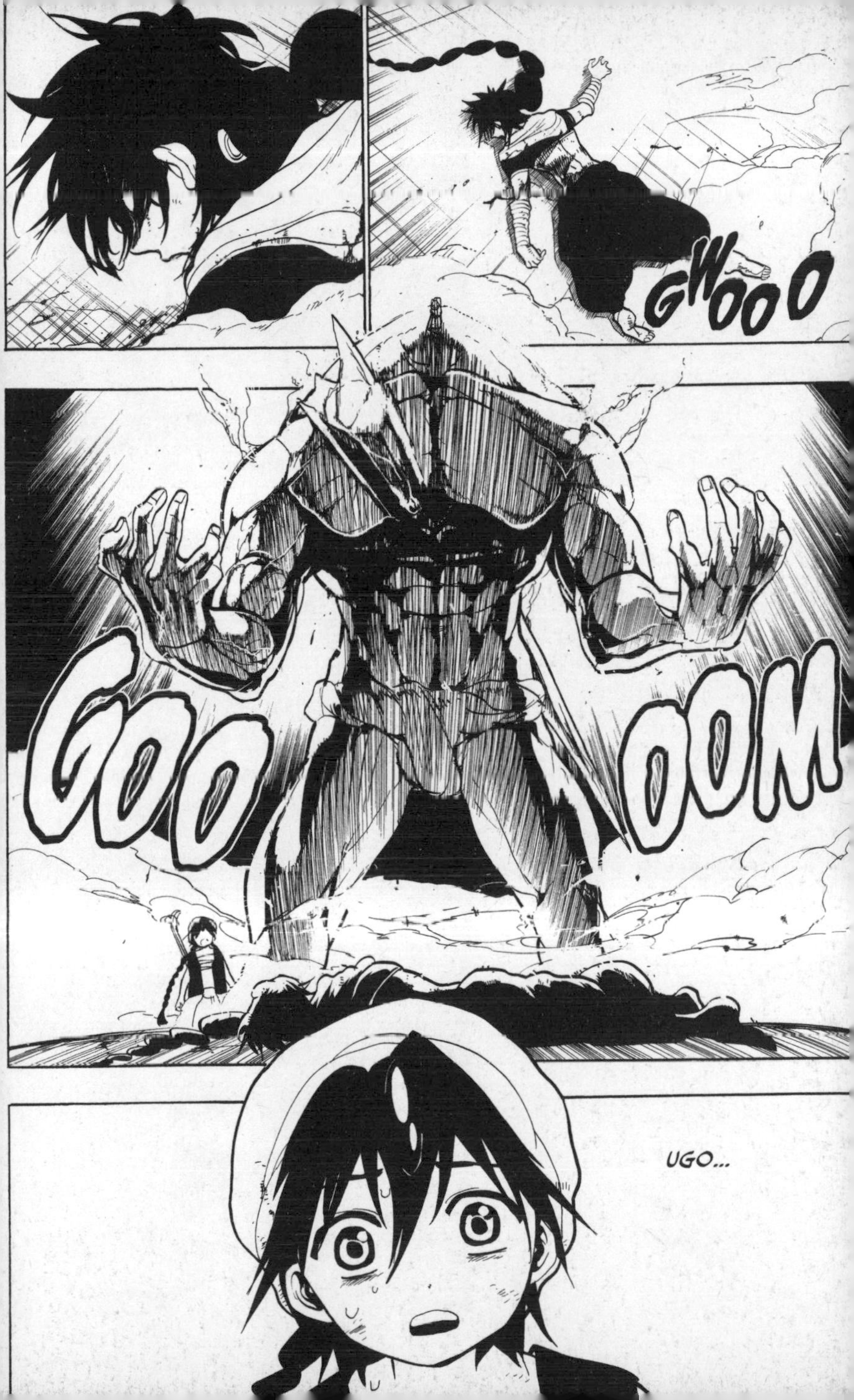
GWOOO
GOOOOM
UGO...

# MAGI
### The labyrinth of magic
## 5

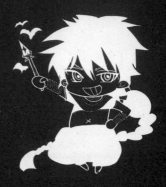

## Staff

■ **Story & Art**

# Shinobu Ohtaka
Shinobu Ohtaka

■ **Regular Assistants**

### Matsubara

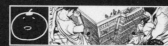

### Miho Isshiki

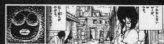

### Akira Sugito

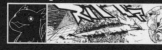

### Tanimoto

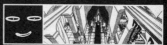

### Maru

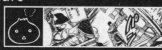

■ **Editor**

## Kazuaki Ishibashi

■ **Sales & Promotion**

## Akira Ozeki
## Shinichirou Todaka

■ **Designer**

## Yasuo Shimura + Bay Bridge Studio

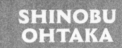

## SHINOBU OHTAKA

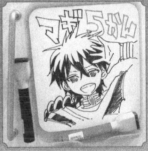

*Magi* volume 5!!

*Let's have some fun!!*

# MAGI

## Volume 5
### Shonen Sunday Edition

## Story and Art by
# SHINOBU OHTAKA

MAGI Vol.5
by Shinobu OHTAKA
© 2009 Shinobu OHTAKA
All rights reserved.
Original Japanese edition published by SHOGAKUKAN.
English translation rights in the United States of America, Canada,
the United Kingdom, Ireland, Australia and New Zealand arranged with SHOGAKUKAN.

Translation & English Adaptation ◇ John Werry

Touch-up Art & Lettering ◇ Stephen Dutro

Editor ◇ Mike Montesa

Printed in the U.S.A.

Published by VIZ Media, LLC
P.O. Box 77010
San Francisco, CA 94107

10 9 8 7 6 5 4 3 2
First printing, April 2014
Second printing, January 2016

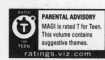

www.viz.com

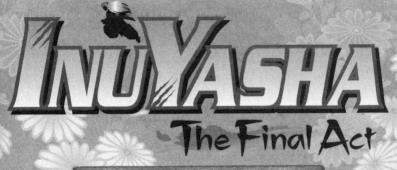
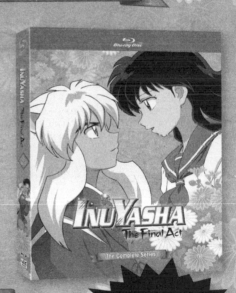

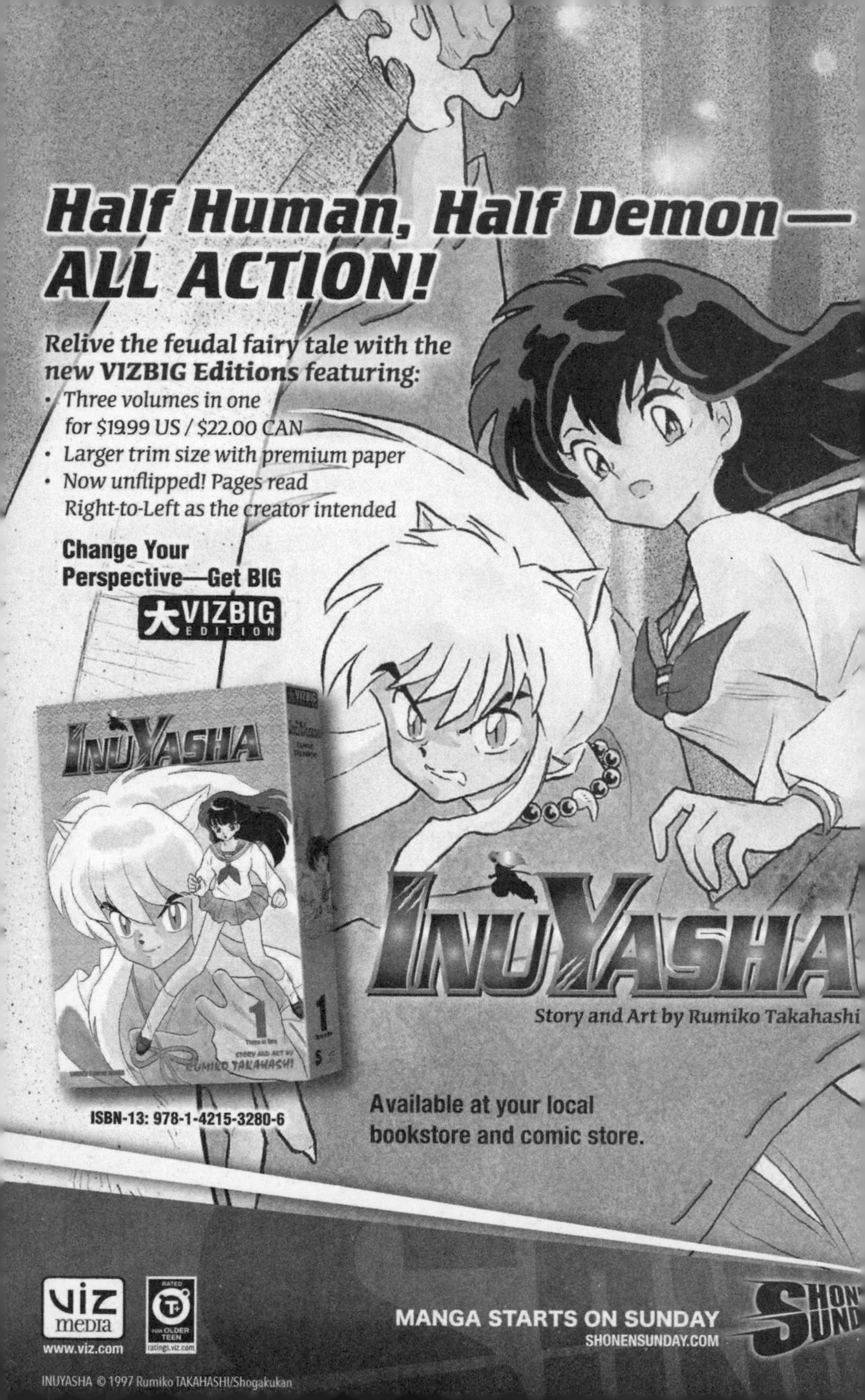
Half Human, Half Demon—
ALL ACTION!
Relive the feudal fairy tale with the new VIZBIG Editions featuring:
• Three volumes in one for $19.99 US / $22.00 CAN
• Larger trim size with premium paper
• Now unflipped! Pages read Right-to-Left as the creator intended
Change Your Perspective—Get BIG
大 VIZBIG EDITION
INUYASHA
1
ISBN-13: 978-1-4215-3280-6
INUYASHA
Story and Art by Rumiko Takahashi
Available at your local bookstore and comic store.
viz media
www.viz.com
RATED T+ FOR OLDER TEEN
ratings.viz.com
MANGA STARTS ON SUNDAY
SHONENSUNDAY.COM
INUYASHA © 1997 Rumiko TAKAHASHI/Shogakukan

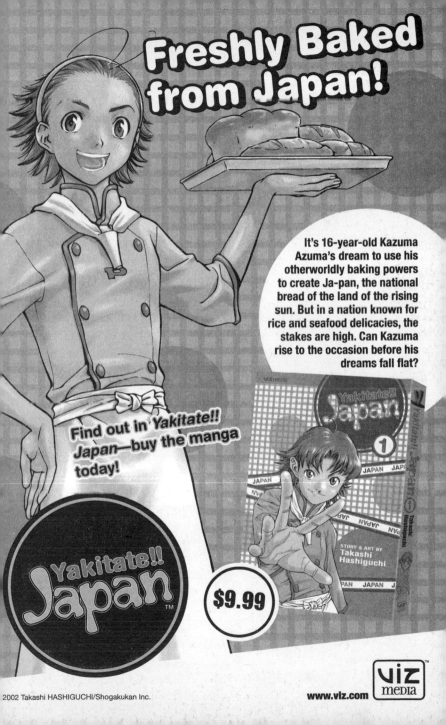

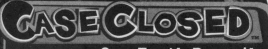
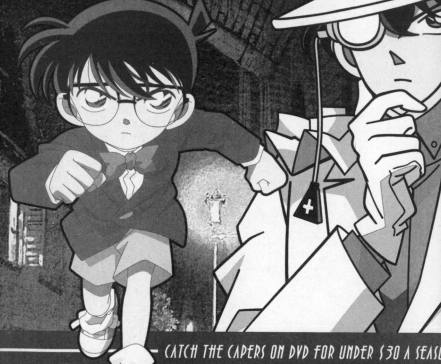
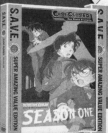
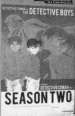
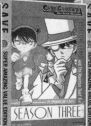
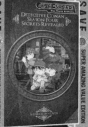
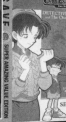

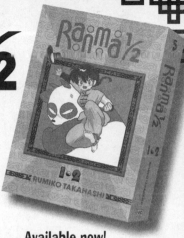

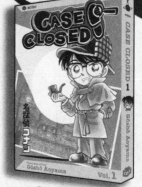

# You're reading the
# **WRONG WAY**

◇◇◇◇◇◇◇◇◇◇◇◇◇◇◇◇◇◇◇◇◇◇◇◇◇◇◇◇◇◇

**MAGI** reads from right to left, starting in the upper-right corner. Japanese is read from **right** to **left**, meaning that action, sound effects, and word-balloon order are completely reversed from English order.

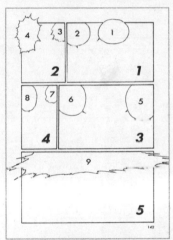

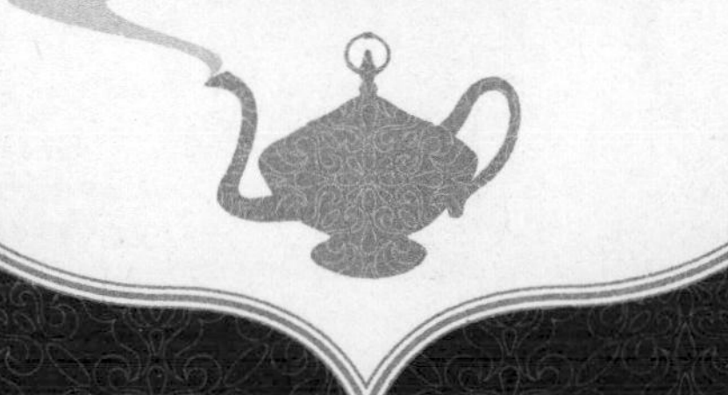